OPERATIONAL MID-LEVEL MANAGEMENT FOR POLICE

Fourth Edition

OPERATIONAL MID-LEVEL MANAGEMENT FOR POLICE

By

MAJOR JOHN L. COLEMAN (Retired)

Kansas City, Missouri School District, Director of Safety and Security
Kansas City, Missouri Police Department, Division Commander
Director of Security at Bannister Mall and
Benjamin Plaza Shopping Complex in Kansas City, Missouri
President and founder of J.L. Coleman Company
Expert legal consultant in Civil Cases involving Private Security
Instructor, Business and Society Course at Webster
University, Kansas City, Missouri Campus
Consultant, Penn Valley Community College
Division of Continuing Education
Development and Instructor of Primary Manager/Supervisor Training
Seminars for Private Security Personnel
Former Senior Vice-President and Principal Instructor
for Assessment Preparation Training, Inc.
Overland Park, Kansas

CHARLES C THOMAS • PUBLISHER, LTD.
Springfield • Illinois • U.S.A.

Published and Distributed Throughout the World by

CHARLES C THOMAS • PUBLISHER, LTD.
2600 South First Street
Springfield, Illinois 62704

© 1988, 1995, 2002, and 2012 by CHARLES C THOMAS • PUBLISHER, LTD.

ISBN 978-0-398-08710-4 (hard)
ISBN 978-0-398-08711-1 (paper)
ISBN 978-0-398-08712-8 (ebook)

Library of Congress Catalog Card Number: 2011033304

First Edition, 1988
Second Edition, 1995
Third Edition, 2002
Fourth Edition, 2012

With THOMAS BOOKS *careful attention is given to all details of manufacturing
and design. It is the Publisher's desire to present books that are satisfactory as to their
physical qualities and artistic possibilities and appropriate for their particular use.*
THOMAS BOOKS *will be true to those laws of quality that assure a good name
and good will.*

Printed in the United States of America
MM-R-3

Library of Congress Cataloging-in-Publication Data

Coleman, John L.
  Operational mid-level management for police / by John L. Coleman
-- 4th ed.
    p. cm.
  Includes bibliographical references and index.
  ISBN 978-0-398-08710-4 (hard) -- ISBN 978-0-398-08711-1 (pbk.) --
ISBN 978-0-398-08712-8 (ebook)
  1. Police--Supervision of. 2. Police--Supervision of--United States. 3.
Police--Personnel management. 4. Police--United States--Personnel
management. I. Title.

  HV7936.S8C65 2012
  363.2068--dc22
                                                    2011033304

PREFACE

The primary principles that are the foundation of this book and the managerial doctrine set forth for mid-level police managers is unchanged, and the ultimate objective is for the effective and professional performance of the defined law enforcement leader. The basic concept aforestated is true even in the current period of time, where managerial leadership must adapt to the behaviors of subordinates in this fast-paced era of almost instant knowledge expansion, coupled with subordinates' attitudes and expectations based on a desire for "instant gratification." It has become increasingly clear during the last few years that law enforcement goals and objectives cannot be accomplished in the absence of well-trained and effective managerial performers. Thus, the nature and content of this text became necessary and important to the ultimate achievement of the basic objective of most if not all police agencies. It cannot and should not be overlooked that the fundamental purpose of law enforcement is to serve the clientele of its community, and this can only be accomplished if all elements of the organization function in a manner that is interactive and responsive to the problems confronted. Therefore, the linchpin between executive and functional-level police (mid-level police managers) must operate within the parameter of an established pattern of standards and goal-oriented job leadership behaviors.

The focal pattern of this text and many leadership books aims to provide not only a framework from which a majority of the ideals and theories germinate but their environmental development. The text will delineate the practical application of Middle Management in its many forms. Some texts have set forth formulas that are projected to achieve managerial success. However, in this age of rapidly expanding informational awareness and technological advancements, it would appear that a fixed or non-fluid criterion would not be adequate. Thus, this text provides a structural application useful to Mid-Level Police Management.

The author has expanded the content of this fourth edition to enhance its requirements as a must read book for Operational Mid-Level Police Management. The addition of the aspects of foundational Leadership Standards and Standardization to the content of this text moves this book further toward the forefront of published managerial material for police management. This fourth edition is clearly written with a dynamic flow of leadership information that will expand the knowledge of its readers. This updated text was crafted with judicious knowledge and a point of focus for clarity of information and useful application to Mid-Level Police Management. It articulates the Development of a Leadership Vision to enhance the establishment of a viable Manpower Usage Strategy that destines the expressed Planning and Organization projections in the text for successful application.

The information content in this book is non-traditional in many respects but yet very familiar to some of the contemporary innovative leadership teachings. It was written to concisely address the issues and characteristics that confront mid-level police managers. Thus, there are references to traditional leadership concepts and practices that the author perceives as contemporary. However, this text has advanced beyond the traditional and ordinary to introduce some psychological and managerial theories not typically applied to a secondary leader. The author has attempted to challenge the traditional concept that workers can be motivated through the efforts of a primary or secondary leader or other job inducements used by management. Motivation as a job performance concept is a self-generated course of action and/or desire on the part of an individual to accomplish a task. Job performance or behaviors prompted by a leader's actions is primarily attainment of responsive actions and not an internal desire to accomplish. Thus, managerial actions result in responsive behavior instead of worker motivation.

Functional-level police employees, like leaders and managers in all strata of the organization, are motivated (inspired) to action by some inner desire or need to perform. A leader may use positive or negative sanctions to induce or manipulate behaviors and performance actions in workers. But in its truest sense, such action cannot be regarded as motivated or self-inspired actions. Motivation is an internal initiative concept individualized to the personal level.

The contextual content of this text is aimed at operational behavior of mid-level secondary police leaders to attain desired performance of line workers through interactive and specifically focused management actions. An acute awareness of personal self is also identified as a prime factor in a secondary leader's ability to direct and control the behavior of others. Readers of this text should perceive a growth in their overall leadership skills and a better awareness of how his or her own personality influences the work environment, as well as how the work atmosphere or environment affects the job performance of functional personnel.

J.L.C.

ACKNOWLEDGMENTS

Many individuals played an essential role in the development of this text. The information presented in this book was gathered through many hours of research by the author, but the guidance inspirations offered by family and colleagues were extremely valuable. Special consideration and notice must be given to Gaynell Coleman (my wife) for motivation and time dedicated to helping ensure the grammatical correctness of the contents of this text.

The development of this text is the culmination of years of experience, research, and training in the area of personnel management. The author acknowledges the dedicated effort and committed assistance provided by Mrs. Rose Garner. Her selfless efforts and time committed is reflected throughout this book. Also, special notice is extended to Sergeant Robert Mesa (Retired) of the Kansas City, Missouri Police Department for the illustrations used in this text. **Thank you one and all!**

CONTENTS

OPERATIONAL MID-LEVEL MANAGEMENT FOR POLICE

Chapter One

INTRODUCTION

ASSESSING POLICE MID-LEVEL LEADERSHIP

The essence of mid-level police leadership assessment has traditionally focused on the actions of leaders to increase productivity and performance of functional workers through the efforts of primary leaders. While the author agrees with this basic approach to leadership study and research, it is believed that a brief self-analysis relative to the *psychology of leadership* would greatly enhance the effectiveness of a leader. During our introductory assessment of police mid-level management, we will also attempt to briefly explore the evolutionary development of interactive human relationships of superiors and subordinates.

The current age of intensely enlighten subordinates has made it necessary for effective Mid-Level Police Management to better anticipate and project actions to productively deal with behavioral and operational changes. Most societal and external influences, to a police agency, have traditionally not been considered a major factor that the Mid-Level Police Managers had to be overly concerned. However, this time of almost instant informational awareness by subordinates emphasizes the need for leaders to be more aware of appropriate managerial knowledge and actions. This awareness must include how leadership approaches have evolved over time and how they must adjust in future.

The *clinical leadership prospective* had its beginning in the pre-Civil War era in this country. It has for the most part been applied principally to technical specialists. However, with the emergence of the Industrial Revolution, the concept became more widely used and accepted. Police management during the decade of the 1950s, like most industries, began to focus on the treatment of workers and the job environment as having a direct bearing on performance and productivity. Since the 1950s, there has been an explosion of training requirements based on a *needs analysis* to keep up with the changing atmosphere of the work place as well as the knowledge expansion of workers. The environmental changes created by many women and other minorities entering police work has also forced an attitudinal change. The attitudinal changes brought about by these events has forced all levels of organizational leadership to reevaluate perceptions and adjust. The advancement of performance skills by workers new to the organization has also forced mid-level police managers and both their superiors and subordinate leaders to change their previous philosophy of *one best person for the job*. They have been required by enacted laws and operational objectives to *cross-train* and involve multiple workers to assure achievement of desired goals.

The clinical leadership approach used by past mid-level police leaders traditionally attempted to enhance performance by both positive and negative incentive inducements. Also, they attempted to utilize the physical work environment as a way of obtaining greater efficiency in workers. However, police leaders and managers of today seem more willing to recognize that while incentives can have a desired effect, its tenure tends to be very limited. They (police leaders) have come to realize that inspirational challenges, coupled with incentive inducements, tend to be more lasting and effective in improving worker performance. The trend during the Industrial Revolution (and well into the middle of the 1900s) was to view workers as mere factors to be used to achieve an objective. The past trend of viewing workers in the same perspective as any other resource tool is no longer practical. Today's functional-level police officers, like his/her counterpart in other industries, is not as willing to think organization first and self-interest second. The reverse of that philosophy seems to be the rule rather than the exception.

The operational sphere of law enforcement in this time of increased threats of terrorism, higher level individual intelligence, and a greater trend toward organizations that operate counter to the policing objective has considerably influenced the actions of Police Management in directing law enforcement actions. The author, as an intellectual theorist, believes that mid-level police management can achieve leadership effectiveness through simulation, which can then be used as teaching aids to expand the performance knowledge of functional managers. The positive aspect of this view seeks to refocus the perception of the problem being confronted from a negative challenge into a motivational and constructive achievement of goals. This may be accomplished by the "old adage" of comparative analysis, in other words, gauging effectiveness by counting positives achievements against the number of failures. But to effectively use this approach, it will require skillful and knowledgeably competent mid-level managers to recognize the opportunities and push forward to help subordinates obtain self-actualization from the challenges and results. In other words, a good mid-level police leader will more often than not see obstacles to success as constructive opportunities rather than as negative impediments to his/her operational effectiveness.

A PSYCHOLOGICAL ASSESSMENT
OF ONE'S SELF AS A LEADER

A psychological look at one's self is non-traditional when discussing leadership and how to be an effective leader. However, it has long been a consideration that effective leaders at all levels of the organization must have a working knowledge of the expectations of others regarding job performance. The psychological awareness question addresses the fact that a leader, no matter what his or her rank status, must have an analytical knowledge of personal expectations and abilities to accomplish the job. In doing the research for this text, the author concluded that awareness of one's own personality traits would benefit a leader in his or her personal interactions and in the acceptance of the behavior of others.

In considering one's own psychological self, there are several aspects that are considered critical by a number of noted psychologists. The self-appraisal of one's psychological self should begin with *the necessary components that combine to create what is termed our personality.* The collective components as identified by such noted psychologists as C.R. Rogers, G.D. Goodwin, and G. Freud are the **Inter-Active Self, the Materialistic Self, the Non-Corporal Self**, and the **Prideful Self**. Collectively, the aforementioned components combine to form an individual's personality. The **Personality** is defined, for the purposes of this discussion as *the habitual patterns and qualities of behavior of an individual, as may be expressed in personal attitude, physical performances, and intellectual actions.* The **Inter-Active Self** has to do with how the police mid-level manager is perceived by him/herself as well as others. These expectations or perceptions will influence a mid-level police leader's behavioral responses and performance manipulation of workers through his/her subordinate leaders. It must be realized that no matter what actions a mid-level manager takes or how perceptually correct his or her performance may be, the person cannot be considered an effective leader if the **followership** of others is not obtained. The **Materialistic Self** refers to a person's desire to obtain or acquire items of perceptual value. The value is usually based on a self-perception of worth. Therefore, it should be noted that a police leader or mid-level manager may value a role assignment more than an acquisition of monetary gain. If this is so, then the mid-level police leader (manager) should realize that noteworthy success and recognition is more important to him/

her than may be the acquisition of bonus incentives. The **Non-Corporal Self** represents the thinking, motivating, and feelings of the leader. It is the creative and intuitive aspects of a person's character that contribute to the spiritual and non-physical parts of the personality. The **Prideful Self** is personal gratification that a person perceives relative to personal importance. It provides the essence for a leader to consider his/her own interest, the part of the personality that gives a leader self-confidence in personal perceptions and/or actions. The collective of these personality components combines to form an effective leader. Therefore, if a positionally placed leader determines that he or she is deficient in either of these component areas, a concentrated effort can be made to strengthen the perceptively weak area. An effective mid-level police manager is not fearful to do the type of self-psychological analysis that will provide an insightful view of personal strengths and weaknesses.

Before conducting the discussion of the psychological aspects of personality as it pertains to leadership, it is essential that the term *self* as a concept be clearly defined as it relates to a managerial focus. **Self**, as a concept of personal analysis concerning a mid-level leader, has a double meaning. The first has to do with formed attitudes, the "I" concept, referring to what is concluded about one's own actions. Also, in this portion of the definition *self* is conceived as a doer, in the sense that certain aspects relate to a non-corporal process such as concentration, memory, and perception. This area basically considers *self satisfaction* as the objective. The second aspect of the *self* definition has to do with the performing portion of the personality; in other words, the consideration of self as a process. *Self* in this phase of the definition is a performance technique. The two components of *self* may be so different in each of the two meanings that it would be best to separate them. It should be clarified and understood that no current theory of leadership concludes that *self* is a dominant aspect which regulates the actions of a leader. But some psychologists who have researched leadership from a psychological perspective do recognize that the *perceptual self governs* the *self* aspect of a leader's expectations.

The above psychological review of personality and self as a leadership consideration represents a serious attempt by the author to account for certain behavioral actions and to conceptualize a leader's personal view of certain aspects of one's own self. The use of the term **doer**, as defined in some psychological texts, does not imply that it is anything other than an identifying associate to the self-analysis process. Productive leaders are not fearful to analyze themselves in attempting to determine how they can become more effective. More often than not, our own individual personality has more to do with positive interactions than do overt actions. Knowing yourself and knowing your limitations will greatly benefit a leader in his or her interaction with subordinates.

MID-LEVEL POLICE LEADERSHIP
(Mid-Level or Operational-Level Management)

A mid-level police manager or leader is directly responsible for the operational duties performed by line personnel. They are the second level of management above the functional workers of the police organization. Their responsibility is limited in scope relative to managers higher up in the organization's hierarchy. Police mid-level managers are considered a primary member of the management team, even though in some unionized departments secondary and line leadership are allowed to join the union. The distinction of being allowed to be a member of the union does not erase the fact that mid-level leadership is responsible for the job performance of others through primary leaders. Operational-level leaders are principally concerned with performance output of others through subordinate leaders and application of rules, regulations, policies, and procedures to achieve the department's basic objective. Since mid-level police managers have constant contact with superiors and subordinates, the middle level of managerial leadership's time horizon for meeting task expectations by operational workers is usually limited. In other words, a second-line leader usually works in the here-and-now aspect of task accomplishment and not just in a visualized future. Secondary police managers must possess a multitude of skills, because he or she supervise functional subordinates through line leadership and also must deal with superiors, who are planners and visionaries. There is a need to know something about the nuts-and-bolts (foundational) operation of line personnel, as well as being able to think and talk strategy with peers and the organization's hierarchy. The skill most essential to operational-level police supervision or mid-level management is the ability to deal effectively with people.

A possession of human skills is an essential aspect of a mid-level leader's ability to perform his or her assigned task. The mid-level police leader is responsible for getting tasks accomplished through and with the efforts of others. The mid-level police manager is expected to perform effectively as a director and controller of subordinates. Effective secondary leaders can demonstrate human skills in the way they relate to other people. Traditional concepts associated with the required skills of an effective mid-level police leader are as an inspirer, facilitator, coordinator, supervisor, communicator, and mediator. All of the skills mentioned are necessary to be an effective mid-level police manager, but an ability to deal effectively with people is by far the most essential skill. A leader possessing adequate human skills will allow subordinates to express their concerns and suggestions without being fearful of offending or incurring the displeasure of a superior. As a manager of people and having sensitive contact with both the functional supervision and the upper level of management, the mid-level leader has to get the tasks accomplished without allowing the almost adversary action of each to affect his/her task performance. Effective police managers will encourage and utilize the input of subordinates to gain the participatory benefit of workers' involvement. Participation by operational-level employees offers the benefits of input by the individuals most aware of the functional concerns of the organization. And, it also promotes increased operational workers' involvement in assuring the quality of the services provided. We need only to remember that subordinates are human and subject to the same job needs as everyone else. The needs being referred to are articulated in a later chapter, where Maslow's "Hierarchy of Needs" is discussed.

Generally, police mid-level managers who possess an adequate amount of people skills tend to know how to effectively deal with others. They tend to be *respected* by their subordinates and in turn are *concerned* about their workers. The use of the terms **respected** and **concerned** does not imply that the leader is easy or weak. It does indicate a projected fairness and objectivity in his/her approach when dealing with subordinates.

Mid-level police leaders who lack the appropriate people skills will often be visibly abrupt, frequently critical of others, and unsympathetic towards worker problems. The leader will often appear to purposefully separate his/herself from others in the organization. The leader who acts in such a manner appears deliberately arrogant in his/her lack of concern for others. The leader with poor people skills tends to be most effective in autocratic situations where they rely only on personal decision-making ability.

New employees require functional-level supervisors and mid-level managers to have an awareness of the importance of people skills. The truly effective mid-level leader is a cheerleader, a coach, and a nurturer, when the situation requires. Along with traits previously mentioned, it is clear that a mid-level police leader must be more than a task master relative to job performances. The mid-level manager must also endeavor to make subordinates want to do the job rather than being forced to; plus, the leader's efforts should enhance employee morale and desire for productive output.

LEADERSHIP: AUTHORITY AND POWER

The authority and/or power exercised by a leader in an organization is more often **positionally placed** and **formal**, meaning that the manipulative controls exercised over functional police supervisors and officers by a mid-level leader is set forth by the organization. However, there is a concept of **informal** leadership within all organizations that should not and cannot be overlooked. Police departments, like other companies, have a formalized structure as set forth in its Table of Organization or developmental charter. In the formally designed structures, leaders at all levels are designated by hierarchical management based upon title and positional responsibility.

Thus, we term this type of leadership as **formal**. **Informal** leadership within an organization, even in a para-military one like public policing, is inter-active people-to-people contacts. This type of leadership is generated by the ability of the person to obtain followership through his/her charisma, job knowledge, or general personality traits. Informal leaders often do not seek to be considered leaders and most generally have the followership thrust upon them. The dominance of a leader, whether formal or informal, will often depend upon the person's desire for the authority and the dis-

"Sally, meet Sgt. Benn and Commander Jerris. Jerris has the <u>Organizational Authority</u> by virtue of his rank and Benn has <u>Influence Power</u> because of his informal leadership control of the unit's line supervisors."

RESEARCH HAS SHOWN THAT BOTH THE FORMAL AND INFORMAL LEADER IS IMPORTANT TO THE PERFORMANCE SUCCESS OF A GROUP.

played ability as gauged by subordinates or willing followers. The need to consider both aspects of leadership is essential, because it must be recognized that the person who has the authority may or may not always have controlling power. And, likewise, the person having controlling power over others may not always possess the authority.

The concept of authority is usually positionally placed and enacted by the organization for an individual to direct and control the behavior of subordinates. A police mid-level manager is granted the options and ability to use sanctions, both positive or negative, to enforce desired behaviors and job performance in others. This, simply stated, is **authority**, and since control is typically synonymous with power, the mid-level manager has the clout to enforce subordinates' actions. **Power**, on the other hand, is an individual's ability to manipulate and/or control the actions of others by their voluntary compliance with the person's stated wants. The ability to obtain the voluntary followership of others may be partially innate, a charismatic ability, or it could be acquired by the person's performance ability. The controlling efforts executed and/or complied with, whether *formal,* or *informal* (*positional authority* or *influencing power*), all serve to affect the job performance of others. And, a mid-level manager must be aware of these concepts and have the ability to utilize his/her personal position and the innate informal power of his/her or another to be most effective in obtaining desired performance behaviors by subordinates. Quite literally, *authority* may be defined as the enforcement controls created by the formal structure of the organization. And, **power** is explained as the informal process of directing and influencing the behavior of others through their personal desire to react.

There is a general **give and take** between the organization's leadership and its functional personnel in accomplishing goals and objectives. The leadership, including primary and mid-level management, desire certain performance behaviors that will result in accomplishment of overall goals and objectives. Operational police officers, like other workers, are concerned with challenging work, job security, positive incentives, and satisfactory accomplishments. Later in this text, the Motivational Theory concepts will be discussed regarding worker behavior and enhanced job performances. An analytical assessment of which entity, *organizational leadership* or the *functional workers,* wins in the conjectured give and take confrontation reveals that neither one is a total winner. Compromise is usually the result, with neither entity accepting what it considers less than minimal.

Because authority is positionally placed, there is no need to analyze it in depth. Basically, execution of formalized sanctions is an upper-level consideration. However, power or authority as a concept and as applied to mid-level leadership generally requires the use of networking skills and a well thought out interactive behavioral approach. The networking skills, better known as political tactics, should be subtle as opposed to an obvious attempt to be popular. It should be recognized that the organizationally sanctioned authority of a leader will determine what approach a mid-level manager must use to be considered a positive networker. In concluding our discussion of **authority** and **power**, it should be remembered that *authority is the right to enforce action and is authorized by superiors to a subordinate,* while *power is the ability to influence, persuade, or inspire actions in another person(s).* The effectiveness of a mid-level manager may rest upon a personal knowledge of each concept and which can be used to a personal advantage in inspiring the performance of subordinates.

LEADERSHIP APPROACH TO DUTIES

A police mid-level leader must consider the perceptual interpretations that subordinates and superiors will view his or her performance actions. The principal benefit to any action taken by a leader can be gauged by the results that are revealed in the job performance of subordinates. In order to better understand the ways in which a leader's approach may influence subordinates' job actions, some objectives and obstacles, both positive and negative, should be identified relative to their effect on the leader's approach to duties. Some of the identified objectives are:

1. **Task Accomplishment**. This refers to the performance approach being geared toward assuring desired task accomplishment through the providing of appropriate information, monitored overview of work, and a clearly defined objective. The desired expectation of efforts must be appropriately articulated and understood by the persons expected to perform the actual work.

2. **Job Satisfaction for Workers**. The leader should, through his or her approach and design of a plan of action to achieve the desired task, consider some measure of job satisfaction for the workers. In an industrial factory, line workers are asked to provide input on production expectation and operational methods and are shown how their contribution fits into the overall finished product. It is recognized that because public police provides a law enforcement *service,* a tangible view of the ultimate results of their efforts are not typically possible. But allowing primary supervisors and line officers some input as to performance methods and the developing of strategies to deal with certain significant problems may provide the challenge to produce job

satisfaction. Functional police leaders who are self-assured and confident in their management ability are not fearful to utilize this approach whenever possible.

3. **Emotional Outlet of Employees**. A mid-level police manager must realize that at times employees' emotions become a factor. It is at these times that an effective leader should have a process that can act as a safety valve for the outlet of the subordinate's emotions. The employee must be allowed to have an opportunity to vent pent-up stressful emotions. This is especially true in police work, where it can be disastrous to allow an officer to carry job or situational stress from one call for service to the next, and so on. Such action may at some point cause the officer to respond inappropriately, primarily because of an overstressed condition.

4. **Establishing Both a Formal and Informal Feedback Process**. The effective mid-level police leader will set into place a feedback process that will allow interactive responses from subordinates. This will allow the mid-level leader to obtain subordinate information as to the effectiveness of the implementation process, the appropriateness of the decision, and/or any developing problems that may be averted.

The areas identified above are certainly not a panacea to effective performance as a mid-level police leader. It is an introductory set of factors that will assist a leader with other more detailed and specific functions of an efficient and effective mid-level manager.

There are a number of obstacles that a mid-level police leader needs to be aware of and in which he/she should plan a personal performance approach in order to minimize their effect. Some of the more notable obstacles that a mid-level leader has to deal with are:

1. **Resistance to Change**. A human being as a species of life is a habitual animal and therefore is not subject to change behaviors in the absence of a need to do so for some reason. By this, it is meant that generally people prefer to do the things they are familiar with. Very few of us seek to face new and unanticipated changes in our lives on a regular basis. Consider, for example, how many of us get up each morning at the same time, go through the patterned process of cleaning up for the day, dressing, and taking the same route to work day after day. This is not to say that anything is wrong with this or that some people don't deviate from doing continually what has worked well in the past. But even when we attempt to be unpredictable, we often establish a pattern of unpredictability that is predictable. In a

study utilizing private security guards at a plant who were reminded each day at the start of duty that they should attempt to be unpredictable in their patrol pattern, it was determined through observation that the physical needs and psychological factors, as well as an inborn tendency to continue what has worked well in the past, soon made their unpredictable actions predictable. This refers to the fact that it could be determined almost exactly when they would do something unpredictable. Therefore, the police mid-level leader must be aware that subordinates do not accept changes without some resistance, whether expressed or not. A mid-level leader should not overreact to this resistance to change. He or she should implement alterations as needed and allow subordinates, if the situation permits, time to adjust and even to question. Explaining a change, if time and the situation allow, does not alter a leader's authority by providing insight to subordinates. It may make his or her job easier and elicit more productivity and effectiveness from subordinates.

2. **Conflict of Objectives**. Frequently, in large organizations with multiple tasks, such as a police operation, it is not unusual for two or more objectives to conflict in some way. The leader must be aware that such occurrences may happen. And, when interactive conflict of goals and objectives occur, the mid-level police leader must assess the conflict areas and devise adjustments to make the activities compatible. Harmonious compatibility should not always be expected in multifaceted organizations with varying task obligations. An effective mid-level leader should anticipate problems and be prepared to effectively deal with or minimize the counterefforts of the goal conflicts that occur.

3. **Conformity Concerns**. The effective police mid-level manager should be aware that the barrier of conformity as a concern is closely associated with *conflict of objectives*. The norms of applied sanctions are typically the processes used to persuade subordinates to accept the goal objectives of the element and the organization. It is not uncommon for peer pressure and/or organizational culture to be just as strong an influence of employee behavior as potential sanctions or incentives. Of course, the conformity pressure that an employee faces can involve influence factors that are less noticeable than an overt sanction. The mid-level manager should be aware of the *conformity barriers* and attempt to assure the informal leaders within the group are a force for desired actions. An adversarial conflict between the formal and informal leader can be counterproductive and make the position leader's accomplishment of task objective through subordinates' efforts very difficult. To overcome or to minimize the effect of conformity prob-

lems, the police mid-level leader must win over the peer group leaders to accept the aims of the unit and the organization. This may be accomplished through networking or employee involvement and/or as a last resort transfer of the nonconforming peer group leader thus creating another informal leader that may be more receptive to conformity to work objectives.

4. **Rumors or Partial Information**. Virtually no department or entity of an organization is immune to the effects of rumors and half-truths. A mid-level police leader should recognize this as a natural barrier to the performance objective of subordinates. Rumors and partial information generally are transmitted along the lines of informal communication (the grapevine) and are seldom openly stated in an attempt to get accurate or complete information. Secondary police leaders who have an interactive and functioning feedback relationship with subordinates will be made aware of the rumor or partial information. The effective and efficient police mid-level manager will inquire of knowledgeable sources to obtain the true and accurate information. This information should then be released to the informal network as well as being addressed in his/her formal processes as a positional leader. The information concerning the rumor should be verified and complete before the leader releases it. If he or she furnishes counteractive data that is not wholly accurate, personal credibility as a knowledge source for subordinates may be destroyed. Remember, rumors usually develop from some source where there is an interest by those spreading the information, which makes it a factor not to be ignored. Rumors and misinformation are typically maintained and enhanced by selective filtering and elaborations as it is spread.

An effective police mid-level leader will recognize the inevitability of the barriers identified in an organizational setting. The leader should make a direct and influencing effort to short-circuit the barriers/obstacles so that goals and objectives of both the unit and the organization are in harmony and achievable. Mid-level leadership in a police organization must be aware of the fact that the barriers to goal accomplishment cannot be totally eliminated. Thus, it will serve the mid-level police leader well to understand the reality of their existence and to attempt to lessen the negative effect. Also, a mid-level police leader should attempt to influence their direction and consequences toward accomplishment of goals and objectives.

The introductory information provided in this chapter was aimed at providing a brief insight into the preliminary areas of mid-level police leadership and management. The following sections of this text are structured and content-focused to provide a more detailed analysis and informative presentation of information. The information presented should enhance the capability and knowledge of mid-level operational police leaders. In essence, the contention of this book is that **effectiveness as an operational mid-level police manager** *can be learned*. Also, that the successful use of the information presented in this text will enhance the performance of both new and incumbent mid-level police leaders.

PRINCIPLES OF PRIMARY POLICE LEADERSHIP

Primary managerial leadership in a police organization is a process whereby a person positionally placed directs others through manipulation or coercive inspiration to accomplish a goal or objective. An efficient and effective police mid-level manager will mentally project the planned accomplishment and the method that must be induced from others to achieve the desired results. The leader must have the ability to influence subordinates to direct their effort toward the desired task achievement. An effective mid-level police leader should generate a desire in subordinates to work toward accomplishment of the goal and objective. There is little doubt that a leader who is ineffective in inspiring a desire in others to work toward a specific purpose is a failure as mid-level manager. Later in this text we will discuss leadership styles and methods of getting tasks accomplished through the work of others. But there can be no assumed measure of success as a leader, if the person cannot have others follow his or her personal directions to task achievement. Therefore, it is clear that the **Principles of Primary Leadership** and the performance characteristics of an effective mid-level manager are synonymous.

Leadership theorists do not agree on a single approach or functional effort that will be successful for all leaders. The fundamental leadership traits that seem most necessary for an effective leader are: (1) **innovation**, *a willingness to venture beyond the status quo for desired results;* (2) **directing force**, *an ability and desire to urge others toward task achievement;* and (3) **patience**, *the capability to be tolerant of the work behaviors of others.* It has been generally concluded that these **Principles of Leadership** are the basic qualities that a successful mid-level police leader must possess. The assumption of most theorists is that if a person possesses the aforementioned leadership traits along with some innate or developed personality characteristics, the individual can perform appropriately as a leader. There is a school of thought among other theorists that certain personal attributes are the foundational basis for effectiveness as a leader. The personal attributes most mentioned are: (1) **Intel-**

lect, *a mental ability to comprehend a situation and the capability to devise a method to achieve desired results;* (2) **Controlled Reactive Perception,** *a developed ability to objectively react to an arousing situation;* and (3) **Assessment and Resolution Skills,** *the need to possess a capability to perceive the essence of a concern and the experienced know-how to formulate a resolutive plan of action.*

Many teachers and researchers in the field of leadership recognize that there is not one universal set of characteristics or traits that make up an effective leader. However, there is a general assumption that certain traits, such as *a zest for the job, a willingness to commit one's self a degree of intellectual ability,* and *the capability to develop and implement solutions to problems,* are typically possessed by effective leaders. The author has attempted to this point to not specifically address personality characteristics, in that many of them may be considered innate qualities. Previously, the psychological qualities and innate abilities of an effective leader was briefly discussed. It has not gone unnoticed how personal trait characteristics influence an individual's leadership ability. However, as a practitioner of the concept that **effective leaders are not born,** this author prefers to focus on areas of leadership knowledge and practices that can be learned. It is simple enough to say that a person who is born with an intellectual handicap will not be an effective leader. But, if we exclude the obvious problems caused by an unchangeable, inborn handicap and concentrate on a perceptually average individual, it is contended that the person can learn to be both efficient and effective as a leader. Public policing is such a demanding field, in terms of knowledge needs and performance capability, that it is apparent that a formalized and practical approach to positive leadership is very necessary.

INSTITUTIONALIZED LEADERSHIP

There is a need for a formalized professional approach to mid-level leadership assessment in public law enforcement. Mid-level managerial police leadership is the foundational area upon which all other organizational upper management must focus. The mid-level leaders for functional management of any organization (law enforcement included) must formulate its attainments of goals and objectives on the performance capability of operational level employees. It is true that top hierarchical management formulates the leadership structure and typically establishes the parameters in which each positional leader will function. And, it is recognized that the very top of the organizational structure and the primary levels of leadership is where the majority of decisions are made. The mid-level managers generally make operational decisions that affect basic work performance, while the organization's leaders make the monumental decisions that affect the overall agency. Most managerial leaders of today are confronted with a multitude of legal concerns regarding employee rights that were only conceptualized and/ or developed in recent decades. Modern leadership at all levels of the organization operates in an environment that is ever-changing.

REQUIRED EFFECTIVENESS OF A MID-LEVEL POLICE MANAGER

Operational management within a police department is a critical and very important position, primarily because it requires a knowledge of functional matters from the operational level while maintaining a leadership position within the hierarchical structure of the department. Each operational police manager must be a skillful leader in the handling and control of departmental resources, both human and logistical. There are times when his or her attention and prime consideration will be the acquisition and allocation of material resources, while at other times an operational manager may have to concentrate on personnel matters and controls. Delegated authority to subordinates of primary functional leadership in various operational matters does not abrogate the manager's ultimate responsibility. The effectiveness with which operational police managers, who are responsible for a functional operation, perform their job will determine the successfulness of the overall department. An operational police manager's behavior in the context of this book is principally from a performance perspective of required **dimensional trait characteristics**. The needs and techniques for the handling and allocation of organizational resources will also be discussed, along with the various methods of skill enhancement.

It is evident that with the exception of direct functional leadership, the position of operational manager is the single most critical job in a police organization. The job requires a mental awareness that is superior to most organizational task assignments, plus an insight into possible future needs or trends and the performance skills to translate all of the qualities identified into desired results through the work of others. Management from the hierarchical level is difficult, but a middle manager in a police operation, who is held responsible for task accomplishment even though he or she may be one or more steps removed from direct or actual control of the task, is exceptional. However, the contention of this text is that an operational police manager can improve his or her job performance skills through a dedicated effort, purposeful knowledge and actual functional experience.

An effective operational leader will recognize that the various goals and objectives of his or her element and those of the overall department will determine subordinate performance aims. Likewise, the individual should realize from a managerial perspective that subordinates' performance productivity depends on direct and indirect leadership controls. And, no matter what the organizational leadership responsibility or authority level, they cannot be separated from one another, primarily because of their interactive and coordinated efforts toward ultimate mission accomplishment. Also, the individual performances of each positional leader should be complementary of the job activity of all others so that objective attainment becomes a mutually shared effort.

The upper echelon of the department is traditionally concerned with the overall organizational operation and mission accomplishment. Functional or line leadership is said to be generally focused on **improving work performance** and **productivity of workers**. Our perception in this book is that an operational police manager functions somewhere between these two focuses. An effective manager at the operational level of responsibility of an organization cannot concentrate personal efforts exclusively in either direction. Upper management views the operational leader as a member of the organization's **decision-making** hierarchy, while functional-level employees tend to view the position as their true link and/or voice to the upper echelon of the department. The perceptions emphasized make it clear that an operational leader should be aware that his or her job performance projects a dichotomy of being influentially involved with two mutually exclusive components.

An operational police manager in our ever-changing society must acquire and utilize as wide a variety of information as possible. This knowledge expansion has become necessary because of the rapid changes in behavioral philosophy of both police clientele and employees. Reactive leadership will always be a major consideration in evaluating the performance of police managers. But there will also remain a **set core** of dimensional trait characteristics that are traditionally used to assess overall effectiveness within an established organizational edifice. Therefore, in this book, we have concentrated on a chapter-by-chapter assessment of the significant and enhancement aspects of these dimensional trait characteristics. Much of the leadership trait information considered important to the enhancement of managerial effectiveness has been incorporated into the documented content. It has been concluded that if the contents of this book are comprehensively reviewed and the information utilized, an operational police manager can noticeably improve his or her job performance behaviors. The expanded knowledge concept projected in this text is based on an awareness that as subordinates' basic needs and behaviors increase in complexity, so to must the leader's aptitude. A positional leader's capability to assess and take appropriate action relative to the non-traditional behaviors must also be improved. It is with this principle concept of possible **self-improvement** by an operational police manager that this text was developed.

It is recognized that the dimensional traits utilized in this text is not all-inclusive as to the essential characteristics of an effective police manager. However, research has shown that of the multitude of possible traits, the nine or so identified and discussed in this book are the most universally used. They are utilized to **test for** or **measure the potential** leadership qualities in promotional processes, as well as the evaluation of incumbent positional leaders. The dimensional trait characteristics chosen for discussion and detailing in this book are: (1) obtaining follow-ships, (2) performance initiative, (3) analysis skill, (4) decision making, (5) strategy projection, (6) communication, (7) logical inferences, (8) job performance controls, and (9) delegation. As is readily apparent, each of the listed areas could be considered indispensable to effective performance by a positional leader in a police department.

The author's concept for enhancing the leadership capability of an operational police manager may not be a totally new idea. However, the basic approach and manner in which each dimensional trait is addressed appear to be somewhat unique. It cannot be classified as a purely clinical approach to leadership, even though only practical and proven techniques are recommended. What the author has attempted to do is take the performance requirements of an operational manager and separate them into interrelated parts that when discussed will simplify the concept of operational leadership and provide an indication of techniques or methods for performance skill improvements. Approaches and concepts closely akin to **scientific management** have been used to strengthen the organizational characteristics that are indelible to law enforcement operations. We are referring to conceptual characteristics, such as **formal chain of command**, **strict lines of authority**, **clarified performance responsibilities**, and **specific organizational goals and objectives**. An operational philosophy of result-oriented functioning that parallels scientific management was also employed as an essential criteria of positional leadership.

It should be noted that in order to provide a comprehensively sound introduction to any adequate discussion of operational management, there are some essential factors that must be set forth. Initially, it must be revealed that operational management, like line leadership, should remain sensitive to the changes that permeate the department. The effective operational police leader will be alert to opportunities to allow both direct and indirect subordinates to express creativity, thus allowing them to grow in their job and maximize their chances of promotional advancement. In addition to opportunities provided subordinates, a truly efficient and effective operational police manager is stimulated toward independent performance initiative, plus a self-reliance on personal capability and know-how, along with the courage to not only accept but also seek added responsibility for difficult tasks to enhance personal abilities.

The primary aspect of an examination of dimensional trait characteristics is to explore and provide techniques or methods that operational management can utilize in daily job performances. Trait characteristics of an operational police manager are used in much the same manner as functional tools to a line worker. The more knowledgeable and practiced the individual is with a certain tool, the greater will be his or her level of confidence in using the instrument. And, in sequence, the greater the level of confidence, the more productive and effective will be the performance of the individual in using that tool.

Earlier in this chapter we identified the dimensional trait characteristics that are typically considered the primary tools of operational police man-

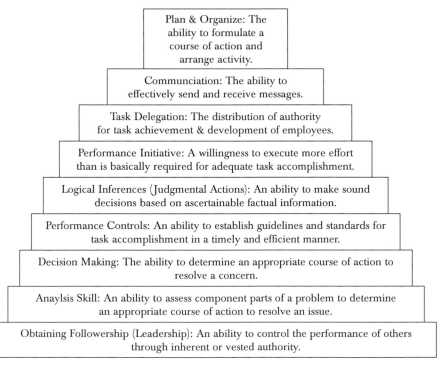

THE BUILDING BLOCKS FOR OPERATIONAL LEADERSHIP SUCCESS

agement. Clarification of what is meant by operational management at this time may be appropriate for definitive purposes and more effective reader comprehension. Basically, we are all aware of the basic definition of management as a leadership phenomenon, but **operational management** is merely the terminology utilized to focus attention on the level of the individual's authority and responsibility. Primarily, an operational manager is responsible for the functional activity of line personnel and its primary leadership. If we think in terms of hierarchy levels of leadership, an operational manager would be a second line leader—a recognized and important member of a department's hierarchical staff, yet sharing an interrelationship to line functions through his or her operational responsibilities. We are not trying to paint a picture of the individual as being neither management nor functional. However, he or she does operate somewhere in between the two extremes, with a noticeable tilt toward managerial philosophy and concepts. The concept of being neither staff nor functional is simply not accurate; an operational police manager is, pure and simple, a member of the management team. But, because of his or her specific knowledge, expectations and leadership responsibilities make for a kinship with line leadership and functional personnel. From this somewhat lengthy explanation of the operational managerial concept, hopefully it will enhance the reader's comprehension of the importance of the leadership trait characteristics discussed.

To further clarify the perspective from which the contents of this text was developed, it should also be noted that the author perceived there to be notable distinctions between leadership and management. It is generally concluded that because the two concepts are used interchangeably (as we use them here), there is no perceptual difference worthy of noting. In a broad sense, the author agrees with this concept; however, in an effort to be as candid as possible, the reader should be aware of the distinction between the two. Basically, as perceived, **leadership** is a much more expansive concept than is management at any authority level of an organizational structure, while **management** is a more focused or narrow form of directional control with specific aims to achieve organizational goals and objectives.

Thus, the primary difference lies in the scope of focus and directional purpose of accomplishing a goal and/or objective. In essence, true leadership need not have a prior specific focus or structured parameters to occur. An individual who is able to obtain the **followership** of others for whatever purpose and for an unspecified period of time must be considered a leader. It may be an intentional or unintentional influence of the behavior of others. Also, it may be accomplished through a knowledgeable effort or an inherently developed ability. While management, on the other hand, is virtually always a purposefully and concentrated effort, existing within preestablished

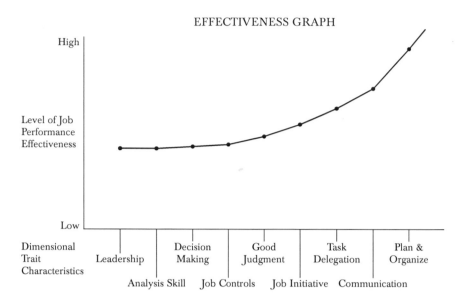

When plotted on an Effectiveness Graph utilizing a curvilinear approach as the basic concept for displaying the sequential mastering of essential managerial skills, the level of Job Performance effectiveness will increase.

parameters and focused for a specific task accomplishment. Generally, personnel management may appear to be not specifically targeted, but a close analysis of what the manager's job entails reveals behaviors and tasks that subordinates are required to achieve under his or her direction. As a further note, **remember it may be for personal goals that a person chooses to follow another person's lead and the individual's objective may have no relevance or consistency with departmental objectives, but it is still a form of leadership**.

Dimensional traits from a **conceptually analytical** standpoint contain moral and ethical criteria that are outgrowths of personal characteristics of an operational police manager referring to the fact that job performance actions of a positional leader have a direct effect on the ethical climate of subordinate personnel. Also, the actions of an operational positional leader must be beyond reproach and must display integrity. It is also an operational police manager's responsibility to preserve and strengthen the logical aspects of his or her personal concepts, through analysis and by developing better ways of cooperative interactions with others. Most positional leaders who are infinitely familiar with and adhere to the concept of dimensional characteristic principles of operational management will generally be more effective managers. The fundamental factors concerned with any specific situation may assist a leader in the selection of the best techniques for efficient job performance behaviors.

The material content of this book is a contemporary view of the fundamental aspects of effectiveness as an operational police manager. The basic intent is to provide both functional and theoretical information for the knowledge expansion and improved performance capability of police managers. We also attempted to anticipate any questions that a new operational leader might ask and then to comprehensively answer these inquiries. Recognition is conceded that in most situations in the field of law enforcement, an operational police manager is a dynamic force. And, through his or her effective performance of certain desired traits, an organization can be more productive and realistically expect to accomplish overall goals and objectives. The material provided in this text has been especially documented to assist incumbent as well as aspiring operational managers. However, like any other informational text, the material presented will only be as effective as the willingness of the individual to read it; if the suggestions and knowledge offered go unutilized, then the material content is of little value to the person. But, on the other hand, if the person chooses to comprehend and use the information to enhance job performance, then there is no limit to how valuable the book might be to that individual.

The content structure has been concentrated in a style and format that should be easily understood and practical from an applicability perspective. Like most textbooks, only a limited amount of information could be provided. Realistically, it would be a virtual impossibility to write a text that would cover every area, problem, concern, or situation that may arise regarding operational management. Therefore, it becomes incumbent upon the reader to supplement the knowledge-acquisition process through other means, such as experience and research, where necessary. For example, we offer some **specific tips** on how an individual can **enhance personal writing skills**, but we also suggest that an individual particularly weak in this area may be well-served to review a text specifically on formal writing practices. In no way do we perceive that the text content of this book is deficient in its material presentation. We simply desire our readers to derive the most productive benefits from the information provided through improved job performance as an operational police manager.

It is important for you to remember during your review of this book that managers are positional leaders who are primarily responsible for assuring that tasks get accomplished through the work of others in the organization. This simplistic statement is applicable to virtually all managers, no matter what industry they are involved in. Most managerial or positional leaders will have in common the responsibility for directing other people. In other words, they will have subordinates whose job performances they are held responsible for. Operational police managers are no different, except on rare occasions. Specifically, some private companies have the luxury of employing two types of managers; the **first** type only manages personnel, while the **second** type controls and accounts for the use of material resources. Budgetary constraints on police departments normally don't allow such latitude of leadership usage. An operational police manager must effectively direct and control (to some degree) the allocation and use of both human and logistical resources within his or her scope of influence.

Chapter Two

OBTAINING FOLLOWERSHIP (LEADERSHIP)

Leadership characteristics as a dimensional requirement for persons in positions of authority and control is the most documented of all identified trait qualities. The obvious reason for this is that principally, without a doubt, it is one of the most critical, if not the primary and/or essential trait characteristic needed by an effective operational leader. The author of this text also subscribes to this basic concept but with some adaptations to the universal perception of leadership. The adjusted concept of which I speak has to do with leadership as a personal characteristic of an individual. Basically, my meaning is this: **the trait qualities or leadership actions taken by a positional leader are worthless unless the individual obtains followership from others**. The old adage that "a leader is only as good as his or her followers" certainly applies. Therefore, the title of "**Obtaining Followership (Leadership)**" is a very appropriate name for this chapter, which highlights the directions and controls exercised as a dimensional trait characteristic of an operational-level police manager.

It is not uncommon in modern-day police organizations for knowledgeable and motivated operational leaders to be concerned with traditional concepts of leadership as well as innovative ways to improve performances. This transition of managerial desires for awareness and enhanced effectiveness can primarily be attributable to improved testing and/or selection processes for promoting police leadership. The "good ole' boy" systems of promoting someone for social or personal reasons has been greatly reduced. Admittedly, it has not departed from some law enforcement advancement processes. However, with increasing frequency, courts at all levels are forcing police departments to set into place promotional processes that can be justified and quantified by objective test scoring, etc. Written tests of the civil service variety have added a sense of fairness to some promotional processes, but they too fall short of getting the best person for the job. Therefore, leading police agencies have had to go to a combination method of scoring, that being a written test and some form of trait evaluation. The institution of the more comprehensive promotional processes have produced a more effective positional police leader, as well as selecting persons who demonstrate a higher level of knowledge and job motivation.

The transitional emphasis of selecting the best qualified police personnel have not halted with the promotional processes but also is applicable to initial employment practices, thus producing a more aware and capable functional-level police subordinate at all organizational plateaus. Most social scientists will agree that the more knowledge an employee has, the less likely he or she is to be easily lead. Therefore, an awareness of appropriate techniques to **obtain followership** of employees and a knowledgeable capability to apply leadership skills is essential, if a police manager is to be effective as an operational leader. As may be apparent from what has been stated thus far in this chapter, the terms **obtaining followership** and **leadership** are considered synonymous and are used interchangeably throughout the chapter. Formally defined, **leadership** means directing or an ability to obtain the followership of others, and conversely, **obtaining followership** is another method of saying the capability to lead other persons.

Obtaining followership like the other dimensional trait characteristics identified in this text must be developed by the police manager. While it is

"Sir, perhaps a utilization of a more conducive interpersonal style would be a better form of leadership."

OBTAINING FOLLOWERSHIP DOES NOT IMPLY A NEED FOR AN APRONSTRING FORM OF LEADERSHIP CONTROL BY A MANAGER.

true that the assigned position produces an inherent authority to exercise directional controls over subordinates, it has been determined that true leadership and productive effectiveness over the long haul must be earned through the performance attributes of the positional leader. Being accepted as a leader requires an acknowledgment of a manager's leadership authority and ability by subordinates. Principally, we are saying that true and effective leadership is a product of subordinates' willingness to follow a positional leader's dictates. Non-effectiveness in obtaining followership does not imply insubordinate behavior on the part of assigned functional-level employees. It may be more subtle than direct disobedience, such as in not automatically looking to the positional leader for guidance in unclear situations, substandard, or merely adequate job performance in compliance with the manager's direction could all be clear indications. Obtaining followership as an operational police manager likewise does not infer a need to short-circuit informal leadership within an element's functioning, nor does it require blind obedience by subordinates. But what it does imply is that the police manager or any positional authority figure be recognized by subordinates as the unquestioned organizational leader from a formal perspective. And, as such, the directions and controls of this formal leader is absolute and binding. A leader in any organization, whether public policing or private industry, should remember that, like respect and confidence, recognized leadership must be earned. It is not difficult to perceive how leadership as a dimensional trait characteristic of an operational police manager may be accomplished. The performance activity of the positional leader relative to leadership style and appropriateness of decisions determines unquestioned followership.

SKILLS OF A LEADER

When considering which performance characteristics can be categorized as universal to all or most effective leaders, there are several that come readily to mind. Traits such as **communication, internal drive to succeed, self-confidence, charismatic attributes, authoritative projection,** and **mental aptitude** are but a few of the numerous factors that go into making an effective positional leader. However, it is plain that with the exception of the leadership imposed by a specific organizational position or title, these influences are clearly paramount to a leader's successful job performance. This is especially true in police work, where approximately 70 to 80 percent of policing involves mental processes and projected authority rather than the actual use of force. The majority of the time that a law enforcement officer influences the behavior of another person, whether manipulating a subordinate or police clientele, the **communicative** and **psychological skills** are predominant.

Leadership skills in the work place are generally not as visible as they may be on a "sports field" or in a playground with kids at school. In the latter areas, generally it is the person with the most expressed desire and energetic excitations that proves to be the leader. In job performances it may be positionally placed, based on task knowledge or an inherent charismatic ability. No matter what circumstance placed the individual in the perceived leadership role, he or she will not be effective in maintaining followership without a conscious desire to influence others. Because the skills of a leader may be found in more basic texts and is not within the contextual scope of this book, we will not analyze it further here, but instead, the specific traits or skills of an effective operational police manager will be detailed.

DIMENSIONAL ASPECTS OF SECONDARY LEADERSHIP

Leadership is defined in totality as a position or capacity to lead others; basically, it is an inherent or vested authority to exert control over the performance or behavior of another person. This classic definition of leadership defines the concept in terms of the overall functions performed by a midlevel positional leader as an individual. The author's contention in this text is concerned primarily with leadership from a more precise and direct perspective. It is approached from the standpoint of a particular middle manager-subordinate relationship that makes up one of the foundational structures of a public police organization. The responsibility of the police mid-level manager is to direct the performance behaviors of subordinates into channels that promote successful achievement of overall organizational goals and objectives.

The dynamics of leadership say that an effective mid-level leader can increase the organization's human resource capacity by inspiring in subordinates a more focused desire to accept the burdens imposed by the organization. It has been said that a leader directs human resources in the form of the power that evolves from their position of authority. There may be an addition or subtraction from the effectiveness of the resources through the leadership actions that motivationally influence subordinate behavior.

Traditional leadership research has tended to be focused on the influences imposed in informal groups, management level groups, and primary leadership associated with major recognized professions. However, the leadership problems and the hierarchical structure of public law enforcement may differ in many important respects from those found in the traditionally researched entities.

The police mid-level manager is a leader by virtue of his or her position in the hierarchy of the organization and the power and authority allocated the managerial position to direct the behavioral performance of subordinates. The power afforded a functional mid-level manager is not necessarily indicative to any personal leadership ability that may be possessed. A mid-level manager should recognize the importance of his or her position of authority in relation to appropriate action and toward the development and maintenance of a secondary police leader's recognized *hierarchy status* in the management chain. The functional-level police mid-level manager should maintain a position of authority by creating the presumption that the power possessed is absolute in the enforcement of organizational policies, rules and regulations, etc. A failure to impress on his or her subordinates that the mid-level manager is in direct and total control of their on-the-job behavioral actions may have adverse consequences. Also, a mid-level police manager in a hierarchical structure such as a public law enforcement operation should help maintain the authority of other leadership and/or managerial positions in the organization.

BEHAVIORAL CHARACTERISTICS OF AN EFFECTIVE LEADER

Secondary police managers, like mid-level leaders in any industry, must display the qualities of leadership traditional to obtaining followership. It must be realized that leaders in any field of employment are effective **not because of task fulfillment by getting people to do what you tell them** but rather because **the task is accomplished by people doing what you tell them**. Upon initial observation there appears to be little or no difference between the two previous statements. But an informed analysis reveals an *order* vs. a *convince* quality of leadership in the statement. In effect, an **order** as meant here is *directing* or *focus dictation*, while **convince** is leadership through perceptual incentive and/or desire to accomplish.

When we think of mid-level leadership, terms like **patience, wisdom, empathy, trust, knowledge,** and **restrained behavior** are common to our consideration. But in considering specific leadership traits or performance areas associated with mid-level leadership, the principal ones are:

1. **Loyalty/Supporting**. Being supportive of upper management, encouraging subordinates, and creating a team spirit.
2. **Job Knowledge or Performance Ability**. Having a basic knowledge of the job, in order to effectively manage the work of subordinates.

3. **Decision Making**. Being courageous in accepting the challenge to express your conceptual plans of action.
4. **Initiator of Action**. Being self-starting in personal actions and directing subordinates toward accomplishing task expectations without upper-management prompting.
5. **Controller of Behavior**. Maintaining control of performances and directing subordinates' actions, thus assuring task behaviors are relevant to accomplishing organizational goals and objectives.
6. **Good Judgment**. Exercising the logical inferences of actions to produce efficient and effective performance by you and your subordinates.
7. **Planning and Organizing**. Analyzing all available information to formulate a workable course of action for subordinates toward task accomplishment and structuring a performance criteria to achieve desired results.
8. **Communicator**. Displaying an ability to clarify task goals and objectives for subordinates, disseminating appropriate data and receiving information from subordinates.
9. **Evaluating**. Assessing the feasibility of task accomplishment and work performance of subordinates. Also, an ability to test the consequences of actions taken.
10. **Honesty and Integrity**. Setting an example for subordinates and assuring personal behaviors are totally objective.

The dimensional characteristics of mid-level managers and the process of obtaining followership is considered essential to formal leadership. Previously, leadership theorists have considered innate personality traits, as well as identifiable learned behaviors, that went into producing an effective leader. However, recent theories and studies of management behaviors have suggested that successful leadership qualities are principally learned behaviors. These learned behaviors are most often paired with an ability to analyze influences and appropriately react to situational factors. It is believed that many of the recent studies of leadership behaviors have focused on classifying the various management traits into a specific behavioral style. As noted elsewhere in this text, the author believes that no one specific style of leadership is best for all situations. The behavior style selected by a leader is mainly dependent upon what the circumstances are and what task needs to be accomplished.

Inasmuch as we have taken a cursory look into some of the aspects of leadership as it applies to the operational mid-level police managers, it is essential that we review some of the applicable **theories of leadership**. Informational knowledge of these theories will enable us to better understand the role of a mid-level police manager and the impact that he or she has on subordinates' on-the-job behavior and performance.

POPULAR LEADERSHIP THEORIES

In order for the operational mid-level manager to gain an appreciable knowledge of leadership, its effect on subordinates, and the perceived motivational needs of the employee, we will examine several of the major *theories of leadership.* The study of subordinate needs and organizational behavior is an analytical look into what typically motivates an employee. Recognizing the importance of the human factor in job performance behavior will be presented in our look at leadership. The operational mid-level manager should realize that only through an understanding of human behavior as it relates to environment and goal accomplishment can he or she make the most effective use of subordinate personnel.

Douglas McGregor, in the 1950s, developed the theory rationale that the traditional organization is one that fosters centralized decision making and is a pyramid type structure. Also, that most organizational leaders such as operational mid-level managers have certain basic assumptions which he titles **"Theory X."** These basic assumptions he listed as:

1. It is the organization leadership's role to organize logistics, resources, and personnel in a structure that requires *close control by supervisors.*
2. It is the organization leadership's responsibility to direct the efforts of their subordinates, keeping them motivated, controlling their job performance, and modifying the behavior of employees to fit the company's needs.
3. The organization's leadership should take an active part in controlling the behavior of subordinates, or the employees will resist the needs of the company.
4. That the typical worker is passive toward work, as work is inherently distasteful to them.
5. The typical functional level employee avoids responsibility and authority. Also, that the worker would prefer being told what to do.
6. That the functional level subordinate is basically concerned with personal needs and not motivated toward a concern for organizational objectives.
7. That most employees are not creative and are normally resistant to change.

The author's conception of Theory X's assumptions concerning most functional level law enforcement officers is that they are incorrect. The agencies that operate on such assumptions create a serious management problem, generally resulting in their failure to motivate subordinates toward organizational goals and objectives.

McGregor also developed the **"Theory Y"** concept, a second human behavior theory, that the organization's mid-level manager's role is to unleash the potential of every member of the company. His contentions under Theory Y were that:

1. It is the leadership of the company's role to organize logistics, resources, and personnel to achieve the goals and objectives of the organization.
2. Job performance can be rewarding to an employee if the environment and working conditions are favorable.
3. The worker's attitude toward the job and job performance is more a product of experience rather than an inherent nature.
4. The potential for motivation, accepting responsibility, and willingness to work toward company goals and objectives are in each employee and that it is the leadership's responsibility to allow the subordinates the freedom to develop his/her ability.
5. That employees generally possess creative skills that could benefit the organization if encouraged by management.

Organizations that subscribe to the **Theory Y** approach usually have within their structure fewer levels in the hierarchy, controls with broad guidelines, and minimal first line supervision of functional activity. The Theory Y agency provides increased autonomy to mid-level managers, first-line supervisors, and functional-level officers. This process allows them to become involved in identifying and overcoming obstacles to achievement of organizational goals and objectives.

It should at this juncture be clear that leadership is a very complex process that involves a complicated interactive relationship and response to influence between the leaders and his or her followers. The process of leadership is affected by a multitude of situations, organizational influences, and personal wants and needs of the components involved. Also, as noted elsewhere in this text, the exercise of leadership may involve many different styles to be effective. It has been said that given all the complications, one may wonder why many researchers focus a great deal of their efforts on attempting to understand all of the intricacies of leadership. The indication is that effective leadership is an important ingredient in an organization achieving its goals and objectives.

During the decade of the 1950s, psychologist Chris Argyris conducted several studies and derived the "Immaturity-Maturity Theory." Argyris's studies and theory inferred that the perceptual effectiveness of management practices on a person's development within an organization depends upon the individual's *personality change*. Personality change occurs as a result of managerial actions within the organizational environment. Argyris suggested a number of changes that may occur if the employee develops into a mature personality within the organization.

As theorized by Argyris, a person within an organizational setting goes through a number of stages during maturation. Beginning with ***infancy***, where a person advances from a passive state toward an increased active state, and ending in an ***adult*** stage, where there is understanding and a capability to control one's activity within the organization, the schematic model as developed by Argyris is as follows.

The Developmental Model from Immaturity through Maturity for Employees in an Organization

1. Passive_____ Active
2. Dependence _____ Independence
3. Restricted between pattern_____ Diversified
4. Erratic, shallow interests _____ Deeper & stronger interest
5. Short time perspective_____ Long time perspective (past and future)
6. Subordinate position _____ Equal or superior position
7. Lack of self-awareness_____ Awareness & control over self

As may be evident by the above model, the principal point is that it is very rare for an employee to develop the stage of complete maturity within an organization. However, it can be concluded that as an employee develops within the organization, he or she is constantly advancing toward the Maturity Stage.

It is unusual, because of the non-transit nature of public police employment, to question whether a majority will ever reach the higher stages of development within the organization. Optimism is not an unusual expectation of police managers relative to employees' maturation within the organization. Managerial leadership in a public police organization typically considers workers as being interested and/or motivated in their job. The job is generally considered a career opportunity that will provide financial employment security and beneficial work opportunity. The perceptual stability of the job and management's desire to limit any type of frequent turnover in manpower is a contributor to allowing employees chances of advancing toward organizational maturity. Public police employment, like many other service-related jobs, by nature is structured to allow individuals little or no control over task assignments and work expectations. Normal public police duties encourage a heavy reliance on organizational leadership for control and guidance, thus slowing the development of employees' advancement from the ***infant*** or ***immaturity*** stage of development.

Some authors have indicated that the job of public police organizations and the managerial structure of the elements' hierarchy forces employees to remain immature relative to worker growth and development. The clear implication is that traditional police agencies are structured to treat employees in a manner that suggests workers fit into McGregor's Theory X category. There must be a fundamental change in leadership's perception, actions, and a willingness to limit micro-managing to enhance the maturity growth of employees.

Doctor Abraham Maslow's "Hierarchy of Needs Theory" is based upon an employee's performance as related to motivational needs. His theory describes man's behavior in terms of a pyramid structure with a five-step process, emphasizing the individual's need system as the source of motivation. The basic contention was that an employee initially works to satisfy the first or primary need and then moves on to the secondary need and so on until all five needs have been fulfilled. If the assumptions of Maslow are correct and a mid-level manager wants to motivate subordinates, then the positional leader's actions must fit the needs of the employee because only unsatisfied needs become a source of direction. The five **need sources** of Maslow's pyramidal "Hierarchy of Needs Theory" are:

1. **Basic Needs**:
   The primary need of man is his basic need for food and shelter. It is believed that in our modern society this need has basically been fulfilled, and that this need transcends the need of the employee to increase assets.

2. **Safety Needs**:
   The secondary need of man, once his basic need for food and shelter has been fulfilled, is the need for safety or security in the protection of what he has, in terms of job, income, benefits, property, and avoidance of physical harm to himself or his family. The employees who are overly concerned with the safety need will tend to be very conserva-

tive and show little or no creativity or flexibility for fear of upsetting the security that they have established.

3. **Belonging Needs**:
The third step in the hierarchy of needs process is a striving for acceptance by fellow workers and a need to be viewed as an important member of the organizational family. This need is manifested in the worker's desire to be friendly with peers. The mid-level manager can aid in the meeting of this need in ubordinates through the use of teamwork involving the employee.

4. **Ego Needs**:
This need has to do with worker pride and desire to achieve some special recognition for his or her performance. It also motivates the employee to contribute to the organization through creativity or exceptional work performance in order to be recognized by peers and superiors.

5. **Self-Actualization Needs**:
The self-actualization needs center on the self-satisfaction or personal goal achievement. The worker's behavior pattern on this need level typically produces creativity that provides a high degree of personal satisfaction.

In reference to Maslow's need structure and the mid-level manager's performance, the positional leader must evaluate personal motivational needs to determine what is required to satisfy the self needs. The police mid-level manager should then address those motivational needs of subordinates. It is the mid-level manager's responsibility to assist subordinate personnel through their hierarchy of needs.

Frederick Herzberg conducted a study that dramatized Maslow's theory. However, his theory focused on organizational behavior and motivation. Herzberg defined two categories of needs that affect a worker's behavior. The categories were named "Motivators" and "Hygiene Factors."

The **Hygiene Factors** are defined as the basic safety and social needs of the employee. The ego need is also a part of the "Hygiene Factor" and is divided into recognition and status. Herzberg has defined **Motivators** as a sense of achievement, challenge, professional development and recognition. He also stressed that these factors have a positive effect on the employee which possibly results in some job satisfaction and increased work performance.

EMPLOYEE EXIGENCY PLATEAUS

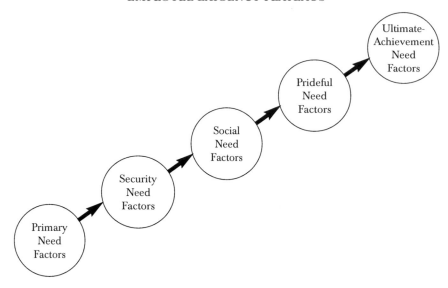

The sequential steps of progression in Maslow's "Hierarchy of Needs" is essential to effective Operational Leadership.

The graphically listed items under the "Motivation-Hygiene Theory" are:

Hygiene Factors	*Motivators*
Salary	Challenging Assignment
Fringe Benefits	Increased Responsibility
Security (Civil Service)	Recognition of Work
Rules and Regulations Supervision	Individual Growth

In our brief look at several of the more noted theories of motivational basic leadership, we have attempted to examine organizational behavior in relationship to mid-level managers.

Baron and Greenberg wrote in their text, entitled *Behavior in Organizations,* that effective leadership in an organization is an essential ingredient for success accomplishment, and with appropriate management it can grow, prosper and compete, but without it, many cannot survive.

Recognition of this basic point lies behind several modern theories of leadership . . . , all are linked by two common theories themes. First, all adopt a *common contingency approach* to this complex topic. All recognize that there is not a single preferred style of leadership and that the key task of Organizational Behavior researchers is determining which leadership approach will prove most effective under which specific condition. Second, all are concerned with the issue of *leadership effectiveness.* They seek to identify the conditions and factors that determine whether, and to what degree, leaders will enhance the performance and satisfaction of their subordinates.

Fiedler's "Contingency Theory: Matching Leaders and Tasks" noted that leadership happens in a social environment and that to be effective, it must function in coordination with other factors in the organization. An effective leader will try to influence subordinates, etc. within the context of the situation and since the situations can co-exist with numerous other dimensions, it may be assumed that no single style of leadership or approach is always best. And, that most effective strategies will vary from one situation to the next.

Fiedler believed that acceptance of the above stated premise lies at the core of a theory of effective leadership he noted as a *Contingency Approach.* *Contingency* as a term associated with leadership focuses on the leader's ability to direct or influence the performance of subordinates toward achievement of goals and objectives. He identified esteem or liking *for least preferred coworker* (LPC) as most essential. This indicated a leader's perception of a worker in a favorable or an unfavorable manner by coworkers. A low LPC person is perceived in negative terms and seems to principally focus on attaining successful task accomplishment. A high LPC person is perceiving this least preferred worker in a positive light and appears to be primarily concerned with establishing good working relationships with subordinates. Fiedler suggests that *low LPC* or *high LPC* leaders are more effective depending upon the degree to which the situation is favorable to the leader's approach. A favorable approach should also provide the leader with enhanced control over subordinates. This, in turn, is determined largely by three factors:

1. The nature of the leader's relations with group members (the extent to which he or she enjoys their support and loyalty),
2. The degree of structure in the task (the extent to which task goals and subordinates' roles are clearly defined), and
3. The leader's position power (his or her ability to enforce compliance by subordinates).

Combining these factors, the leader's situational control can range from very high (positive relations with group members, a highly structured task, high position power) to very low (negative relations, an unstructured task, low position power). In concluding the consideration on Fiedler's Contingency Theory, it should be indicated that low LPC leaders (ones who are task-oriented) are superior to high LPC leaders (ones who are people-oriented) when situational control is either very low or high. In contrast, high LPC leaders have an edge when situational controls fall within the moderate range. Assessing mid-level management in terms of Fiedler's theory, it is a reasonable assumption that leaders whose individual style are not compatible with the conditions within their group of subordinates would experience a number of job-related problems. Conversely, leaders whose styles are more of a match with the situational aspects and expectations of subordinates will encounter fewer problems and less job-related stress.

Vroom and Yetton developed a theory they called "Normative Theory: Decision Making and Leader Effectiveness." They theorized that a major task performed by leaders is decision making and that it is one of the defining characteristics of leadership. Vroom and Yetton's theory suggests that, similar to the fact that there is no one best style of leadership, there is no one single best method of decision making. And, that a major task facing leaders is choosing the specific decision-making approach that will maximize potential benefits but limit potential adverse effects. They identified "**Potential Strategies for Making Decisions**."

AI (Autocratic)	Leader solves problems or makes decisions unilaterally, using available data.
AII (Autocratic)	Leader obtains necessary information from subordinates but then makes decisions unilaterally.
CI (Consultative)	Leader shares problems with subordinates individually but then makes decisions unilaterally.
CII (Conservative)	Leader shares problems with subordinates in group meeting but then makes decisions unilaterally.
GII (Group Decision)	Leader shares problem with subordinates in a group meeting; decision is reached through discussion to consensus.

Regarding a primary police mid-level manager utilizing Vroom and Yetton's suggested theory of decision making, it is difficult to conclude that this suggested strategy in and of itself would be ideal. Like the styles of leadership, the situation and circumstances at the time will determine which method may be best. Basic existing data indicate that the **Normative Theory** provides some useful guidelines to functional level leaders for selecting an approach in decision making. The theory may also provide a more comprehensive understanding of leadership and the things that a leader can do to enhance his or her effectiveness.

Inasmuch as we have taken a comprehensive look at the basic theories of leadership to gain an insight into what makes an effective leader, the content of this chapter will now focus on the technical and practical aspects of leadership by a mid-level police manager.

LEADERSHIP DYNAMICS

The operation of leadership as a dimensional trait is comprehensively defined as a capability to obtain and maintain followership from others. Primarily, it is positionally placed authority to exert control over the job performances of subordinate personnel. This basic definition of leadership details the dimensional trait as to the overall job behaviors performed by an operational police manager as an individual. The principal focus of this text's content is a concern with leadership as a specific characteristic. It is discussed from the prospect of an operational police manager's functional demonstration of those measurable dimensional traits that make a positional leader effective. The basic responsibility of an operational police manager is to direct the behavior of subordinate personnel toward efficient and effective accomplishment of overall departmental goals and objectives. The dynamics of positional leadership informs us that a productive police manager can elevate personally directed human resource capability by getting subordinates to readily accept and perform the tasks imposed by the department. It is perceived that an operational leader in a police department has personnel resources in the form of personal authority that evolves from his or her positional duties. There can be a productivity increase in the effectiveness of human resources through the managerial actions taken by the positional leader with respect to incentives that influence subordinates' behaviors.

Traditional researchers in the area of police management have centered on the influences imposed by the formal organizational structure and the primary leadership actions associated with administrative functioning. However, the managerial problems and the hierarchical functioning on a police manager may require more specific operational detail than those found in the traditional leadership texts. By functional definition, the operational police manager is an organizational leader by virtue of assigned responsibility within the structure of the department, plus the operational powers allocated to the managerial position to control the behavioral performance and use of resources by subordinate personnel to achieve desired results. The power allotted an operational police manager is not indicative of any personal ability of leadership that the individual may or may not possess. An operational police manager should recognize the significance of his or her positional leadership in relationship to appropriate actions. Further, that an enhancement of leadership ability and maintenance of the operational manager's position as a recognized member of the department's hierarchical echelon is advantageous. An operational police leader should maintain his or her position of authority by creating the presumption that the power possessed is absolute in the enforcement of departmental directives, rules, and regulations. A failure to impart this perception to subordinates that the manager is in directional control of their job performances may produce negative consequences. Also, an operational police manager in a hierarchical structure such as a police department should support the authority of other leadership positions in the organizations. Since we have provided a preliminary view into the aspects of leadership as it applies to operational-level police management, it's now essential to analytically assess some popular theories of leadership. A comprehensive awareness of these philosophies and practices will allow for a better understanding of the role of an operational police manager and the impact that the individual has on the achievement of desired goals and objectives by subordinates.

"I don't know Sally but there is something about our new leader that does not inspire confidence in his leadership ability."

A PROJECTION OF A LEADERSHIP ABILITY AND JOB DESIRE IS CRITICAL TO OBTAINING APPROPRIATE FOLLOWERSHIP OF SUBORDINATES.

Requirements of Leadership

The position of leadership held by the mid-level leaders of an organization places the individual in a situation of moral obligation to adhere strictly to the highest standards of integrity and honor that is expected of subordinates. These high standards are expected of a mid-level manager by both subordinates and superiors. The formal leader moral code must be above contention, as personal behavioral conduct will be evaluated under (1) *what actually occurs,* and (2) *what is perceived by others.*

Responsibilities of Leadership

It goes almost without saying that the position of mid-level manager obligates the individual to provide leadership and direction to his or her subordinates. Basic responsibility is defined as an obligation of a person to perform specific duties associated with the assigned position. Job responsibility infers that the tasks delegated to others do not release the delegating mid-level manager of the accountability to get the job done. Simply stated, an assignment responsibility of a positional leader is a required task. A required task of every mid-level manager is to provide direction and guidance for the employees under his or her scope of authority. To be a good and effective mid-level managerial leader, the individual must have the qualities of *persuasiveness, intelligence, flexibility,* and *good judgment.* These qualities are all traits and characteristics that aren't necessarily hereditary but can be learned or developed.

Every mid-level manager has a primary responsibility to enforce the rules of the company. The mid-level manager should also provide the subordinates with the opportunity for personal growth and professional development. Further, the positional leader should strive to overcome the personal traits or leadership weaknesses that hamper effective performance as a mid-level manager. Additionally, most of the leadership responsibilities of a functional mid-level manager have been identified as qualities inherent to the position.

Characteristics of Leadership

It is a traditionally accepted concept that the organizational performance of a functional mid-level manager determines in certain respects the behavior and reflective attitudes of subordinates, peers, and superiors. The mid-level manager affects those attitudes and behaviors through personal leadership characteristics and duty performance. While it is true that the mid-level manager's environment, to some degree, affects the display of what we term *effective leadership characteristics,* the individual must endeavor to keep the positive aspects of these influences in the forefront of his or her performance.

There are a substantial number of characteristics that we associate with positive or effective leadership. The author has identified several characteristics that are essential to the effective performance of a functional police mid-level manager. The more important of these characteristics are as follows:

1. **The ability to motivate subordinates**. The effective mid-level manager must be able to motivate/inspire subordinates' job performances. It is in this area that subordinates' interest and the overall interest of the organization are at its closest point. Also, it is at this juncture that the level of employee productivity or work output is created and the primary criteria upon which the mid-level manager's effectiveness is measured. The author prefers to reference this leadership characteristic as the *ability to inspire* because it is concluded that motivation in its purest sense is internal to each individual.

Recommendation: It is recommended that a functional police mid-level manager practice some measure of participatory management or democratic leadership, whenever possible, to strengthen personal skills in this area.

2. **A subordinate-oriented perception**. By subordinate-oriented perception we are referring to an approach where consideration is given to worker satisfaction and comfort, when it does not conflict or hamper organizational goal accomplishment. Many studies have shown that high worker satisfaction and high productivity are synonymous. However, it must be emphasized, at this point, that employee satisfaction and comfort should not supersede the overall accomplishment of the goals and objectives of the agency.

Recommendation: The police mid-level manager on occasion should mentally project him- or herself into the subordinate's position to see how to make personal actions more employee oriented. Also, a formal process should encourage the submission of suggestions by subordinates on how the assignment can be improved both from a personnel and an effectiveness standpoint.

3. **Technical job knowledge**. The effective functional mid-level manager must be technically competent in the work that is being supervised. This competence is essential to the individual's ability to assist a subordinate when needed or to provide *on-the-job* training. Technical

knowledge or competence does not imply that a leader must be able to do the job better than subordinates, only that the mid-level manager should know the parameters of the job and what is needed to perform it effectively.

Recommendation: The police mid-level manager can improve his/her technical knowledge and competence by assuring that each has a working awareness of all the policies, procedures, rules, etc., that affect subordinates' positions and assignments under their span of authority. The functional mid-level manager should also be well versed and up-to-date on the latest techniques for performing as a public police officer. Furthermore, he or she should have some knowledge of the laws (local, state, and federal) governing a law enforcement officer and line supervisor's actions. The mid-level manager can increase personal ability in this area through extra effort and review of appropriate documentation, etc.

4. **The ability to communicate effectively**. Being able to comprehend organizational directives and to communicate the information to subordinates is an essential function of a police mid-level manager. The functional mid-level manager of today also should be able to effectively relay the suggestions, complaints, or the feelings of subordinates to upper management. In a modern-day police operation the mid-level manager may be called upon to communicate at any given social or professional level, from a derelict frequenting a public area to the heads of major corporations.

Recommendation: The mid-level manager should constantly practice the techniques of effective communication in both written and verbal form. The mid-level manager should assess his or her ability of presenting information by the number and nature of the questions that are asked after a presentation. The writing skills should be practiced as often as possible by writing something and reading it several hours later to evaluate its content and structure. The use of a tape recorder is effective for verbal communication training; for example, taping a mock staff meeting or presentation, then reviewing the tape in search of ways to improve the effort.

The principal makeup of the functional mid-level manager's basic on-the-job personality is a combination of all of his or her leadership characteristics. Each play a major role in the development of personal leadership ability and effectiveness as a functional police mid-level manager. Very few people truly lack the capability to perform in a leadership role, if they knew how.

The individual needs to recognize the areas of weakness and use the suggested techniques to strengthen those traits and give him- or herself the confidence that is so necessary. The positive or successful character traits observed in other positional leaders should be reviewed and structurally adopted in an effort to refine his or her own techniques.

Improving Leadership Ability

The police mid-level manager should strive for perfection in personal efforts as a positional leader in the organization. The functional mid-level manager shall assure that all of the leadership characteristics that make leaders effective become a permanent part of his or her performance and personality.

Effectiveness as police mid-level manager is a learned behavior, as we previously stated. It is also a developed skill that must be maintained through constant effort. This repeated effort to improve personal leadership ability is synonymous with the phrase *practice makes perfect.* We, as human beings, all make mistakes and mid-level managers are no exception. But a mid-level manager's attempts to constantly utilize positive leadership characteristics will offset the mistakes.

Attempting to improve personal ability to lead does not necessarily mean that every mid-level manager in the organization must do everything the same way. When we talk about the practice of using positive leadership characteristics, we are referring to the things that are *favorable* to individual personality, subordinate attitude, and the attitudinal climate of the organization. But there are certain universal concepts that are applicable and should be employed by all mid-level managers. First, mid-level managers should utilize every opportunity to employ positive leadership practices. Second, they should be knowledgeable of areas of needed improvement in their personality and correct them. Third, they should always be attempting to sell themselves to subordinates while advancing personal beliefs and faith in their leadership ability.

Remember that effectiveness as a leader is established by gaining confidence, trust, respect, loyalty, and desired job performance of subordinates.

LEADERSHIP BEHAVIORS

There are a number of behaviors that go into making an effective and efficient leader. The areas cited are typical to all fields of employment. Public police, because of its unique aspects, generally present mid-level managers with some problems that are unusual to other employment fields. The aspect of action-seeking employees, non-specific situations dealt routinely, quasi-military lines of command authority, and unrealistically defined expectations of clientele are but a few of the unique characteristics confronting police mid-level managers.

An analytical assessment of the behavioral qualities, concluded as important to a public police mid-level manager, should aid in specifying the leadership expectations of a position leader. First, a leader must display **a great deal of tolerance** in his/her dealing with subordinates. It is important to recognize that not everyone will perceive, think, or complete a task as the mid-level leader might. There should be a *tolerance* to look beyond the actions to the intent and the results. And, if the results are not all that is expected, be willing to examine the communicated directions to see if they were sufficient. In other words, don't be so quick to blame but rather consider the possibility that the failed results may have been caused by miscommunication, instead of an error by a subordinate.

Second, a leader should **seek to obtain participatory action from all subordinates**. The inclusion of subordinates into the decision-making process, when possible, will frequently increase their desire for the success of the task. It is recognized that not all decisions, especially in policing, can be made in a participatory forum. Time availability, circumstances, and the situation will determine the urgency, etc., of the decision. In those situations requiring immediate action, the leader will be expected to make *autocratic decisions* based on his or her experience, knowledge, and desired results. But, if circumstances and time allow participation of workers in decisions, particularly those concerning task accomplishment, the results will more often than not prove favorable. An involved line worker or supervisor is more likely to work harder to implement a decision that he/she had a hand in making. Also, it is more likely that the decision will be feasible and results oriented because it involved those who are most familiar with the *nuts and bolts* of the problem. The police mid-level manager, as well as the employees themselves, will develop more confidence in their ability as workers. A recognition of the anticipated finished results or an awareness of what the ultimate achievement goal is should motivate positive action in workers.

Third, the police mid-level manager must seek to avoid the **leader-centered syndrome of *"do it my way"* because might (positional authority) makes right**. It's not unusual for a newly promoted leader to go through the so-called **"God Syndrome."** But after the initial euphoria which is promulgated by positional power, the mid-level manager must begin to recognize that subordinates have ideas and knowledge that should not be overlooked. Intellect and judgmental knowledge is not an exclusive ability reserved for those who ascend the hierarchy of an organization. *It is similar to the story of*

NEWLY PROMOTED LEADERS OFTEN FEEL ALL POWERFUL, POSSESSING UNLIMITED KNOWLEDGE AND AUTHORITY.

a newly promoted mid-level manager, who sat down the day after his promotion to analyze his advanced job knowledge to perform as a section leader. An objective assessing of his job knowledge revealed that he possessed no more performance wisdom or actual behavior know-how than he did the previous day before his promotion.

The only real difference was that he was now responsible for not only his performance but for the job behaviors of a number of other people. Recognizing that job knowledge is not the exclusive province of a positional leader will allow a mid-level manager to access the wealth of knowledge and talents of subordinates. A leader must feel secure and comfortable enough in his/her own leadership ability to not be threatened by the knowledge or point of view of subordinates.

Fourth, a leader must have **a comprehension of the limits of personal authority**, meaning that the individual should be aware of the parameters of his/her behaviors, as well as the interorganizational politics required to be most effective. Positional leaders at all levels within the agency are subject to the competitive and interactive foreplay that occur in the organization. The leader must recognize that personal actions, both on and off the job, will be scrutinized by superiors and subordinates. We recognize that organizational leaders are human and as such are subject to the same failings and weaknesses of everyone else. But somehow an ethical miscue by an organizational leader is viewed with more disdain than if committed by a worker-level employee. Thus, a mid-level leader must consider that the job carries a higher visibility and responsibility for personal actions. It is also pertinent to be aware that the higher up the organizational ladder a person goes, the fewer advancement positions exist. Therefore, there is a more intense and direct competitive effort to position oneself for the reduced number of promotion possibilities. If a positional leader is unaware of the management interplay or unwilling to engage in the networking process, he or she will typically not advance past the competitive testing level within an organization. Internal networking has less to do with effective subordinate management than it does with getting pertinent leadership ideas accepted by the hierarchy of the organization.

Fifth, an effective leader must **assure emotional control by learning to tactfully deal with personal hostility, as well as the hostility of others**. The emotional stability of a leader is essential, especially during those times when he or she is confronted with the unexpected. Subordinates and superiors are usually not tolerant or will have no confidence in a leader who seems to lose control in what may be termed as a *crisis situation*. It is recognized that no matter how much we plan or what the expectations may be, leadership within an organization will, to a great degree, be reactive to unanticipated events, etc. Also, a leader should not allow his/herself the luxury of expressing personal hostility at a hierarchy directive or a subordinate's actions. A leader must objectively view the situation, consider the influences, and react appropriately. His or her actions should not be biased or reactionary to a personal feeling of hostility. Likewise, a leader should not overreact or respond in kind when a subordinate expresses hostility. The person should be brought under control by a leader's display of restrained patience and instructional comments directed at defusing the person's expressed hostility. Controlling one's emotions in these circumstances will often take an almost superhuman effort not to display personal feelings. But an efficient and effective leader is predominantly a self-controlled and tactful person.

Finally, an effective behavior leader is a **self-starter who does not let disappointments rule personal actions, as well as continually striving for performance success and increased job knowledge**. Those objectively advancing to leadership positions within the organization will often possess an inert quality of being self-motivated and somewhat ambitious. These qualities most often manifest themselves in a self-inspired person who seeks to be the best that he/she can be. They most often are persons that look for and attempt to take the next step on the road to success. These individuals tend to be less restrained by uncontrolled or unanticipated setbacks. An effective behavioral leader will *accept the things that cannot be controlled* and will *seek to compensate through the things that can be manipulated via personal efforts.* Enhanced job knowledge is not a new or innovative concept of leadership. It is a necessity in this modern era of rapidly advancing technology and employees who are more informed and self-centered relative to what the job has to offer.

Traits of an Effective Leader

The effective police mid-level manager as a positional leader will most often possess a number of traits that are considered common in good functional leaders. As Iannone states, "Possession of any particular traits certainly does not assure that a person is a good leader." The effective mid-level manager must possess a number of the qualities identified in the following list of behavioral traits, coupled with the personality and characteristics of leadership (previously discussed). The following list of leadership traits will make a positional leader an effective police mid-level manager if he or she possesses qualities of each.

1. **A zest for the job**. Showing a marked enthusiasm for the position and all that it entails in the organization.
2. **A lack of complacency**. Displaying a desire to advance in the organization by attempting self-improvement and increased job performance toward that end, within the bounds of fairness and controlled behavior.
3. **An inherent aptitude**. Having and using good judgment when making decisions. Typically refers to *good common sense.*
4. **A genuine affection for others**. Presenting a positive type attitude about subordinates, peers, and superiors. Basically displaying an optimistic, not a pessimistic, attitude.
5. **A competence of job performance**. Possessing the job know-how that gives him or her the confidence to supervise others actually performing the task.
6. **A sense of honor and integrity**. The mid-level manager must gain the trust of their subordinates and be viewed as a role model by keeping their professional and and personal life free from discredit.
7. **A high level of patience**. The ability to control personal anxiety, frustration, and hyperactivity relative to the mistakes and vitality of subordinates.

8. **Effective communication skills**. The ability to communicate effectively to all levels of the organization in both written and oral form.
9. **Reliability or consistency of performance**. The effective mid-level managers must have a quality of dependability. Subordinates, peers, and superiors should feel that they can rely on them to do what they say and to perform in a professional and efficient manner.

While the above prioritized list of traits are considered essential by the author, there are a number of other characteristics that should be a part of the effective mid-level manager's personality. Some of these traits are **empathy, adaptability, courtesy, modesty**, and **self-control**.

The identified traits are all considered as essential personality characteristics of a good leader. However, it is not practical to assume that any one person will be well endowed with an abundance of all of these traits. As previously stated, effectiveness as a positional leader is generally a learned skill. Therefore, to improve personal abilities and the chances of being successful, a new or incumbent police mid-level manager should make a special effort to make certain that each of these traits is an everyday part of his or her performance as a mid-level manager.

Styles of Leadership

The way that a mid-level manager imposes authority or enforces decisions will determine personal effectiveness. The mid-level manager's leadership approach will of course be dictated by basic personality and temperament for the job. Leadership is said to be a cooperative endeavor between the leader and the followers. By this, I mean that to have an effective leadership there has to be an alliance of sorts. Simply stated, **a person is not a leader if no one is willing to follow him or her**.

The three basic approaches normally associated with leadership or the enforcement of authority are the **Autocratic**, **Democratic**, and **Laissez-Faire**.

The Autocratic Leader

The Autocratic style is a *leader-centered*-type approach to leadership. This type of leader is often referred to as "Authoritarian," meaning that he or she makes all the decisions without subordinate participation. The authoritarian leader usually has a forceful personality and has to feel in control of the situation. There is little doubt as to who is in charge or who has the last word. This approach is most effective in crisis situations where decisions need to be made without equivocation. And, directions need to be carried out without question or hesitation. The best and most effective military leaders in combat conditions are the Authoritarian or boss-centered type leaders.

The Democratic Leader

The Democratic leader is better known as a "Participatory" leader, referring to the fact that he or she allows subordinates to have a say in decision making when the situation permits. This type of an approach is becoming more commonplace in recent years as we seek to capitalize on the insights and knowledge of the functional-level employees. Most of the major organizations in this country hold scheduled meetings and solicit suggestions from workers to improve productivity and quality. The techniques of Participatory leader can produce positive results. The involvement of subordinates in the decision-making process can serve to motivate (inspire) them. The employee satisfaction created by the process is important and undoubtedly the social conditions play a major role in the response of subordinates toward leadership. Participatory leaders encourage input and mutual understanding of subordinates, and control employee behavior through emphasis on goals and training.

This type of leader is most effective in non-critical kinds of situations that allow time for considering alternative courses of action. The biggest shortcoming to this approach is that in emergency type situations, decision making and leadership control become very difficult. It is also important to note that the more people involved in making a decision, the longer it will take to achieve a true consensus or agreement.

The Laissez-Faire Leader

"Laissez-Faire" is the name universally used to characterize the Free-Reign leader. In this type of leadership approach, the mid-level manager allows each of the subordinates to do whatever they choose, thus establishing very few limitations on their actions. The teamwork concept of organizations does not lend itself well to the free activity functioning of individuals. This type of leader is usually a positional leader in name and position only because he or she provides little, if any, real leadership for subordinates. A Free-Reign or Laissez-Faire leader is most effective when subordinates are performing properly; then it is best not to interfere, if the desired results will be accomplished.

A close analysis of each of the three leadership approaches reveals neither is ideal in every situation. *True leadership situations are seldom purely one or the other but are usually a combination of all three depending on the circumstances.*

CHOOSING A LEADERSHIP STYLE
THAT IS BEST FOR YOU

In every problem or circumstance requiring a decision by the police mid-level manager he should select which of the approaches to be used in the situation. The approach to be used should be made on the basis of an assessment of the subordinates' temperament and the particular circumstances. Environmental factors such as organizational policies, sensitivity of the problem and the pressures of time, etc., should also influence his decision. Accordingly, the specific style of leadership approach that a police mid-level manager should employ in handling a particular situation can't be dictated by any specific theory of leadership.

Thus we conclude that the best style of leadership for a line police mid-level manager is a combination of all three. It is a principal responsibility of a functional-level leader in a law enforcement organization to determine the technique of leadership that will best accomplish the job.

DEVELOPING A LEADERSHIP STYLE

Basically, there is no one best style for positional leadership in most situations that necessitates a decisive course of action by a police manager. Each problem should be assessed individually, with the resolutive alternatives also considered before selecting which of the leadership styles that can be most effectively used under the circumstances. The approach to be used must be made on criteria of an evaluation of information relative to the manager's subordinates' attitude and the situational influences. External influences such as departmental directives, need for confidential control of information, and the allotted time frame are all factors that will affect the decided-upon style and action. Principally, a particular leadership style that a police manager should utilize in dealing with a specific concern cannot be predetermined. To date, there is no known formula for deciding a generic leadership approach to problem solving.

Therefore, as will be made clear in the following section, the best approach to leadership for a positional leader in a police organization may be a combination of all three styles. A primary responsibility of an operational manager in law enforcement functioning is to decide on a method of leadership that will best accomplish the element's objective. What we are referring to in this text is a **situational leadership style**, which depends as much on the circumstances as it does on the individual personality of the positional leader. Another term sometimes used to describe situational leadership has been **contingency control**, which infers that no specific philosophy approach is ideal for dealing with every form of organization problem encountered, personnel or logistical.

Situational leadership informs us that instead of attempting to apply any one best style of subordinate control, that most effective police managers have found that a **pattern-type leadership** is best. By pattern type leadership we are referring to the manager's analysis of the circumstances and influences on the subordinate and situation at the time, thereby letting the pattern or sequence of events determine his or her leadership action. This approach is neither modernistic nor innovative, as it has been used in professional type jobs for some time. Attorneys and physicians, for example, deal with clients on an individual basis and thus apply different styles of guidance control in each situation. The police manager should realize that he or she will have to deal with a variety of differences relative to personnel and clientele in each situation that is handled. Therefore, it would be illogical and less effective to choose one form or style of leadership upon which to base his or her overall personal job performance.

However, because the author hasn't recommended one particular leadership style for all situations, this does not imply a non-endorsement for the use of the three basic approaches as may be called for. On the contrary, it is extremely important that an operational manager is totally aware of the particulars of each style and utilize one of the three leadership approaches as dictated by the situation.

SYNOPSIS

The position of leadership held by mid-level police managers in an organization places the individual in a situation of moral obligation to adhere strictly to a high standards of integrity and honesty that is expected of his or her job assignment. A police leader's adherence to skilled leadership techniques should be above contention, because personal behavioral conduct and job performance will be evaluated by what actually occurs, as well as what is perceived by others. It goes almost without saying that the position of a police manager obligates the individual to obtain follower-ship and provide direction to his or her subordinates. A police manager's job responsibility infers that the tasks delegated to others do not release the delegating managerial leader of the accountability to get the job done. Simply stated, an assignment responsibility of a positional leader is a required task. A required task of every mid-level police manager is to provide direction and guidance for the employees under his or her scope of authority. To be a good and effective manager, the individual must have the qualities of persuasiveness, intelligence, flexibility and good judgment. These qualities are all traits and characteristics that aren't necessarily hereditary but can be learned or developed. A managerial leader should also provide the subordinates with the opportunity for personal growth and professional development. Further, the mid-level managerial leader should strive to overcome the personal traits of leadership weaknesses that limit his/her effective performance as a middle manager.

The effective mid-level police manager will most often possess a number of traits that are considered positive attributes in good leaders at all levels of the organization. An effective middle manager should possess a number of the qualities identified previously as behavioral characteristics or traits. The leadership traits listed as essential for an effective managerial leader were: (1) A zest for the job; (2) A lack of complacency; (3) An inherent aptitude; (4) A genuine affection for others; (5) A competence of job performance; (6) A sense of honor and integrity; (7) A high level of patience; (8) Effective communication skills; (9) Reliability or consistency of performance; and, (10) The ability to project to subordinates, peers and superiors a feeling that they can rely on him or her to do what they say and to perform in a professional and efficient manner. Accordingly, the specific style of leadership approach that the police manager should employ in handling a particular situation can't be dictated by any specific concept of leadership. Thus, we conclude that the best approach of Obtaining Followership (Leadership) for a police manager will be dictated by the situational. It is a principle responsibility of a mid-level police leader in a law enforcement environment to determine the technique of leadership that will best accomplish the job.

Chapter Three

ANALYTICAL SKILLS

An operational police manager's **analytical** or **problem assessment** skills are not traditionally discussed in terms of being one of the behavior components that are inseparable from effective job performance. But for the researchers of managerial behavior, who attempt to analyze operational-level police management through its basic and individual components, the **analysis skill** is critical to a positional leader's day-to-day performance. It is also recognized that an individual consideration of analysis as an essential of managerial leadership is not commonplace in most police environments. However, when we add the term **problem** as an adjunct to analysis, then the usage becomes more familiar, especially in staff operations or promotional testing. For our purposes in this text, the terms **analysis**, **problem assessment**, and **problem analysis** are used interchangeably because indeed they are synonymous. Problem analysis for a positional leader in a police department becomes the forerunner of all effective managerial actions or decision making. Therefore, the traditional concept of analysis not being considered an inseparable behavior component of job performance is not accurate. This becomes evident when we consider that all appropriate police action or reaction requires some recognition of what the concerns are and what solution is needed to deal with the situation. In a police department the situations requiring recognition or evaluation by an operational manager may range from a simple assignment adjustment to an emergency life-or-death decision.

A clinical definition of analysis within the specific framework that we will concentrate on in this chapter as it relates to an operational police manager's performance is **a direct association and comparison of facts from relevant sources; the identification of pertinent criteria and a determination of applicable kinships of data to obtain sufficient information for a sound practical decision**. In other words, it is the gathering of sufficient and relevant information upon which a good decision can be made. Primarily, simple decisions such as what personnel to assign to which task **area may** appear not to require an analytical use of problem-solving methods. But an assessment of individual officers' personalities and the activity of the specific assignment may dictate which person is assigned to a given unit, etc. However, a more obvious duty-related problem that would require sufficient information in which to make a sound decision is an arrest situation where facts are not clearly apparent. The potential retribution of legal action makes the second example an obvious situation where the utilization of an appropriate problem analysis is essential before rendering a decision that would result in action. But, as is evident in both situations, a problem-solving method of data gathering must have taken place in order for a sound and practical managerial decision.

The above information was presented as a brief introductory look into analysis as an essential characteristic component for efficient and effective police managerial performance. But in order for us to present analytical skills more comprehensively, a detailing of **managerial problem solving** and the **art of problem analysis** from a specific methodical approach would be beneficial.

MANAGERIAL METHODICAL ANALYSIS

Conceptually, the specific method or technique that each individual manager will use to gather factual information upon which to make a decision will vary as a result of personal characteristics. These variations may be due to a number of factors, such as mental ability, time frame allowance, availability of information and a host of other ingredients. Although the basic problems faced by operational police managers around the world is a constant, the solutions arrived at will be keyed to the individual positional leader and the specific department. It would not be practical for us to attempt to address all the possible remedies that may be employed to deal with particular police problems. But it is possible to set forth a basic mental process or technique that is practical for virtually every operational-level police manager to use in obtaining adequate data to render a sound and comprehensive decision.

The starting point of any analysis process aimed at determining a resolution or course of action to deal with a problem is to disassemble the concern into smaller parts. Just as it is easier to study a picture or a document one section at a time, so too can a problem be better analyzed if it is separated into constituent concerns. This is not a radical or new idea; it is one that normally takes place whenever we mentally address a problem. However, we as

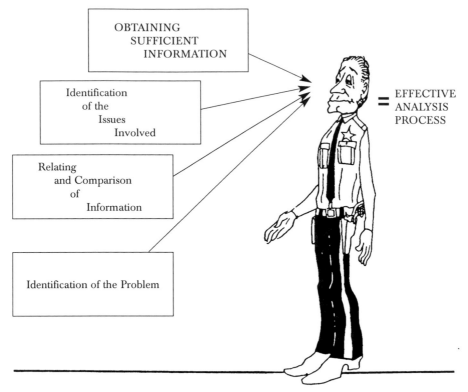

AN OPERATIONAL LEADER'S ABILITY TO ASSIMILATE INFORMATION IS ESSENTIAL TO EFFECTIVE PROBLEM ASSESSMENT.

a general rule don't consider our deliberations over a problem as compartmentalized processing of its component parts to arrive at a solution.

It appears that our thought process is an agglomeration of all the concerns at one time. This is not accurate, because when examined resolutive thought processes are generally well-organized and somewhat chronological. For example, an operational police commander arrives at the scene of a break-in where the suspected person is perceived to be still within the dwelling. The functional-level leader explains the situation and the resources he or she has available at the scene. The operational police manager quickly assesses the information and immediately dispatches officers to cover likely exits from the building. The assistance of a K-9 team or whatever specialists that are needed or available to scour the dwelling is requested. Even though the manager's analysis and reactive decision only took a few moments, a comprehensive assessment revealed the problem-solving process was structured and orderly. A possible sequence of the thought process was:

1. The person was still believed to be in the dwelling;
2. How best to contain the person in the building for apprehension and to prevent escape;
3. What are the likely avenues of escape;
4. Need for officers to cover the possible escape avenues to apprehend the suspect if he or she leaves the building;
5. Which officers to send to cover the areas;
6. What resources are available to search the interior of the building, etc. and a number of other fleeting concerns that were considered prior to deciding what actions to take.

Note: It is recognized that traditionally the functional leader at the scene would have had the responsibility for directive actions. Our scenario is for explanatory information.

As you can see from the above simplistically brief scenario, that in what we routinely think of as a natural reaction, instigated by training and experience, is really an analytical process. The main focus of this or any analysis of a problem is to reduce the situation into smaller problems/components that are easier to comprehend and resolve, rather than attempting to deal with all of the concerns at one time. The disassemblage of a problem into smaller parts is a very constructive and creative method of resolving issues, basically because it involves handling simpler concerns that require less analysis to postulate a solution. This breakdown of techniques involves the seeking and determining of the meaningful relationship that links the pieces together for resolution of the whole problem.

Nearly all mental analysis of problem situations will go through the above constructively descriptive process for appropriate resolution. The segmented processes of problem analysis to achieve a solution are considered productive aids to the interpretation of the situation being scrutinized. The previous information relevant to analytical thinking and how a police manager arrives at a decision is not easily discernible to the average person, because he or she does not as a common practice engage in clinical-type thinking, where each decision is dissected as to how and why it was arrived at. So, to better enable the operational police manager to understand the **techniques of analysis** and to provide the steps whereby a positional leader can enhance personal performance in this component characteristic by which a leader's ability is measured, the following are the four sequential processes of problem analysis.

1. **Separate Problem and Whatever Adjective Data That Is Available into Distinguishable Components**. This is accomplished by bringing to mind all of the major issues within the problem to be resolved. Just as you can separate a bacon, lettuce, and tomato sandwich into primary component

parts, by placing the bread here, the tomatoes there, the bacon over to the side, and the lettuce someplace else, so too can you analyze a problem in the same fashion. By realizing this and being able to utilize that knowledge regarding problem solving, an operational police manager should achieve a more comprehensive awareness of the situation. This improved awareness should enhance job performance ability in this dimensional trait area. The example of the sandwich can be used to further clarify the **divide and conquer** approach to problem analysis and/or resolution. The components of the sandwich are collected and prepared separately before they are placed together to form a finished product; so too is a problem when it is viewed and approached from a clinical analysis perspective.

2. **Evaluate and Assess Each Component of the Dissected Problem in Conjunction with Relevant Data Until a Comprehensive Awareness Is Achieved**. An operational police manager needs to analyze each individual problem as to the scope and effect of it on the overall concern. The smaller problem concentration concept does not require a computer-type mindset but, rather, a channeling of mental resources toward a limited concern, thus allowing a more rapid and effective solution to the component problem. Our previous example of the sandwich can again aid us in understanding this process. For instance, by concentrating and resolving **how thick to slice the tomatoes** before concerning yourself with the bacon, one portion of the overall problem can be quickly solved and set aside. However, if the person vacillates back and forth between the component concerns within the overall problem, he or she is much more likely to take a great deal of time to arrive at a workable solution. As indicated previously, the operational police manager who directed subordinates' personnel via the functional leader to appropriately "seal off the building" to assure apprehension of the suspected person had to sequentially deal with each minor detail or component before reacting to the overall problem. **It must again be stressed that in relationship to the time required, the evaluation and assessment of component concerns is so small as to be virtually unnoticeable as being separately performed.**

3. **Conceptualize the Interrelationship of the Component Parts of the Situation, as Well as to How They Will Need to Interact in Order to Properly Focus the Entire Problem**. The conceptualization of interrelationships and interactions simply means that the operational police manager should be aware that: (a) the concerns must be separated for more comprehensive understanding; and (b) the component parts must be perceived as a chain of events for a workable solution to be achieved. Principally, this is because, to resolve a problem no matter what its complexity, the individual must understand the relationship between components and how the res-

olution of any portion of a concern will affect another. If no perception of interrelationship is considered, then the positional leader may make the problem, as a whole, worse by improperly resolving only a portion of it. It must be remembered that the entire spectrum of a problem must be maintained if an individual's decision is to be appropriate. The sandwich example can again serve to illustrate our meaning. Consider what the consequences may be if the effect that a slice of tomato will have on a piece of sandwich bread if not perceived. By placing it next to the bread, an additional problem may be created, because the interaction of the sliced tomato's fluid on the bread will weaken the exterior structure of the sandwich, which in all probability would not hold the other component parts of the sandwich together. This would seem to be an over-simplification of a vital step in the problem analysis process. However, when viewed in its totality of the analysis process, the steps that an operational police manager goes through to make a decision is also not complicated. The problems and the solutions may be complex but not the basic analytical process. What the decision maker must remember is that the **basic laws of physics** apply: for every action there is a direct reaction, as well as an adjacent action. Thus, the counteraction and/or interaction can be just as vital a concern to an analysis process as any other function.

4. **Scrutinize and Visualize the Entire Problem Censorious, Yet With a Discerning Perception of Expediency and Effectiveness**. It follows that in the course of analyzing a concern, the individual thoughts at some point must focus critically to put the whole situation into one picture. No sound problem-solving decision can be made until the positional leader studies and comprehends the so-called "Big Picture." As previously noted, a leader's study of the problem and the decided-upon actions to deal with it may take only a few moments. The mental processes to resolve a situation need not be long or arduous, but they will nevertheless be sequential in order to formulate a true picture of what is needed. In a number of operational situations when a police manager is called upon to make a decision, he or she can't afford to have overlooked any portion of the problem. Like a military leader in combat conditions, when an operational police manager makes a wrong assessment and thus an incorrect decision in a field situation, a life may be endangered during the course of events. Therefore, a conceptual awareness of the entire problem is a must before directing resolutive actions.

The previous steps have offered a comprehensive picture of an analytical thought process where a concern is taken apart to better understandable form. The previous information has also shown us that most of what we do involves some sort of problem and a sequential cerebral process to deal with them. Prior to the example set forth in the previous information, most persons would not consider that the making of a simple sandwich was a problem that they mentally resolved before doing it. But, as was pointed out, an understanding of analysis or problem analysis is a comprehension of the sequential intellectual processes that occur automatically and often subconsciously. This understanding will enable an operational police manager who is faced with a problem, where a solution does not come readily to mind, to perceive the situation in a manner more conducive to effective resolution.

APPLICABILITY OF MANAGERIAL ANALYSIS

When should an operational manager demonstrate the skills associated with the problem analysis component of positional leadership? The question seems to answer itself; principally, the problem analysis skill is employed when there is a problem. However, it's not that simple, because recognition that a problem exists is not always easily discernible. We are not talking about the mental processes of analysis, as detailed previously in this chapter, but rather the applicability of its problem-solving aspects toward making an effective decision. From a practical standpoint, the subject of this portion of the text should be entitled the "Detection and Identification of Problems" by an operational police manager. No specific action toward analytical resolution of a problem can occur until a person, or in this case an operational police manager, perceives a difficulty. Our venture into the primary phase of problem solving is a contention that alertness and vigilance is required to detect the unmistakable signs of trouble. This will allow the police manager to take appropriate actions at the earliest possible time to resolve the issue. It is no secret that the longer most problems go undetected and undealt with, the more entrenched and difficult they will be to deal with when recognized. Admittedly, early detection may or may not prevent the problem from escalating in seriousness, but awareness can enable the problem to be handled sooner because of the added analytical and preparation time afforded the positional leader.

Recognizing That a Problem Exists

Conceding that the information presented previously relative to the detection and identification of a problem is accurate, the first logical step is a practical method of recognizing a problem. To perceive what is an actual problem means to become alert to the existence of a particular concern or difficulty. Most positional leaders who become proficient in recognizing real and potential problems are sensitive to their perceptual feeling that something is amiss or not quite right. This quality exists in most functional-level or street officers (some call it a "sixth sense"), but in reality it's an alertness to things within their scope of job performance that something is contrary to the norm. An operational police manager's alertness of expectations and a willingness to investigate the "not quite right" feelings that most problems will generate sets the stage for **how to recognize a problem**.

To become proficient and adept at recognizing a problem concerning their operation or personnel, an operational police manager must have the knowledge acquired by constant effort. This is not easy where personnel actions are concerned, considering the changeability and mood variations of most people. But, to be effective, an operational-level manager should be so aware of personnel and environmental factors that the slightest change in behavior or performance activity will register, either consciously or subconsciously. This subconscious recognition generally manifests itself as a feeling of uneasiness, etc. A problem-detection ability can be learned or enhanced like most of the skills used to assess the effectiveness of a positional leader. Some of the telltale signs that a concern or difficulty exists that requires resolution, as offered by social scientists in the field of problem solving, are:

1. An uncomfortable feeling toward something or some situation; that "not quite right" feeling.
2. A feeling of pressure to accomplish something in a specified time frame; the pressure may be real (external) or self-imposed (internal).
3. A perception of a need to alter or change something to improve results or to accomplish a desired objective.
4. Perceiving obstacles to effective element operation or goal achievement.
5. A perceived resistance by external influences to effective changes to improve and enhance operation of a specific project.

A simple synopsis of the above list of telltale signs is the positional leader's perception of a disconsonant relative to commonplace situations. The most effective and productive operational police managers will get into the habit of reacting to these disconcerted auras about operating conditions. The person's reaction (examination) of the concern will reveal that a problem situation exists and needs to be properly identified and defined. A problem situation is generally referred to in clinical terms as a **problematical condition**.

Once a problematical condition is recognized, then an operational police manager should undertake the chore of **identifying the problem**, which is the next sequential process a positional leader must perform in the application of managerial analysis.

Identifying the Problem

When a problem has been recognized as existing, a primary job of the operational police manager is to determine what the real concern may be and the extent of the problematical condition. The problem must be identified in terms of the situation, inasmuch as symptomatic factors may not always be the answer to achieving a true picture of the concern. A differentiation between the issue of concern and the actual problem generally is only the primary step in the identification process. An operational police manager must deal with a number of other tasks directly affecting **problem identification**. The individual manager must distinguish among the issues that present themselves, i.e., what the overall problem to be resolved is and what the component concerns are. Frequently, a positional leader will perceive a splinter concern and assume it's the total problem. The leader will usually react to resolve it, only to find out later that it was but one of several issues or that it was only a symptom of the real problem. Under the methodical review of analysis stated earlier in this chapter, it was clarified that these splinter concerns must be addressed before the total problem can be resolved. But an operational police manager must avoid the assumption that the first concern or symptom that manifests itself is the real problem.

Future manifestations is another reason why positional leaders often have difficulty perceiving the actual or total concern that needs to be resolved. By future manifestation, we are referring to the problems that don't readily surface, the ones where symptoms and splinter concerns appear well before the main issue is identifiable. A simple example of this is when a traditionally average employee, in terms of on-the-job behavior and effectiveness, suddenly appears to become difficult to deal with and whose performance falls below expectations. The stated problems will normally be visible long before a recognition that the real problem was alcoholism and that the other transgressions are only a part of the total concern. This example shows quite clearly that until the real or total problem is identified, a true analysis and/or workable solution cannot be obtained.

An investigative approach must be undertaken by the operational police manager to determine the totality of the problem. The manager's skills in this area should involve an ability to recognize that related concerns or the issues that correlate in time frame and substance may be the signs of a bigger underlying problem. Therefore, it is apparently obvious that the person must be able to differentiate between symptomatic concerns and the real problem. The following list of questions are provided as a guide to the type of investigative inquiries that an operational police manager should pursue in an effort to identify the problem.

1. What are the concerns that are aggravating the individual's interest; both conscious and subconscious feeling?
2. What are the desired results relative to the concerns?
3. What external or internal pressures and interests are affected by the situation?
4. What precipitated the perceived problem(s)?
5. What are the obstructions to achieving expectations?

It is recognized that some of the questions asked above would not be easily answerable by the operational leader. This is particularly true in law enforcement, where the temperament that we seek in a police officer becomes a barrier to obtaining such information. The personality and internal strength that is demanded of an effective police officer will impede his or her willingness to share personal problem type information. Nevertheless, the areas focused on by this list of questions need to be addressed before success can be anticipated. When the individual manager has answered these questions (or ones of a similar nature), he or she can more effectively focus on the identity of the total/actual problem that needs to be resolved. It must be remembered that the character of the inquiries posed will depend upon the specific nature and type of concerns that are readily visible. Once the problem has been identified, the positional leader must then clinically examine the issues in order to clarify the concern. The examination of the total concern under analysis is commonly referred to as **diagnosis of the problem**.

DIAGNOSING THE PROBLEM

Diagnosis of a problem is a synonymous way of referring to a dissection and defining of the concern under review. We recognize that this appears to be a somewhat circular statement in a chapter where the central theme is on improving an operational police manager's analysis skills. However, in our approach to diagnosing a problem, there is more concentration on defining the concerns rather than dissecting the issue. Therefore, the author's recommended approach to this phase of **problem detection and identification** is basically an **interpretation of the identified issues**. Clinicians in the study of problem solving traditionally refer to the interpretation of an issue as the most important step in the resolution process, primarily because the way in which we define a problem will have a considerable effect on how we go about resolving it. To consider any attempt to resolve the issue without an accurate diagnosis of the concern is tantamount to trying to construct a house with no concept of the structural plan (i.e., blueprints, layouts). In other

A POSITIONAL LEADER MUST ASSURE THAT ALL FACTS ARE OBTAINED AND
INTERPRETED BEFORE AN ANALYSIS PROCESS CAN BE CONSIDERED.

words, an understanding of the parameters, such as what is wrong and the causal factors, are essential components in the overall analysis process.

A diagnosis of the problem represents a clinically systematic review of the issue. Unless there is a comprehensive interpretation of the concern, the effectiveness of the analysis process cannot be relied upon. The reality is if an operational police manager's analytical skills and subsequently his or her problem-solving abilities are to improve, the individual must know how to develop a clear concept of the issue. This will enable the person to focus attention on obtaining essential and pertinent data upon which to make a decision. An operational police manager must seek to avoid the pitfalls of many of his or her predecessors by believing that initial observations alone are sufficient for diagnosis of a problem. Lessons learned the hard way have shown that an investigation is needed to gather adequate information to effectively understand and define a problem.

The essentiality of a **diagnostic understanding** of a problem is an analysis process. An operational manager's performance can be summarized by stating, **the primary purpose must be to increase the awareness of the individual to a point where there is a clear and accurate understanding of the circumstances in which the problem exists**. This interpretative comprehension is a necessity because of the mental effort it takes for the appropriate accounting of all the influential information about the concern.

A positional leader (police manager) will not be able to accomplish this without all the important factors being accurately understood and interpreted. Diagnostic understanding may be accomplished through absorption of essential concerns of a problem into the intellectual functioning of a manager during the decision-making process. Proper classification requires the detection and recognition of relevant factors and their interrelationship, in addition to the development of a mental picture of the operational problem situation in the mind of the police manager/problem solver. Who, then, must comprehend and interpret the pattern of concerns? The previously mentioned diagnostic actions will:

1. Allow the avoidance of time-wasting on non-related features.
2. Enable the individual to concentrate on the real issue.
3. Allow a better assessment of goal achievement.
4. Help the individual to have a clear perception about what he or she is attempting to accomplish.
5. Make information-sharing about what is needed easier.
6. Allow smoother coordination of effort with others.
7. Boost the self-assuredness of the decision maker.
8. Clarify the problem that needs resolution.
9. Often reveal alternatives or resources in which to combat the problem.
10. Provide for the postulation of an effective course of action to reveal the problem under consideration.

Most operational managers who are desirous of accomplishing the resolution of a situation will typically start resolving each peripheral concern that is encountered without finding out what the real problem may be. This type of "eager beaver" approach could be detrimental to the ultimate solution needed. Therefore, the next logical step in the analysis process is the acquisition of factual information.

Obtaining Adequate Factual Information

An appropriate diagnosis of sequentially analyzed data requires sufficient factual information upon which to make a decision. With rare exceptions, most operational police managers and other positional leaders are fairly intelligent and mentally stable persons. Even so, most can't provide a respectful number of pertinent facts about a situation that they have not gathered prior information about. It is true that some very good guesses and assumptions can be made from general knowledge and perceived features, but actual accurate facts will be lacking. And, a leader at any level can't be expected to analyze a situation until he or she has some facts to scrutinize. Therefore, the obtaining of sufficient data is essential to the applicability of managerial analysis.

After the existence of a problem has been **recognized, identified**, and **diagnosed**, an operational police manager must then endeavor to ascertain all available facts relevant to the concern. The obtaining of related information should not only include factual data but also whatever peripheral knowledge that is available. The gained information is critical to the formulation of any resolutive actions. Generally, most resolutive actions appear to be simplistic as a result of a positional leader's failure to obtain and understand all factors relating to the problem. Many of the conclusions reached that were originally perceived as practical and effective were proven at a later date to be flawed, because the initial assessments were made without sufficient factual information.

Principally, the acquisition of ample information is the key to obtaining sufficient facts for an operational police manager to be able to properly analyze a problem before making a decision. Then it follows that our text concentration must now focus on the primary information sources available to a police manager. All of the areas identified in the following material offer a different perspective of the situation. However, as a collective body of information, they traditionally provide adequate knowledge for a manager to formulate a practical and soundly based decision.

First, the various **policy and procedural documents of the department** will provide essential factual information as to whether the situation is within organizational guidelines. Second, **independent research sources**, such as books, legal opinions, and personal observations, can add immensely to the manager's knowledge needs. Third, a **police manager's superiors** can provide important wisdom as to what may be desired from a hierarchy leadership standpoint. Fourth, in most situations the information shared by **peer-level managers** who have handled similar problems in the past can offer a direction or guide to an effective solution. Fifth, the attitudinal aspects or environment of the department may in some ways affect the solution arrived at. Sixth, an operational police manager's **subordinates** in a participatory leadership climate, where time and circumstances permit, can add invaluable insight into a particular situation in which they are involved. Seventh, the **priorities** of due dates and the importance to the department will affect time availability for the collection of sufficient information. As is readily apparent from the foregoing, a number of information sources are available for use by an operational leader to obtain sufficient data.

SYNOPSIS

In order for an analysis process to be as effective as possible, it must be a deliberate and meticulous procedure—one that requires a sufficient amount of time to consider each component of a problem situation as a separate entity. A **sufficient amount of time** does not necessarily mean an extended period. The time frame may actually be very short; the only criteria is that adequate opportunity exists to consider all aspects of the concern and to take in as much available factual information as possible. The example of the operational police manager sizing up the problem of the suspected person on the inside of a dwelling and directing action took less than a minute or so. But in the context of what we mean by **sufficient amount of time**, the time frame was immensely adequate.

The recommended dissectional approach to the resolution of problems is essential to a comprehensively effective method of dealing with concerns. In other words, the simplicity of resolving smaller issues in a sequential process should culminate in an overall effective solution to the concern being considered. The disassembling of a problem is nothing new; it is a function that takes place automatically in most mental processes. However, a conscious awareness of specific areas by an operational police manager will enhance his or her analytical skills and thus improve the person's ability to effectively deal with problems. The applicability of problem analysis sequentially goes through such stages as **recognition**, **identification**, **diagnosis**, and **factual information acquisition**. Once the analysis has been adequately accomplished, the next logical step is **decision making**. We will deal with decision making as a process in Chapter 5.

Chapter Four

LEADERSHIP STANDARDS AND STANDARDIZATION (FUNDAMENTAL ASPECT OF MANAGEMENT)

Leadership Standards in law enforcement management is foundationally formed by the tradition of the past and the needs of a changing society. The established customs or rules that form a set of standards may or may not be based on hard rules or facts. They may simply be a practice that is easier and effective in certain situations; however, their consistent usage in a particular circumstance may quickly form a standard by which actions will be measured. Leadership standards are rules and behaviors that direct mid-level police managers to relate to certain actions, desired objectives, or evaluation criteria by which accomplishments can be assessed. The leadership standards may be intangible, as in the case of employee morale. Thus, it must be emphasized that standardization is merely the function of determining and maintaining performance standards.

It is apparent that nothing can be gauged or evaluated without an established criteria or standard to be judged against. The standards of criteria are usually a set of convenient or applicable elements of the behavioral actions or desired results. They must be capable of setting forth the various degrees and attributes for which the standards exist. Therefore, there is little practical significance in setting standards that cannot be discriminated accurately from randomly articulated criterion. Leadership standards tend to be an analyzed codification and classification of prior causal and effect behaviors. An effective managerial leader must recognize that standards of directional influence are necessary to assess the influences, behaviors, and results achieved via leadership standardization. Simply put, the standardization of mid-level police leadership in a law enforcement organization could not occur without specific criteria to measure behaviors against and to judge the results achieved there from.

BEHAVIORAL STANDARDS AND THE
FUNCTIONS OF MANAGEMENT

The requirements of a mid-level police manager to formulate and adhere to established standards of criteria are universal to every form of leadership. However, for a police manager such standards are quintessential because they enable the mid-level police manager to improve the quality of his or her leadership performance. Basic managerial standards are a set of criteria for appropriate performance of leadership functions. The structural management functions are the innovative planning, organizing, and directing of the task behaviors of others. The standards of leadership referred to should be accomplished under traditional situations that have been previously identified and articulated.

Innovative Planning is the capacity of foundational determining for a productive basis of action. The creative planning efforts must be focused on the achievement of identified objectives. For example, Community Policing is a fairly recent concept of law enforcement's directed efforts to address the needs of a centralized area, as opposed to the previous theory of utilizing the same approach throughout the city, town, or village. Creative anticipation and projections endeavor to address such concerns as what must be done, how will it be accomplished, when will the performance occur, who is responsible for the action, what essential factors must be used, and a number of other critical questions of similar nature. Therefore, *innovative planning* for a mid-level police manager mandates a determination of the components, strengths, and results of his/her projected leadership functions. The anticipated projection should assess its possible influences on the situation. Also, appropriate planning should proportion the standards into a collection that will maximize desired results. Thus, appropriately applied leadership standards related to desired performance interactions must exist if leadership effectiveness is to be achieved. Remember, a productive creative scheme always includes some extension of past criteria that carries through to the present and projects into the needs of the future. The quality of the analysis and projections depends a great deal on the accuracy and appropriateness of the leadership standards. Also, the form and manner in which the standards are assessed will affect the quality and precision of the measured results.

Organizing in relationship to mid-level police leadership standards is the behavioral action of creating or providing those foundational conditions and interactions that are a requirement for effective execution of a performance plan. Specific circumstances and interrelated actions must be present and/or available prior to the functioning of either phase of an innovative plan of action. From a results perspective, organizing involves an advance supply and allocation of foundational performance components and inherent influences, as identified by the projected plan of action. Thus, it becomes clear that organizing for mid-level police management depends on leadership standards and the assessments thereof.

Controlling as a concept relative to standards of leadership is the function of governing and directing behavioral actions in accordance with the mandates of an Innovative Plan. The aforestated indicates a requirement for standards to assess and focus the performance behavior of a leader. Subordinates must be provided with criteria for the assessment determination of the expectation for effectiveness and desired accomplishment. These should measure task performances or relative progress toward the completion of the objective. The delineated standards will ensure the coordination of effective behavioral actions. There should be leadership standards and components of job performances by which the results of a leader's behavioral actions can be gauged throughout the plan's execution, as well as to evaluate the end results. Corrective action, if needed, is unlikely to be effective in the absence of measured results during each phase of a leadership plan of action. Articulated and accurate leadership standards most assuredly affect the controls that are so necessary for performance plan execution. Controls within the parameters of leadership standards are therefore an essential consideration in the determination of directed mid-level managerial expectations. Attempting to set leadership standards enters into and affects the direction of subordinate behaviors and leadership functions in many other ways.

Managerial Delegation within the scope of leadership standardization concludes the perspective definition of functional management at the level of operative performance. Subordinates and many administrative executives, as it relates to leadership standards, relegate the general concept of delegation into a tangible perspective—in other words, a clear understanding of why delegate tasks and to whom will delegated power be allocated. The order of delegation should be the hierarchy of function, the responsibility for action and/or the authority between perception and primary operational performance. Hierarchy leadership provides assistance to functional personnel in the performance of their duties. Plans of actions are transmitted by organizational leaders to functional staff who are required to cooperate, organize, and execute the set forth course of action.

The ultimate delineation of Creative Planning is found in the foundational performance of functional personnel. For this reason it mandates the application and use of appropriate leadership standards. Primary functional performance tends to be commonplace and repetitive, whether mental or physical. As a consequence, at the functional level, leadership standards tend to be more physical or actual rather than conceptual or theoretical. In other words, it is where the "rubber meets the road." It is evident that the influence of leadership standards or standardization is pervasive in police management and operation.

REQUIREMENTS OF LEADERSHIP STANDARDS AND STANDARDIZATION

Leadership standards and standardization must comply with certain decreed criteria. Some of the standards set into place and used are determined by the compulsory needs of the particular problem or concern. Yet, some leadership standards may be considered typical or general and adaptable to most managerial situations.

The so-called "General Standards of Leadership" must be applicable to any situation. A generalized standard of leadership should be applicable to the evaluation of particular characteristics in all of the organization's management situations and under most conditions of the concerns that exist. Information concerning the coercive energy and results of the action under different circumstances will not be readily comparable otherwise. It would be easier to interpret and apply the information if a generalized standard of leadership with universal components of assessment were used. The primary universally essential attributes have to do with the following traits:

1. The general standards of leadership should be **constant**. A varying of standards skews the effect and the evaluation results of the measured applicability of the criterion. For example, positive results are less likely if the guidelines or the rules of the game are constantly changing.
2. The standard of leadership utilized must be **reducible** to a permanent set of criteria. The items or components of measurement must be capable of being documented into a form that others can understand and use. It is essential that an organization standard be useable and adaptable to others in a like situation or position to gauge behaviors and performance.
3. Standards of leadership in a police organization must be **reproducible** as a measurement for managerial performance at several leadership levels. The military type infrastructure of a police organization reflects the repetitive nature of leadership obligations, depending on the level of responsibility.
4. Being **representative** of the task obligations and job accountability is an essential term associated with leadership standards and connected with mid-level police management. Setting a standard that is applica-

ble only to a first line supervisor would not epitomize the measurement of leadership standards for a mid-level police manager.

5. The leadership standard utilized must possess the trait of being **applicable** to the position being measured and the performance task expectations. For example, an evaluation of the running speed of an individual is not applicable and useless when evaluating the speed at which a person can crawl. The prior statement indicates the essential nature of what is to be assessed and why the method used is critical to establishing the relevance of a standard of leadership.

6. The leadership standard must be free from **ambiguity**. There should be little or no doubt as to the interpretation of the behavioral standard. Equivocation or double meaning for terms of measurements or other considerations of task performances can be misleading as a standard of leadership.

Leadership Standards for a mid-level police manager should be reasonably constant. The accuracy and effectiveness of the standards will typically be continuously affected by the environmental and social inducement influencing police activities. Standards are typically criterion set forth for optimum conditions and interactions under a given or predictable set of circumstances. Changes or variations that do not allow adequate time for adjustments, etc., may negatively influence standards though they may be flexible. Fixed leadership standards are reflective of static or stable performance conditions. To some degree leadership standards must be flexible, although unstable measurement traits or standards tend to lesson the effectiveness of managerial and operative assessment.

Parameter guidelines of leadership for any level of management must be classified, systematically arranged and documented. The formation of an established list of leadership standards should occur as soon as the trait area is identified as relevant to the assessment of the job performance of an organizational leader. It should be remembered that it is not the purpose of leadership standardization to make static or to hinder performance behaviors. Its primary purpose is to prevent or reduce the chances that whatever progress, etc., that have been made from being lost. There is little doubt that the concept and practice of leadership standards are conservative in nature. They essentially are put forth to assist leadership in moving forward and not slipping back to using non-positive or non-productive traits or behaviors. Organizing leadership standards into a formalized document facilitates management's need for information regarding leadership behaviors and functional performances produced therefrom. Thus, it is essential that the evaluation standards can be reproduced with whatever accuracy that may be required. If the standards cannot be reproduced, it may not be possible to develop an evaluation instrument that will assess with adequate correctness the traits to which the leadership standards relate. The leadership standards must, of course, be reflective of the most effective and productive current knowledge and practices. There must be the capability to apply the leadership standards quickly and efficiently to any problem or measurement to which they relate.

As has been articulated above, the formulation and use of leadership standards/standardization in law enforcement is essential to the effective performance of a mid-level police manager. The old axiom that says, "You don't know where you are going unless you know where you have been," is certainly applicable to developing or establishing standards. In other words, to set and utilize standards and measures to guide job performance is essential to universal leadership application throughout the organization. Also, the performance efforts of a police manager can be more efficiently focused on accomplishment of desired tasks. Thus, it is conclusive to note that the quality of managerial leadership is closely associated with the superiority of the standards used to guide managers. Most managerial concerns can be solved or adequately addressed through planning, organizing, and operational controls exerted by management.

THE ORIGINATION OF STANDARDS

It is apparent from the previously stated information that initially all standards must be based on the results they are designed to achieve. The standards are the concretion of some accomplishment of law enforcement's primary managerial objectives. All elements and forces in a police organization must be proportioned, related, and coordinated with one another in a format that will make possible an effective achievement of objectives. Management is usually unable to meet all requirements completely in most cases, because there are usually factors that are beyond the control of established standards. Nonetheless, it is true that standards of behavioral measures, policies, functions, environment, personnel, and performances derive their characteristics and validity from evaluation tools.

Of course, there is a point of diminishing returns regarding the development of assessment standards. It is therefore costly in terms of manpower and efforts to identify, define, and refine standards. Generally, there is no scientific methodology that indicates that all performance evaluating standards must have precise accuracy. Standardization of behavioral measures requires only that the desired solutions should produce results that are satisfactory within the quality parameters of the concerns. It is unscientific, as well as ineffectual, to produce assessment measures that have no redeeming qualities regarding appropriately structured managerial behavior. The aforementioned concept structures traditional thinking concerning the requirements of performance standards and therefore relates to all other measures associated with managerial guidelines.

There are many sound objectives that justify the origination and/or development of the compilation of performance standards into an evaluation instrument relative to the standardization of managerial dimensional components. Remember, managerial procedures should coordinate the performance of management functions via the specification of concurrent or sequential operational job performances.

HOW LEADERSHIP STANDARDS ARE DEVELOPED

Executive leadership in law enforcement as it is in other businesses has the managerial and social responsibility for developing and improving work standards for all levels of the organization. Many believe that this responsibility is inherent in its managerial functioning in today's society. The obligations include edification of both positional leadership and functional-level personnel as to the standards by which leaders will be judged and subsequently what they should or will expect from the job performance of subordinates.

The development of job performance measures for law enforcement leadership tend to progress through certain stages of evolutionary growth. The various stages have been designated the pioneering stage, the exploitation stage, and the stabilization stage. The **Pioneering Stage** is the phase in which new and innovative concepts of motivation and functional patterns and growth emerge to ensure task accomplishment. At this stage a leader will develop or enhance performance techniques to guide or foster the behavior of subordinates. Furthermore, a leader will take the developed techniques into standards by which to measure future leadership performance of managers at the various levels being assessed. The **Exploitation Stage** is the facet of the process in which the components of the standardization process have been developed to the point where it is understandable and useable to accomplish the projected task of guiding and measuring the performance skills and behaviors of law enforcement management. The **Stabilization Stage** is the phase in which the novel and creative processes of leadership components are secured. Thus, the use of the developed standards becomes a benchmark by which a manager or other organizational leader can gauge their job performances. Stabilization is also the stage at which the maximum practicable limits of assessment (at each point in time) have been reached.

The rapid expansive growth in the specialized need for law enforcement services has caused a parallel increase in the requirements for leadership standards. The process will be repeated as the needs and the requirement to police today's society changes. This cycle may have a great effect on the kind and ability of the management required by a law enforcement agency. It will have an equally measurable effect on the various standards that the organization should establish and maintain.

The tendency in law enforcement today is toward decentralization rather than the centralization of authority and responsibility. This has occurred generally to be more responsive to the various needs of society and to emphasize individual accountability. The managerial leader who is accountable for the results of the operation under his/her command must be provided whatever authority is necessary to accomplish the task. It includes the initial power to make decisions concerning the method by which the results will be achieved. Each mid-level police manager is responsible, accordingly, for developing the best method for his/her operation. Further, a mid-level police manager should evaluate personal job performance via the criteria or standards derived from the components of his/her actions and the results of the subordinate's task accomplishment. If the mid-level police manager is to accurately assess him or herself as a managerial leader, then it is essential that the person closely examine some of the aspect of his/her role in the organizational hierarchy and what those obligations entail.

ESSENTIAL ROLE OBLIGATIONS FOR AN EFFECTIVE MID-LEVEL POLICE MANAGER

The middle-level managerial leader for a police agency is a responsible key member of the managerial efforts in the achievement of desired organizational successful accomplishment of its goals and objectives. An effective mid-level police manager must possess and competently demonstrates the following leadership trait characteristics (further discussed throughout this text): good judgment, integrity, initiative, courage, patience, flexibility, and a number of other qualities. Most organizations will readily admit that the first-line supervisor is the main organizational leader who gets tasks accomplished by the base-level workers. However, the essentiality of the mid-level manager's role in perpetuating and assisting both superior and subordinate persons to perform effectively cannot be overlooked. Thus, it is mandated at this point to articulate a few of the lesser discussed task obligations of a mid-level police manager that are necessary to help assure successful achievement of organizational goals and objectives.

Initially, we discuss the term "intermediary" as used primarily in the context of a first- or second-level supervisor's role responsibility especially as principal or primary operational leaders who shields both management and functional-level workers from the routine of each element's respective operation. However, it is plain from the information presented in various managerial studies that a buffering to some degree occurs at every leadership level of the organization. Thus, we recognize that a mid-level police manager has an obligation to mediate and translate performances between his or her superiors, peers and subordinates sub-leaders, and sequentially the functional-level workers to accomplish organizational goals and objectives. This does not imply that directives or suggestions will he filtered by the mid-level police manager, but rather that information relayed will he couched in a form that is most understandable and acceptable to the respective level for which it is intended. It should be clearly articulated and appropriately relayed whether the specific performance action is directed to superiors or to those appointed under his/her organizational leadership position, explaining the behavioral approach that will be used.

Although at this juncture, we are not specifically addressing a mid-mevel police manager positional obligation, it is essential that a brief reminder be set-forth to ensure clarity of the manager's role and subsequent action toward achieving organizational goals and objectives. These areas of task obligations and the basic skills of leadership are essential knowledge for all levels of police management.

Task Obligations

Middle management, as previously discussed, refers to the handling and leadership of personnel and organizational resources. This does not imply that a mid-level police manager needs to possess great technical skills in the areas being overseen, whether directly or through the direction he/she provides to sub-leaders. middle-level managers and the functional leaders, primary or secondary, under his/her control and/or direction are traditionally not employed as technical craft persons but as first or secondary leaders of base level workers.

This would appear to be a contradiction, especially in light of the fact that most police organizations tend to promote the best workers or perceptually most skilled employees. This concept has and continues to be the modus operandi throughout the various levels of leadership within a police organization. It is generally agreed that we need to recognize and reward the efforts of our best employees even though several studies have shown that generally the better worker level performers do not translate into the more effective and efficient leaders. Although, a mid-level police manager's work habits and task performances are a clear indications of the individual's positive organizational commitment and motivation; it should be recognized that while these qualities are important to a leader's makeup, that they must be considered in conjunction with the leadership characteristics which are suggestive of an overt ability to effectively direct and control the behavior of others.

Most people have heard a leader or two say something like, "I would not ask anyone to do anything that I would or could not do myself." This sounds good and the concept makes the person seem like an outstanding and caring leader, but a focused analysis reveals that if a leader can perform worker-level tasks as good as or better than subordinates, especially technical or skilled jobs, then the performance-level employees are sub-par or the manager and his/her direct report leaders are not efficient or effective. It is critical to note that the type of positional leader who is expected to have equal or greater skills than worker level subordinates is considered a "crew leader." And, "crew leaders" are not considered a manager or a person having true leadership responsibility; they traditionally focus on personal or individual job behaviors and to a minute degree, the interaction of a few other workers. A manager or leadership person in an organization must think in terms of the collective behavior of others toward accomplishing organizational goals and objectives. The mid-level police manager does not need to be highly skilled in the area that he or she is providing leadership; he or she must, however, have a working knowledge of the fundamentals of directing and controlling the performance of others, as well the ability to coordinate his/her operation with other organizational elements. An effective manager should maintain a basic and current knowledge of any changes in organizational goals and objectives, as well as any interactive techniques, and procedures concerning the collective operations within the police agency. The mid-level police manager is also expected to have organizational knowledge of the overall goal achievements, plus a basic awareness of the interpersonal skills and scientific knowledge techniques of managerial leadership regarding his or her sphere of responsibility.

The management knowledge areas that a mid-level police manager is required to be aware of during daily operations are hereinafter briefly explored. The identified knowledge areas are not exclusive to a middle manager, but they are critical to the effectiveness of any organizational police leader. The required managerial knowledge areas being referred to are:

The knowledgeable awareness to formulate a plan of action: The currently more aware managerial leaders, whether in law enforcement or some other industry, must be able to effectively project the available resources and subordinate manpower toward accomplishing the organization's goals and objectives. From this projection and assessment, the mid-level police manager is expected to develop a functional plan of action for that will ensure accomplishment of tasks by those he or she is directing. The knowledge required for a managerial leader to be effective as a planner has been articulated in the chapter discussing "Decision Making." The middle manager must also have an intimate awareness of what information is needed, how much data to obtain, and how the decision will correlate with other organizational entities before developing a plan. The managerial leader should further demonstrate an ability to analyze and interpret the collected information as to what is the most effective and efficient use of the identified resources to achieve desired results.

Further, the mid-level police leader, as a managerial planner within the organization, must be able to look into the future of his or her scope of responsibility and forecast the coming needs and adjustments. An effective manager should then demonstrate the management skills necessary to be able to anticipate problems and make decisions to resolve them prior to the situation occurring. Additionally, the managerial leader must be aware of possible organizational changes or adjustments of the goals and objectives that will affect the task accomplishment of those assigned under his/her span of control and formulate strategies that will compensate for these modifications. *In essence, one of the principal functions of a mid-level police manager is the anticipation, planning and ensuring the task performance behaviors of subordinates to achieve organizational effectiveness.*

The awareness and foresight to ensure that subordinates are adequately knowledgeable of how to accomplished the tasks they are assigned. An effective mid-level police manager must have the ability through managerial know-how and leadership efforts to ensure that necessary training for subordinates is provided. Whether the training or knowledge sharing is externally presented or participatory on-the-job training, relayed by incumbent subordinates, the more accomplished managerial leader will assure that their personnel are adequately trained. Effective managerial leaders recognized that training is a never-ending process, especially in the area of law enforcement where court decisions, laws and procedural techniques change almost daily. The effective manager must maintain a current knowledge of these changes and ensure that develop knowledge skills necessary to train subordinates for improved efficiency are available and utilized.

A demonstrated ability to control and direct job actions of subordinates: mid-level police managers must have the knowledge and ability to control the performance behavior of subordinates if they are to be effective as a managerial leader. A second- or third-level police manager must learn to use appropriate management control techniques to direct subordinates to a successful conclusion of their performance. There has to be a thorough awareness of the rules, regulations, policies and procedures of the organization, so that the dictates to subordinates will be in compliance and focused on the agency's goals and objectives. An effective managerial leader knows the value of disciplinary actions, both positive and negative, to reinforce desired behavior in employees. It is natural to expect that some errors of performance or misbehavior by subordinates will occur. Thus, a primary measure of a competent management leader is the ability to deal with these performance exceptions by leading and guiding the employees toward the desired organizational goals and objectives. It is clear from the above information that effective police managers must enhance their required knowledge in the areas of the specific responsibilities and functions in order to be effective. There are other informational areas in the dynamics of the work place that a managerial leader must have knowledge so as not to violate any applicable employee rights or constitutional safeguards.

SYNOPSIS

The most efficient mid-level police manager in today's society must not only possess at least a workable technical knowledge of personnel management skills and traits characteristic of an effective leader, but he or she must also have a practical knowledge of *the basic motivational needs of subordinates.* An effective managerial leader should understand all the legal and moral ramifications of his or her position concerning the responsibilities and liabilities for actions affecting subordinates and the organization. Secondary managers should acquire a basic knowledge of the legal parameters of leadership actions concerning subordinate employees so as to avoid becoming an unanticipated liability to the organization in the form of lawsuits against the company because of a perceived managerial action or inaction. The efficient and effective mid-level police manager will direct and control a subordinate's job performance behaviors through motivation and/or manipulation within the accepted parameters on the job.

The information provided in this text articulates the critical nature of establishing managerial criteria upon which a leader can focus and thus manage toward. These criteria or exemplars are closely aligned with the Characteristics of Leadership as is the Behavioral Standards and managerial precedence's discussed previously. It is a traditionally accepted concept that the organizational performance of a mid-level manager determines in many aspects the job behaviors and demonstrated attitudes of his or her subordinates, peers, and to some degree, superiors. A productive manager affects those attitudes and behaviors through personal leadership characteristics and duty performance. While it is true that the police manager's environment, to some degree, affects the display of what we term *effective leadership characteristics,* the individual must endeavor to keep the positive aspects of these influences in the forefront of his or her performance.

There are a substantial number of Behavioral Standards, Functional Performances, and Personal Characteristics that we associate with positive or effective leadership. The author has identified a number of these characteristics throughout the text that are essential to the effective performance of a functional mid-level police manager. It is imperative to note the essential importance of these characteristics as they relate to the efficient and effective operational performance of an organization's manager. The ability to motivate subordinates is the foundation of any leader's performance ability and this becomes even more focused in the field of Law Enforcement. The effective managerial leader must be able to inspire the subordinates' job performances. It is in this area that subordinates' personal motivations and the overall interest of the organization are at its closest point. Also, it is at this juncture that the level of employee productivity and work output is created and the primary criteria upon which the mid-level police manager's effectiveness is measured. It is recommended that the functional mid-level police manager to some degree practice participatory management or democratic leadership involving his/her primary supervisory leaders, whenever possible, to strengthen personal skills in this area. Therefore, it should be noted when the text discusses Role Obligations, Task Mandates, Awareness of Responsibilities, and Demonstrated Ability, we are referring to a leadership approach where consideration is given to worker satisfaction and comfort, when it does not conflict or hamper organizational goal accomplishment. Many studies have shown that high worker satisfaction and high productivity are inseparable.

Chapter Five

DECISION MAKING

A decision made by an operational police manager is an affirmative course of action that has been selected to resolve a problem. The selected actions are generally chosen from among a number of available choices. The circumstances under which a police manager will have to make decisions will vary as widely as the different situations that confront law enforcement. Normally, to discuss decision making, an author will approach the subject from a methodical step-by-step sequence, beginning with detection and analysis. However, inasmuch as we have dealt with those areas in the previous chapter, they will not be further detailed here. Also, in most operational situations faced by a police manager, circumstances may develop in which there is usually no apparent opportunity for a meticulous analytical approach to the problem at hand. It appears in those occurrences that the manager is relying primarily on experience and instinctive intuition to deal with the problem. However, as stated in the previous chapter concerning analysis, no matter what the time frame, there is usually enough time to identify the problem and the type of decision required, even though we may be talking about fractions of a second. Remember, a weak or inadequate decision is usually better than no decision at all, when one is needed. An inability to make timely and effective decisions has been determined to a great many, so designated, positional leaders.

An operational police manager who desires to maintain the positional respect of subordinate personnel should attempt to get all the available factual information on the problem under consideration, decide on a course of action, and then commit to a decision. A police manager must at all times keep the overall achievement of the department's goals and objectives in mind while contemplating the decision. The individual also has a positional leadership obligation to assure that any decision made is based on accurate, complete, and factual information. An operational police manager's final or problem-solving decision must be comprehensively reviewed in coordination with the functional policies and procedures of the department.

Problem-resolving actions in police organizations are typically very formally structured regarding the leadership position occupied by an operational manager. In most military and paramilitary operations, such as public policing, the authority to implement action is based on the level or extent of the recommended action. For example, an operational-level manager does not usually possess the final authority to terminate a subordinate. He or she can relieve the person from duty for cause, pending a final decision by top departmental management, i.e., the chief of police, etc. This does not lessen the fact that the manager was required to make a decision—only that the decisive actions were cloaked into a recommendation instead of a final resolution. Therefore, in a traditional organization, such as a police department, there can be no set formula to assure that a proper decision will be made in every case. It is perceived that through training and acquired knowledge, by way of departmental directives **coupled** with experience, the individual manager can employ sound judgment in making a decision.

Nearly all action taken by an operational police manager during the course of his or her job performance is a result of some form of decision made by the individual. The decisions made need not be complicated or critical to the element's operation, and the so-designated "life-or-death" functional decisions are hopefully few and/or seldom required. But there is never a guarantee that what may seem like a simple or routine decision may turn out to be monumental from the perspective of the police department's operation. It is noteworthy that while top-level management decisions traditionally are recognized as affecting more people and tend to muster a greater reaction, it is the decisions made by an operational manager that deal with and/or resolve a majority of the functional or personnel problems of the department. In law enforcement, unlike other types of organizations, an operational manager is recognized as an individual whose responsibility includes making critical decisions daily. And, yet, police managers are still required to make the same type of routine operational and the less sensitive tactical or non-tactical decisions as their counterparts in other industries. However, because of the behavior-controlling nature of police work, most operational-directed actions are essential to citizen or subordinate safety and survival.

The previous statement relative to less sensitive tactical or non-tactical decisions was not to imply that these types of managerial actions, whether personnel related or operational in nature, are not important. To the contrary, it should be noted that these types of determinations are more complicated than may be initially considered. They may appear to be one-dimensional, meaning the resolution can be limited to a single isolated concern, but this will not diminish the essential nature of their effect on the organization's overall performance. So-called simple decisions, as to which personnel to assign to handle a particular problem, may have far-reaching effects on productivity, unit capability, and a host of other factors. So, what may seem like a one-dimensional decision, i.e., placing "A" and "C" on the same assignment, may on the surface appear simple, but the resulting fallout can prove that concept faulty. Therefore, it must be concluded that no matter what the concern, an operational police manager must not consider the resolution inconsequential and unworthy of deliberation.

To this point we have discussed decision making in a rather abstract introductory mode as it applies to an operational police manager. However, before proceeding further, a textbook-type or formal definition of decision making should be offered for the reader's contemplation as he or she reads through this chapter. **Decision making** is defined as **a process whereby an individual willingly makes a choice of available alternatives after careful and comprehensive consideration of the situation**. Some authors on the subject go so far as to say that **a decision is a form of judgment between ends and means to accomplish desired goals or objectives and that the process can be classified as an intellectually assertive act**. Toward our goal of detailing a comprehensive review of decision making and how an operational police manager can better understand it, plus enhance personal performance in this area, the text content will now focus on the cornerstones or the very edifice upon which a logical and effective decision is made.

A STRUCTURE OF DECISION MAKING

In order to present a comprehensive and detailed discussion of the internal application of decision making and how each component interacts into an effective process, we must examine the entire procedure. To perceive the structure and process of making a decision, the beginning should be with a determination that a problem needs a resolution and a comprehensive analysis of the concern. But, since both of those areas were explored in-depth in the previous chapter, we will only identify and highlight the first two steps before more thoroughly detailing the other stages of formalized decision making. The initial two steps can't be eliminated from our discussion here, because the foundation of a decision-making edifice is determined in these stages. The author has compressed the structural procedure into a five-step process for easy analysis and practical. The five distinct components of decision making are **detecting and identification of the problem, analytical**

assessment of the problem, development of alternative resolutions, determination of the most appropriate action, and **taking action on the resolution selected.**

1. **Detection and Identification of the Problem.** The basic step for any positional leader in the resolution of a concern is to know that there is something amiss. After the situation requiring action has been uncovered, then the process of finding out what the real concern is and defining its relevance to the overall situation is undertaken. In this step, an operational police manager can't rely only on visual observation or the verbal information provided by subordinates, etc. He or she must also, to some degree, depend upon intuitive assessment of the situation. It seems as if we are saying that beyond the actual facts received, an operational manager must use a "best guess" method. This is not the intent. We are merely saying that experience and intuition should be used in conjunction with factual information when detecting and identifying a problem. Also, since virtually everything we do requires some type of decision, there is no practical way of determining or outlining when and where a police manager may encounter a concern that needs addressing.

Most police operational leaders are as a matter of routine placed in situations where they are accountable for making practical and realistic determinations. These decisions are required to resolve the concerns that generated the need for the resolution. Thus, the expectation of problem detection and identification is a relatively essential function of the operational manager's responsibility. Traditional managerial texts dealing with decision making refer to this area of concentration as "problem recognition." It is obvious that any decision-making edifice, whether we refer to it as "problem recognition" or "problem identification and detection" begins with this foundation as its starting point. The detecting and identifying step of the process leads almost effortlessly into the analytical or second stage of decision making.

2. Analytical Assessment of the Problem. The second stage of the decision-making process is a diagnostic review for classification of the problem. It also provides a directional focus that an operational police manager must use to gather sufficient factual information to make a logical and sound decision. The process should be clinical approach to evaluate the concern for determination of its nature and possible resolutive actions. The analytical assessment of the problem will indicate the hierarchy level of the police department at which the final decision should be rendered. Further, a clinical review of a concern is essential to clarify what information is needed to make an operational decision. Without this type of diagnostic review, the effectiveness of the decision made can't be reasonably assured.

A diagnostic analysis of the problem means a determination of why the problem exists in terms of both cause and effect. The analytical assessment must include who or what identified the problem that needs resolution. If some directive is being violated or needs compliance, then the intent and expected results must be examined and considered. Likewise, if the problem is focused by upper management, the areas of concern need to be addressed relative to their expectations before a comprehensive diagnosis can be considered complete. An effective operational police manager will recall that all good decision-making processes are dependent upon the individual awareness of the factors that caused the resolutive actions to be taken.

A noteworthy phase of analytical assessment is the **acquisition of factual information** from which stage three, the **developing of alternatives**, are derived. After the detection, identification, and diagnosis of a problem, the next logical sequential step in the concern's resolution process would appear to be data acquisition. This means a search for and the collection of available information relative to the concern from which a strategy of action can be developed. These strategies of action are more commonly referred to as "seeking alternatives." Exploration of these strategies of actions into workable alternatives will be discussed further in the following stages. However, once the concern has been recognized and diagnosed, the police manager must assure the acquisition of sufficient information to render a sound deci-

"Hey, this does not seem too difficult."

THERE IS NO MAGICAL SOLUTION TO EFFECTIVE DECISION MAKING. IT'S ACCOMPLISHED THROUGH A CLEARLY DEFINED AND STRUCTURED PROCESS.

sion. This point can't be overemphasized. When discussing the obtaining of sufficient information, we are talking about not only relevant factual data but also the observations and conclusions of others who are in a position to provide insight into the situation.

A number of positional leaders in all fields tend to make quick or snap decisions that often prove inadequate when all the facts are in. An operational police manager should avail him- or herself of all the information sources within the department; these inceptions usually include **directives** (documents and traditional practices), **research information**, **superior dictates**, **opinions of peers**, **logistical availability**, **environmental factors**, and **subordinates' input**. This list is not all-inclusive, but it provides a strong base for an operational police manager's acquisition of factual information. The obtaining of sufficient data leads automatically into the use of the information in a decision-making process. The use of the information gathered translates into **developing alternative resolutions**.

3. **Developing Alternative Resolutions**. The generation or formulation of alternative actions to resolve a concern in a police operational situation is a basic means of determining the proper resolution process. Principally, choices of alternatives provide an operational police leader with varying courses of actions. Of course, there can be no absolutes in terms of fixed alternatives, especially when dealing with internal personnel problems or the ever-changing focus of emotional concerns in operational situations. Thus, the assurance that alternative courses of action are available to an operational police manager when dealing with a law enforcement or personnel problem is essential for effective job performance. The determination of effective alternatives is often a search for the best of all available choices. Frequently, however, these searches for choices will often bypass what may be the most effective alternative without a conscious effort of an operational police manager to methodically seek the most appropriate resolutive actions.

An operational police manager will find that in a lot of situations requiring some type of decisive action for resolution, available choices are readily visible. While in other cases of concern, there can be either an abundance of alternatives from which to choose, or the reverse, where there appears to be no acceptable resolutive choices. It is this variance of available alternatives, depending on the situational circumstances, that can determine the effectiveness of job performance by an operational-level police manager. Whether it is simply making a choice between numerous alternatives or generating solutions by a so-called "spontaneous idea method," either way there is no specific **rule of thumb** to guide the operational police leader. Some researchers in decision-making assessments have professed a few general rules for selecting and/or formulating resolutive alternatives. Some of these rules are:

Brainstorming as many choices as can be perceived. It is much more conducive to arriving at the best possible solution by choosing from more alternatives than is needed, rather than from too few possibilities.

Don't limit alternatives to a focus that is too narrow for effective creative type thinking. If an operational leader automatically excludes relevant areas of concentration, he or she may overlook an alternative choice that is most conducive to resolving the concern.

Once choices have been conceived, don't be afraid to adapt them. An operational manager should not routinely dismiss alternatives because they fail to perfectly fit the concern. Conceived alternatives may need to be given a second or third look, if time permits, when modifications may make them a more resolutive possibility.

Seek participatory input from others whenever possible. Realizing that in police work an operational manager like a functional-level leader can't always seek the opinions of others before developing and selecting an alternative. Like the military leader in a combat situation, a police leader must be ready to make and require execution of instantaneous decisions in certain functional situations. However, when time and circumstances permit, the individual should have the self-confidence in personal ability and/or authority to feel comfortable in seeking suggestions from other knowledgeable and involved persons.

Allow time for reflective and inquisitive review of the choices arrived at. It is no secret that often our ideas or suggestions will look different to us in the **cold light of day**. This generally occurs whenever there is confusion or concern that the alternatives available or selected are not the best of all possible choices. By this, we are referring to a **manager's** need for contemplation over the alternative chosen. As before, if time allows, write down the possible alternative resolutions and mentally leave them for a period of time before returning to assess which one will best resolve the problem or concern. More often than not, your perspective will not change, but there are a few occasions where a factor that you may have overlooked will come into focus.

Attempt now to allow the resolution alternatives being considered to become an either/or choice. This type of dichotomy approach will severely limit an operational police manager's latitude of action. Either the leader will utilize a particular course of action or the individual will do nothing. The latter alternative may be inappropriate as a resolutive choice for a positional leader to take no affirmative action. Especially, when a decision is needed, this can be detrimental to the manager's survival in a police organizational setting.

As is perceived from the few guidelines cited above, there can be no developed fixture of **rules** or **processes** that is ideal for all concerns or situations faced by an operational manager. The six rules cited above* may be useful in an environment where time and lives do not hinge on immediate decisive actions, but they are less practical or beneficial to an operational police manager who responds to a functional crime scene where a situation requires decisive action. The development of alternatives as in the assessment and identification of problems must be completed in the intellectual processes of the individual. Therefore, it's appropriate to say that mental preparation through practice, experience on the job, and departmental procedural knowledge are an operational manager's best assets during an emergency situation. In other words, like most skills, a police manager can improve personal ability to bring into focus alternatives for problem resolution through increased knowledge and experience. The elevation of his or her intelligence level in the purview of procedural parameters and suggested actions are developed by a comprehensive review of departmental directives. While enhanced familiarity generally comes with job tenure and some specifically focused situational training sessions, they would also advance the manager's experience acquisition.

4. **Determination and/or Selection of the Most Appropriate Action**. Once the other stages of the decision-making process have been determined and available alternatives identified, the concern should be effectively dealt with. An operational police manager should consider the alternatives in conjunction with the time frame priority, logistical requirements, financial considerations, and other factors that will influence the resolutive outcome of the problem. The choice of which alternative to select must be made with the previously mentioned factors in mind, as well as with the ultimate goal of resolving the concern.

The chosen alternative most generally will come down to a dichotomy of choices, not in terms of an **either/or situation**, but rather a choice between two closely related alternatives, which when conceptually viewed will both resolve the problem to some degree. The author refers to this as "a choice between legitimate alternatives."

An operational manager's choice between **legitimate alternatives** should be made with clinical precision to assure that the most effective one is chosen. The basic assessment of choices to resolve an operational issue is essential to the individual's overall effectiveness as a decision maker. A contention that is so primary that it seems unnecessary to relate, states that it is **the single most crucial area to decision making after problem analysis**. The positional leader's clinical type evaluation of identified alternatives should be accomplished in a virtual pragmatic manner. The positional leader should carefully review the positives and negatives of each operational alternative toward the concern's resolution. Of course, under a clinical and purely logical forum, the individual would simply total up **the pluses** versus **the minuses** and select the one with the highest number of positive attributes and the least number of negatives. This seems very simple, which in point of fact it is, but this simplistic version of alternative selection does not take into account any variances in the factors considered. Realists in the **art of personnel management** know that **there are no exact absolutes** when dealing with human emotions regarding problem resolution. And, about 90 percent of an operational police manager's decisions will involve some form of human reaction or logistical resource usage, whether it concerns an internal police personnel matter or the reaction of police clientele (victims or suspects) in a functional situation.

The clinical review process outlined in the previous paragraph is not as simple as it sounds, even in situations not directly associated with active human emotions. The various choices identified, whose advantages and disadvantages have been comprehensively examined, must be assessed against other criteria before a final workable solution is determined or selected. The criteria most typically identified are:

1. Whether the alternatives under consideration will most effectively contribute to goal accomplishment;
2. What the economical cost is to the department to implement the alternative versus the benefits derived from a resolution of the concern;
3. Whether the selected alternative's implementation lends itself well to a logistical availability of the resources of the organization; and
4. Whether the chosen alternative positively affects the overall agency's operational objective in conjunction with an affirmative solution of the problem being considered.

After all of these considerations have been given due mental process, a particular choice or a series of alternatives may be perceived as most effective for the problem's resolution. In cases where one choice clearly stands out as best for concern resolution, there is no problem in selecting the appropriate alternative. However, when several alternatives appear to be satisfactory or where more than one apparently needs to be employed to effectively deal with the concern, an operational police manager needs to list all of the recommended alternatives for consideration for appropriate assessment. If his or her decision is final on the choice of alternatives to resolve the concern, then one must be chosen for implementation. But if the individual decision is for the consideration of higher ups, then the listing of these multiple alternatives should be in the form of prioritized recommendations. Documenting possible alternatives focuses the text's emphasis onto our final recommended stage of the decision-making process, which is **taking action on the resolution selected**.

5. **Taking Action on the Resolution Selected.** In any process the prior developmental action of an individual is meaningless unless the end product produces some type of affirmative activity. The same principle is applicable to decision making. All of the other stages discussed in this chapter are not worth anything until decisive action has been taken. This phase of decision making is more aptly referred to as "implementing the decision" and is the concluding step that an operational police manager utilizes in completing the resolution to a concern. We recognize that a resolution process can be extended to include such phases as **obtaining a positive reaction to the decision, checking the results of the decision**, and many others. However, for our purposes in this chapter, we are concerned with making appropriate choices and taking actions on the selected resolutive effectuation. Managerial actions beyond the scope stated is discussed under the auspice of another dimensional trait characteristic.

In providing this clinical look into decision making, this text does not want to imply that determining resolutive action is always an arduous and painstaking process of some duration. Generally, an effective operational police manager, especially in functional situations, must make decisions quickly without hesitation or reservation. He or she is not often afforded the opportunity for lengthy contemplation when a life may hang in the balance. Thus, by having to make the decision in a relatively short time span, an operational police manager will at times have to settle for solutions that are not totally researched but yet satisfies the need. As previously noted, the individual is forced to choose what appears to be theoretically appropriate or what circumstantially seems most effective for resolving the problem at hand. The reality is that the choice made is often somewhat better than several other alternatives for resolution of the problem but may be deficient in some other area. Seldom will a guesstimated alternative be ideal or satisfactory for resolution of the concern in every respect. Therefore, at this stage of the decision-making process the police manager's preference is the key factor. Of course, the individual's preference should be swayed by the concern's resolution and favorable versus unfavorable consequences. The main consideration in this phase of decision making is that an alternative choice is made and a course of action taken. The natural tendency is to choose the least risky alternative relative to the manager's personal image and/or likelihood of failure. The **risk-taking** aspect of decision making is the point at which efficient positional leaders are separated from less productive ones. The willingness to **commit thyself** or to **be decisive** in taking action to resolve an operational or functional concern is an observable trait, which should be considered critical to the effective job performance of an operational police manager.

MID-LEVEL DECISION MAKING AND PROBLEM SOLVING

As before noted, selecting an alternative or deciding to take action is not an easy aspect of leadership. The process of decision making most typically is accomplished during the interactions of a number of factors that may affect the planned action or the results. Generally, these influence factors are unclear as to complete information or possible impact at the time that the decision is to be made. Leaders in any type of organization, including a police department, are considered decision makers because the nature of their responsibility is to get things accomplished through the work of others. Primarily, many of the decisions made in an organizational setting are strategic in nature. Organizational leaders also make critical selection regarding his/her element's structures, command control systems, and use of available resources. The police mid-level manager must make a decision as to the functioning of his or her element and subordinates in an effective manner that fosters the overall achievement of organizational goals and accomplishment.

Every operational police mid-level manager who expects to obtain and keep the respect of subordinates must learn to get all the facts on a given situation and then commit to a course of action. The mid-level manager must also consider the overall accomplishment of the organization's goals and objectives relative to the decision. Also, when the mid-level manager makes a decision based on accurate and complete information, which has carefully been reviewed in reference to the end result, the decision should be final.

Alternative selection is the process of identifying concerns and choosing an action to resolve them. Decision making in a formally structured organization such as a public police department involves the use of the authority to implement the action that was decided upon. Also, the positional structure of the organization dictates who is responsible for making the needed decisions. This positional makeup does not, however, establish a set formula to assure that proper decisions are made in every case. It is hoped that acquired supervisory knowledge and procedures will assist the new or incumbent functional-level mid-level manager in applying good judgment when making a decision.

Virtually every on-the-job action taken by a mid-level manager is accomplished because he or she made a decision. The decision may be so simple and so consistent that it is made as a matter of routine and not perceived as a specific decision. By the same token, the decision may be monumental from the perspective of the organization, one that will affect the entire operation of the agency. The *need for* and the *importance* of decisions made by management are traditionally recognized by all elements of the organization; not so are the decisions of the functional-level middle manager. But yet, a majority of the problem solving from an operational or personnel standpoint is accomplished through the decisions made by the mid-level manager.

Mistakenly, the only decision perceived to be made by mid-level management are those of a routine, unimportant, and tactical nature. This perception of a mid-level manager's responsibility for and performance in the decision-making process of the organization must change. Upper management of the organization must take note of the everyday decisions made by functional-level middle managers and how these decisions affect the overall operation of the organization.

It should be noted, however, that tactical or operational decisions are more complicated than initially perceived. They are generally one-dimensional, but this does not diminish their importance to the effectiveness of the organization's overall performance.

The obvious conclusion is that a decision is a judgment, no matter at what level in the organization it occurs. It is a commitment to one course of action selected from among two or more alternatives. There always has to be some type of decision made in every situation; even if the person does nothing, he has made a decision. **The decision was to do nothing**. The test of the effectiveness of a manager concerning the decisions that were made: (1) Were they sound? (2) Were all the facts received? and (3) Were all the alternatives considered?

Some theorists in the field of police management feel that only people at the executive level make decisions. The contention of this text is not in agreement with that concept. This author believes that important decisions are made at all levels of the organization, although it is recognized that the initial impetus of the chain of events that led to a managerial decision might have started at the executive level. Examples of common decisions made at the functional-management level are: what resources to assign to which patrol area, or what amount of on-the-job training is needed by operational subordinates, and many other similar type decisions. Some decisions are more critical in nature and some less, but all have an impact on the operation of the organization. Therefore, efficient managers make appropriate and effective decisions based on the need for the element's goal accomplishment. Their decisions should be made from a consistent process of a clearly defined procedural pattern for receiving, reviewing, and analyzing all pertinent data before making a decision.

When we consider previous information, it is clear that in order to examine effective decision making from a functional mid-level police manager's point of view, we must first look at a secondary leader's behavioral style of problem solving and/or deciding on an appropriate course of action.

STYLES OF LEADERSHIP
CONCERNING DECISION MAKING

As emphasized throughout this chapter, the process of decision making is not a difficult task. However, the manner in which decisions are arrived at and the various leadership styles affecting the process can be somewhat more challenging. It is generally recognized that decision making is **risk taking**, but yet an essential part of leadership. An indecisive person is most often a poor leader and an ineffective performer in whatever task that's attempted. Hersey and Blanchard' articulated **Tell**, **Sell**, **Consult**, and Join as points along a continuum for styles of leadership. The terms utilized by Hersey and Blanchard very closely parallel this author's descriptive analysis of decision making, as it corresponds to styles of leadership. The styles of decision making related to a leader's methodology are:

1. **Selfish or Autocratic** is the style of decision making that is self-centered. In other words, the leader formulates an action based solely on personal perceptions and directs its implementation without consultation or input from subordinates. The leader fully expects and anticipates subordinates to carry out the action without question, which in critical situations, where time is limited, may be the difference between success or failure.

2. **Agreement or Obtaining Endorsement** of subordinates relative to decisions made by a police mid-level manager. The leader makes a decision based on facts known to him or her and then attempts to convince subordinates to accept the idea. The concept here is to gain acceptance rather than mere surrender or compliance of employees to the decision rendered. Many leaders, when exercising the agreement form of acceptance, will generally *sugarcoat* the decision or present it in a manner that is most favorable to the employees. It must be understood that the leader will make the decision on his or her own, but does not try to force feed the idea to workers. A number of leadership theorists disagree with this form of action implementation, citing the fact that if the decision is made solely by the leader, then action on it should not be an option of subordinates. The leader who chooses to use this form of decision making and implementation process should be cognizant of the potential for resistance by subordinates. The deci-

sion itself must be feasible and understandable to subordinates if a leader attempts to convince others to buy into his/her ideas.

3. **Participatory or Consultation** with subordinates in decisions made by a police mid-level manager. This type of decision making usually occurs in *non-urgent* situations where a leader has ample opportunity to consider the input of others. The leader who solicits a participatory decision still must realize that the ultimate responsibility, for the *decided upon action,* rests with him or her. A participatory decision offers a number of advantages over those made by an individual: more points of view are involved, a number of perceptions go into the decision, and there is less chance of essential factors being overlooked. The old adage, *"two heads are better than one"* is true, if the time frame of the decision isn't a prime factor. Another factor that must also be remembered is that *"it's harder for two heads to make a consensus decision than it is for one."* It should be recognized that the greater the number of participants in a decision-making process, the greater the amount of time needed to reach even a consensus, and possibly a lot more to achieve a complete agreement. In this style of decision making, the leader will usually not decide upon action until subordinates, etc., have been consulted for input. A leader can appear weak or indecisive, if he or she use the participatory input for more than an information source to be considered in making the decision. A self-assured and confident leader is not afraid to use participatory decision making when circumstances and the situation allows.

4. **A Shared or Delegated Style** of decision making is when a leader assigns the authority to decide a course of action to a subordinate. This type of decision making can be effective, if adequate information is provided the employee designated to decide the course of action. The leader choosing to utilize the delegated style of decision making must fully understand that the ultimate responsibility for deciding an appropriate course of action cannot be abrogated by him or her. A delegation style of decision making can be innovative, in that the selection of the designee will often bring with him/her a fresh or new approach to solving a concern. Inasmuch as the principal task of a police agency is controlling the behavior of others, creative decision making may be somewhat limited. The above statement is true because of the unpredictability in the behavior of people thereby making the use of untested or creative methods of handling people in behavior-controlling situations hazardous. Also, policing leaders recognize that law enforcement officers frequently are confronted with problems and concerns that they have no previous experience upon which to base an effective course of action.

A secondary police leader must assure that he/she considers alternatives before deciding on a style of decision making. The mid-level manager must be cognizant of the requirement to develop specific parameters for his/her decision making. A consideration of which situations require a decided upon action and what style is best are prime factors in the overall decision-making process.

Situational Recognition Regarding Decision Making

Police mid-level managers are continually placed in situations that require logical and realistic decisions, which when put into action will resolve the problem or situation. Therefore, it is reasonable to assume that true problem analysis, including recognition and decision making, are two of the supervisor's most important duties. But in assessing any structure or procedure, and *decision making as a process,* we have to begin with a basis upon which to build or start from. Thus, indecision making the basis upon which a police mid-level manager starts is **recognition**.

The inadequate performances of subordinates or equipment and the development of flaws in operational processes are clear indicators that a problem exists. Many times the variation in the behavior pattern of these entities is so small that they are barely detectable. However, experience has shown that the longer a problem goes unrecognized, the more difficult the solution will be when it is detected. This does not imply that every small variation in a person's performance is symptomatic of a problem. In fact, it is considered normal for some variance in a person's day-to-day actions.

However, if the supervisor detects what may be perceived as a pattern starting to develop or that there are some external contributing factors, then recognition of the problem is essential. But it should be remembered that an alert, effective mid-level manager will usually find a potential problem in more situations than he or she has time to handle.

Also, directives from upper management must be considered under the Recognition-of-Problems category. Even though in a strict sense the problem was not detected by the secondary manager, from a practical standpoint, the decision-making process for a solution is the same. Remember, a good decision made by a manager depends on his or her being aware of the factors that caused the decision to be made. The circumstances of the situation will determine whether any decision by the mid-level manager is practical. Once it has been recognized that a problem requiring a decision does exist, then the second step in the mid-level manager's decision-making process is the "acquisition of adequate information."

Acquisition of Adequate Information

Once a problem has been identified, the mid-level manager must then undertake the ascertaining of all available data related to the situation. The gathering of relevant data will not only include facts, but also the opinion of others may be needed when subjective decisions are to be made. Initially, many decisions seem to be simple at first glance because the supervisor quickly assimilates and assesses the consequences of all of the facts affecting the problem. A number of decisions that were thought to be sound and practical have been made, only to be proven at a later time not to be so, because the initial determination was made without the necessary information. Since adequate information is needed for the manager to ascertain sufficient facts to make a decision, then it is safe to say that effective communication is essential to decision making. The principal sources of information available to the functional level mid-level manager to obtain adequate data to make a sound and practical decision are **organizational directives**, **research sources**, **management**, **peers**, **environment**, **subordinates**, and **priorities**. Each of the areas identified provides a different perspective of the problem, but collectively sufficient information is obtained for a practical solution. The principal informational source areas identified and defined are:

1. **Organizational Directives**: The various policy documents of the organization (General Orders, Memorandums, Standard Operational Procedures, Duty Manuals, Rules & Regulations, etc.) will provide valuable information as to whether the situation is within organizational guidelines.
2. **Research Sources**: The information gathered from this area may range from legal opinions arising out of labor laws, etc., to the opinions of published experts in the field.
3. **Management**: The manager's superiors can add valuable insight into what it is that they desire in cases where they initiated the action. Also, organizational goals and objectives are generated from the top levels of management of the organization.
4. **Peer Level Managers**: In unusual situations and circumstances, information shared by peer managers who have handled similar problems in the past may provide a clue as to a sound and practical solution.
5. **Environment**: The attitudinal climate of the organization and even the physical surrounding of the organization may have an influence on the decision that has to be made.
6. **Subordinates**: As previously stated during our discussion of Participatory Leadership, when time and circumstances permit, employees who work in the particular situation can add considerable information

to the process. The principle is *collective assessment* with a lot more brains involved.

7. **Priorities**: Priorities in the case of decision making are directly related to timing. Priorities of action must be set depending on the amount of time available to the police mid-level manager.

The areas cited are not all-inclusive of the sources of information available to the mid-level manager, in order to obtain sufficient data for a good decision. Also, there is no specific formula to tell the primary leader when he or she has sufficient information to make a decision. The best test is for the supervisor to answer all the questions that come to mind about the situation, then a logical/feasible decision can reasonably be expected.

Assessing the Information Received

It is believed that regarding a problem-solving situation, the best process in evaluating data is to review the information, select an alternative and then leave it alone for a full day before analyzing it again. This process is valuable, but it can only be accomplished in cases where time permits. After the wait, the decision maker should review the data and the selected alternative to determine if it is the best decision. The wait also allows the person to take a second look, almost the same as obtaining a second perspective of the problem and recommended solution.

Another positive practice in analyzing data for a decision is to allow someone else to review the problem, the collected information and the proposed solution to obtain their opinion and input. Discussing the factors with several persons has the same effect and there are greater possibilities of obtaining an effective and workable solution. But the decision maker should be aware of the pitfalls of obtaining a group decision, such as the extreme amount of time that is required and the differences of opinions.

The critical factor in assessing data from several sources is how much weight each should be given. The author recommends that the police mid-level manager not be overly concerned with the weight factors but rather that he or she prioritize the source areas that are being considered. By doing so, the affecting factors to the decision will be addressed in the order of their importance. The next priority will be moved to only after the influences of the higher one have been met and considered.

The dictionary states that to analyze a thing is to separate it into individual parts so as to determine the nature of the whole by examination of the components. This basically is what a mid-level manager does with the collected data prior to making a decision.

The logical final step in the decision-making process is committing one's self to an alternative—in other words, making a decision. In some writings, the final step to decision making is thought to be implementation, but this author concludes that the actions taken to carry out the decision are separate from the actual decision-making process; also, that the critical area in making a decision is not selecting the alternative, because no matter what the subject or situation, we each have an opinion on it. The important focus, as far as managerial decision making is concerned, is with the person's willingness to take the risk and commit to an alternative.

ASSESSING A MADE DECISION

Assessing the action to be decided upon, its potential effect and ultimate results, is generally considered an essential process of the decision maker. It is considered quintessential to a leader's effectiveness to determine if an implemented action achieved the desired results. The evaluation process should occur, if possible, before completion of the process to determine whether planned actions are proceeding as expected. For example, if the decided upon action is flawed or not being implemented as planned, it will be more difficult to correct after completion than during its progression. A simple analogy of this is a rocket that is aimed one degree off course will be further out of line with the object the greater the distance it is allowed to travel before correction. In other words, one degree off line at the launch point may mean a target miss of several hundred miles. But if an early evaluation shows that the projectile is misaligned, the easier it will be to correct. In other words, the sooner an error is discovered, the better. The aforementioned statement is simplistic, but nevertheless it clearly illustrates the need to evaluate a decided upon course of action before the concluding results. This is not to imply that a final assessment should not be made to determine the ultimate results as to the accomplishment of the desired action. And, then to make whatever alterations as may be needed to successfully achieve the desired end.

Evaluating an enacted decision follows the same suggested format as assessing performance actions toward a planned objective. First, the assessment should take into consideration whether or not the ultimate results of the decision and subsequent action(s) achieved the anticipated objective. More often than not, a planned action initially made will exceed or fall short of the intended results because all influence factors and interactive consequences are not primarily known. Second, as in the law of physics, *for every action there is a reaction,* the implementation of a decided upon action may cause a corresponding reaction that may be a hindrance to desired results. Take, for example, a police officer or line supervisor who decides to reroute traffic around a hazardous area at his/her place of employment, but in doing so, the persons are detoured through an area not designed for heavy foot traffic. The detour causes unanticipated delays and damage, none of which was initially foreseeable by the police officer or supervisor. In other words, a decision to solve one problem created another that now has to be dealt with. Thus, when evaluating a decision to be made or one already implemented, the leader should attempt to foresee other difficulties or impediments caused by the decided upon action. Third, an effective and efficient leader or decision maker should evaluate planned actions to gauge the cause and effect of the concerned solution. It is recognized that not all relationships and affected influences can be perceived before action is taken. But through a clinically objective assessment of planned action, some valuable insights and empirical data will be gained. Conceivably through such a perceptual examination, it is believed that decisions can be made to resolve a concern while minimizing peripherally generated problems.

There is no panacea of assessment actions that will eliminate faulty decisions or provide information to assure a decided upon action is totally workable and effective. The leader can only set into place evaluation methods that should be objective and practical, as well as being specifically designed for the decision being evaluated. All decided upon actions that are to be implemented should, if possible, undergo the evaluation process as stated. It must be realized that within each decision and its assessment, there is a measurable result that should aid secondary managers in achieving a desired outcome.

Risk Taking by Committing to a Decision

It should again be emphasized that putting him- or herself on the line, no matter what decision that a secondary leader makes, involves a certain level of risk. The risk in this sense is if his decision is bad or unsound, it will damage his/her credibility. The other side of the coin may also be risky to a midlevel manager who is too conservative or afraid to make a decision for fear of being wrong. The manager will appear to lack innovative skills, or even worse will be considered indecisive by staying with past solutions or failing to act when the situation dictates action.

A functional-level police middle manager is considered effective based on a willingness to take necessary chances appropriate to the positional status in the organization. A manager should view the *committing to a course of action* to make a decision in a *positive manner,* such as a challenge or opportunity to display personal skills, as a leader worthy of the position. The manager should avoid the negative perception that each decision puts his or her position or status at some degree of risk of disenchantment within the department or organization.

The logical conclusion to our discussion of the willingness of a functional mid-level police manager to commit to a decision is to point out which of the following is the greater risk to his or her image as a decision maker. The risk areas are: (1) failure to make any decision; (2) making a snap decision without all the ascertained facts; and (3) making decisions that are based on personal assessment of the facts, even though the action may sometimes be in error. Obviously failing to make a decision when one is needed is more damaging to the supervisor's status or image than the other two areas. And, in turn, the making of a "snap decision" that is wrong is inherently more detrimental and improper than making a decision based on available facts.

In conclusion, it must be stated that any decision reached has to be made effective through action. In other words, once the supervisor selects an alternative and decides to implement it, he or she has to motivate the subordinate to carry out the decision. This presents no problem in situations requiring an autocratic style of leadership exercise of authority. However, in situations requiring discretionary actions by subordinates, it is important that the manager is able to present the decision in a manner that it is perceived as *our decided upon course of action.* The decision also has to be palatable and understandable to upper management. Meeting these objectives is also likely to increase the quality of the decisions made by functional mid-level police managers. Decisions should not be designed purely to aid the leader in making his or her job easier and better but rather to more effectively achieve the organizational objectives.

Finally, there are two areas worthy of repeating before concluding our discussion concerning decision making for a functional mid-level police manager. A managerial leader should (1) avoid appearing indecisive by failing to make a decision in a timely manner and (2) should avoid making snap decisions without obtaining adequate information. The operational police mid-level manager should look at the positive aspects of decision making, inasmuch as they can lead to favorable recognition by upper management. Also, by utilizing the process of decision making outlined in this chapter, he or she will be an effective problem solver and decision maker as a mid-level manager.

MID-LEVEL PROBLEM SOLVING

The ability to identify and determine a solution to problems or concerns is an everyday occurrence that extends beyond the process of decision making. The actions of the operational mid-level police manager in problem solving, like that of decision making, is an essential task of leadership within the organization. Some theorists speculate that problem solving is one of the most critical parts of a manager's task. A police organization at the secondary level of leadership is principally concerned with personnel and logistical matters related to performance. Also, a mid-level manager is obligated with the task of maximizing the use of allocated material and human resources. The action of problem solving is a demand of leadership that is continuous and ongoing, because in law enforcement, as with other employment fields, the concerns resolved today will reoccur tomorrow, possibly with a different set of variables and consequences. Thus, the solution utilized to solve the problem today may be unsuitable for a similar problem tomorrow. The process of effectively dealing with the prevention, control, and reduction of crime is dynamic. It is somewhat fluid in nature, inasmuch as the offenders very often are different in their methods and techniques, thereby necessitating a variance of actions by public law enforcement in its policing approach.

Many law enforcement officials believe that a methodological approach to deal with problems faced by public police is the best procedural process of resolving the concerns typically encountered. A methodological procedure is the reaction to one another by components to determine a solution. The components are usually interrelated in their goals and objective focus. William F. Roth, in his book titled, *Problem Solving,* identified three processes he designated as "System." The systems identified by Roth were (1) Social System, (2) Technical System, and (3) Socio-Technical System.

A Social System as it relates to secondary police leadership is a collection of persons interacting to accomplish a common objective. And, that any function contingent upon working together toward a common purpose is a social system. Therefore, collectively, an entire police organization can be considered a social system. Thus, the components led by secondary managers are likewise a social system. The significance of this as a consideration in problem solving is that a leader can effectively utilize the interrelated nature of subordinates working together to deal with or resolve a problem. A secondary leader in a police organization should seek to utilize the interrelated tasks of subordinates in a focused effort to solve whatever problem that occurs.

A Technical System was articulated as a combination of two or more methods or entities to achieve a desired quality and quantity of goods or services. Methods (techniques) include a tangible focus that may be necessary to the actual accomplishment of desired goals or objectives. For example, a police mid-level manager recognizing a need to provide policing protection or preventive efforts at an event being held in his/her assigned area must appropriately react to solve the problem. The manager then designates an officer or officers through the primary leader to perform on-site patrol or a line beat coverage of the area in an effort to perform on-site patrol or a line beat coverage of the area in an effort to deal with the perceptual problem. At the time the police mid-level manager set up the interacting efforts to deal with a perceived concern there was no tangible problem in existence. The assumption being made is that the mid-level manager established the method of dealing with the forthcoming need based on obtained accurate information, efficient use of available resources, and an experienced awareness of how to resolve the perceptual problem. The essence of the Technical System of problem solving by a line police mid-level manager is that of transformation of techniques or methods into action by subordinates to solve a problem. Mental projection and awareness of performance capability within certain parameters of actions is the most concise articulation of a technical system of problem solving.

The Socio-Technical System is identified as a number of persons and methods, including materials, interacting to produce a specific amount or quality of goods and/or services to assist in the accomplishment of goals and objectives. The goals and objectives are defined and parameters established by the leader who seeks to resolve the problem via the socio-technical system. A socio-technical system is most always embedded in a larger system. It is part of the organization that focuses on the services provided from the basic level through ultimate goal attainment. In a police organization, a socio-technical system can either be an *open* or *closed* system. Open refers to the fact that resources utilized will be obtained from the environment or the organization as a whole in its effort to resolve the problem. The closed system refers to the fact that the leader seeks to utilize no resources beyond those already assigned or available to him/her. For example, in an open system the leader may request a tactical team or response type squad for assistance in dealing with the concern, while in a closed system the leader will rely only on the resources that are internally available to his/her element.

Problem solving by effective leaders is viewed as a preplanned approach and something normal to general operation. Thus, problem solving is treated as an integral and continuous part of a mid-level police manager's job performance. A secondary leader should use problem solving as an opportunity for learning and development both personally and for subordinates. Problem solving is a central core of leadership activity for a police mid-level manager. A number of leaders treat unexpected problems as abnormal occurrences and attempt to ignore them or react to a concern only when they have reached the crisis stage. The leaders that consider unanticipated problems as abnormal, view them as disrupting normal operations requiring the need to concentrate both human and material resources on finding a solution. Leaders who antic-ipate the unexpected and try to predict what they will be in advance and pre-pare for their arrival or react to them as a normal course of events will tend to be more effective as a mid-level police manager.

OPERATIONAL MID-LEVEL POLICE MANAGERS SHOULD ALWAYS BE CONDSIDERING AN ALTERNATIVE PROBLEM RESOLUTION

As stated earlier, upon making a decision regarding the resolution of a problem and its most probable cause and effect on the organization, the managerial leader should immediately begin the consideration of an alterna-tive. The reason for his or thinking of another method of dealing with the identified problem is not a matter of how meticulously a managerial leader decided on the solution, but rather that there is always the possibility that an adjustment or alternative resolute action will be needed. Some may conclude this as a creative venture into problem solving and decision making. How-ever, it is only the realization that things and situations may change, thus, making it necessary that the proposed solution be altered as well. The typi-cal conception as a resolute behavior in the handling of a problem seems to be to try to resolve the concern by determining a course of action that is most conducive and the easiest to accomplish. This suggestive approach follows along the line of determining the best possible, which may mean that often the first answer to manifest itself is inviolable and then pursuing it generally because there is a tendency to not expend perceptually more time and per-formance effort that would be needed to conceive of additional alternatives from which to choose.

Most operational mid-level police managers recognize that it takes time, patience, and a performance effort to conceive and develop worthwhile alternative solutions. However, the fluid dynamics of most managerially han-dled problems dealt with by a mid-level police manager clearly reflect the need for a flexible approach to problem solving and decision making. The traditional concept of "simply concluding that the most readily available solution should be selected can be a bit misleading." Because time and re-source limitations, as well as the constraints of the organization, more often than not mean that the concept of best or most conducive is relative to the situation and external influences. Ordinarily, alternative recommendations to resolve a problem may not be evaluated for the most desirous balance of effectiveness and efficiency, because of relevant constraints and influences.

When a managerial leader resolves a problem, it should be through a course of action that is most compatible with the goals and objectives of the organization and must meet his or her need to be effective as an operational mid-level police manager. The concept or a solution being adequate or acceptable has been used as indicated or the custom of settling for a decisive action that accomplishes the task well enough but may not provide the best possible resolution. For example, the utilization of a piece of cardboard as a patch to stop a leak in a roof may initially work, but it is not the best possible solution because of the structure of the temporary stoppage and will be ineffective in a very short time span. Some managers who claim that this action allows them time to determine a more long-term solution often use the temporary or "quick fix" method of finding a solution. The old axiom of "any port in a storm" may be sufficient in an emergency, but an operational mid-level police manager should always keep in mind that the problem you fail to handle today or put off until another occasion will require the time and effort that was not expended at the initial recognition and handling of the concern that needed to be addressed. It is significant to recognize that a "quick fix" method has been criticized as a passive technique, because it fails to consider the need for the long-term problem resolutions that augments improvement and growth.

As we have noted, a problem is best resolved whenever the most conducive and resolute action toward implementing a possible solution that will effectively deal with the concern in line with the goals and objectives of the organization. Operational mid-level police managers are believed to have made the most of their opportunity to utilize available resource when they methodically research alternative problem-solving behaviors through carefully formulated observations and quantitative considerations before choosing a solution. Another resolutive action worthy of consideration as we discuss problem solving is that a problem may dissipate when the circumstances in which it exists are altered, so that the concerns are no longer components of the equation that makes up the perceived difficulty. It has been theorized that Problem Dissolvers are said to seek perfection, inasmuch as, they actually alter the structural context of the system in which a problem needing resolution exists. Police managers at all levels of the organization who solve problems by altering the circumstances in which they exist rely on whatever combination of measurable assets and other resources available to get the job done.

Some noteworthy theorists and authors in the area of managerial problem solving have set forth the concept that the determination of whether or not a solution is best can only be determined by implementing the resolute action and then evaluating its long-term effectiveness. Simply stated, the conjecture that "time is the true test of any solution." Until implemented solutions have not had time to prove their worthiness, a police manager can rely only on his or her personal assessment relative to the efficiency and/or effectiveness of the decisive action taken. Generally, the resolute action implemented should totally resolve the differences between the actual and the desired outcome in a smooth and timely manner. However, should operational police management not be convinced that the problem has been completely and accurately identified, then they must reevaluate the problem, the situation, the influences, and resolute actions decided upon and implemented. In this method the leader may perceive an element previously overlooked, which will allow him or her an opportunity to try another solution that may have been previously identified and dismissed as insufficient to adequately resolve the problem. This is typically called "recycling" and should continue until all conceivable solutions have been reasonably evaluated and assessed for its possible effectiveness or until the circumstances/influences related to the problem changes to the degree that the presently viewed resolutions are no longer feasible. If the problem continues through the recycling effort, then it is suggested that the leader consider the approach of redefining the problem before attempting to decide on any action to resolve the concern.

DECISIVENESS IS ESSENTIAL FOR SUCCESS

A standardization definition of decisiveness is **a decision maker's willingness to make a choice, depict individual assessments, execute alternatives and to commit to a personal preference**. As is articulated by the definition, an operational police manager's ability to choose a course of action to resolve a concern is paramount to the conclusive process of decision making. The committing of his- or herself to an affirmative alternative involves a certain amount of risk to the person making the choice. There is little consequence as to what the nature of the decision, it still represents a jeopardy to the manager's credibility. Naturally, there are more negative consequences related to making a bad or illogical decision than to selecting a perceived good or effective choice. A perceived good decision that effectively resolves the problem will tend to depict the positional manager in a positive perspective, one who is an efficient leader and who has a positive job performance knowledge. The positive portrait projected by the individual's job performance is such that top departmental leadership will perceive the police manager as a capable and desirable positional leader. However, it must also be stated that all of the things mentioned above may be opposite of what could be the result of a decision rendered that is perceived negatively.

AN EFFECTIVELY UTILIZED DECISION-MAKING PROCESS WOULD AID A POSITIONAL LEADER IN DETERMINING WHICH PROBLEM TO PURSUE.

The issue of decisiveness as it relates to an operational police manager has several components. However, the ones that most challenge an operational leader are those with time frame parameters to make the decision and a required tenacity of commitment after the choice has been made. Both components relate directly to the manager's willingness to persevere without fear of defeat or error. In other words, when talking about decisiveness, we are referring to individual courage. In fact, it is a truism to say that **decisiveness is a form of courage**. This seems an inconsistency, especially when we consider that human behaviorists tell us courage is not a personality trait that can be taught, but yet, experience has shown that decisiveness as a leadership trait in operational managers can be effectively learned. Assuming both of these concepts are true, then what we are talking about regarding **risk taking in decisiveness** is personal confidence in ability as opposed to courageous actions. However, in learning how to be decisive, the police manager must keep in mind that the ability to make quick decisions and a steadfast adherence to the alternative decided upon is not an end in itself. They are, however, an asset in critical operational situations. Also, intellectual speed in deciding what should be done often eliminates wasted time and an erosion of subordinate confidence in the manager's ability to lead. There's a number of other peripheral things like cost, frustration, etc., that may be avoided when decisions are made without unnecessary delays. Tenaciousness in assuring a decision's implementation can also be an asset. Vacillating when making a decision by an operational manager can be costly to the individual in terms of respect for job performance capability and could further jeopardize the safety of subordinate personnel and/or police clientele.

Remember that when a commitment has been made, based on a quick decision, and a course of action taken that indicates a need for change, based on new or additional information, and that change is not forthcoming, this can be perceived as a negative performance trait. A manager's failure to make a decision adjustment can be injurious to the concern he or she is attempting to resolve. Therefore, an operational police manager should strive to assure that sufficient information is known prior to rendering a decision and that a mental adaptability is maintained toward choices as required for effectiveness. So it would be fair to say that good judgment or logical considerations are absolutely essential in deciding and implementing a course of action. The capability to assess the requirements for a decisive course of action develops with experience. And, it may be quintessential to ascertain whether or not an advantage can be gained by a conjectured decision instead of a more deliberate and time-consuming one. A person who is normally considered cautious will by nature be a hesitant decision maker. Thus, a positional leader who is cautious by nature must make a special effort to overcome this hesitant tendency. As an operational police manager, the individual should be reassured, because rendering timely decisive actions creates a certain amount of respect. Also, an increased development of the exercised **judgment skill** can be a benefit of the practiced endeavor.

A positional leader at the operational level of management is perceived as effective because of an ability to positively deal with a concern and a willingness to take appropriate action. A police manager should take pride in the ability to make timely decisions and the positional authority afforded him or her as an organizational leader. A positive view of individual status achievement is worthy of personal pride, because generally only about 7 to possibly 15 percent of an organization's work force advance to a managerial level. This joyful consideration of personal accomplishment must translate over to decision making, where an operational police manager should look at the committal of one's self to a decisive course of action in a positive manner. It should be realized that each time he or she makes a decision, it is an opportunity to show personal skills considered essential in a positional leader. Also, it is a displaying of the confidence and/or the courage of facing and effectively dealing with the challenges of the job.

The perceived potential damage or reacting in a decisive manner must not take precedent over the pitfalls of being indecisive. An effective operational manager should be aware of the causal factors of indecisiveness and make a special effort to avoid them. Some of the identified causes are:

1. No clear concept of what the concern is;
2. A lack of awareness of the scope of the problem;
3. Insufficient alternatives available for an adequate solution;
4. A lack of procedural knowledge for deciding an issue;
5. Incorrectly perceiving the positives and negatives of the situation; and
6. Lack of preparation before attempting to make a decision.

All of the above areas, as well as many others, contribute to a person's indecisive reactions. A police manager can combat these detrimental aspects of decision making by:

1. Being confident in a personal ability to render logical decisions;
2. Avoiding a temptation to hesitate, by reviewing the why and quickly assessing the positives versus the negatives to assure effectiveness of the decision;
3. Following a pre-established format for decision making, such as the one outlined previously in this chapter; and
4. Determining the perceived best course of action to be implemented with courage and self-assuredness.

It is recognized that every decision does not require nor is benefitted by an affirmative course of action. There are many occasions where procrastination may be a favorable approach to decision making. But those occasions are generally very rare and are indicated in the procedural processes that will clearly focus the need for a delay prior to a choice being made. There is no specific or ideal set of criteria that can be listed to tell a manager **when** or **when not** to be decisive. Each situation must be evaluated on its own merit and circumstances against the perception of being **indecisive**. Indecisiveness as a dimensional trait characteristic of a manager is traditionally considered a weakness in positional leaders.

SYNOPSIS

Positional leaders in every conceivable organization, including police departments, have as one of their daily responsibilities and/or functions reactive decision making. The need for the decision may originate from the upper management structure, a personal perception of needed action, or a suggestion/recommendation from subordinates. But regardless from whence the required decisive action comes, an operational police manager must deal with the concern and attempt to resolve it in an effectively positive manner.

To a great degree, the effectiveness of the manager's performance ability is gauged by his or her capability to make and render decisive actions as needed. A knowledge of how to make a decision may not be enough; an operational police manager must become proficient in performing the skill. As previously noted, a practiced effort, on-the-job experience, and the courage to act are the best methods for enhancing decision-making skills. Like most other things, sufficient practice will make decision making a skill that can be developed to a point where an effective process is almost automatic.

Primarily, there is no essentially right or wrong way to make decisions. The procedure outlined in this chapter is merely a practical guide; each individual manager will have to assess his or her own personality as to what is personally effective. While the author perceives a sense of comfortability that the five basic steps outlined are generally universal, he is also aware that variations are possible and in some cases advisable. Some texts on decision making refer to the addition of an individual's personality as the "personal equation variable." It should be understood that making a logical and sound decision requires a practical and methodical approach. However, the "personal equation variable" adds the elements of ethics and morality to the individual's deliberations and the decided-upon course of action.

The decision-making process noted is a modified scientific technique that has proven to be effective over the years by positional leaders. The primary steps to remember are identifying and formulating the concern, defining the problem, gathering sufficient factual information, analysis to choose a course of action, and implementing the decided-upon alternative. As a conclusive note to our comprehensive look at decision making from an operational police managerial perspective, it should be revealed that any course decided upon must be made through the mental process of developing an affirmative course of action and then having the courage to implement it. An operational manager has to assure that actions decided are within the capability of subordinates who must carry them out, as well as being acceptable to his or her superiors. Of course, meeting these stated criteria will only serve to strengthen the quality of the manager's decision.

As noted, the rendering of decisions that are creditable and responsive to the need to resolve a concern, as well as effectively and efficiently solve a problem, is a primary component of all levels of police management because it requires choosing between different courses of action each of which may resolve the problem to varying degrees. Modern-day police decision makers in addition to dealing with a rapidly changing society and employees who are more knowledgeable than ever before, have to contend with external influences that continue to encroach at an accelerated rate. Today's managerial leaders are faced with the aforestated challenges, along with the multidimensional requirements for flexible thinking. A number of elements contributing to the complexity of decision making, as well as some of the influences have been identified as an advance number of standards, such as intangibles, creditability risks, extend impact of the action taken, hierarchical influences, traditional decisions to similar situation within the agency, and the goals and objectives of the organization. Contemporary police management as decision makers needs an adaptable pattern of analysis, based on the capability to perceive contributing factor both vertically and laterally.

Two factors essential for remembering by an operational police manager regarding decision making are:

1. To clearly and comprehensively understand the parameters and as much of the ascertainable data as possible; and
2. To avoid the appearance of being **indecisive** concerning a commitment of one's self to a specific alternative to resolve the issue.

An operational police manager should approach decision making from a positive perspective of showing his or her skills in this critical dimensional trait area. Upper organizational management often makes their assessment of operational leadership based on the effectiveness of the individual decisions made by positional leaders.

Chapter Six

JOB PERFORMANCE CONTROLS

Job performance controls in private industry will usually fall under the auspice of a specialist in quality control. But in law enforcement organizations, such as a police department, standards like quality control, productivity and timely accomplishment of goals and objectives are a responsibility of management. Public service elements, like police, generally have neither the resources nor the operational requirements that are conducive to utilizing a quality control specialist. This doesn't imply that police departments do not, as a rule, have a special element that acts as a check to insure peak efficiency, because, most generally, the major police departments will encompass some type of audit or inspection unit for that purpose. However, such traits are generally considered a second or specialized form of operational control and usually provide only observed information. They normally don't have the power to institute actions that will affect functional-level employees' job performances. Therefore, operational management via functional leadership is the primary organizational component that is responsible for quality standards and job performances of worker-level personnel.

When job performance controls are discussed, there is a tendency for the discourse to gravitate toward **quality control** of work output. But, in reality, task controls in police work have to do with several factors that are traditionally influenced by the efficiency and effectiveness of management. The basic tenet of positional leaders in police departments with closely controlled budget operations is that the real asset of job performance controls can be assessed in terms of employee satisfaction, quality work output, and task accomplishment. As will be noted and further discussed later in this chapter, there are several other factors pertinent to a comprehensive review of job performance controls. In the past, police departments' upper management operated under the same philosophical approach as private industry. The somewhat dated ideal of which we are referring was based purely on enhancement of quality controls. This concept was that to be of any real value

111

the varied overtures to work controls should be directed primarily toward the maintenance and/or enhancement of an overall accomplishment of organizational objectives. Ultimately, this concept cannot be overlooked in an assessment of the job performance controls relative to the dimensional trait characteristics of a modern operational police manager. However, the restrictive parameters of the stated concept must be expanded to include all the areas identified in this chapter.

Social scientists and most top-level police officials have recognized that when a specialized element or an operational manager's control actions are limited to a quality objective, its efforts are generally unnecessarily wasteful, especially when **quality discipline** combines so adeptly with other leadership aspects of the total job performance control of subordinates. Also, if the premise exists that a special quality control is required to eliminate subordinates' errors and to increase productivity, this is tantamount to an admission that there is a notable lack of managerial effectiveness and that the stated perception of leadership ineffectiveness is permeated throughout the hierarchical structure of the department.

Controlling within an organizational environment, whether it's as broad as job performance control or as restricted as quality control, is a clear indication that some efforts have been made in the behavioral directing of employees. Work standards, rules, regulations, and codes of ethics would not be necessary if all operational police personnel were perfect. But the reality is that there are no perfect individuals for performing in every aspect of law enforcement; therefore, controls are necessary, even though positional leaders typically recognize that perfection is unlikely and will possibly never be achieved. The department's hierarchy, at various levels of management, and functional personnel all plan and work toward that type of performance expectation. There also tends to be some general expectations that managerial controls and documented directives are implemented so that subordinates will not falter in job performance. Realistically, an operational police manager should be aware that ultimate achievement is seldom, if ever, obtained but at the same time realize a person will usually only accomplish to the maximum point of his or her focus, meaning that **if an individual does not strive for perfection, he or she will never achieve perfection**. As a result of the managerial leadership of a police department not being perfect and subordinates at descending levels also not being perfect, it is essential to establish and exercise controls to prevent errors or to locate and correct miscues as they occur. When we consider the basic imperfection of man, then miscues of behavior and job performance can be predicted and/or anticipated. This is not to imply that because non-perfect people make mistakes that these errors are acceptable or not preventable for the most part. Experience has shown that a monitoring of what is occurring and a feedback system to short-circuit errors can be effective in adequately controlling job performance. An effective operational manager will maintain a fairly close and intense directional control over subordinates, etc. to prevent miscues from occurring and/or dealing promptly with those that do occur. As comprehensively covered in the chapter on "Communication," any type of appropriate job performance controls relies primarily upon a significant communicative flow. This essentially accurate informational flow travels both upward and downward in the established chain of command; also, this non-distorted informational exchange needs to be both precise and timely for appropriate management control.

As individual managers and subordinates differ from one another both at the peer and hierarchy levels, so too do their perspectives of what constitutes adequate job performance controls. Most managers interviewed believe that as much information as possible or available should be provided to the subordinates initially so that their behavioral performance will be as near perfect as possible. Thus, the individual can avoid costly time and effort correcting mistakes caused by a lack of insufficient of information. However, there are a number of managerial leaders who foster a belief that a subordinate should be provided only adequate and/or sufficient parameter details necessary for job performance. Their contention was primarily based on goal achievement, noting that the ultimate responsibility for the correctness of the task outcome is his or hers. Thus, the individual as a positional leader should not expect a perfect job outcome and must be prepared to step in and provide additional direction, etc. to guide the task results to a more conducive objective accomplishment through follow-up controls.

Thus far in this chapter we have attempted to provide the reader with an introductory perspective into job performance controls as they relate to the organizational leadership concept. But in order to better formulate a comprehensive discussion of job performance controls as an essential dimensional trait characteristic of an operational police manager, the functional aspects and influences must be detailed.

A LEADERSHIP RESPONSIBILITY

Job performance controls, most traditionally referred to as **management quality** controls, are considered both an upper hierarchy and an operational-level managerial responsibility. Work controls are a concept that administratively provides for acceptable standards of task accomplishment. Typically, job accomplishment may be a delegated requirement and thus is in the hands of another department employee. But as noted in the chapter on "Delegation," **authority as a basic obligation can be assigned to a subordinate, but that ultimate responsibility for satisfactory goal achievement remains with the positional leader**. Performance or result control of a task is nothing new for organizational leadership. Some form of directed work outcome has been around as long as man himself. No matter what level a manager functions at, he or she cannot abdicate the responsibility of job performance controls regarding the fulfillment of subordinates' objectives. Therefore, the concept of this dimensional trait characteristic must be given emphasis by an operational police manager, because the effective performance of the individual hinges on the resultful outcome of the subordinates' actions.

One factor influencing an operational police manager's critical need for enhanced capability in this dimensional trait characteristic area is the steadily declining availability of logistical and human resources for public agencies during the past decade. The outlook for future budgetary allocation appear just as bleak or even worse. Therefore, a more productive and effective use of subordinates' job performances is mandatory. Police organizations of all sizes have placed a **measured emphasis** on its leaders' effectiveness by the committed time of subordinates and the requirements for repeat efforts. In other words, it reflects negatively upon an operational manager if a significant portion of a subordinate's available work time is taken up by having to redo an improperly accomplished task. This is doubly true when an operational police manager through job performance controls could have prevented most, if not all, of the needed corrections. As noted earlier, public organizations such as the police seldom enjoy the luxury of employing an efficiency expert or a quality control element that specializes exclusively in establishing standards that will result in overall subordinates' performance effectiveness. Budgetary constraints make it necessary for the positional leadership of the organization to perform such essential tasks. Public entities such as a police department cannot allow their hierarchical personnel to be concerned only with managing logistical resources and the functional handling of subordinates. Operational-level management at every departmental strata has to combine job performance controls into his or her traditional administrative duties.

Job performance controls generally relate to a police manager's obligation as a positional operations leader to direct and regulate subordinates' task behaviors; this direction and control being specifically targeted at managerial actions that are essential for effective and efficient work accomplishment. These operational functions will enable the manager to perceive and use available resources in the most productive manner possible to meet established goals and objectives. In other words, there should be an awareness and use of these traditional managerial responsibilities to augment leadership functions into recognized task standards. As previously stated, an administrative focus that emphasizes job standards as a normal function of positional leadership is not a revolutionary concept. However, our contention in this text is to isolate and feature job performance controls as a separate dimensional trait characteristic and to emphasize the realization that it can be enhanced in managerial leadership of a police organization through knowledge and specific effort. Management controls, as they are more traditionally perceived, have a primary purpose and focus for appraising the most effective utilization of departmental assets toward achievement of defined goals and objectives. Virtually every organization, whether public or private, will typically have some form of formalized task management or job performance controls. These established departmental controls or requirements are a natural recourse of structural communication channels within a systematic organization such as a police department.

The aim of our discussion of the attributes and the capability for enhancement of managerial performance in this specific dimensional trait characteristic must now shift to the practical aspects of performance controls. In order to obtain a more comprehensive perspective of this managerial characteristic, the primary essence of leadership requirements for domination of subordinates' performance behavior must be clarified. Thus, we should clarify the definitional edifice within which our practical discussion will focus. The parameter definition of which we refer is **the developing of processes to monitor and/or control task activities and accountability of subordinate personnel**. These definitive limits should also include the managerial actions taken to regulate the accomplishment of tasks coming within the vista of the individual's leadership responsibilities.

PRACTICAL MANAGEMENT CONTROLS

As a leadership responsibility, practical managerial performance controls relate directly to the establishment of procedures that will appropriately delegate tasks and will inherently develop a monitoring system to assess the ultimate work achievement and the step-by-step regulation of the process to meet the objective. The necessity for and the amount of performance dominance exercised by an operational manager will demonstrate the person's perceived authority as the individual categorically responsible. This clearly establishes the operational manager as the person expected to review the task's progress and to take the actions necessary to guide the results of a delegated job to successful conclusion. The previously mentioned information vividly illustrates that an operational manager within a police organization is expected to display a great number of skills and performance techniques in order to be considered effective as a positional leader.

Though organizational hierarchy doesn't traditionally consider job performance controls, quality controls, or management controls, a top dimensional trait characteristic requirement of a leader, they will readily admit that without the qualities so prevalent in this trait characteristic a positional leader is destined to fail in effectiveness. Principal to effectual performance as an operational police manager is the development and utilization of control standards of job behaviors for subordinates. As may be clear in our use of the terms **standards** and **controls** in this chapter, we are referring specifically to the guidance and directional authority exercised over subordinates. Of course, the purpose of such guidance and direction is aimed at achieving a desired result.

The pyramidal type hierarchical structure of most police organizations establishes the authority of a manager by virtue of his or her position in the department's edifice. The positional roles reflect the inherent power of influence over subordinates' job performance and thus a direct responsibility for both productivity and quality control. An atmosphere of dominance in the form of job performance control must be reflected throughout the operational and functional responsibilities of a police manager. We have concentrated in this text on the leadership controls exercised over performance expectations of personnel. This is necessary because of the broad aspects that could be linked to job performance controls and the obvious overlap of this dimensional trait with other characteristics discussed in this text. The interrelatedness of each of these essential traits often depend upon one another for true effectiveness by a positional leader. However, a job performance control process is basically a positional leadership function from an operational perspective and usually includes both operating and productivity dominance, although it must be emphasized that the involvement of the two stated entities are in a comparative format, typically for the purpose of evaluating the effectiveness of leadership controls of the positional leader.

Normally, when we think of operation planning to achieve results in an organizational setting, it is formulized and structured for fairly rigid adherence to established procedures. But as mentioned earlier in the text, police managerial effectiveness may be contingent on the adaptability of the positional leader to the unanticipated or unexpected factors. Therefore, it is safe to say that an unyielding tenacity toward a preformulated plan of operation may not be conducive to overall goal achievement in the most effective manner possible. The ability to adjust a plan once it has been formulated and implemented is an essential element in a police manager's job performance control of subordinates. These controls of which we speak are designed to monitor progress (where changes can occur if necessary) and to establish a completion date (to assure timely achievement of results). A failure to implement or utilize such controls will more often than not result in failure of objective attainment relative to specifically desired results and time frame availability. There is generally a productivity reduction resulting from the subordinates having to backtrack over completed work to correct errors or to make adjustments so that desired goals will be achieved. Plainly speaking job performance controls are designed to short-circuit mistakes or to correct sidetracked projects to achieve desired results in the first time. This quite simply is **managerial effectiveness** by a police manager in an operational environment.

Because of the complex nature and variety of the problems dealt with by an operational police manager, his or her effectiveness as an organizational leader requires a performance equilibrium. This harmony of effort is generally between traditional leadership controls (preplanned) and a readiness to respond to role activity (reactive functions). Role activity, as used in this context, refers to basic responsibilities and duties of an operational manager to effect the results of subordinates' performance behavior. The individual role responsibility of an operational police manager is a critical component of organizational effectiveness. The basic essentiality of an operational positional leader's control over the logistical and human resources of the organization is not a simple matter and should not be misjudged. Whether the manager is a direct factor in functional-level performance or has secondary accountability through the delegated responsibility of others, the individual exercises an immeasurable influence on the productivity of the organization. This is true, because it has been shown that the most effective method of job performance controls are developed as a result of observing the behavior activity of subordinates. The viewing of actual performance enables the positional leader to combine preplanned directions with reactive controls to more effectively assure task accomplishment. As the author previously noted, **much of a job performance control process is informal and reflective of certain aspects of the social dynamics of a leader/subordinate relationship**.

From the operational perspective of a police manager, the development and implementation of job performance controls are a pre-established set of influences. These influence factors are designed to evaluate and/or appraise a subordinate's progression regarding desired results. The predetermined controls or influences serve to regulate the subordinates' performances that require accommodation in order to fulfill objectives. **Time in motion** studies have shown that the most efficient methods of result achievement and the judicious use of manpower are the leadership controls exercised during the actual process. The traditional influence factors that we refer to in association with establishment of job performance controls by an operational police manager are:

1. Due dates,
2. Progress checks, and
3. Follow-up checks/dates.

The noted job performance controls will allow a manager to monitor the task being performed and to guide it toward a successful resolution. The primary control procedures employed in the process provide for an adjustment in variances from the anticipated behavior norms. And, the use of performance controls will aid in the acquisition of needed information throughout the process, which should help in development of criteria for anticipated projects. Therefore, an effective operational police manager will use job performance controls to establish, evaluate, and enhance the performance of subordinates.

So as to provide a more comprehensive portrayal of the traditional job performance controls utilized by an operational police manager, the three previously identified influences are detailed.

I. **Due Dates**. I tis standard that any effective administrative leadership functioning will be required to meet assigned time frame obligations. Completion of designated tasks on a timely basis is essential to a police manager's effectiveness. Most assignments are delegated with a specific time frame in mind for completion, as well as the desired results. This is true with any type of industry. The problem develops when the positional leader assigning or delegating the task **assumes** the person being given the assignment is fully aware of his or her desires without being actually told. Subordinate personnel usually are not "mind readers" and can only evaluate and react to the information provided. Therefore, it should remain uppermost in a leader's mind that when assignments are made that adequate comprehensive information should be provided to include an established date for completion. Timing in task fulfillment is an essential component of virtually all of the duties of an operational manager. Obviously, the establishment of **due dates** are critical to job performance controls of an effective operational police manager. His or her efficiency as an operational leader depends on the utilization of this influence factor to satisfactorily accomplish departmental goals and objectives in a timely manner. There are several critical areas that need to be reviewed when discussing the **setting of task completion dates**. These considerations are:

A. **Allowance for a sufficient completion time frame**. An effective positional leader will consider and build into his or her delegation of tasks to subordinates an adequate time for their research and reaction. It must be remembered that appropriate and sufficient data is not always readily at hand. Also, it will take time to assimilate the information into an understandable and useable format to meet objectives. There should also be a time allotment that affords the subordinates an opportunity to adjust and correct miscues or to gather additional data when there is an insufficiency of information submitted. The anticipation of a need for additional effort to improve the final product is simply a sound management practice when a task has been delegated to another person.

B. **The positional leader should allot time for his or her analysis of the results submitted**. An allowance time for comprehensive review by a manager must be a prime consideration when establishing a due date. Typically, the positional leader will be concerned with personal compliance in meeting corresponding due dates set by his or her superior. Therefore, in order to submit an acceptable product that fulfills personal responsibilities for ultimate task accomplishment, additional time must be allotted. Thus, in addition to the time allowance for subordinates' research and development, a leader has to consider a personal comprehensive review and analysis period. As noted before, the project may need to be returned to the designee for additional work or correction of mistakes.

C. **A manager should provide for an adequate amount of time to document personal recommendations and/or add input to the submission**. The effectiveness of an operational positional leader is assessed by the quality and productiveness of subordinates. This can be said to be a truism, but let us not forget that the quality of the work is most generally filtered through him or her. Also, a leader's superiors will traditionally appraise the individual's personal knowledge and leadership awareness based mostly on administrative recommendations and/or decisions. Common sense indicates that faulty or inadequate analysis will more than likely produce poor and unacceptable responsive actions. Also, in most highly structured and well-documented organizations, such as a police department, recommended actions will be presented in written form. Formal writings, as detailed in the chapter on "Communication," inform us that not only must the recommended actions be clearly delineated but so does the reason why the individual endorsed the course of action. Going beyond a "piggyback endorsement" demonstrates to the positional leader's superiors that the results had been assessed and an insight into the overall project was obtained. The documentation of a manager's recommendation must not be a haphazard process, nor should it be an arduous task. However, because of its importance as stated previously, a time allotment in **due date setting** is essential to an operational police manager's perceived effectiveness.

D. **Delay of documented responses**. In most organizational environments, including law enforcement, there is a transition time requirement, meaning that there is generally an interval period of time required for administrative paperwork and/or documentation to go from one office or hierarchical level to the next. This is true even in situations where all involved parties are in the same building. For example, if a manager sets a **due date** for July thirty-first to receive a project that has been assigned to a subordinate, the positional leader cannot expect to complete his or her recommendation by the end of the workday on that day and transfer the documentation to a superior for review on that same day, especially if the material is voluminous and his or her superior had established a **received-by date** of July thirty-first. If documentation is transferred via an intradepartmental mail system, the positional leader should allow for at least one day's travel time from one office to the next. However, if the recommendations are normally hand-delivered by the individual, then a closer allowance of travel time can be gauged. But in either case, the **due date** established by the positional leader should take into account this influence factor as well as the other three previously identified.

In professionally structured organizations, such as major police departments, effective managers will seldom assign a task down through the chain of command without some type of time frame requirement. Successful and effective leaders know that in order for information and/or project results to be useful, they must be timely. Thus, an operational positional leader will generally have no choice but to set some form of assignment **due date schedule** for subordinates that will accommodate his or her submission requirements. Even in those rare occasions where upper management does not establish a return date on an action, the operational manager should. This will establish constraints that will focus a subordinate's effort and assist in project tracking and accountability for the operational manager. There are persons in every organization at all hierarchical levels (managers, functional leaders, and workers) who are procrastinators, the type of individual whose philosophy appears to be why do today what you can put off until tomorrow. The problem is that tomorrow seems to always produce its own set of problems or concerns. There is also the individual who tends to be an effective crisis performer in a highly structured environment, such as a police department. This type of person is aided by a formal due date because of the job performance controls it offers.

> II. **Progress Checks**. Utilizing a formalized and structured schedule of checking on how a task is being performed is a job performance control that is common to every hierarchical level. It may be as simple as asking a subordinate how the work is proceeding or as formalized as requiring a structured report (orally or in writing) at specific intervals of time. It should, however, be made perfectly clear that the strategy of most organizations is to focus performance controls on results rather than the process. In a sense, that may be the way to proceed because it is the ultimate results that we are concerned with, of course without side effects, etc. they basically apply the adage, "I don't care how you achieve it, just get the job accomplished," or "The end result will justify the means." This concept may work in some private organizations but not in public law enforcement, where every action or inaction is answerable to the citizens being served. Also, because of the power that the police generally exercise and the potential for its misuse, public scrutiny makes ongoing progress or process checks a mandatory requirement of effective management.

It is often very difficult and sometimes impossible to undo inappropriate or misperformed tasks; therefore, positional leaders should establish **progress checks** as job performance controls. If a project is constantly under scrutiny or analytical review, the less likely for costly errors or inadequate performances to go unnoticed through the entire process. Besides, a pattern of managerial examinations of performance proficiency by subordinates will make it possible to correct errors early in the process. It is also likely to pre-

"This is not what I wanted, there is not enough detail in this report."

"But, you did not say to put any details in this report, you only said you wanted the number of occurrences."

ARTICULATING EXPECTATIONS IS ESSENTIAL TO MEETING GOALS AND OBJEC-
TIVES, BUT KNOWING HOW TO SET PARAMETERS MAY BE JUST AS CRITICAL.

vent mercurial job performance behaviors by subordinates. Therefore, it is plain that in addition to establishing of **due dates**, an implementation of a consistent system of meticulous progress checks are critical to the effective-ness of positional leadership. This influence factor is critical as a job perfor-mance control and may be considered essential to the dimensional trait char-acteristics of an operational police manager.

   III. **Follow-up checks**. The managerial influence factor of setting **fol-low-up checks** are more typical of what comes to mind when sub-ordinate job performance controls are mentioned. This particular influence refers to the actual methods traditionally used by an operational manager to stay aware of task accomplishment; also, to determine if work planned or scheduled achieved the desired results in the manner expected and that the quality of its outcome was sufficient. Establishing **follow-up checks** is simply a matter of formalizing scheduled dates and times to review the results of a project subsequent to completion. Assigned or delegated tasks are utilized to achieve certain results, and an operational-level manager cannot know if the solution met or continues to meet the objective without subsequent checks. In addition to affording the positional leader an opportunity to adjust activity based on the possible fluidity of the concern once it is completed, it also provides an opportunity for evaluating the job performance outcome and control system. This will establish an appraisal process for future planning and/or handling of like situations.

In order to accomplish the desired consequence, the **follow-up process** should be structured in a manner that will focus attention on the factors that have an impact on the results. Setting follow-up dates is an important factor in an operational police manager's demonstration of a job performance control characteristic. Without a doubt, there are few functions of an operational police manager that have a superior effect on the results of subordinates' task behavior than a consequential checking procedure. **Follow-up checks**, defined in the context that we are referring, primarily means **the developing and scheduling of formalized times that the manager will check through appraisal methods to assure satisfactory outcome of assigned or delegated tasks**. An operational-level manager must remain sensitive to and knowledgeable of the usefulness of the data obtained by way of a formalized after-action review. **A follow-up process** by a positional leader provides a clarification of subordinates' efforts and graphic displays of managerial concerns for the ultimate consequence of the task achievement. This is essential if the manager is to ascertain whether the informational transfer **prior to** and **subsequent to** the work completion was appropriate. Remember, much of the individual's display of job performance controls depends on the outcome of delegated subordinates' efforts.

The planning and execution of follow-up sessions to assess job performance and results are considered a critical component of a positional leader's exercise of leadership controls over subordinates and events under his or her span of influence. A positional leader's execution of managerial job performance controls illustrates that the individual is concerned for subordinates' behavior. It also tends to demonstrate a desire to assure that informational transmittal is accurate and will be assessed to make certain that operational directives are complied with. Job performance controls through a follow-up process by a manager shows an awareness that he or she retains final responsibility for tasks delegated to subordinates for accomplishment. There is no pre-established interval of time that a particular manager can use in setting possible follow-up dates. The individual positional leader will have to assess each situation and outcome on its own merit to determine time frame allotment and/or the period of time that a specific completed task will need to be monitored. The only suggested consideration that can be offered is that by aligning the time frame sufficiently close to the result outcome, needed adjustments will have a positive and/or productive effect.

In our summary of the three most utilized influence factors in job performance controls by an operational police manager, we should reflect to some degree on the basic purpose of managerial dominance of subordinates' task behavior. First, the stated influence factors provide the operational police manager with a comprehensive and timely perspective of the results of a task accomplishment from which the individual can react. Second, they will afford the positional leader with the opportunity to more precisely assess the outcome and determine a course of action to overcome or eliminate negative aspects of the final consequence. Third, these influence factors will aid the manager in achieving ultimate effectiveness from the efforts of subordinates' job performances. These influence factors, universally, most typify what is termed job performance controls in an organizational environment.

MANAGERIAL CONTROLS AND BEHAVIORS

Operational control in a public law enforcement environment can be strictly established and maintained if the mid-level manager was to oversee all actions of functional personnel. This is not practical in public policing in this era of fast-rising calls for service and an ever-expanding crime rate. The basic term *control* implies that functions will be checked, tested, regulated, verified, and adjusted when needed. The control processes that are most common in public law enforcement and major corporations are: (1) qualitative analysis, a basic assessment meeting performance goals and objectives; (2) a long-range plan, a strategic course of action that is future oriented; (3) budget evaluation, assessing the cost effectiveness of its operation; (4) performance appraisals, measuring the action of personnel against expectations; and (5) regulations and procedures, establishing guideline parameters for job behaviors.

Leadership requirements are no longer considered strictly an upper administrative level knowledge need. **Managerial Controls** is a concept that is comprehensive analysis of a familiar task, one that we traditionally don't associate with training for functional mid-level management. Though the concept and the emphasis placed on it here in this text is updated, its actual performance and use by effective mid-level police managers is as old as leadership itself. The concepts that we will be relating to are usually only taught or presented in management level courses and books. Likewise, strategy and implemented actions from the perspective of estimated activity and future operational needs have been areas that are generally considered primarily an upper management function.

The ongoing economic conditions and the tight budget allocations have reduced the manpower availability in most public law enforcement organizations. This reduction of manpower is being felt not only in the line elements of the organization but in the management elements as well. This downward manpower trend or more cost-effective use of resources practices have meant an increase of job responsibilities and functions for each organizational member at every level. Police organizations do not enjoy the luxury of having the functional police mid-level manager only be concerned with the handling of subordinates. A line supervisor now has to also assume the administrative duties of a mid-level manager associated with planning and controlling of work.

Managerial controls, referring to the traditional management performance concept, will enable the functional police mid-level manager to take the actions that are necessary for more effective operation. They will help a secondary manager to view and utilize the logistical resources efficiently and effectively in accomplishing the objectives of the organization. The administrative functions of managerial requirements bring together the various management responsibilities of a mid-level manager in a coherent manner, so that the primary positional leader can best measure the appropriate use of resources against the goals to be accomplished. Traditional leadership controls or performance requirements are organizationally established and have formalized channels of input and responses.

In this we will examine the basic nature of managerial controls such as structuring and directing subordinates' activities and responses. Second, we will discuss some of the components of the administrative operation and management of subordinates by a functional positional leader. The basic functional aspects of each of these areas will be comprehensively discussed.

A MID-LEVEL MANAGER'S ROLE REQUIREMENTS

Total Quality Manager (TQM) is simply a more identifiable way of perceptually viewing performance of an all-around leader. The TQM leader is a person who considers and appropriately reacts to every aspect of leadership. This text has attempted to focus on the nuts and bolts of mid-level police leadership, and it will simplistically identify and articulate the managerial aspects of primary police leadership. Therefore, TQM will not be comprehensively addressed as a concept because, as the text discusses the role expectations and appropriate task performance of a mid-level police manager, it also will have articulated the context of the management idea it represents.

Initially, a police mid-level manager's role expectation is identified by the interaction and relationship with superiors and subordinates. The secondary police leader is also a position that requires a certain amount of coordinating of efforts. The mid-level manager's element does not operate in a vacuum. And as such, it is typically only one of several components of an organization. A secondary police manager must be willing to do a self-analysis of personal job behavior and the performance accomplishments of subordinates to accurately determine his or her abilities as a leader.

Second, an effective police mid-level leader must specifically identify the job requirements of his or her position as a member of the organization's management team. The mid-level police manager should also identify and comprehensively understand task expectations of subordinates. The identification of job requirements should be continuous and an ongoing process of a managerial leader. The assessment should be directed toward determining what is best for his or her element as a contributing component of the organization. This evaluation must be undertaken through the use of the most accurate and comprehensive information available at the time of the assessment. The mid-level police managerial analysis should be accomplished in a proactive mode of anticipated needs or job requirements for subordinates to achieve goal expectations. Pre-planning and/or strategy projections for a mid-level manager's areas of responsibility is a principal requirement of leaders at all levels of the organization. A police managerial leader must view his/her area of task responsibility as extending into the foreseeable future.

Third, the informational needs of a managerial leader in a police organization are normally structured into the positional authority of the job. In other words, the managerial job description established for a police mid-level manager's position usually determines the amount and flow of operational information needed for performance effectiveness. However, it must be recognized that leaders at all levels of the organization are responsible for assuring essential information beyond that which may be preordained by the position. The mid-level manager is held responsible for communicating needed operational information to subordinates in the form of technical knowledge, performance directions, and organizational policies. The aforementioned data is considered essential to appropriate accomplishment by functional employees. A secondary police leader should also remain aware that effective communication is a two-way process. He or she must realize that employee feedback is essential if the informational requirements of the position are to be achieved. An effective leader must be willing to assess:

1. What information is needed to appropriately do the job.
2. What informational data subordinates need to appropriately function.
3. Where and how the information needed can be obtained.

The effective mid-level police manager will think through these questions and determine the answers that should make him or her successful as a leader.

Finally, the police mid-level manager must realize the importance of maintaining an open and progressively functional relationship with subordinates, superiors, and peers. The leader should seek to cultivate both the formal and informal processes of the relationships. Too often, a secondary police leader will depend on the formal interactions to provide the essentials of relationships with the identified entities. However, as noted in the chapter on "Communication," the informal interactions and/or information exchanges can be just as important and critical as the formal processes. An effective manager will first determine what the expectations are demanded of each entity relative to his/her position. The police mid-level manager will then utilize the expectations to develop and establish personal goals and objectives for his/her position. The objectives of the position the leader interacts with should also be determined, so that personal actions will assist them in achieving their expectations. As a leader in the management chain of the organization, an operational manager must be willing to transfer tasks to subordinates. He or she should be aware that the assumption of a leadership position entails the acquisition of tasks beyond personal duties. A managerial police leader is responsible for not only personal actions but the actions of all his/her subordinates and their functional teamwork, as well as the coordination with other organizational elements. It is generally recognized that the higher up a person goes in an organization's leadership structure, the greater the need to delegate. The need to shift demanding work loads begins at the functional police manager's level because the number of task responsibilities and job requirements noticeably increase when the duty of overseeing the work of others is assumed. Delegation as a specific leadership dimensional trait area, which an effective police mid-level manager needs to employ, will be discussed later in this text.

Managerial controls as a leadership obligation refers to a developmental process whereby assigned tasks and job performances can be monitored and the proceedings regulated toward goal accomplishment. The controls also reflect the responsibility of the police mid-level manager to take action toward reviewing the results of delegated assignments and projects.

Effective operational leadership within an organizational setting require a great number of skills and techniques for effective job performance, not the least of which is the development and maintaining of standards of performance and control functions. The term *controlling* within this context means directing or guiding actual performance toward a desired conclusion. The positional leadership obligation of a mid-level manager inherently reflects the authority and thus the control of the functional level subordinates. Controls in one form or another permeate the entire edifice of managerial performances. However, the area of specific controls referred to in this section have to do with a mid-level leader's direct command over employee performance from a managerial perspective.

Essentially, a managerial control process from a functional standpoint involves a comparison of *operational planning* and *productive performance information,* to evaluate the efficiency and effectiveness of the operation. However, strict adherence to a formulated operational plan may or may not be compatible with overall effectiveness of the managerial control process. The adaptability of an operational plan is an important component of a managerial control process, because a lack of goal attainment may be due to an inappropriate plan rather than a subordinate's performance.

The effective operational police mid-level manager must balance the aspects of traditional leadership authority concerning planning and results against personal role responsibility in a managerial control process. The importance of the mid-level police manager's role in the control of a subordinate's job performance cannot be taken lightly. The secondary leader's role as an observer of subordinate job behavior under various conditions is sometimes the best method of assessing and controlling performance. Much of the job performance control process is informal and indicative of certain aspects of the social dynamics of a superior-subordinate interaction.

Managerial controls from the practical standpoint of a police mid-level manager is the establishing of some predetermined objectives whereby he or she can measure the employee's progress toward goal accomplishment, plus some regulatory measures that provide for adjustments during the process for determination at its conclusion what were the actual results. Simply stated, this process reflects the establishing of **progress dates**, **due dates**, and **follow-up dates** whereby the supervisor can track the work being performed and assure it is directed toward a successful conclusion. The basic process provides for correcting deviations from desired performance objectives and to obtain information through a process that will aid future planning of activities. Thus, the effective functional mid-level police manager will utilize the *managerial controls* developed to appraise and improve the performance of his or her subordinates.

It appears appropriate at this juncture to take an exacting look at those controls specifically under a mid-level manager's scope of influence. There should also be an examination of both the logistical and personal control responsibilities of a primary positional leader in a police organization.

INCREASING SUBORDINATES' PRODUCTIVITY

One of the skills seldom addressed, when assessing the performance of a mid-level police manager, is worker productivity. It typically is an assumption that if a leader performs appropriately in all traditionally dimensional areas of leadership, that he or she will be effective in worker productivity. This assumption, while frequently accurate, is not always true. An effectively functioning mid-level manager and satisfied workers do not necessarily translate into increased productivity. By analyzing the relationship of performance to job output, we can gain a proper perspective of productivity and which aspects of leadership behavior can be directly attributable to subordinates' functional actions. Public police agencies have not traditionally considered productivity as a prime factor in evaluating its leaders. This was due principally to the fact that law enforcement by nature is a reaction to inappropriate behavior. However, in the current era of restricted budgets and rollbacks in available human resources, being able to *obtain more from less* is essential. Almost universally, in public law enforcement, the number of calls for services has dramatically increased, while allocated resources and manpower have remained the same or decreased. This has required law enforcement leaders at all levels to be attentive to the need to increase productive output of functional personnel. Productivity has been a premiere issue in the private business sector since the Industrial Revolution. Private industry has always been aware of the need to produce more and better quality goods and services while limiting the use of resources. Now and in the decades to follow, productivity will become a prime factor in evaluating the performance of law enforcement and its leaders.

Productivity can rightfully be defined as a performance measure of available resources as it relates to output or achievement. During the latter part of the 1970s, **pro-active** policing was a rallying cry of progressive forward-thinking law enforcement agencies. This innovative **buzz phrase** soon regressed into the reality of task accomplishments measured by increased demands. Available resources or supply input generally refers to both human and material factors that influence outcome. Law enforcement outputs are the services provided by the policing agency. Productivity as a performance measure should indicate to police mid-level managers how efficiently they are utilizing the department's human resources to meet the needs of the community. As can be perceived from the above information, **productivity** is not a term that fits easily into a performance measure of law enforcement. However, it is a factor that must be integrated and appropriately applied if an advancing work load is to be achieved with *status quo resources.*

Law enforcement has attempted to meet the need of a rising crime rate and increased calls for services by requiring functional-level police officers to work more effectively and faster with fewer people. This has not solved the problem, as more and more citizens have indicated a need for **Community-Oriented Policing**. Community-oriented policing is essentially a request for police officers to take more time when addressing issues or interacting with people. This concept effectively distorts using productivity as a measure of a leader's effectiveness in getting multiple tasks accomplished through the use of available resources. A traditional formula for determining productivity is the calls for the tasks and products (services) to be utilized to be divided the output by the input (resources used). Job performance, as articulated earlier in the text, is the effectiveness in which expectations, goals, and objectives are achieved. When task objectives (timely responding to and handling calls for services) are increased and effectively handled, then meeting productivity demands have been accomplished by a public police agency.

Some social scientists question the ability of a leader in public industry to increase productivity through workers. Their basic contention is that more effort and finances should be committed to the problem in the form of human and material resources, rather than attempting to motivate increased actions in workers. The contention that allocating more resources to address the rising problem of crime certainly has some merit. But it should also be realized that at some point the commitment of increased resources will need to be restricted and efforts of workers will have to offset the downsizing or cutbacks. It has long been recognized that it's the police mid-level manager's job to maintain or increase the performance production of functional level employees.

RELATING TO SUBORDINATES

People skills, as previously noted, are much more essential in today's work force than in past years. The temperament and expectations of modern workers differ greatly from generations of the past. The philosophy of *what can I do for the betterment of the organization* has been replaced by *what can the organization do for me.* The principal goal of a leader's human interactions efforts to satisfy employee needs and to assure achievement of organizational objectives by workers. Primarily, a mid-level manager should consider the goals and objectives of his/her element and the organization as paramount. The needs of the workers (police officers) and the supervisor-subordinate is secondary, inasmuch as the organization's work accomplishment is ultimate. This is not to imply that a police middle manager should get so busy accomplishing tasks that he or she forgets about the needs of the subordinates. It has been speculated that the most employees initially bring to the job are enthusiasm and optimism. This positive zest for the job and its task accomplishments are soon displaced if the mid-level manager fails to take the time or effort to develop the human relations aspects of the leader-subordinate interactions. An efficient and effective primary leader will assure that his or her people skills are develop and utilized to achieve a positive human relationship with subordinates.

The quintessential nature of a positive relationship with workers is mandated, today and into the future, if a mid-level police manager is to be effective. When attempting to develop or establish a leader-subordinate relationship, the mid-level manager needs to adhere to some basic guidelines. Robert N. Lussier, in his book, *Human Relations in Organizations,* cited nine factors that should be used by leaders when considering their people skills. The areas cited are:

1. Being optimistic
2. Being positive
3. Being genuinely interested in other people
4 Displaying a cheerful appearance
5. Addressing people by their nature
6. Noticeably listening to people
7. Providing assistance to others
8. Being thoughtful and deliberate in actions and
9. Attempting to create a win-win situation in your dealing with others.

These are but a few of the things that an individual as a police mid-level manager can do to enhance personal people skills.

It is recognized that there is no perfect leader-subordinate human relationship at all times and in all situations. The secondary manager should attempt in all interactions to attain a harmonious relationship, even in those situations where differences exist. An efficient and effective leader frequently seeks the opinion of others, whose idea or approach to a concern may differ from his or her own. It's those recognized differences and adaptive adjustments, as needed, that make a leader or manager most effective. Also, the attentive consideration by the organization's leadership of the opinions of others fosters increased morale and a sense of self-worth in subordinates. The police mid-level manager must be cognizant of the principal need in human beings to feel worthwhile and to have their utterances listened to.

The aspect of maintaining a positive relationship with workers does not imply that the mid-level manager needs to be charismatically popular with subordinates. It does indicate a professional approach by the leader and a perceptual compatible interaction with subordinates. Some managerial texts have indicated that the mere nature of police management excludes any real friendships between leaders and subordinates. The author disagrees with this statement, because it is believed that if both leader and subordinate are aware of their role, and seek not to attempt to utilize friendship to manipulate a decision or action in the other, then a friendly relationship can exist. This is, of course, exclusive of a romantic type relationship that tends to imply a more intense involvement. It must be realized that none of us live or work in a vacuum, so personal interactions and friendships do occur. The stress factor of a leader-subordinate friendship type relationship tend to center around the ability to separate professional behavior from personal interactions. The friendship relations between superior and subordinate seem to work best when at-work interactions are separated from off-duty behaviors.

THE POSITIVE SELF-CONCEPT

Primary managerial leadership's handling of subordinates relates to all the concepts and factors previously set forth, but the single most important aspect of managing functional workers may be a *positive self-concept* by a leader. It is believed that a positive self-concept can be achieved even though it is recognized that a true and objective evaluation of yourself may be very difficult. If the police mid-level manager will comprehensively and objectively (1) *identify personal strengths and weaknesses in leadership behaviors,* (2) *establish realistic and attainable performance objectives,* and (3) *implement purposeful and deliberate actions to improve areas where improvements can be achieved,* he or she could construct a positive self-concept. Once a leader recognizes that an enhanced self is needed, it is said that half the battle of acquisition has been won.

There is little doubt that the successes achieved in life can most often be directly linked to an individual's belief in personal self. Therefore, the *positive self-concept* can comparably be referred to as a *self-fulfilling prophecy.* This author does not wholly subscribe to this notion, because it is through the meaningful behavioral approach and actions that desired outcomes occur. This then may be perceived as a result of a positive attitude, but it may be that if you think you desire something and then work at achieving it, a desired outcome is possible. The results cannot be guaranteed, but they are possible. The major factor in a positive self-concept is a belief in one's own ability and efforts to utilize personal talents to accomplish a desired objective. The self-belief (positive self-concept) comes from a "Search for Excellence" in one's own performance actions through enhanced behaviors. This means that each time an act is performed by an individual, it should be performed better than the time before, inasmuch as the person accomplishing it should be a little more knowledgeable about its positive attainment. It is a generally held conclusion that people with a negative perception will be less successful than those harboring a positive attitude. The author believes that this has more to do with performance efforts than with any supposed mystical psychic energy created by negative thoughts. Persons with a positive outlook and expectation tend to put forth more noticeable effort in the belief that desired accomplishment will be obtained. Thus, the attainments are due to actual efforts instead of a psychic energy. The converse is usually true of pessimistic or negative thinkers. Therefore, the supposed *self-fulfilling prophecy* is nothing more than a perceptual outlook and efforts toward achievement.

A leader should develop a positive self-concept and thus can enhance personal expectations and performance. First, an effective leader should utilize personal non-corporal philosophical beliefs to aid him or her in developing a positive attitude and subsequently an enhanced job performance. Second, a mid-level manager needs to be able to accept less than desirable results and quickly react or respond to correcting and improving the outcome. A secondary leader's job is managing the work performance of others, and anytime actions are gauged by the efforts or behaviors of human beings, the end result cannot always be predicted. By accepting failure in this context does not in any way imply that poor performance is acceptable but rather that mistakes will occur and are understandable. However, miscues should be corrected immediately. Most often, they occur because not everyone has the same level of expertise or job knowledge. The main emphasis in dealing with setbacks or errors for a mid-level manager is placed on a leader's ability to rebound and advance from the error. Third, a police mid-level leader must cultivate and advance his or her ability to gain knowledge from each situation and/or job-related experience. A majority of successful leaders interviewed by the author agreed that it is absolutely essential that a mid-level manager profit from each encounter as it relates to job performance. The process of learning from miscues and/or successes will make a leader more comfortable in typical job actions. And, the adjustments made to deal with unexpected situations, etc., should teach the leader how best to react to unanticipated actions in the future. There is little doubt that *trial and error* is a well-known learning method that should be a consideration for all leaders. Finally, the effective mid-level police manager will purposefully seek to control personal inappropriate behaviors and negative considerations that may in some way inhibit his or her job behavior. A leader must recognize that even his or her own nonverbal expressions of negative reactions to organizational rules, regulations, policies, and procedures will affect their acceptance by subordinates. As a human being, a leader must anticipate that some organizational actions are not going to be totally agreeable to him or her. But it is the effective leader that will control personal emotions and behaviors, to project a positive reaction to operational practices presented.

It can be clearly shown that a leader's attitude and the manner in which he or she interacts with subordinates in a job situation noticeably affect task accomplishments. If a secondary leader has a positive attitude and establishes high standards of behaviors for subordinates, it is reasonable to expect leadership effectiveness. As has been previously noted, the workplace climate or atmosphere influence the attitude and behavioral performance of workers (police officers). There may be some difficulty in controlling the job climate, inasmuch as the organization's hierarchy actions directly affect the perceptual work atmosphere. However, it can be shown that an optimistic projection by the secondary manager has a direct effect on the perception and behaviors of functional level employees.

Positive Leadership and Interactions

An effective police mid-level manager, in addition to performance in the areas previously discussed in this text, needs to be proficient, positive, praising, and interacting with subordinates. The traditional term for this much needed managerial ability is called **Incentive Leadership**. Incentive leadership is defined as the recognition and praising, in the presence of others, the efforts and/or performance of an individual. Positive, open praising of an individual is beneficial to the esteem of the person and will typically enhance the performance behaviors of the subordinate. Recognition and positive comments about a subordinate's performance behaviors and attributes will prove most beneficial to primary leadership. Positive recognition by a police mid-level manager has been shown to be a powerful performance inducement. Many leadership theorists indicate that it may be the most enduring of all the motivational tools available to a line supervisor. Inasmuch as it costs nothing, it is certainly cost-effective to the organization.

A leader must be aware of the parent-child syndrome within each of us. And, as such, most adults do not react as well in situations where they are dominated by another person, whether it is a positional leader or not. In a work situation, people recognize the dominant role of a leader, but it is still not a comfortable feeling for an adult to be submissive to the control of others. An effective leader needs to be aware and sensitive to the emotions of workers that are controlled by others, even in a work situation. The requirement of leadership dominance by a mid-level manager is essential to organizational effectiveness. The leadership efforts are needed to guide and focus employees' performances toward task accomplishment. The leader's comments at times will need to be corrective and even negative to assure appropriateness of a subordinate's job behaviors. But even during those times when corrective measures are taken, a leader needs to be aware that positive encouragement or stroking will enhance the supervisor's performance ability in getting tasks accomplished. Thus, a functional police mid-level manager should utilize positive subordinate stroking whenever possible. A police mid-level manager should, whenever possible, deal with subordinates in an *adult-to-adult* manner. The adult-to-adult interaction allows the leader to convey the necessary information and/or instructions while allowing the subordinates to react in a perceptual positive manner without feeling demeaned. A leader must learn to control his or her behavior and transact leadership dictates and expectations in a behavioral mode that's conducive to adult-to-adult communication with subordinates. The leader must grow and develop in the positional role to a point where he or she is able to create a perceptual **win-win** situation for subordinates. Positive verbal encouragement is only one of the vital attributes that is not typically associated with basic leadership or middle management. Performing in an extroverted manner is also conducive to effectiveness as a mid-level police leader.

The Extroverted Leader

A leader who is experienced as an *extroverted leader* or has been assertively trained to face up to and appropriately deal with the concerns facing a person in authority will be effective as a mid-level manager. The secondary leader's extroverted ability will allow him or her to appropriately deal with anxiety-producing situations in a productive manner. The police mid-level manager so endowed will be able to express emotions, solicit favors, and provide and receive compliments. Also, a leader should be able to effectively turn down unreasonable requests, as well as solicit behavioral changes in others. Essentially, a leader that possesses an extroverted behavior characteristic is more confident in his or her personal ability and self-assurance of the capability to effectively perform as a mid-level manager. It is primarily a process whereby a mid-level manager has the focused ability or learned skill to articulate emotions and concepts while directly soliciting what is desired to appropriately perform. Extroverted behavior as a term when associated with positive leadership refers to a direct, straightforward, and deliberate displaying of self-confidence as a leader without being offensive.

Subordinates of an extroverted leader tend to be more confident in the individual and can effectively anticipate what are acceptable results, because the leader is open about personal performance expectations. Being aware of the expectations of his or her work performance allows a subordinate a degree of comfort, in that he or she has knowledge of what is expected. Personal openness for a leader is not unique to the functional police midlevel manager. However, the networking concerns that seem to impregnate the upper levels of leadership in an organization is less noticeable at the secondary managerial position. Typically, the higher up in an organization a person elevates, the fewer positions there are to be filled. Thus, networking is more important, and an open, honest sharing of ideas and perceptions may become more of a detriment. The police mid-level manager's role in the organization's structure is the leadership position where true extroverted behaviors are an asset.

Responsive Leadership

Responsive management refers to leadership that attempts to project and anticipate job-related concerns before they occur. Reactive leadership responds primarily to events after they have occurred. A responsive mid-level manager seeks to be ahead of the actions required to effectively perform as an organizational leader. Police leadership at the operational level is thought to be principally reactionary to problems and events related to law enforcement. A police mid-level manager must focus on adjusting to the ever-changing climate in the workplace and the shifting task objectives of subordinates' job obligations. The basic priorities and goals of the organization do not change, but the pattern of crime and criminal activity causes unexpected actions that must be reacted to in a timely manner. The shifting nature of a police officer's job will focus leadership efforts not only on operational matters but the workplace environment as well. The police organization's top leadership causes a downward spiral of responsive actions by all levels of the agency.

Pro-active policing has long been a catch phrase in public law enforcement. It primarily refers to the efforts of the organization to predict and react to prevent policing situations before they occur. For example, *it is anticipated that the local entertainment area will have an increase in street robberies during the next two weeks.* Pro-active policing may mean *saturating the area with marked patrol units or setting up several sting-type operations to apprehend the offenders in the area, etc.,* to prevent crimes or to arrest perpetrators. The main emphasis is to anticipate and implement action to deal with the problem. Responsive police mid-level managers are generally aggressively analyzing information and projecting future performance needs of subordinates. The idea is simple enough: *forecast potential concerns and then implement actions to avoid the problem.* The responsive leaders tend to consider their subordinates more humanly than do some other leadership types. This type of leader will focus on treating their subordinates in a manner that will not cause dissatisfaction. Responsive leaders view functional-level employees as valuable resources to the organization and its task accomplishments.

The responsive police mid-level manager does not fit the traditional role of being purely a reactive leader. He or she tends to be somewhat visionary in personal considerations for the future performance needs of subordinates. Earlier in this text it was noted that the top echelon of a police organization was more visionary, while the lower levels focused on the real and tangible. However, the responsive secondary leader does not entwine very concisely into the mode of being merely a reactive leader. The leader's unique ability to adapt to the changing environment and demands of the job makes him/ her at times seem weak as a manager. This is a misconception, because contrary to initial appearances, the individual generally is self-confident in personal leadership ability and will allow the *risk-taking* visionary approach to handling concerns by involving subordinates in forming work strategies and achieving job expectations.

ELEMENTS REQUIRING CONTROLS

Before a comprehensive review of the dimensional trait characteristics of job performance controls can be considered complete, a discussion of the **elements requiring control** must be undertaken. The job performance of each member of an organization must fit into certain prescribed functional parameters. These functional limitations are then combined into an overall achievement of organizational goals and objectives. The operational manager has a basic responsibility to assure the specific objects within his or her scope of influence are controlled and directed toward goal accomplishment. The simplest way of identifying the elements of which we are referring is to categorize them as: (1) human resources (personnel); (2) material resources (logistical); and (3) financial (cost expenditures). But a simple identification of the managerial objects of control is not sufficient to clarify their importance or to provide a course of action for a manager's positive effectiveness concerning each area.

Each of the identified areas will be explored as to its impact on the organization and a police manager's responsibility from an operational perspective. However, before we get into the specifics of the individual areas, it is important to emphasize that job performance controls are a form of **risk reduction** for a positional leader. Whenever a manager is given a task objective, he or she assumes a certain responsibility and/or risk that events or situations may hinder its achievement. This is typically true of any positional leader's function; that should be clearly understood. The leader's basic concern must be to prevent or reduce the chances of failure to an absolute minimum. This is usually accomplished through comprehensive planning and the exercise of precise job performance controls. Most effective positional leaders do not just sit back and let things happen prior to implementing control type actions. Generally, that's like "closing the barn door after the horse has escaped." An effective operational police manager will utilize performance controls to guide and structure subordinates' task results beforehand. As stated in the chapter on "Decision Making," most positional leaders will recognize the possibility of risks, if a problem is allowed to continue. But it takes a knowledgeable and assured leader to control actions beforehand to reduce the possibility of subordinates' job performance miscues. Risk reductions concerning job performance controls take internal leadership courage. As a further note prior to discussing each area individually, a manager should realize that **risk-reduction controls** may not stop a certain problem, but it will usually enable the person to be better prepared to deal with it. The text will now detail an exacting perspective of the job performance controls previously identified as being directly under the vista of influence of an operational police manager.

I. **Human Resources (Personnel)**: Job performance controls by an operational manager generally begin with determination of whether or not sufficient manpower is available to accomplish the task. From that point, it enlarges into areas of worker regulation and personnel accountability, etc. It is appropriate to note that the basic obligation of an operational police manager is to assure that there are adequate personnel under his or her span of control to meet organizationally assigned objectives. And, that these directly controlled personnel are sufficiently trained and qualified to do the job. After the primary job performance controls of numbers of personnel and productivity output have been met, the human resource leadership role of the operational police manager becomes more atuned to need fulfillment. These **need-fulfillment objectives** are for motivational purpose to enhance job performance and behavioral controls. There are also a number of organizational requirements interspersed with subordinates' personal need controls that come within the vista and influence of an operational manager.

The human resource controls under the influence of an operational leader are divided into three main topic areas. These topic areas are administrative, mobility, and incentives, all of which could easily be categorized under a heading of motivation in terms of job performance controls when positively utilized to increase subordinates' behavioral productivity toward goals and objectives. In order to better focus and clarify the topic areas identified above, we will list some of the universally accepted tasks associated with operational management.

A. Administrative.
  1. Personnel record maintenance (employees' files)
  2. Subordinate appraisal (performance evaluations)
B. Employee Mobility.
  1. Job transfers (intraorganizational movement for enhancement of knowledge and job satisfaction)
  2. Promotions (recommendation to advance deserving and qualified personnel)
C. Incentives.
  1. Salary increases (merit raises for productive subordinates based on a department-established criteria)
  2. Disciplinary action (positive or negative as a training tool to enhance behavioral performance)
  3. Separation from the department (termination or resignation for the good of the organization and/or the subordinate)

We have listed but a few of the tasks associated with each topic area that fall within the scope and control of the operational manager. There are numerous others that could have been indicated, but we chose to list only the more universally utilized ones. Positional leadership must be cognizant of the parameters that governs human resources and job performance control within a police department. A realization that certain external influences such as environmental and departmental directives can noticeably affect an employee's performance behavior. Concerning personnel management controls, this is true inasmuch as police organizations are no different from most other agencies. A requirement for job performance controls is a must if work standards of productivity are to be achieved. These work standards of which we refer are organizationally induced to control personnel behavior throughout the department through such controls as **job description, quality of work performed and/or quantity of productivity, personnel behavioral guidelines,** and **subordinate evaluation systems.**

Of the elements of controls essential to the effectiveness of an operational positional leader, human resources (personnel management) is certainly the most important. As stated numerous times, the effectiveness of a manager and the productivity of an organization toward meeting its goals and objectives rest on the performance of the operational-level personnel. After a comprehension of the essentiality of human resources usage to a manager's job performance control trait characteristic, it is sequentially a necessity to now discuss the material resources (logistic) standards as a factor.

II. **Material Resources (Logistical)**: Material resources accountability relative to job performance controls characteristics of an operational police manager is concerned primarily with acquisition and maintaining of sufficient supplies and equipment for subordinates' functioning. Managerial answerability for the logistics under the scope of his or her influence serves to focus attention on productive inefficiency due to misuse or inappropriate use of material resources. The current era of constricted budgetary parameters, especially in the public sector has made logistical **accountability** and **management** nearly as critical as the use of human resources. A police manager's logistical control responsibility also is concentrated in the direction of the flow of supplies and essential resources to the appropriate department components. The basic control influence dealt with relative to the direction and monitoring of material resources are:

A. **Transmittal of Material Resources**. The basic control influence involves the formalized routing of operational equipment along directional channels to the appropriate elements for effective use. The directional focusing of the material resources to the proper components should expedite transposition and make more effective use possible. Misrouting of materials is a waste of time and the manpower necessary to handle the erroneous transmitted resources. The transmittal of material resources also includes the proper addressing or designating of the routed logistics. The directing of logistics to the department component that can most effectively use them is a more cost-effective utilization of material resources.

B. **Meeting Time Frame Requirements**. Assuring that material resources are received as expeditiously as possible by the element needing them is paramount. Therefore, it is absolutely essential that an operational police manager make sure that established schedules and time commitments are met when allocating and/or dispersing material resources. This is also essential when directing or developing time frame sequences for the achievement of departmental goals and objectives. Time frame obligation is a mandatory component of job performance control for an operational police manager when departmental logistics are involved.

Principally, whenever there is a discussion of material resources use in an organizational setting, the deliberation invariably shifts to the degree of influence type of control focus. Referring to the measuring and balancing of productivity versus the perceived positive attribute of the task accomplishment, an ascertainment of output standards for the services provided is an important control consideration for a positional leader. It should be remembered that a primary focus of departmental leadership through material resources control is that there should be a match between equipment usage and task results. Productivity and quality output mandates a consideration of logistical expenditures as a way of determining effectiveness of established job performance controls, thus directing our discussion into the third category of elements requiring controls: **cost expenditures**.

III. **Financial (Cost Expenditures)**: The general budgetary parameters of most police agencies have been referred to numerous times in this text. Therefore, it should be no surprise that financial controls is a prime factor in an operational police manager's direction and guidance of his or her span of influence. Public organizations, because of their need for accountability of funds usage and tight control over budgetary allocations, have ingrained cost-expenditure parameters in every phase of its operation. The operational positional leader then becomes the obvious choice for overseeing and exercising job performance controls relative to financial limitations. Each managerial leader of an operational component is allocated a certain amount of funding in which to operate his or her element. Performance and cost expenditure control then become mandatory if effectiveness versus capital outlay is to be achieved. Some of the controls traditionally used by positional leaders to maintain accountability of allotted funds are: (1) formalized accounting procedures, such as account ledgers and requisitions; (2) frequent audits of fund expenditures; and (3) projected justification reports when preparing the budget request. These are but a few of the restrictive measures that can be used to control cost expenditures by an operational police manager.

No matter what the particular functional behavior or result accomplishment, an underlying factor that mandates managerial consideration is the economics of the operation. Economics in police operations is typically always evaluated in terms of cost expenditures versus productive output of service to the department's clientele. It is evident from the above information that the financial cost expenditures are absolutely essential to operational police managerial job performance controls. As a final note concerning the effectiveness of job performance controls on expenditues, it should establish a clear portrayal of the difference between cost effectiveness and the expense of desired results.

It is a natural and obvious conclusion that most police managers are aware of their various control responsibilities, relative to an operational-level manager's obligations for control of subordinate performances, material allocation, and the need to function within certain parameters of cost-effectiveness. This includes not only a **basic knowledge of** but also a **practical use of** that information for effectiveness of his or her operation. A preponderance of the information gathered in formulating which controls would be most effective will be obtained through personal observations as the manager performs prescribed duties. A positional leader needs a continual flow of pertinent information to plan and implement the best control system. An operational police manager must also seek to avoid overcontrolling subordinate personnel, as this will often stifle creative and innovative actions, but he or she should maintain an appropriate monitoring position for overall effectiveness.

ADEQUATE INFORMATION

An effective operational manager will make certain that a sufficient amount of details are received by subordinates to appropriately accomplish delegated tasks. The receipt of adequate or a sufficient amount of information relative to assigned tasks is a control device, though often not perceived as such by operational managers. However, it is not **atypical** for a positional leader to delegate a task or assign a job by providing only minimal detail information. As previously indicated, this can be time wasting and economically detrimental to operational performances. The insufficient informational details will generally be substituted for by the subordinate during his or her efforts to complete the assignment. The problem arises when the employer translations or the substitute data is not what is necessary for desired results. Projected results will then be inappropriate or ineffective in meeting requirements. An effective operational police manager must project him- or herself into the role of the designee to determine what information is needed to fulfill the task requirements. The providing of sufficient and appropriate detail information is a form of job performance control, as it sets parameters for an acceptable submission format and results. Further, the providing of adequate facts will regulate a task's process by structuring the work to be accomplished and supplying the subordinate with a guideline for desired activity. Therefore, when considering job performance controls by a police manager, the providing of adequate information should not be overlooked.

Job performance controls is a required responsibility of every police leader, even though the fact that he or she may be available and observant will generally project an initial dominance over the task activity. Performance controls in a highly structured environment is a logical sequence of requirements and an obligation to regulate task results. And whether we call them performance controls or operational standards, they should be established and made known to the designee prior to subordinates' behavioral actions. The positional leader who only reacts when a subordinate job behavior fails to accomplish predetermined objectives is utilizing the exceptional principle of leadership—in other words, **crisis management** or **reactive leadership** instead of preplanned and calculated job performance controls. An operational police manager can improve his or her performance in this dimensional trait characteristic by a recognition of the need for ongoing and result-oriented guidelines that will produce a desired outcome, plus a cognizant reaction to preplanning operational controls with the same zeal that he or she **plans** and **organizes** subordinate expectations. Remember, job performance controls are just as important to goal achievement results as is functional productivity. **A recognition and practice of job performance control is the key to effectiveness in this managerial trait area.**

SYNOPSIS

Most public agencies such as police departments will rely on operational managers to set job performance controls and/or quality standards to achieve desired results. Tight budgetary constraint in public organization does not usually allow for efficiency or quality control experts as a separate entity. Quality of work, productivity expectations, and desired results are all primary job functions of an operational leader. Concerning leadership responsibility, a manager's job performance controls are traditionally referred to as management quality controls. Management controls as a job performance guideline is a traditional concept in law enforcement. It has a prima ry purpose and focus of appraising the most effective use of departmental assets. Some of the practical management controls that may be utilized by operational police management are: (1) due dates, (2) progress checks, and (3) follow-up checks. There are also a number of controls utilized by operational-level managers to monitor and regulate task results. To simplify the categorizing of these control elements, they are comprehensively listed under three specific areas: (1) human resources (personnel), (2) material resource (logistical), and (3) financial (cost expenditures). An effective police manager should also assure that adequate information is provided to regulate and control the outcome of task achievement. The furnishing of sufficient data is a recognized control influence available to an operational police manager. The recognition and practice of appropriate job performance controls are the key to improving managerial task accomplishment in this dimensional trait characteristic area.

Chapter Seven

MID-LEVEL MANAGEMENT OF
FUNCTIONAL-LEVEL PERSONNEL

A mid-level police manager in a law enforcement organization is responsible for providing leadership for a specific unit or element and its assigned personnel. This management or leadership is over basic level performances that includes scheduling, training, and productivity expectations. A secondary leader's task is diverse in nature and complex regarding task accomplishments through the inspiration and manipulation of others. There is a long list of skills attributable to the makeup of a successful leader, many which have been identified and discussed in this text. The author has attempted to address all of the readily associated skill requirements as well as some that are not typically mentioned. For example, the Conceptual Skills needed by a police mid-level manager is not usually discussed as an essential trait of leadership. However, it is felt that at least a cursory acknowledgment of this characteristic was critical to the personality of an effective leader. A Conceptual Skill is said to be an ability to recognize the organization's goal and objective and what part of his or her element plays in helping to achieve the desired results. Any form of conceptualizing involves the leader's mental ability to think through a problem and develop a strategy of action to achieve a positive accomplishment.

The content of this chapter will reflect some of the areas of focus that come readily to mind when thinking of a functional mid-level manager's handling of subordinates in a public police setting. The textual content will initially begin with a discussion of employee problems and subordinate motivation. The concerns of employee leadership confronting the functional mid-level manager may range from simple on-the-job matters to individual personal crises that affect job behavior.

An organization's principal resource and certainly the most costly component are its employees. Therefore, the managing of workers is the most important aspect of any leader's job. Most organizations, including public police, have a major concern about making its employees as effective and productive as possible. On one side of the issue, companies strive to inspire employees to work harder and be more effective, while on the other end of the continuum, the workers are seeking to enhance personal gains and increase leisure time. This is not to imply that the two views are in conflict, because they both seek a better quality of goods and services while attempting to enhance the job performance of workers. The real test is to achieve a mutuality of expectations and goal efforts. By doing so, both service and product industry can readily recognize the benefit in terms of balanced cost and performance effectiveness. However, it has not gone unnoticed that today's employees seem less committed to an organization's ultimate goal than in past years. Also, employees today, such as functional-level leaders/workers, seem more willing to change jobs, to be absent from the job more frequently, and other factors considered not favorable to a career-oriented organization. Additionally, there seems to be a greater disinterest in hard work, increased productivity, and/or loyalty to the employer.

Legal actions have put both supervisors and managers in the picture as codefendants for perceptual wrongs, leading to court settlements for actions of subordinates. Therefore, laying out a plan of services to be provided and assuring the appropriateness of actions by employees is very important. Modern police leaders must analyze the service needs of the community and design a plan of action that will be adhered to in providing sufficient public protection.

MANAGERIAL RESPONSIBILITY

Traditionally, it is not perceived as a direct responsibility of a mid-level police manager to provide a cure for an employee's personal problem. However, if the problem manifests itself in a subpar job performance, then it becomes a requirement of line supervision and secondary management to seek desired behavior through referral or managerial action. Referring or recommending someone to seek external specialized help for a personal problem is far from easy. Recommending to an individual that he or she could benefit from some type of treatment, or the administering of some form of behavior modification action, whether disciplinary or not, will *not* typically be well received. The mid-level police manager should be tactful but decisive in personal actions to correct the inappropriate behavior.

The common sense question at this juncture concerning a functional mid-level police manager's dealing with subordinates is, *How do I detect or recognize an employee's problem?* The functional mid-level manager can recognize problem employees through their actions or inactions on the job. If a subordinate's job performance behavior is abnormal from the expected responses or is a deviation from the person's regular habit pattern, that may be the surest and most detectable indication of problems. The employee problem may be either of two types: (1) the subordinate is having personal or psychological problems or (2) the subordinate is experiencing a job performance problem.

Typically, an employee undergoing **personal** or **psychological** problems may display abnormal on-the-job reactions, contrary to his or her normal pattern of behavior, some of which are listed below:

1. **Overly Assertive Behavior** is a type of frustrated action where the employee engages in some form of aggressive action excessive to the norm. In a job setting, this action may be through arguments with other employees, gossiping, or running down the organization and its members.
2. **An Apparent Lack of Interest** may be a resolve that what is can't be changed, virtually giving up without making any effort to alter or improve an undesirable situation.
3. **Tense or Apprehensive Behavior** is typically characterized by the employee's fear and uneasiness. The employee's apparent discomfort and related behavior will tend to continue, no matter what the circumstances.
4. **Rationalization of Actions** is a term associated with the defense mechanism, where the employees will attempt to justify all of their actions through unreal or manufactured reasons. It should be noted that the rationalizations may not be readily realized by the person him/herself.

It should be noted that personal or psychological problems can divulge themselves in a number of other behaviors that are too numerous to identify. The essential thing for a secondary leader to note is that the behaviors are abnormal and in some way affecting the person's job performance.

What is traditionally termed **Job Performance** problems by functional level employees will generally have its foundation in the personality of the particular individual. The most noticeable of the negative job performance behaviors are:

1. **Tardiness**, being habitually late in responding to or carrying out assignments.
2. **Lack of personal initiative**, providing no more effort than is absolutely necessary to do the job at hand.

3. **Carelessness**, both in the handling of equipment and job performance. Also, the individual will typically make an excessive number
   of mistakes.
4. **Lack of motivated teamwork**, generally preferring to go it their own
   way, attempting whenever possible to work contrary to other organizational members.
5. **Preoccupation with influences outside the workplace**, attention
   span for organizational detail tends to be limited, desire to focus concentration and outside interests.
6. **Lackadaisical work efforts**, displaying a noteworthy lack of effort in
   job performance, attempting only to meet minimum standards and
   waiting until the very last moment before doing the job.

The above listed job performance problems are only a few of an infinite
number of negative behaviors that a troubled employee may display.

DISTRIBUTION OF WORK

Workload distribution is a process by which a police manager will assess
the task(s) to be accomplished and accordingly assign it equally among workers. It is recognized that task assignments cannot always be equably allocated. However, he or she should divide the work load or task obligations as
equally as possible. By doing so and assessing future needs, the total number
of workers needed may be minimized. The process utilized to equalize work
loads is conceptually simple. First, the leader will determine and analyze
which tasks are to be accomplished. Second, he or she should ascertain the
number of police officers needed to efficiently and effectively provide the
service. Third, the work load is divided by the number of officers needed by
**time of day, area to be policed, and the level of service mandated by
a crime/call-for-service analysis**. This process is a simple and straightforward formula for distributing work load, but it becomes more complicated
when you have to consider the public's expectations, the available manpower, and the financial commitment needed to effectively perform the tasks. A
needed consideration is, as noted elsewhere in this text, the community's
general expectations of the police and its cost-effective use of public funds.
Thus, there is typically little room in a police element's budget for widespread creative variants, etc. The concept of *cost effective* is based on the fact
that there is usually little or no revenue produced by police services. Although it is recognized that there is a need for public police, no one, as yet,
has developed a workable formula to measure public protection's true suc-

"This work is very easy."

"Rommy, I know you are the primary supervisor and I as your superior must tell you that the work load should be more evenly distributed."

AN EFFECTIVE SECONDARY LEADER WILL ASSURE THAT THE JOB TASKS ARE BALANCED FOR MORE EFFICIENCY.

cess. If a police operation is truly effective, it prevents more offenses than will ever be known or perceived. Also, the equal dividing of police services among workers will generally mean greater efficiency and reduced idle time for functional subordinates.

The distribution of protective duties among functional police officers is not a simple matter. The inconsistency of human actions makes the behavior-controlling task of public police officers unpredictable. In fact, there are a number of alternative ways that a behavior-controlling element, such as public policing, can respond to accomplish a task. In other fields of employment, management theorists have used such studies as linear or dynamic programming to project and balance worker availability to achieve expectations of production output. Public policing, because it does not produce a tangible or measurable product, is not ideally suited for quantitative evaluation. Secondary managers in the field of public police traditionally utilize an incremental job-assignment process. In other words, tasks to be accomplished are simply added to ones already being performed in order of occurrence and need, relative to the services to be provided.

GENERAL CONSIDERATIONS

There are a number of general considerations that need to be examined when viewing secondary police managers. Each area of focus is essential to the overall positive makeup of a secondary leader whose principal responsibility is getting tasks accomplished through the work of others. It is the appropriate mixture of these qualities and/or essential behavioral actions that form what is termed an effective leader.

Ethical Behaviors

The primary question to be asked when looking at ethics as an issue related to a secondary leader's makeup, may be, What is the definition of ethical behavior? Ethical behavior is defined as human actions in respect to right or wrong and good or evil from a societal perspective. A major factor that seems to manifest itself when there is an attempt to define ethics or ethical behavior is the term ethical values. We recognize values as a learned trait, usually developed early in life, where there is a principal standard or quality that is regarded as worthwhile or desirable. It can be a moralistic attitude associated with the job. Clay T. Buckingham wrote in his 1985 article, "If I believe that human life has limited value, let's say limited by what it can contribute to the common good, then my concept of right or wrong will reflect this conviction. Thus, our whole moral and ethical concept of right and wrong stems from this thesis-antithesis of good and evil." Therefore, considering this information relative to second-level police managerial leadership, there should be a consideration of the performance behavior of leaders on and off the job. The question concerning the ethical behaviors of leaders is whether or not an employer should consider the non-duty-related actions of a leader. The job-related nature of public law enforcement mandates a degree of honesty and integrity. Thus, it is not out of line to hold police leaders to a high degree of ethical behavior, both on and off the job. Perceptual right or wrong and good or evil actions of a leader affects how superiors and subordinates view the individual's personal character. The old adage "Do as I say, not as I do" is not sufficient for workers of today. Recognizing this, it should be noted that ethical behavior on and off the job is an essential part of being an effective leader.

Appropriate Resolutive Action

An effective leader at any level of the organization is expected to be able to mentally formulate a plan and then to assure its execution in dealing with a concern. There are a number of identified steps in such a process, which is integrated throughout this and other leadership texts. However, the author does not feel that the concern resolution process can be overemphasized when providing leadership direction for line supervisors or mid-level managers. Initially, the secondary police leader must recognize and define the limits of the concern. Simply stated, this means that a situation or circumstance has to be perceived as causing difficulty or concern. The leader can then select the appropriate alternative to achieve the desired goal and objective. Second, the leader should gather facts related to the concern and then formulate some assumptions as to its effect or limits, etc. The acquisition of facts is somewhat self-explanatory because you as a leader cannot be sure that a concern is a problem until you have obtained relevant influence factors. Drawing assumptions as to its limits and effect is essentially visionary of what the real scope of the concern may be. An identified focus and a possible direction of resolution efforts are needed if the concern is to be adequately resolved. Third, a leader should develop alternative solutions for the identified concern. A mid-level police leader or manager should assess what actions his or her subordinates could take to resolve the issue or concern. Frequently, there appears to be a number of solutions that are readily visible. However, many of these resolutive actions can cause a negative reaction. In other words, an action taken to solve one problem may cause another, as yet unidentified, concern. For example, Officer "A" is told that several times a day he is to check the rear doors of the businesses in the Center City main shopping area, which is consistently left unsecured by workers. However, in order to check the rear door, Officer "A" must leave his visible patrol area for up to ten minutes to get to the rear alley to check the security of the doors. The needed police action for the rear door has now been resolved, but this has created the problem of leaving his normal patrol area unprotected for ten or more minutes. When the officer leaves the main patrol area, the amount of criminal activity, such as street robberies, assaults, etc., noticeably increases. Fourth, the police manager should analyze and compare the possible solutions or alternatives to determine a feasible and effective resolutive action. It is through this analytical process that a definitive plan of action that will not only resolve the concern but can fit within the realm of appropriate consequences. In other words, perform an action that will solve the initially identified concern without creating a new one. Further, regarding most problems or concerns, there is usually more than one way to address an issue. Therefore, the leader must make a choice of which resolutive action to use based on need fulfillment, feasibility, and applicability. Finally, the effective leader should assure that he or she implements the concern resolutive action decided upon. Remember, a decided upon action that is not enacted may be like a tree falling in the forest. If nothing is affected by its falling and no one saw or heard it fall, then for all practical purposes, the tree did not fall, or did it? In other words, if it was not noticed, then it's as if it never happened. The most useless information in the world is knowledge or data that is known but never utilized. It was often said during the Cold War years that an "unused weapon is a useless weapon." The above identified concern resolving skills are considered necessary to the understanding and implementation of performance expectations of an organizational leader. This understanding typically guides a leader's problem assessment process, as well as structuring it into the context of the goals and objectives of the organization. Conceptually speaking, a leader's Concern Resolutive Process should aid his or her understanding of organizational goals, envisioning or anticipation of required actions, and proactive planning and behavior within task expectations.

Establishing a Command Climate

Command climate, as identified here, refers to the need for the mid-level police manager to assure a work atmosphere that is conducive to positive performance by subordinates. Employees tend to work better and be more productive in situations where they feel their efforts will be appreciated. Effort appreciation in the sense of command climate refers to leadership's recognition of job performance. In most organizational structures, discipline, much like communication, is a formalized process from the top down. Wrong behaviors or unacceptable performances are expectedly undesirable and their resolution is generally a process that's inbred into the functional fiber of an organization. It is a formal process that is established procedurally within an organization's structure, and it is generally established and formulated to be administered from the top of the organization leaders utilize to gauge and/or establish a command climate within their sphere of control.

1. **The mid-level police manager should make an assessment of the organization's command climate**. A leader should be cognizant of both his/her personal actions and the organization's hierarchy philosophy that affects the perceptual attitude of workers. The police mid-level manager should be able to perceive what effect the organization's hierarchical actions will influence his/her subordinates. The leader must be attuned to grapevine information and the concept of subordinates as to their fit into the organization's overall goals and objectives. By this assessment of the organization's atmosphere toward the perceived positive treatment of its workers, a manager can gauge his or her actions. If upper management is perceived by workers to be uncaring or nonresponsive to the needs of lower level employees, then the

mid-level police manager must assure that his or her recognition of subordinates' actions are visible. The leader should never let his or her actions, in any way, appear to conflict with the overall philosophy and/or goals and objectives of the organization's hierarchy.

2. **An effective leader should identify the climate areas he/she can and desire to influence**. It is recognized that a mid-level police manager's sphere of influence relative to a subordinate's hiring or firing is usually limited to making recommendations of actions within his or her authority and responsibility. For example, if employees are dissatisfied with their level of pay, the mid-level manager typically can not affirmatively affect this area of the organizational climate. However, the secondary work leader traditionally can affect the atmosphere of cooperative teamwork and the job performance recognition of the workers. Therefore, from the above, a secondary leader should identify work behaviors and job recognitions as areas he or she can effectively influence. The mid-level police manager should undertake the needed actions to perceptually affect an employee's environment in those areas that can be affected. A positive effect on the work atmosphere of workers can influence the worker's productivity. The Western Electric study during the early part of this century proved that attention to workers can have a positive effect on productivity. Even though the experiment (Hawthorne Study) was a failure relative to the production level of the test group vs. the control group when the physical environment is changed, it was successful in proving a positive interaction between workers and recognition of their work. The bottom line as to the results of the study was that a noticeable effect on subordinates' attitudes and job performances was achieved by recognition of work output.

3. **A leader should establish clear expectations/goals for each area that he or she wishes to affect**. The developing and implementation of clearly defined paths of operations toward desired achievement is fundamental for an effective leader. By climate area, we are referring to the atmosphere which is conducive to a subordinate's motivation to aggressively achieve positive results. An effective leader wants a high level of productivity from subordinates; thus, the mid-level police manager must promote a positive work climate. A positive work climate should project an environment and incentive perception that reflects an atmosphere which is conducive to desired employee behaviors. For example, a leader establishes an aura of positive recognition of workers, which is visible to all subordinates, for good work and/or incentive points that can be converted into additional time off, etc.

Defining goals and objectives is a classic leadership prerequisite for an effective leader in the directing of subordinates toward meeting expectations. Like the Western Electric study of the early 1930s revealed, workers are motivated by attention and recognition, as well as by financial incentives and/or job challenges. The mid-level police manager, because of both direct and indirect daily contact with functional-level workers, are certainly in the best position to influence the perceptual climate or atmosphere of subordinates. When clearly stated, the desired job expectations typically establish a climate conducive to performance productivity.

4. **Once identified and clarified, the leader must implement actions to positively influence the performance climate**. The leader should assure that he or she executes a plan which recognizes that a positive command climate must be created from the top of the organization down. This means that the hierarchy of the organization should realize the importance of the environmental climate or work atmosphere that exists. Organizational leadership must realize that the temperament of employees of previous generations, where loyalty to the organization and non-questioning acceptance of hierarchy action, is no longer the norm. Modern employees are more likely to ask why or to think first of their personal wants or needs before considering the organization's goals and objectives. Therefore, the top management of an organization should seek to create a working climate or atmosphere that is work positive.

The mid-level police manager should always be aware that his or her actions in dealing with subordinates create a behavior pattern that is discernible to other subordinates. The "Do as I say and not as I do" adage is no longer an acceptable action of superiors. The leader should use performance behaviors that are positively perceived as expected actions and conducive to non-negative interaction. The mid-level police manager's actions must be positive and innovative in meeting the expectations of both subordinates and superiors.

DEALING WITH SUBORDINATES' PROBLEMS

The functional mid-level police manager is an unparalleled factor in the troubled subordinate's ability to deal with job-related, problem-causing situations. The responsive nature and temperament of the mid-level manager's personality traits provide the key to his or her being able to effectively guide the employee through the problem by means of discipline, counseling, or training. The mid-level police manager that is attempting to deal with the job performance of a problem subordinate may utilize either one or more or a combination of the methods identified. The particular method(s) that will be employed will depend on the nature of the problem and the perceived approach that will yield the best results.

A majority of the literature on functional management tell us that a secondary leader begins taking action because of a recognized problem and the action taken is to correct the problem. It must be realized that the secondary police manager is treating the symptom rather than dealing with the cause. By treating the symptom and not the cause of the problem, it is likely to resurface in another form, if not the same behavior. As with any problem, the cause must be eliminated if the mid-level manager is to avoid a reoccurrence. In the attempts to determine the underlying cause of the problem, a leader has to display exceptional listening skills and the patience to hear out the subordinate and not pre-judge him/her.

The foundational causes that permeate the misconduct of a subordinate are as important as the behavior itself. The most practical attempts by the mid-level manager to prevent repeated acts will require some knowledge or perception as to the cause, as well as a specific effort to eliminate the motive. Being a positional leader in the hierarchical structure of the organization makes it extremely difficult for the mid-level police manager to retain an objective attitude toward the misbehavior of a subordinate. However, if the leader's initial approach to the situation is an attempt to uncover the cause, as well as correct the behavior, then his or her effectiveness in this area should increase. However, if the functional mid-level police manager takes the analytical approach to dealing with a problem subordinate, then there are several factors that he or she should be aware of. The following listed areas are some commonly perceived as underlying causes of subordinate deviate behaviors. The author has also provided Solution recommendations for corrective actions for both supervisors and secondary leaders.

1. **Violations of rules, regulations, and policies because of a faulty perception**. The assumption here is that the employee would not have violated the established documented guidelines if he or she had a complete knowledge and understanding of the directive.

   Solution: The supervisor or mid-level manager can eliminate this problem by assuring that each subordinate receives a copy of all applicable directives and that each has a clear understanding of the intent and purpose of the rules, regulations, and policies.

2. **The employee's emotional posture toward the directives, peers, superiors, and the organization**. The belief is that the subordinate is violating the established guidelines because of a negative mental approach to the areas cited.

Solution: A positive occurrence associated with the organization will quickly improve a person's attitude. Also, strict and harsh disciplinary action will often garner compliance but not an attitudinal change.

3. **Inadequate or inappropriate behavior because of an insufficient skill level**. The subordinate's unacceptable performance is due to his or her lack of ability to perform at the level required. The general perception that the person does not have the mental aptitude to do the job is often an overused phrase in quasi-military organizations, but it is not always wrong. The required mental aptitude to do the job may be an area that is foreign to the developmental knowledge attainment by some subordinates to date.

Solution: Specific training aimed at the deficient areas of the employee's knowledge, and if training fails, perhaps a transfer of the subordinate to an area more suited for the person's aptitude and skill level. Discharging the employee, if all else fails, is certainly an option, but one that should be undertaken only as a last resort.

In most work situations there will only be a small percentage of the organization's human resources whose duty performances will be contrary to the accepted norms. These problem personnel must be dealt with quickly and effectively, if the mid-level manager is to prevent their behavior and attitude from adversely affecting other functional-level employees. As previously stated, the secondary manager is usually ill-equipped to deal with personal or psychological problems of employees where the cause is external to organizational operation. The secondary leader should attempt to obtain the confidence of the subordinates and respond to them individually concerning the problem on a personal, one-on-one basis. A middle manager should also assess the concerns as presented by the subordinate and recommend the employee to a suitable person or agency to handle the problem. Unless there are some other mitigating circumstances requiring disciplinary or training action, the employee must feel that it is his or her choice to seek the help.

Therefore, in a mid-level manager's attempts to deal with functional subordinates having job performance problems, it is generally concluded that he or she must deal with the overt behavior of the employee through recognized traditional methods. The actions taken will depend on the level of authority delegated by management to administer corrective actions and, whether disciplinary, counseling, or training should be perceived by the employee as prompt, fair, and appropriate.

A comprehensive discussion of each of the traditional techniques for dealing with and correcting undesirable job performance behavior in subordinates is required. Therefore, we will attempt to adequately address each method individually.

Discipline

Discipline is defined as the action taken by functional leadership or organizational management to correct perceived abnormal performance actions or behavior of employees who violate established rules, regulations and policies of their organization. The disciplinary action can range from a verbal reprimand by the immediate supervisor to termination of employment. The nature of the offense and the established practices of the organization will be the key to the severity of the discipline.

A mid-level police manager should approach the situation of a subordinate's discipline for misconduct with a compassionate, legalistic, objective, and effective view. First, in terms of the compassionate view, the leader should have some feel for how the disciplinary action will affect the subordinate, his or her family, and the integrity of the organization. Second, a legalistic perspective allows the leader to view the discipline from a legal standpoint of what the limits are within which action must focus, concerning the subordinate's civil rights and the law. Third, the mid-level manager must assure that the disciplinary action taken is not biased to the individual and that it is consistent. Fourth, managerial leadership should evaluate and view the discipline as to its effectiveness for correcting the misbehavior.

Responsibility for Administering Corrective Actions

Unlike the perception of who is primarily responsible for finding a cure for an employee's personal problem, it is clearly the responsibility of the functional mid-level police manager to enforce the guidelines of the organization through the primary leader. But on most occasions in an organization, this is done through directives, both verbal and written. However, there are times when it becomes necessary for the secondary leader to exercise his/her delegated disciplinary powers to enforce these rules and regulations. In most quasi-military structured organizations such as a public police operation, the mid-level manager has authority to administer minor disciplinary actions such as written warnings, verbal reprimands, etc. But in cases of a more serious nature where discipline could be costly to the employee in terms of lost wages and/or benefits, it is upper management's responsibility. In these serious cases the middle manager will usually make a recommendation, but final authority rests with the organization's leader.

Concerning the specific power of the mid-level manager to administer discipline, Pfiffner and Fels conclude "that there can't be any specific guideline for management which will work well in all situations. Though the ultimate authority to impose severe penalties such as dismissal, transfer and suspension lie with a higher level of management the immediate supervisor and secondary leader must be supported in their recommendations that these actions be levied."' The term discipline commonly denotes a perception of unpleasant actions taken against an employee for some act or violation. However, in point of fact, effective discipline is a form of training to foster compliance with established organizational norms. Discipline should not be a purely punitive measure and can be administered in either of two forms, positive or negative.

Positive Disciplinary Action:

Under the concept of what is actually being referred to when we say positive discipline, that term may not be appropriate. The term discipline to most of us usually denotes a punitive form of action, which is not always the case. As in positive discipline, which means an action that is considered favorable to the employee and the organization in correcting deficiencies and on-the-job miscues. Per the previous statements, the author is aware that the majority of job performance misbehaviors are caused by the lack of knowledge or misjudgments as opposed to intentional misconduct. Thus, mistakes in knowledge, etc., should not be dealt with in a negative forum, because this will affect the subordinate's attitude. The feeling that, I made an honest mistake but instead of teaching me to do it right, the organization tries to hurt me in some form. This type of perception by organizational employees soon manifests itself in an attitude of it's them against us and thus comes additional labor and/or union problems.

Positive discipline is a state of affirmative productive training to correct deficiencies and to maintain a constructive favorable attitude on the part of functional level employees toward the organization. Positive discipline is also the attitudinal pressure that peer members exert upon an employee who is deviating from the norms, to conform with established rules, regulations, and practices.

Therefore, it is extremely important for the functional mid-level police manager to be totally familiar with the concept of positive discipline and to use positive disciplinary methods at every opportunity to correct an employee's improper behavior. A mid-level manager must realize that discipline should not be a method of getting even with the employee for misconduct or to punish him or her for a mistake. It is basically to teach or train the employee so that the same error will not be repeated.

Remember, no matter what the discipline or punishment is for an employee's error it will not undo the mistake, it can only serve as a lesson for the future.

Negative Disciplinary Action:

Negative disciplinary action more closely conforms to the general perception as to what is discipline when used to correct an employee's error or misconduct. It is a perception that persists not only at the functional level of police organization but at virtually every management level. The feeling that we punish wrongdoers whether the error was intentional or not is very prevalent in quasi-military type organizations. The organization's primary and mid-level managers must get their "pound of flesh" for the mistake. This is not intended to say that negative discipline has no place or should not be used to deal with problem employees or misbehavior. Quite the contrary, negative forms of discipline can be very effective in correcting misbehavior and deterring future like behavior. However, some theorists in the field of leadership and management will tell you that negative disciplinary methods should be resorted to only after positive methods of adjustment have failed; also, that the negative discipline used should be on a "graduated scale." By this we mean that if a subordinate violates a perceived minor rule, why suspend him or her for a week when a verbal warning may do the job. In other words, why use a sledgehammer to kill a fly. The graduating scale concept refers to the fact that if a "verbal warning" was given a week ago and the employee repeats the misbehavior, then perhaps the primary leader and the mid-level manager should then graduate the discipline up to reprimand and so on until the desired results are obtained. This is not to infer that just because the police officer was suspended for a week the last time, that he or she should be suspended for two weeks this time. The option of the amount of discipline recommended should be left to the individual recommending it. However, the use of a graduating scale of discipline will let the employee know that continued improper behavior will increase in its negative effect until the misconduct is stopped.

Some of the traditional methods of perceived negative discipline available for use by functional-level supervisors and mid-level managers are:

Warnings–verbal and written.
Reprimands–verbal and written.
Loss of compensation–fines, suspensions, or demotions, and
Loss of employment–forced resignation or termination.

In most police organizations when the level of negative or disciplinary action reaches "loss of compensation," the mid-level manager can only make recommendations, with the final decision resting with upper management. A factor often overlooked, but one that is very real when discipline reaches the "loss of compensation" or "loss of employment" level, is that both the employee and the organization come out losers. The organization loses when it suspends an employee because of the manpower loss during the time, even though it is temporary. The employee and his or her family loses because of the financial loss of earnings to the family's budget during the suspension. The effect of the loss of income to the wage earner, even for a short time, generally needs no additional explanation.

Disciplinary action by a functional mid-level police manager is only one form of action available to guide the employee through problem situations. A second method (and one that is much emphasized in formal training of operational mid-level managers) is "Employee Counseling."

Employee Counseling

The counseling of an employee in an on-the-job setting is defined principally as the giving of advice and/or making recommendations in a formal leadership mode. Traditionally, the leader-subordinate counseling session is a form of interpersonal, face-to-face communication that takes place between a positional leader and a subordinate. The actual counseling session is a verbal exchange between the two principles and should possess some degree of confidentiality, outside the view of others. The mid-level police manager must be aware that his or her every word or gesture during the counseling session may in some way affect the perception of the subordinate being counselled. Therefore, the mid-level police manager should pay special attention not only to being cognizant of what he or she says to the employee but also how it is said. The leader's attention to the content of the session should further extend to the body language and responses of the counselee, to determine how the session and the information is being received.

An effective functional mid-level police manager must develop and cultivate personal skills as a counselor. It must be realized that each session may have some similarities, but that because the principles and/or the issues are different, so too will be the emphasis. If knowledgeably and purposefully done, the counseling session will be very effective and productive. The effective leader-counselor will be aware of his or her normal personality traits and tailor personal techniques and actions during the session to fit a traditional operational posture. For example, a normally soft-spoken and not easily excitable leader may distort a counseling session by shouting and pounding on the table to get a point across. The reverse would be true of a normally vocal and excitable person. The leader-counselor should also be aware of the morale of the person being counselled, as he or she should be in every situation requiring a leader-subordinate exchange. In addition to all the previously listed factors, a mid-level manager needs to consider and be conscious of the timing of the session. Timing is essential to most areas of effective management and, thus, is no less critical to subordinate counseling. If the counseling is given too soon, some of the needed impact may be missed because the problem may not have been fully realized. And, likewise, if it is given too long after the problem, the situation may have corrected itself and thus eliminated the perceived importance of the counseling.

The author has, to this juncture, attempted to define what is a job-related counseling session and provided some insight into the areas that an effective leader-counselor should be aware of. It is critically important that the midlevel police manager be familiar with the reasons why subordinate counseling is so essential to effective functioning. On-the-job counseling of employees is important for a number of reasons, principally to: (1) motivate work performance; (2) correct unacceptable behavior and establish a compatible working relationship; (3) aim the employee toward problem solutions, if one is needed; and (4) provide confidentiality of the exchange. Each of these areas are fairly clear as to their respective importance and structural makeup in an organizational setting.

Recommended "Subordinate Counseling Session Structure"

The following is a step-by-step process that the author recommends that a functional mid-level manager of a police operation utilize in the counseling of a subordinate. The nature or need for the session may affect the content of the information, but this should not alter the basic structural process. The step-by-step process is:

Step One. The mid-level police manager who is to conduct the counseling session should plan for it. By reviewing all pertinent data and assuring that all of the facts are accurate and up-to-date, he or she should make notes or a list of the subject areas he plans to cover in a prioritized or smooth-flowing order that he feels will be most effective. He should plan an estimated time span for the session. The police manager's effectiveness as a counselor will depend in large measure as to how step one is carried out.

Step Two. Initially, the leader should attempt to put the counselee at ease. The value of this tactic is evident, as most effective speakers will attempt to put their audience at ease with light conversation or a joke. However, in a serious on-the-job counseling session I would not recommend telling a joke. But light conversation in which the subordinate interacts verbally will lessen his apprehension about the session and thus be more receptive to the information. The attempts to put the employee at ease should be limited in time span, as too much light conversation will appear to be a stall and add additional stress to the situation.

Step Three. Briefly discuss some of the favorable things that the counselee has done. The mentioning of some favorable traits or performances of the subordinate will bolster his confidence and create a perception that it is not a total put down of him. It is important to the employee's self-esteem to know that the good things that he has done have not gone unnoticed. This feeling will allow him or her to be more receptive to challenges to his negative behavior with the recognition that positive changes or corrections will not go unnoticed. This step, like step two, should not be carried to excess or the true emphasis of the counseling session will be altered.

Step Four. The leader should discuss the specific areas that necessitated the counseling session. He or she should adhere to the pre-plan as outlined in step one, making sure that each area is adequately covered. The mid-level manager must, whenever possible, state specific examples of the employee's behavior to illustrate the point. For example, "On March 24th, you reported two hours late for assignment." By doing this he/she will assure that the subordinate clearly understands the supervisor's point. At the conclusion of the leader's information presentation he or she should pause to ascertain if the subordinate wishes to say something. The employee's explanation points or rationalization should be limited and the leader/manager must not become involved in a point-counterpoint debate over the issue, because the time expended in this back-and-forth exchange will limit the time available to cover the other areas.

Step Five. Once step four has been completed and the areas of needed improvement or adjustment have clearly been identified to the subordinate, the leader-counselor should provide some suggested methods that the employee can use to correct the deficiencies. This step would not be applicable if the counseling session were for reasons other than a problem situation or performance improvement. Just as a leader/manager was told in step four to provide specific examples of the negative behavior being referred to, it is suggested that specific things that the subordinate can do to improve the situation should be recommended by the leader-counselor. For example, the employee is generally late because of tie-ups on the freeway. The leader-counselor recommends, in order to correct the problem, that the subordinate leave for work several minutes earlier and take an alternate route that is less congested with traffic and a fewer frequency of accidents.

Step Six. The effective leader-counselor will ask questions after the problem areas have been laid out and offer some suggestions of how to correct them. These questions should be designed and structured for the purpose of determining whether or not the employee has a clear understanding of what the supervisor has said and meant. The leader/manager at this point should assure that the subordinate fully comprehends what the problems are and what can be done to correct them.

Step Seven. The effective mid-level manager will set into place some managerial or management controls to check the results of the proposed changes. He or she does this by setting follow-up dates or response reports to check the employee's activity. These managerial controls should include some follow-up counseling sessions to strengthen what was initially set into place or to modify the process, if needed.

Step Eight. The leader-counselor should give the subordinate an opportunity to bring out any points that the person feels are important and might have been overlooked. The employee's responses should not be limited only to the situation being discussed but should be open for any issue that the counselee feels needs to be addressed with the immediate supervisor or mid-level manager. The leader-counselor should respond appropriately but should not become involved in an external discussion to the point that he or she is put on the defensive by the subordinate. Being put on the defensive, even about another issue, will effectively take the edge off of what the supervisor wanted to accomplish during the subordinate counseling session.

Step Nine. The employee should be told in very plain and specific language what will occur from a disciplinary standpoint if improvements are not made in the problem areas. The middle manager should attempt not to be threatening but yet make it clear what will or could happen if corrections are not made.

Step Ten. The leader-counselor should conclude the counseling session with positive comments about the employee's abilities and how the improved performance will fit into the overall goals and objectives of the organization.

The above identified steps are not complete in all the things that need to be considered by a functional mid-level police manager conducting a counseling session. Not present in these recommended steps are several essentials to effective communication techniques that the mid-level manager should be aware of and exercise during a counseling session. It should be clearly understood that in order for a counseling session to be productive, the mid-level manager has to communicate effectively, employing all the necessary skills. Some of the more important of these skills in a counseling session are: (1) eye contact—looking at the subordinate when talking or listening to him or her; (2) voice control—using a voice tone, volume, or rate of speech that allows easy comprehension; (3) language—assuring that the words and terms used are common to both the counselor and the counselee; (4) body language—making sure that the movement and gestures of the counselor don't detract from the information presented.

It should be evident from the foregoing that an efficient and productive counseling session is not a simple process, but it can be most effective if properly used. The conjecture of effectiveness can be accomplished through training as a method of dealing with a subordinate's performance problem.

Training

Training as a method of dealing with employee performance problems should be as basic as showing up for work. It has been pointed out that the majority of job performance problems confronting mid-level managers and primary managers stem from a lack of knowledge or understanding on the part of the employee. This problem is most effectively addressed through training, whether it be formalized organizational in-service training or informal day-to-day interactive instruction and training provided by the secondary leader.

It would be beneficial for us to obtain a real perspective of training and its present status in public law enforcement. Essentially, training refers to the presentation (to a person or group) of information that can be used to enhance knowledge and performance. In law enforcement, a great deal of formalized training is provided for new or incumbent police officers. There are some small public law enforcement agencies that require less than 300 to 600 hours of formalized training. Most experts will readily admit that training in the area of public policing has continued to expand to meet the needs of police personnel. Traditionally, police organizations will utilize specially selected trainers to provide most of the in-service or initial training that continues to increase. The instructors are usually chosen because of his or her tenure and job performance, which does take into account their ability to teach and actual knowledge of the subject areas. The operational mid-level police manager must realize that training is one of the principal functions of the position and that it contributes greatly to overall subordinate performance. This on-the-job, day-to-day training also adds to the employee's (1) safety, (2) adjustments to problems, and (3) job satisfaction. Further, a real advantage to this managerial training is that it re-enforces things already learned and the subordinate is experiencing firsthand what is being taught.

The principal purpose of managerial training is to enhance the subordinate's performance and potential to perform. It also increases the employee's chances for growth and development within the organization. This training can be either of two basic techniques: Direct or Indirect. First, Direct Instruction is when a leader explains how to do something in specific language directly to the subordinates to assure their understanding and compliance. For example, "Officer Jones, you will place the suspect's hand behind him/her, with palms facing outward when handcuffing. By doing so, there is little or no opportunity for the arrested person to pick the lock on the handcuffs." The second basic technique is Indirect Instruction, where the subordinate is given temporary increased responsibility and authority to facilitate personal growth and development in the organization. For example, during the mid-level manager's absence, Supervisor Jones is appointed acting secondary leader. This not only enhances the subordinate's self-esteem but it also teaches through hands-on actions. He/she learns how to perform as a middle manager. This will further advance Supervisor Jones's perspective of his or her own job by having a chance to view it from his or her immediate supervisor's vantage point.

The success of a positional leader such as a functional mid-level police manager does not depend on a personal ability to train subordinates, but his or her effectiveness can be affected positively or negatively by the efforts and capabilities.

A Managerial Training Model

As previously noted, training should be an ongoing and never-ending process in a police organizational setting. This is especially true where the courts and legislators seem to make almost daily changes in the legal parameters or performance guidelines for public law enforcement. These changes are mandated because public policing as the action arm of the criminal justice system is charged with maintaining control and order in our society. Many of the things that can be traditionally analyzed and addressed about training subordinates by a mid-level police manager have been discussed. However, there is a specific training process that appears most consistent with the aims of public policing. This sequential process is not new, but it has been shown to be effective in gathering essential data on potential issues and then assuring appropriate distribution of the information to targeted personnel. Also, it provides a follow-up procedure to insure desired understanding and application.

In most police organizations, the supervisor and secondary manager are responsible for basic level on-the-job training. The training conducted by secondary leaders is usually situational day-to-day teaching regarding performance skills and behaviors. The teaching aspect of a secondary leader's duties is a process of developing a method of training incumbent officers in the skill areas necessary to effectively perform the job. Some organizations provide its leaders with a formalized and structured process of information to be disseminated through in-service training sessions, while other agencies distribute training bulletins, special directives or procedural memorandums, and leave the method of presentation, etc., to the leader/instructor. This on-the-job training is generally referred to as interactive workplace instruction. Most organizations have a separate agency-wide in-service training process that is conducted once or twice a year by a specialist in the area to be covered.

However, in addressing the interactive workplace training conducted by primary managers and first mid-level managers, a four-step process is recommended. First, the leader needs to ascertain the concern that requires addressing and then determine the objective the training is expected to achieve. Second, the leader or manager should prepare for the training by gathering pertinent information and determine the time to be allotted as well as the environmental setting. Third, the police leader/trainer must assure that the training is timely presented and disseminated in a way that is clear and understandable. Fourth, an effective leader/trainer will establish a feedback or response process to assure that the information presented is understood and useful to the officers. If possible, the police mid-level manager conducting the training should develop a way to measure and assess the results of the teaching. Some of the keys to effective training by a mid-level manager in a police organization are as follows: (1) put the learner at ease; (2) create an interest in the information to be presented; (3) present information at a normal pace that is easily understood; (4) obtain feedback through interaction with learners during the process; (5) select a training location that is not distractive; (6) through practice and effort, allow the learners hands-on learning, if possible, for gradual skill attainment; (7) correct errors by learners without embarrassment or criticism; and (8) compliment and/or encourage efforts by the trainees. These are but a few of the things that an effective functional mid-level police manager/trainer needs to incorporate into his or her interactive workplace training.

Stimulating Job Performances

Stimulating job performance is not a new or unusual term concerning inspiring functional workers to perform as desired. However, the use of the term stimulating as it relates to worker task performances is something new when used in this context. The more traditional term of employee incentive-induced job behaviors is the term motivation. The author does not wholly subscribe to the notion that leaders can motivate job performances, because in the purest sense motivation is basically an internal drive. Therefore, a mid-level police leader can induce efforts through incentive actions or inspirational efforts, but the only one who can truly motivate a worker to perform is the worker him/herself. However, inasmuch as the term motivation is the traditional term used to articulate the process of work inducement, the contextual content of this text regarding stimulating job performances will use the terminology associated with motivation as being synonymous with inspirational task inducement. Simply stated, the term motivation will be used as is typical when talking about stimulating worker job behaviors.

The traditional concept of motivation, in terms of a manager's efforts to entice subordinates to perform appropriately, refers to the influences that can be used to stimulate desired responses in employees. Human motivation is basically tied to both the physical and psychological needs of the individual(s) concerned. The job of the organization through its mid-level manager is to induce the functional-level subordinates through primary leadership to perform productively in a way that their personal needs, as well as the agency's objectives, will be met. The effective middle manager will recognize that the individual needs of employees will vary from one person to the next and so will the specific motivational requirements.

A majority of the texts dealing with the subject of Motivating Subordinates associates performance inducement or motivation with the "why" of human behavior and Maslow's "Hierarchy of Needs Theory" as previously discussed. But, because we traditionally associate work inducement with need fulfillment and attainment of desired goals by employees, it should not be interpreted that addressing these will motivate the employee. Psychology tells us that often certain needs of a person are unknown to them, and until these unconscious stimulators are met the person will not be totally induced to perform.

A leadership knowledge of these psychological influences on job performance inducement is important to a mid-level police manager, but true motivation from a personal perspective is limited to an individual charismatic ability. Also necessary is the recognition of the status-esteem need of the subordinate and assuring that each employee under the mid-level manager's control have an understanding of how his or her efforts fit into the overall mission of the organization.

A comprehensive examination of the areas that are most accessible and manipulated by the mid-level police manager in his or her effort to motivate subordinates reveals:

1. **The secondary leader's charismatic ability** is the principal tool that a functional-level middle manager has to motivate his or her subordi-

"What else can I do to motivate desired job performance?"

STIMULATING JOB ACTIONS THROUGH INSPIRATION DOES NOT MEAN CATERING TO ALL DESIRES AND WANTS OF SUBORDINATES.

nates outside of the organizational influences. In virtually every employment field you will find that the mid-level managers who are best liked and respected by their subordinates are the best motivators. We are not inferring that simply because an individual is liked by subordinates that he or she is any better or the most effective leader. An operational mid-level police manager's close association with subordinates may result in other difficulties, but for job-inducement purposes it is ideal. During combat operations, soldiers who genuinely cared about their leader were much more willing to follow him into dangerous situations than those who were just carrying out orders.

2. **Being cognizant of the status-esteem needs of subordinates** is a requirement for each individual's ego needs to be a consideration of the mid-level manager in attempting to motivate a subordinate. A person is generally much more willing to perform, if he or she believes that their efforts will not go unnoticed and that some form of incentive can be obtained. For example, a senior subordinate is much more likely to be inspired if periodically, during the middle manager's absence, he or she is appointed as acting secondary leader. This feeds the person's ego need for *status-esteem,* as the subordinate recognizes that his or her tenure and abilities have not been overlooked by the leader and the organization. Thus, the subordinate is motivated to live up to the higher expectations of the position.

3. **Employee understanding of how his/her job efforts fit into the overall objective** is important to the subordinate's motivation. Studies have suggested that factory workers tend to be more motivated when they think in terms of their contribution to the finished product. For example, an assembly line worker feels that his or her job is more important when thought of in terms of "the **Wiggets** that is inserted into **Socket X** holds the **Deflector** together that makes the whole **Gizmo** work properly." This perception is not different when applied to a public policing operation; all of us have a need to feel that what we do means something and makes a difference. Therefore, the functional mid-level police manager should assure that subordinates understand how their performance fits into the overall mission achievement of the organization. Plus, it re-enforces his or her awareness from time to time and will enhance the subordinate's job-induced efforts and the leader's effectiveness at all levels of the organization.

THE TWO FORMS OF ORGANIZATIONAL LEADERSHIP

Theorists in the area of leadership practices have cited two basic forms within most organizations. The forms of leadership identified are said to be **Direct** and **Indirect**.

Direct Leadership is the managerial or management control that is exercised at its lowest possible level. For example, a middle manager's control over functional- or work-level personnel is considered direct leadership. Likewise, a primary- or third-level manager's control over an immediate subordinate is also considered direct leadership. Therefore, managerial control when exercised over an immediate subordinate, no matter at what level of the organization, is termed direct leadership. Direct leadership within an organization involves the planning and operational control of the daily activities of immediate subordinates. The planning and control aspect of leadership being referred to concerns the quality of work, productivity, and the logistical management of items used by subordinates to do their job.

Concerning the role of *direct leadership,* it's a truism that subordinates do not always perform as expected or desired. A secondary leader concerned with the planning, controlling, and assessment of the performance behaviors of immediate subordinates must be constantly alert to the need to exercise direct action. The leader must be concerned about perceptual failures of subordinates to: (1) meet established performance goals; (2) assure the cost-effectiveness of tasks within his/her scope of control; (3) determine what quality control criteria is needed; and (4) develop a strategy to prevent and/or compensate for performance failures, as well as logistical problems.

Indirect Leadership refers to managerial controls that are accomplished by working with or through others in the organization. Much as the designation implies, it is leadership filtered through one or more levels of organizational management. The organizational management referred to need not be beyond the second level of management. An indirect leader, as an organizational manager, engages primarily in getting things done indirectly through other people. An indirect leader, at one time or another, carries out all the duties of direct leadership in addition to the management processes associated with a secondary managerial position. *Indirect leadership* involves setting performance goals and objectives for more than immediate subordinates. It is generally concluded that once plans have been made, organizational task accomplishment becomes important to an indirect leader. Typically, this means formulating and/or coordinating resource people and equipment in the most effective manner to achieve desired goals and objectives. This type of non-sequential leadership also involves the interrelating of resources, both human and logistical.

The secondary leadership that is one level above direct management also involves the inspiring of workers' performance and confidence in the managerial hierarchy. Inspiring, most generally referred to as motivation, involves directing through communication and leadership. It's concluded that when employees' motivation is low, their performance will be substandard. A substandard performance is unacceptable, whether caused by low morale or insufficient ability. Therefore, it is imperative that both direct and indirect leadership foster employee motivation. As indirect leadership is extremely important to the organization, it is essential to management control. Additional elements involve feedback of results through a follow-up process to correlate accomplishment with planned actions.

It is clear from the above information, relative to direct and indirect leadership, that overall focus of an organization's managerial process involves planning, organizing, inducing, and directing job performances. All of these functions are considered an integral part of the organizational leadership regardless of the type of organization or the level of management involved. Leaders in all positions of the organization are concerned in part with task accomplishment via the efforts of others.

All police mid-level leaders or primary managers must possess certain skills in order to perform effectively as a leader:

1. He or she must possess an ability to comprehend the interaction of the multi-elements of the overall organization. There should also be some conception of where his/her operation fits into the organization's operation and then utilizing this knowledge to correlate his/her element's efforts with that of the other organizational components.

2. He or she should possess sufficient knowledge skills of the task being overseen to adequately manage its accomplishment. This means that the leader must possess some technical knowledge concerning subordinates' performance expectations, etc., to determine training needs and to assess worker job behavior.

3. He or she must possess the human skills to motivate and inspire subordinate job performances and to understand both the motivational and performance effect of leadership behaviors on workers.

Common Stimulators

Job stimulators, as with most other things, will vary from individual to individual and from profession to profession, depending upon various factors such as personality, environment, financial status, and many others. But, generally one of the three Common Stimulators listed below is basic to virtually every situation; they are: (1) Fear, (2) Inspiration, and (3) Incentive.

Fear

This form of job stimulation has its roots in the apprehensions that a person may have for a change in what he or she believes is the status quo. A change in status could be a loss of job, transfer of assignment, temporary loss of pay through fines or suspensions, demotions, etc. The total spectrum of what a person may be fearful of is too numerous to mention, but from the things that have been listed, it is obvious that **fear** is a very real and strong stimulator. To some degree, each of us is motivated by one fear or another. The effective leader will recognize *fear* as a stimulator and use it to the best advantage but tempering its use, because the overuse of fear as an inducer can be detrimental. It would be counterproductive to have subordinates who were in constant fear, as this would stifle creativity and other valuable assets of employee self-initiated activity.

Inspiration

Inspiration as a stimulator is looked upon as those influences that are internally generated by the employee but having some direct correlation to on-the-job activity and recognition. For example, the employee is inspired to do a certain job particularly well because the boss will recognize his or her efforts. The primary factor in **Inspirational Stimulation** is *self.* The overall aim of the motivated performance may be to achieve some goal, but the fact that the effort was self-induced puts it in the Stimulation Category of Inspiration.

Incentive

If the organization is to stimulate an employee outside of internal drives, then an object or condition must be *offered.* This *offering* is known as an **incentive**. A mid-level manager should primarily be interested in using incentives to stimulate their subordinates' effective and productive performance of duty. When we normally think of incentives as it relates to the workplace, positive benefits, such as increased pay, more time off, status enhancement, praise, promotions, and other forms of rewards traditionally come to mind.

While it is true that the functional mid-level police manager has little or no control over most of the things that we normally conclude as positive incentives, he/she should utilize those areas that can affect the motivation of subordinates. The mid-level police manager in a public policing operation is in the best position to stimulate job performance in subordinates through the use of status enhancement and praise, with a great deal of influence on the employee's promotion chances. From the factors identified, it is a fair statement to say that *incentives are without a doubt the primary stimulator of most employees, either in the negative or the positive form.*

MANAGERIAL ELEMENTS OF TASK ACCOMPLISHMENT

The primary focus of managerial leadership as it relates to task accomplishment by subordinates is structured around performance results. In a police operation, a leader, whether managerial or supervisory, the *Elements of Task Accomplishment* involves **Controlling**, **Management**, **Obtaining Followship**, and **Command Execution**. Each of these elements integrate into a *leadership style*. However, for the purpose of diagnosing the components of managerial action in obtaining desired results, each will be reviewed separately.

The most common approach to analyzing managerial elements, as they pertain to task accomplishments, is to review individual leadership traits. Such an assessment suggests that inherent personality attributes may be the basis for the effectiveness of the previously identified leadership traits. These traits are not considered by this author as inherent personality attributes. They are learned skills that can be enhanced or improved upon. There is little doubt that charisma or intelligence is inherent and that they can have an effect on a leader's ability to *obtain followership*. But the traits, as noted previously, are all qualities which focus principally on enhanced leadership skills. Some leadership trainers have expressed a contention that a majority of potential leadership attributes are inherent. Such a claim seems to devalue the need to train individuals to assume leadership roles in the absence of certain inherent traits. The clear implication of the "**Inherent Theory of Leadership**" is that we should devise a method of identifying and assessing leadership potential during infancy rather than providing leader development training later in life.

As stated previously by this author, **effective leaders are made, not born**. In other words, the effectiveness of a leader is learned and, as such, is not solely dependent upon certain inborn qualities. Certain qualities such as shyness, timidness, and intelligence can be a hindrance to an effective leader should he or she be unable to learn how to perform exclusive of such inborn traits. Intelligence should not be considered a trait in the sense of the others that were identified, because the inborn lack of a certain level of intelligence is the same as being born with some other form of handicap. It means the individual must learn to utilize other personal attributes to compensate for the missing or the limited bodily function. If a person is unable to learn and execute the skills of leadership, then he or she cannot be a leader. But intelligence aside, it is believed that other inborn hindrances can be overcome through personal efforts and training. It is contended that, for example, shyness in a person can be overcome and the person can be taught to function overtly, thus averting shyness as a hindrance to job performance. This author was a very shy person, but in recognizing this early in life, I took every opportunity to address or interact before groups of people. I started with small groups at first, friends whom I personally knew, and then I was able to work my way up to teaching seminars on a national basis, etc. This is not to say that every shy person or those with some other inborn hindrance can overcome the problem, but it does illustrate that traits normally associated with leadership can be learned. The managerial traits previously identified and concluded by a number of leadership theorists need to be discussed in terms of their relatedness to task accomplishment by a positional leader.

1. **Controlling** is concept of leadership. It refers to controlling the behavior of others in guiding the successful achievement of desired goals and objectives. Controlling as a term in leadership is recognized as *the ability and authority to enforce action.* Enforcement in any type of leadership mode means power, power to mandate action, through both potential sanctions or inspiration. Both are incentives that are primary to a leader's authority to enforce subordinate action. The idea of controlling and use of authority by a leader can generate conceptual differences when analyzing *behavior control* as an enforcement concern. Frequently, the impact of leadership authority has been considered confusing when viewing the overall concept of managerial power within an organizational setting. It is clear that the idea of power and authority are closely akin to the concept of managerial leadership. *A police mid-level manager must realize that he or she is a managerial leader within the organizational structure. Any individual may be considered a leader if he or she has the responsibility for the work performance of others. However, the individual is then recognized as a component of the managerial leadership of the organization.* Some authors in the field of management indicate that power, authority, influence, directing, and controlling abilities are indistinct when viewed as leadership concept or trait.

It should be remembered, whether *managerial control* is termed power, authority, or influence, that the use of such controls is a leadership resource, which may or may not be used. The exercise of controlling authority, positionally placed, could possibly assure achievement of desired objectives by subordinates. Thus, simply stated, controlling may be termed behavioral influence of others. It is power that allows a primary supervisor or middle manager to enforce compliance of subordinates toward task accomplishment.

2. **Management** is a broad concept that has to do with allocation of resources, both human and logistical, for task accomplishment. It is considered a more precise designation of directing subordinates than leadership. Management is believed to be specific in nature and focus is concerning the accomplishment of goals. Success or failure of an organization to achieve its goals and objectives can usually be traced to the effectiveness of managers. The management of human resources is a difficult task and should most often be situationally based. The three styles of management that are best known to use and in which most performance theories concerning leadership are based are: (1) Autocratic, (2) Participatory, and (3) Free Rein. Each of these styles has previously been articulated in this text. Rensis Likert, in his writings during the 1950s, indicated that *to appropriately evaluate an organization's management and its managers the process should emphasize a consideration of the entity's use of both human and logistical resources.* Perceptually, the control processes for decision making is generally focused at the upper management levels of the organization. Authority and control, like communication, typically flow down the organization's structure through a formalized process. Thus, it can be said that the organizational management as a component of the **Managerial Elements of Task Accomplishment** is an integrated and formalized process.

Ideally, there is a degree of interaction between management and functional-level workers. This usually induces worker motivation through participation and involvement in establishing the element's goals and objectives. Also, there is a greater degree of perceptual responsibility and accomplishment at all levels of the organization. The mid-level police manager's role as perceived by most upper organizational leaders revolve around: (1) *production of workers, establishing and implementation of performance actions;* (2) *creativity in the development of practical processes at the functional level;* and (3) *the interaction of his or her elements with other components of the organization.*

3. **Obtaining Followership** is generally identified as leadership; it refers to a characteristic or trait that's traditionally associated with the theory of classical management. The characteristic being referred to is the defining and articulating of the *purpose* and the providing of *motivation (incentives)* for subordinates' performances. In order to focus and clarify followership as a component part of the **Managerial Elements of Task Accomplishment**, it is necessary to discuss both purpose and *motivation* as each applies to management/leadership in the aforementioned context.

A. **Purpose**: An effective managerial leader in an organization depends on how knowledgeable he/she may be of the importance the middle manager's role is in the accomplishment of overall goals and ob jectives. The primary area of knowledge being referred to is the aim or desired intent of the organization in providing goods and services. Within an organization, as objectives or targets are developed, there should be a corresponding change in priorities to match the alterations. The majority of the changes occur most noticeably at the middle police managerial level of the organization. The police mid-level manager must also project future performance needs of subordinates in order to plan strategies to meet the anticipated requirements. All managers and leaders in an organization need a functional knowledge of the entity's goals and objectives, as well as a comprehensive awareness of his/her element's purpose in contributing to the overall task accomplishment of his/her element's purpose within an organization's structure, he or she cannot effectively motivate subordinates to achieve desired expectation.

B. **Motivation**: Fostering employees' performances to meet expectations through a process of positive and/or negative incentives is a general definition of motivation. Motivation as a management or leadership term most typically involves *incentives, fear,* or *inspiration* to obtain desired employee performance. But as noted by many theorists in the field of management, **motivation is an internalized process**. Thus, motivation of workers is not wholly accurate, because a leader can only initiate action or provide inducements to obtain responses based on incentives or sanctions; therefore, a leader cannot truly motivate subordinates. In other words, motivation from a purely clinical perspective is a behavioral attitude. And, as is generally recognized, attitudes are not readily changed by incentives or sanctions. Incentives and/or sanctions can alter actions and reactions by a person to a situation or object, but the internal feeling, bias, or attitude may not change. For example, the various civil rights acts have provided sanctions to prevent certain biased job actions. We recognized certain overt prejudice acts have been reduced, but it is also realized that the predisposed negative attitudes that fostered the past behaviors have not been altered. However, in order not to deviate too far from the generally held notion that leadership actions can motivate job performances, the text will utilize behavior influences and motivations as interchangeable concepts.

Therefore, in using behavioral action inducements and motivation interchangeably, the theories of Maslow, Herzberg, and Argyris can be utilized to interrelate the concept to Managerial Elements of Task Accomplishments. The classical view of motivation as a performance producer in workers relates to a leader's ability to use personal behavioral actions to generate desired subordinate responses. Workers generally differ in many respects, such as desire to perform and personal expectations. Thus, it becomes the obligatory responsibility of a middle manager to direct and coordinate individual employees' job behaviors into a pattern that will produce the desired task accomplishment. Only when a managerial leader comprehends and adequately uses motivation (performance inducements) as it relates to subordinates' job actions can he/she be considered effective.

4. **Command Execution** is synonymous with the use of leadership power or authority to induce job behaviors. It is recognized that command execution, as an enforcement tool of management, needs to be clearly defined. Workers, by tradition, will accept and cooperate with a leader's use of power to command action. The organizational structure and operational philosophy should be delineated to all employees in a manner that clarifies positional authority of its leaders. Leaders at all levels of the organization need to be aware of which areas and decisions he or she is responsible for. Likewise, the leaders must be knowledgeable of which functions and/or obligations are beyond their scope of authority. The responsible leader in a command execution situation should (1) *know what performance objective needs to be accomplished by subordinates;* (2) *establish or develop a method to achieve desired results by subordinates;* and (3) *identify the operational limits within which both the leader and subordinates must function.* Therefore, it can be inferred that command execution is the scope of authority exercised by a leader in an organizational setting. Police managers and leaders should assure that command execution is authorized for performance at the lowest possible level that it can effectively be administered. In other words, **Micro-Managing** by upper-level managers or leaders is usually wasteful of time and resources. It also typically adds unnecessary bureaucracy to an already overburdened system.

Task accomplishment is generally focused around operational goals and performance standards. The basic composition of an element's makeup and interaction with other organizational components are essential to effective task accomplishment. The leader or manager needs to possess some job knowledge in order to effectively direct job performance of subordinates.

There is a level of tenure required by a leader to be appropriately respected by subordinates and to be able to efficiently appraise their job performance.

SYNOPSIS

It is clear from all the foregoing information that **Effective Leadership of Functional Level Employees** is the primary reason for the existence of a mid-level police manager in an organization. And, it is also true that the overall effectiveness toward the accomplishment of organizational goals and objectives depends on how well the mid-level police manager handles functional employees through primary leadership. In our brief look at several of the more noted areas that a motivational leadership such as a mid-level police manager is confronted with in his/her directing of subordinate personnel, we have attempted to examine organizational behavior as well as individual task accomplishments of the leader. Inasmuch as we have taken a comprehensive look at the basic considerations of mid-level leadership to gain an insight into what makes an effective leader, the text of this chapter has focused on the technical and practical aspects of leadership by a mid-level police manager. The position of leadership held by the mid-level leader or secondary managers of an organization places the individual in a situation of moral obligation to adhere strictly to the highest standards of integrity and honor that is expected of subordinates. These high standards are expected of managers at all levels of the organization, as well as primary supervisors and functional-level subordinates. The formal leader's moral code must be above contention, as personal behavioral conduct will be evaluated under *what actually occurs, as well as what may be perceived by others.*

It goes almost without saying that the task performance of a mid-level police manager obligates the individual to provide leadership and direction to his or her subordinates. Basic responsibility is defined as an obligation of a secondary leader to perform specific duties associated with the organizationally assigned position. Job responsibility infers that the tasks delegated to others do not release the delegating police leader or secondary manager of the accountability to get the job done. Simply stated, an assignment responsibility of a mid-level police manager is a required task. A required task of every managerial leader is to provide direction and guidance for the employees under his or her scope of authority. To be a good and effective managerial leader, the individual must have the qualities of *persuasiveness, intelligence, flexibility,* and *good judgment.* These qualities are all traits and characteristics that aren't necessarily hereditary but can be learned or developed. Every mid-level police manager has a primary responsibility to enforce the rules of the organization. The managerial leader should also provide the subordinates with the opportunity for personal growth and professional development. Further, the secondary- or mid-level leader should strive to overcome the personal traits of leadership weaknesses that hamper the effective performance of him or her as a organizational manager. Additionally, most of the leadership responsibilities of a secondary-level manager have been identified as qualities inherent to the position.

Chapter Eight

LOGICAL INFERENCES
(JUDGMENTAL ACTIONS)

Judgmental actions as a dimensional trait characteristic of a positional leader in general and a police manager in particular is a frequently used term. But even with all of its recognizability as an essential component of leadership, there are few texts that definitively discuss it as a distinct character trait. The use of the term **judgment** is a misnomer when talking about the positive aspects of managerial leadership. **Good judgment** is the more recognizable terminology phrase that appropriately conveys the desired leadership characteristic that is being referred to. For the purposes of our discussion, **judgment** and **logical inferences** will be used interchangeably as the dimensional component, inasmuch as they are synonymous. Good judgment or logical inference as a positive trait of police management is defined as **the demonstrated ability of a leader to make assumptions and/or render decisions that are fundamentally appropriate for the situation based on accurate information that is reflective of factual data**. The above definition just about says it all in terms of effective logical inference as a critical component of operational management. What has been stated is that common sense and sound perceptions should be used in making a decision or determining a course of action. **Common sense** should not be considered synonymous with the exercise of good judgment, because it is basically an intellectual attribute rather than a behavioral trait.

Positive judgment displayed by an operational police manager has to do with the **feasibility of achieving an objective**. In order to gain a true perspective as to the essential nature of effective logical inference during our introductory probe into it as a favorable trait characteristic of managerial leadership, we will look at **feasibility** as a **core element** of this dimension. Primarily, in determining usage possibility, the leader must first assess whether the desired objective and/or proposed action is consistent with the basic goals of the department. Implementation of incompatible procedures or rendering decisions that are contrary to establish organizational policies would be counterproductive and considered poor judgment. Further, because most leaders do not operate in a vacuum, it is necessary that planned actions be conducive to the coordinated efforts of other departmental elements. Also, the proposed action must be appropriate to deal with the concern and have a logical chance for effectively being completed. It does no good to implement an action that falls short of accomplishing its objective or cannot be adequately performed by subordinates, etc. From this, it is easy to perceive why **feasibility** is the **core** of good judgment and that it aids in the transcending of merely adequate performances, particularly noticeable in the accomplishment of short-term goals and objectives.

As noted in other texts on the subject, a manager's logical inferences are usually very apparent and thus much more subject to scrutiny because of their visibility and effect on operational consequences. Assessment of a leader's dimensional skills in this dimensional trait characteristic is inherently difficult because of the varying nature of operational responsibility and the level of organizational components that his or her actions may affect. Therefore, there may be conflicting evaluations on the effectiveness or quality of an operational manager's judgmental skills. Line leadership or subordinates may feel the actions showed poor judgment because it negatively affected functional morale, while upper management could perceive it as positive because of its adherence to established departmental policy. Like most dimensional traits discussed in this text, a single display of illogical inference will not typically be detrimental to a manager's career, but it could seriously damage the individual's perceived capability in the eyes of upper management if the poor judgment was critical or perceptually harmful to the department. Thus, no matter what the decision to be made or the action to be taken, an operational police manager should give his or her response due consideration in order that a logical inference will be rendered.

Managerial judgment is a characteristic that is often used when assessing an individual for a leadership role. The term does not seem to surface much in the individual's daily operation, unless a mistake or improper action is taken. Then, the manager's evaluation and judgmental assessment was poor, thus resulting in the inappropriate action. It's no small wonder that the evaluation of a potential leader's judgment is considered so important that many departments tend to assess the individual's entire behavioral performance to determine his or her skills in this dimensional area. When viewed from the perspective of a person's entire job performance, it's a collective trait that sort of encompasses and functionalizes all of the other dimensional characteristics of a positional leader. Logical inference or good judgment is not a particular trait that is unique to operational management; it's an art that's practiced at every level of the organization. All leadership actions depend upon some type of information assessment that results in a logical inference. Obviously, a leader's judgment is not the only factor employed when taking action, but since it's usually a prime element, it may be given credit for the decision. If the occurrence was positive, then it was a good judgment, but if the action taken turns out not so well, then a negative display of this trait was demonstrated. We realize that one decision is not a true assessment and should not be considered a descriptive indication of the leader's skill level in this dimension, but the reality is that it will affect the general perception of the individual.

Logical inferences generally will have an effect on much more than the determination of a decision; it also tends to influence our perception of the quality of the course of action. It is said to be somewhat of a controlling element in the implementation of actions and the resulting product. A resolutive conclusion aids in focusing the direction of action; however, it will not guarantee completion; neither will a comprehensive assessment or the exercise of what we may term **good judgment**. As previously indicated, logical inferences is a product of the situation, one that is typically a collection of all of the dimensional trait characteristics of a positional leader. It is virtually impossible to determine beforehand which trait area will be responsible in a particular situation or set of circumstances. An individual's judgment, good or bad, is a consequence of a number of complicated mental factors that usually defy clear delineation. This lack of comprehension of the logical inference process is not a detriment to managerial action. Common sense and perceptual use of information taken in will often result in the exercise of good judgment by those so inclined. Inappropriate judgmental actions by an operational police manager are generally a result of limited time frames and an inability to effectively assess adequate information. Primarily, **logical inferences** has been said to be a pairing of factual information with the perceptual morals of the decision maker and the personal evaluation of the leader's performance choices.

An introductory examination of logical inferences as a critical and important leadership trait can't be concluded without it being made clear that simply because judgmental actions are considered a psychological process does not imply a correlation of mental ability. In other words, very intelligent leaders can and will make some poor judgments, and conversely, persons with limited scholastic aptitude can display surprising logical inferences. The reverse of the previous statements are also true and admittedly often a fact. Intellect is a mental quality that may be given much of the credit for a manager's knowledge acquisition from which a judgment can be rendered and thus an appropriate decision. It is also a psychological procedure that is used to process acquired informational knowledge by assimilating their meaning. Therefore, it becomes obvious that knowledge is more an acquisition of factual information than an inherent mental capability. Basically, a person's perceived mental intellect is an ability to translate obtained data into comprehendible morals and/or useful information. It may be these ethical choices that hinder a significant correlation between a person's intelligence quotient (IQ) and his or her effectiveness in making logical inferences.

INFLUENCES ON LOGICAL INFERENCES

The fact that most people, whether they are in a leadership position or not, tend to exercise a great deal of logical inference implies that the process is not uncommon unless negatively influenced. The influences will oftentimes dominate a person's better judgment and result in a course of action that is not considered a logical inference. This text will review several of these influences and their effect on an operational police manager's good judgment.

Pressures that Affect Logical Inferences

The pressures of time frame allotment, management desires, etc. can be a hindrance to perceived good judgment. An operational police manager has to respond to the events or circumstances that provoke the exercise of choices, as well as the pressures that are ever-present in organizations. Some psychologists and several social scientists tell us that in order to make sound and practical decisions that are perceived as logical inferences, a positional leader needs to be confident and at-ease, because rendering an appropriate decision requires a cool deliberation of the facts. As with all mental processes that a person performs, when a judgmental action is contemplated, it undergoes a filtration through the individual's intellectual system. This filtration process may noticeably alter the course of action to be taken. For example, an operational police manager responds to the scene of an accident that's two or three blocks from a hospital. The victim is bleeding profusely and the functional leadership and officers at the scene are having a difficult time stemming the blood flow. An ambulance had been summoned via police radio but indicated that it would require approximately 10 to 15 minutes before it could arrive at the scene due to environmental factors. The operational manager at the scene made a judgmental decision to have the victim transported to the nearby hospital via police vehicle, even though established procedures say "the victims of accidents, etc. will be provided first responder aid and maintained at the scene until the arrival of ambulance paramedics." The pressures that are in play in this scenario are plain and the positional leader's actions were clearly dictated by the time frame pressure of the ambulance's E.T.A. (estimated time of arrival) and the victim's possible loss of life because of excessive bleeding. The same principles apply when an operational police manager's superior wants something in a given amount of time. The leader's actions will be affected by **what** the superior wants and **when** she or he wants it. Independent judgmental actions will be limited to operating within the parameters forced by these pressures. If a manager allows the stress of these pressures to agitate him or her to the point of emotional distress, then the cool and calm deliberation needed to render a good judgment is lost. Increased feelings of aggravation confuses the mental filtration process that correlates information and may cause decisive actions to be taken for emotional reasons rather than a factual assessment.

The ebb and flow of human emotions are not a constant and thus may exert limited influence on judgmental decisions, if the operational police manager is aware of them. The conflict of the mental pressures that may negatively effect an action can be controlled if the manager will allow time for the tensions produced to decrease. The human constitution is a unique entity, inasmuch as the longer a person lives with a pressure or stress, the less influence it will exert on the individual's intellectual processes. Obviously, we are not talking about stresses or anxieties that result in a physical malady. Generally, a person's mental adaptability will permit the individual to cope with or resign personal self to a fact that cannot be changed. This allows him or her to form a conscious capability to function around the stress-producing problem. This author is aware of an experience that clearly illustrates this point. In the mid-1960s, a soldier received orders while on active military duty to respond to an army post in the Midwest to prepare for assignment to a combat zone in Viet Nam. Initially, when the orders were received and for several weeks thereafter, anxiety and apprehension caused emotional stress and/or distress at the possibilities. However, because the military move of the infantry division he was assigned to was delayed several additional weeks, he mentally adjusted to the fact that the assignment was coming. After his acceptance of the move as a fact, most of the anxiety that had filled those early days dissipated and a sort of anticipation took its place. Needless to say that during the early days when anxiety and apprehension were at their peak, his logical inferences were somewhat affected by the mental pressures. A police manager will not always enjoy the luxury of allowing time for an ebbing of emotional stresses pressures. Therefore, through practice and a concentrated effort the individual must train him- or herself to act exclusive of the internal and external pressures. The pressures cannot or should not be completely overlooked if their influence will affect what is desired or appropriate for dealing with the concern. There are several factors that are principally the cause of the pressures and stresses that we have been discussing. The following text identifies five of these very pertinent influences.

1. **Physical Factors**. These are real and/or tangible obstacles that produce a limited duration of emotional influence on a leader's ability to make what is termed a logical inference. If the obstacles are controllable or can be manipulated by the positional leader making the decision, then their effect on good judgment can be minimal. But if the barriers are transfixed and cannot be altered or easily bypassed, they may have a more lasting effect. These static objects are called **stationary physical factors**. The stationary physical factors will have only a temporary effect; as previously noted, the positional leader will normally adapt to the uncorrectable impairments. Typically, once these adaptations are made the supposed "bad judgments" will cease, that is, of course, if the manager's logical inferences were not faulty for other reasons.

Physical factors affecting logical inferences during job performance may be the result of environmental conditions, actual structural objects, logistical considerations, disease or illness, physical fatigue, and a host of other elements. As is readily discernible from the physical factors identified, each may have at least a short-term effect on individual judgment. Some, depending on their permanency, can have a lasting effect on a leader's logical inference ability. Environmental conditions, such as weather, location, etc., can surely influence the parameters and speed with which a course of action is decided upon. Structural barriers most assuredly will alter a proposed planned consideration, such as availability of equipment and funds for operational functions. These will influence a police manager's choices, thus affecting judgmental decisions. Sickness, injury, and handicaps are realities in modern police operations, inasmuch as public laws tell us that we cannot discriminate in hiring on the basis of physical abnormalities alone. Fatigue or physical tiredness on the part of the leader makes his or her stress tolerance much lower and will therefore affect the individual's ability to render logical inferences. Physical fatigue also impairs our ability to concentrate and to reason; the loss of either of these capabilities will hamper sound judgmental decisions and/or actions.

These are but a few of the physical factors that may influence logical inferences. However, a recognition of these factors as potential detriments, and that mental or emotional compensation is needed for them by a positional leader, will aid in negating their effect. Adjustments for these factors alone does not guarantee the exercise of good judgment on the part of an operational manager. As stated, logical inferences are not a giveaway; they are usually arrived at through cool and calm deliberation over the facts and influences affecting a situation. But, as originally stated, physical factors are but one of the pertinent influences that affect the manager's dimensional trait characteristic of good judgment.

2. **Anger**. Hostile emotions or anger is defined as a strong reaction of displeasure over a situation or event that usually is displayed in antagonistic behavior. It is an eruption of a person's temper in a negative reaction. The anger that is generated may be held in check or there may be an explosive display of temper. Either way, the leader's reasoning ability is impaired, thus exerting a hindering influence on judgmental actions. Exerted anger is like any other bad habit; the more often the person allows him- or herself a display of temper, the greater the frequency with which it will occur. Our discussion earlier about fatigue as a factor that can and will affect a person's emotional state of mind and will in turn alter his or her deliberation ability correlates with anger. Temperament and displays of temper are synonymous and is an important element in the way that a positional leader will respond. Some social scientists have said that behavioral displays of temper are inherited and is thus difficult to alter. However, the general consensus, with which the author concurs, is that the display of temper or anger is controllable through concentrated effort and practice, and that logical inferences cannot be assured if a manager allows his or her actions to be influenced by hostile emotions.

In an organizational setting, it is apparent that a display of an eruptive temperament is harmful to a positional leader's effectiveness as an operational manager. Both subordinates and superiors will lose respect for the person's ability to react logically in heated situations and that personal emotions will rule the individual's decisions. Guidance or control of subordinates and situations is a primary factor in considering the effectiveness of a manager. However, it is a natural assumption that if the individual cannot control their self, then how can they be expected to control others? Anger as an influence on logical inference produces some concern, in that it will adversely affect a manager's judgmental actions. Emotional response will often cause the person to bypass obvious logical reactions in favor of less appropriate temperamental ones. Hostile temperament will more than likely form a barrier that blocks the normal cool and calm deliberation of factual information. This fixation of thought process will result in many resolutive avenues of actions being hindered by the monopoly of vindictive behavior.

A positional leader cannot allow personal indulgences in hostile or aggressive behavior brought on by anger to hamper his or her exercise of logical inferences. A person initially cannot stop from becoming angered over a situation or event that is displeasing, but the individual can control what reaction manifests itself. A period of time to allow physical arousals to subside will reduce irrational or emotional reactions that may be considered bad judgment under the circumstances. A concentrated effort and practice will enable eliminating explosive eruptions or temper. When anger is controlled in an operational manager, another factor that tends to negatively influence logical inferences on the part of a positional leader has been neutralized.

3. **Frustration**. Frustration, as does other physical factors, hinders an operational police manager's ability to make logical inferences because of the distress and/or anxiety created. Although the feeling of frustration is more akin to **anger** when considering its effect on the mental process of decision making, frustration typically manifests itself in expressions of aggravated behavior, but it is also not uncommon for **apathy** or a **resignation** that failure is assured. An effective operational manager will not allow barriers or setbacks to arouse a defeated attitude when confronted by a seemingly unattainable solution to a problem. Behavioral psychologists have indicated that frustration creates the same type of emotional blockages as does anger and should be dealt with in a similar manner. In other words, frustration is basically displaced anger.

Frustration is almost a natural occurrence in the logical inference process of positional leaders of a police department. Operational police managers and their superiors are typically goal-oriented and high-achievers as is evident by their level of advancement. So when obstacles develop that negatively influence objective accomplishment, it is not out of place for these individuals to feel some level of frustration. It is the manner in which they deal with the frustrations and the level of influence that are allowed to affect judgmental actions that determines the manager's effectiveness in this trait area. The well-informed and mentally prepared leader knows that barriers and problems appearing to have no solution will arise from time to time. The operational manager also is aware that his or her performance behavior must compensate for these factors and work around them. At the same time, an operational police manager must realize that his or her challenge in dealing with frustrated feelings should be to recognize and make accommodation for them.

Most effective operational police managers realize that there is no magical or surefire way to avoid some form of frustration in his or her job performance. However, the more successful and productive operational managers will deal with frustration as an anticipated aspect of day-to-day job performance. Job frustrations can be a consequence of too many tasks in too short a time frame, barriers to satisfactory assignment completion, unreasonable demands of actions, and numerous other situations. An acceptance that perfection or successful conclusions to concerns are not always possible will enable an operational manager to deal with these natural frustrations and to use a rational approach to rendering logical inferences where necessary.

4. **Unfamiliarity**. A lack of knowledge about an event or situation is one of the surest ways of imposing a negative influence on a person's use of good judgment, because how can an operational manager or any positional leader be expected to provide a logical inference regarding a matter when that individual lacks a total perspective of what the situation involves. The mental pressures of reacting in the "dark" amount to a **best-guess approach**. Thus, regarding lack-of-knowledge decisions, most leaders will tell you that they are typically ineffective and that poor judgmental actions are usually the result in such cases. A leader new to an operation will generally require a great deal of repeat information and will typically install his or her own style of administrative action. This is usually done to compensate for or combat the lack of knowledge that he or she initially has regarding the operation or situation.

An unfamiliar awareness of the specific circumstances of a concern creates a natural tentativeness, and this conjectural perception sets up an anxiety that affects a leader's emotional state. As previously noted, a confused or distressed mental process will dramatically influence an operational police manager's exercise of good judgment. This should be considered a surety, because factual information that is comprehensive and accurate must be available before a leader can demonstrate a reasonableness of choices in selecting any alternatives. Unfamiliarity has a double-edged influence when considering negative factors that affect logical inferences. First, because good choices can't be made in the dark (meaning without adequate knowledge), there is a **strangeness** about the concern that prevents what we may term good judgment. Second, clarity of circumstances is essential, referring to the fact that without a comprehensive knowledge, there is an unfamiliarity, which fosters confused mental processes. As may be evident, the **double-edged sword of unfamiliarity** is plainly a factor that must be eliminated if an operational police manager's judgment is to be considered positive.

A knowledge awareness that eliminates the unknown has always been a critical element to man. The uncertainty and apprehension that surrounds a lack of clear understanding has delayed many potential positive benefits to mankind over the years. This me principle of information requirements exists for a leader who has to make a choice. Generally, it is logical to assume that an experienced operational manager with reasonable intelligence can make a guesstimation relative to most job-related events or situations encountered and be correct about 80+ percent of the time. Obviously, a guesstimation cannot be considered a good judgment method of decision making. Further, being correct in deciding a course of action only 80 percent or so of the time is not sufficient for an effective positional leader.

5. **Fear**. Fear or apprehension as a pertinent influence factor in an operational police manager's demonstration of logical inferences is closely related to unfamiliarity, because unfamiliarity will typically generate apprehension that most assuredly will affect the exercise of good judgment. Fear can cause a distortion of facts, which may result in some confusion and thereby prevent an effective display of perceived logical inferences. Being afraid of failure or to take a risk on an unproven idea can be a detriment to the exercise of good judgment. The positional leader may be apprehensive that a proposed course of action will adversely affect his or her superiors' perception of individual abilities. A fearful leader will typically stick to conservative methods that may be less risky to perceived career opportunities, even though the individual may know it is not the best approach to handling a concern. This is an exercise of less than good judgment, because it is known not to be the best approach. However, fear is the most common factor that exists today in most organizations and which negatively influences the demonstration of good judgment.

Many modern scholars in the areas of leadership and management recognize that **fear** in the work place is the most potent incentive of all. Whether it is a fear of losing one's position or the loss of prestige, it's a motivator that must be considered and dealt with if a positional leader is to be effective. Fear as an influence factor is just as applicable to a police department as to a manufacturing plant and to the positional leaders. The term **expectation** when used as a justification for not deviating from the norm in order to improve performance is an indication of fear. Before we talked about time frames and superiors' desires as actual influences on logical inferences, they too represent a form of instilled fear to judgmental actions. The concession to the pressures that they present is a form of giving-in to fear, which may be a negative influence on the operational police manager's exercise of good judgment.

It tends to be easy for a positional leader at any level of the organization to acquiesce to the pressure of fear associated with judgmental actions, traditionally dictated by personal risks, and instead rely on the traditional aspects of expectancy and expediency as justification in an organizational setting. However, over the long term, a police manager must be aware that the perception of his or her ajudged actions will be on results and not on the why. Therefore, to be an effective leader, a manager must be willing to put individual prestige, etc., on the line by doing what is known or perceived to be best. As indicated, effective leadership requires a certain amount of risk and the courage to put decisions to the test. Managerial and leadership skills are traditionally measured from a dimensional trait characteristic perspective. Thus, if a leader is to be evaluated regarding effectiveness of job performance, then his or her logical inferences must be reviewed and a proper evaluation of the judgmental actions must be considered.

DISPLAYING DESIRED JUDGMENTAL ACTIONS

Judgment is basically a rationality of decisions and actions based on quantifying factors. Concerning a leader's job actions, both rational and irrational influences play a part in any decision-making process. The degree in which the decided-upon action may be considered rational will depend on its effectiveness and the feasibility of carrying it out. The rationality of any decision is clearly tied to the consideration given to the consequences of the action and the availability of positive alternatives. Rational is another term that can and often is used as a synonym for judgment. More often than is usually anticipated, the extent to which an operational police manager's judgmental action corresponds exactly with departmental goals will depend on the degree to which the organization's objectives relate to the individual's desires.

When the text refers to rationality of action and consideration of consequences, it is equating and/or interjecting the personal assumptions of an operational manager into the exercise of judgmental actions, the reality of which is that a logical inference of a course of action is nothing more than an assumption based on, hopefully, appropriate information. But in attempting to analyze how and what a perceived logical inference can be made by a positional leader, we should not overlook the fact that an abundance of information may not on all occasions be available. In the cases where more information is desired but unavailable, the operational manager should project data based on at-hand facts and their indicated trend. This projection is similar to **hedging**, which is defined as a minimalization of risk or error. There is no way a manager can totally eliminate **risk taking** in decision making when judgmental actions are required. But through a rational projection process where assumptions are made based on available data, negative judgmental assessment is greatly reduced.

The terms that have been used in this chapter to identify judgment clearly indicate it as a positive and demonstrable trait characteristic of an operational police manager. They also display the perceptual close correlation between logical inferences and leadership effectiveness. Thus, an inescapable conclusion must be that logical inference is primarily a job equilibrium process that an effective operational police manager should consider in all as-

"Sir, apparently here is your problem, the Breaker Switch is off."

FAILURE TO APPROPRIATELY ASSESS A SITUATION AND THE <u>CURRENT</u> CIR-CUMSTANCES BEFORE TAKING ACTION COULD PROVE INJURIOUS IN LAW ENFORCEMENT.

pects of his or her performance.

So much of what an operational police manager does is reactionary, where there is little time for contemplation and lengthy review. **Crisis management** has become almost second nature to effective police leadership in functional situations. It often seems that a police manager moves from one crisis situation to the next, rendering decisive actions based on his or her personal judgment. Policies and directives set forth by the department can't be written to cover all situations, so some judgmental actions are required. The appropriateness of an operational police manager's logical inference will depend on the influences and factors detailed earlier in this chapter. Prior experience in the handling of like or similar concerns will add to the manager's ability to have his or her actions perceived as good judgment. As a final note to our review of logical inferences (good judgment), it would not be comprehensive to conclude our discussion without acknowledging that judgmental actions can be improved through concentrated effort, experience, and knowledge acquisition. And, that there is also a possibility of an inherent quality to judgmental performance ability, just as **common sense** displays are a natural characteristic of some individuals, so too is **good judgment**.

LEADERSHIP PERSONALITY:
A MENTAL INFERENCE FROM BEHAVIOR

Trait Characteristics has been explored and discussed to some degree in an earlier chapter relative to an operational mid-level police manager's development and display of personality behaviors that are conducive to effective leadership. When we approach the consideration of managerial leadership in association with management's obligation to exercise **Good Judgment** or what is most often addressed as **Common Sense**, the focus quickly aligns itself with Logical Inferences as a prime component of an effective and efficient managerial leader's makeup. The author has concluded that it would enhance the contextual content to delve into the *psychology* of a management leader's growth in the area of his or her Judgmental Action, along with the aspects of its practical application, which was previously articulated in this chapter. To appropriately explore logical inferences from the perspective of an individual's personality, the subject area will be addressed from what is perceived as mentally the general makeup of most people, which includes managerial leaders. The text will then venture forth into what is considered the foundational basis of most judgment actions. In other word, to discuss the mental structure of people as leaders and how opinion-based actions are determined before implementation. A number of responses might be given to the question, "What is the mental composition or self-sameness of people?" The response might be based on physical appearance, emphasizing the similarities and the variations in a person's physical edifice. Consequently, there maybe a need for definitive particulars and these descriptors would depend on the nature of the observable credits that were considered significant or worthy of clarification. Such characteristic traits as physical appearance and overt behaviors should be included as aspects of the person's anatomy. Instead of bodily structure, the performance behaviors that a mid-level police manager would perform might be highlighted. Therefore, instead of describing the actual bodily structure, the identifying person should talk about the mannerism of which this individual leader is capable of exhibiting. The edifice of a person or thing generally refers to the permanent physical structure of the individual or object, whereas performance refers to what task they accomplish and how they interact, develop, or are altered.

Logical Inference when viewed from a leader's personal psychological perspective. An articulation could be set-forth that the characteristic behavior of a mid-level police manager is how an individual would generally respond in most like situations. For example, the leader may be dominant, aggressive, or optimistic depending on the circumstances. Inasmuch as a layperson generally will know little of the mental makeup of an individual or manager, there in all likelihood might be some difficulty in assessing the psychological structures and processes underlying the observed behavior. Performance behaviors such as demonstrated demeanors and communication skills should have a physical projection, and thus would be comparatively straightforward to observe in a managerial leader. It is also more difficult to recognize an individual's psychological make-up and performances that underly his or her behavior, although such a composition must exist. This is because, like most dynamic edifices, it is necessary to try to imagine what the underlying causal factor is like, due to the fact that it is not directly observable. Rather the mental composition and behaviors consist of hypothetical factors such as motives, habits, and a self-defenses posture. Any attempt to go beyond the observable behaviors to the underlying mental motivation and task processes may project an abstract view of the leader's personality as it relates to Logical Inferences.

Personality from a Logical Inference perspective is not simply how the person acts. If we say that a mid-level police manager is aggressive, we refer to an observation that he/she behaves in a pugnacious or advancing manner. By merely saying that he or she is aggressive, we are pointedly referring to the person's superficial acts without reference to the personality trait characteristics that produce them. Concerning these psychological determinants that influence a leader's Logical Inferences is the basis of what we are trying to conceptually grasp and comprehend. Because personality involves the trait characteristics that determine action, the problem is to observe and interpret these behavioral mannerisms adequately and conceptualize how they interrelate with the Judgmental Actions of an operational mid-level police manager. The problem is the same for other scientific disciplines concerned with the nature of mental behaviors. The thought processes of the reader presumed to be constant and straightforward, consequentially, it would seems fanciful to propose that this process is made up of many shifting influences that affect the psychological perception of what information that is being obtained or perceived from what the person is reading. Thus, without an internal grasp of the reader's mental make-up, we can only theorize about what information will be obtained by the person. Likewise, it would not be a stretch to conclude that a person's mental makeup and the effect of external influences will garner differing Judgmental Actions from different managerial leaders, inasmuch as each individual's personality and informational background will vary in one form or another. These should be considered practical consequences of speculations about the basic foundation of Logical Inferences, which are commonplace.

Like most actions that are first conceptualized as to their results, the judgmental behaviors aforementioned can be viewed in a similar way; human performances can be understood by theorizing the existence of certain supposed situations that can never be tangibly viewed. A clear example of this is the concept of motivation. No one can observe a motive directly. It is not a scientific or measurable condition of a person's makeup, although it may depend to some degree on body chemistry, which is generally not gauged in relationship to human task performance. Judgmental action is a conception of what is best at the time given the circumstances and the situation. But even though it is an action that is not a tangible or solid object, never-the-less, the result of conducive Logical Inferences have observable effects. For example, a person crossing the desert is perceived or inferred to be thirsty if he or she has gone without watery fluid for a given period and if the individual's behavior is evidently directed toward obtaining a drink of water. The presence of the thirsty motive is not an unscientific concept merely because the desire for water cannot be directly observed.

Logical Inference can be deduced from its causes and effects. Since characteristics of personality can be known only from their directly observable behavioral actions in given situational circumstances, the performance demeanor must somehow be observed in the person in order to study his or her judgment personality. Such deportment develops naturally out of traditional job behaviors and situations. If the behavioral action has occurred previously, it can be determined through inquiries or other past informational knowledge. Or, the knowledge acquisition can be obtained by observing the leader's behavior in specific situations in order to create a basis of inference about what the individual's judgmental action will be in a particular circumstance. The assessment of an operational mid-level police manager's personality traits and performance characteristics will continuously be discussed in considerable detail, throughout this text, as they relate to the impact of Logical Inference on job behaviors. It is sufficient at this juncture to bring to focus that there are a variety of behavioral actions, which serve as sources of information concerning the personality. If we endeavor to introspectively determine more about an operational mid-level police manager's personality and what influences or perceptions will affect the judgment actions of a managerial leader, as well as what motives or procedures he or she will follow to solve a problem, we need only be aware of past affecting pressures and subsequent actions. A unique feature of man as an object of study is his or her ability to articulate unseen perceptual concerns that will mentally influence his or her judgmental behaviors. This capability for introspection also provides an opportunity for the individual managerial leader to recognize the influence of certain external factors and thus, allows him or her to adjust personal Logical Inferences to accommodate for the undesired impact of the particular stimulus. It must be clearly understood that introspective views shared by managerial leaders or any persons doing a self-analysis are not always true indicators of reality of an individual. Because we as human beings have one concept of ourselves and the world or the actions we take in certain situations may indicate something totally different. But highly significant insightful information can be gained from the perspective shared by the person. Thus, we should consider that if the introspective report is taken literally to express inner mental or personality processes, it is sometimes misleading, either because the internal distorted view does not tell what is really taking place or, for some reason, he or she does not feel comfortable with telling the whole truth. Either the processes that are actually occurring are not available for a true introspective analysis, or the person may wish to portray his or her experience so as to present him or herself totally in a more positive light. Thus, the use of introspective analysis regarding Judgment Actions by an operational mid-level police manager must be tempered with the realization that it does not always provide an accurate indication of internal motivations and effects, and it must be augmented with other information, which can help in the process of determining a true Logical Inferences portrait of the individual.

To thoroughly explore introspective analysis of a leader's Logical Inferences and an individual's self-perception when providing an insightful articulation of his or her personal examination, we should view this from the perspective in which a Judgment Decision was made. For example, consider the situation where some time in the past the manager decided on a judgmental action, and later it was learned that not all the influence factors were available at the time the action was taken, thus the leader's performance was revealed as inappropriate to deal with the real situation. Consequentially, he or she was personally embarrassed, which became known to the organization's leadership and peers. And, even though the information about the inadequacy of the influence data was made known and the individual leader's commenting that the misjudgment was not his or her fault and that he would not let this affect personal judgmental action in the future, we all recognize this is not wholly true. Even though the individual leader and others recognize that no misstep would have been made if the information had been correct and complete, it is not reality to believe that this will not affect his or her judgment actions in the future. If we examine the psychological aspects of what could be perceived from an individual's personal concept and motivation, a leader's introspective reporting of his or her view of personal behaviors and possible future effects will quite probably differ significantly from other knowledgeable persons providing an insightful analysis. If the introspective verbal report from the leader is taken at face value, it indicates that he or she is not overly concerned about the misstep that it was caused by the inadequate information upon which the Judgment Action was based and whatever loss of creditability the manager may garner. But such an interpretation fails to be realistic in the face of his/her feeling the need to let it be known about the inadequate information primarily received and the verbal expression that this will not have an effect in the future. This reminds us of the poetic saying, the person "does protest too much." In spite of statements to the contrary, the mid-level police manager appears more than a little concerned with the misstep from the misinformation and the subsequent judgment action. It can be anticipated that in the future the individual will not as readily make judgmental decisions and may in all likelihood require addition verification of received information. This adjustment in Judgmental Actions has been referred to as **"reaction formulation."** The combination of probable future embarrassment caused by behavioral actions and the comments of explanation that included a denial of concern reflects to a different interpretation about the feelings than would be obtained by simply taking his or her introspective analysis at face value. Quite likely, anxiety is a more probable reaction, which would be reasonably expected, even though the police manager providing the introspective analysis is unlikely to admit it.

The content of his or her comments may clearly indicate that the mid-level police manager is overly upset or concerned. However, the behavioral reactions that this text is projecting clearly reflect that the person is dealing with some degree of discomfort over inappropriate judgment action. It is from just such contradictions that Logical Inferences about psychological processes such as *defense posturing* are made. In this defense posturing, the person is believed to be attempting to deceive him- or herself and others about a personal feeling of peril that would accompany a judgmental misstep. Such a personal deceptions is a self-protecting concept that is present in all of us to one degree or another. It is important to note that a denial of distress and the *reaction formulation* establish the sorts of none tangible processes referred to earlier in the text's articulation of personality relative to Logical Inferences and job behaviors.

SYNOPSIS

The more appropriate expression of what may be most desired as a leadership characteristic for an operational police manager is good judgment or logical inference, rather than just **judgment** as a measurable trait of management. A comprehensive view of positive judgment by a police manager indicates that feasibility may be considered the **core** of good judgment. Managerial judgment is a dimensional trait characteristic that generally is a frequent assessing component of leadership skills. It is typically not a term daily used in managerial functioning but tends to become commonplace when evaluating desired leadership skills or job performance appraisals. Judgmental actions/logical inferences will typically affect much more than deciding a specific course of action, because most managerial actions are influenced by the leader's perceptual judgment.

Influence or pressures will often dominate a positional leader's exercise of good judgment. These pressures may be **time allotment for a project's completion**, a **manager's desires**, and a **host of other influences** both actual and psychological. The introduction of psychological influences that affect logical inferences brings into perspective five pertinent natural pressures that tend to distress judgmental action. These commonplace influences are **physical factors**, **anger**, **frustration**, **unfamiliarity**, and **fear**.

An appraisal of **displaying judgmental actions** is primarily a rationality of decision making focusing on the quantitation of influential factors. Rationality of logical inferences is based on consideration of consequences and the availability of positive alternatives. A logical inference is nothing more than an assumption based on appropriate information. However, arrival at a proper assumption may need to be through projection of action, with a foundation on accurate available data and indicated trends. Taking judgmental actions based on assumptions is risky, but it is not possible to totally eliminate all **risk taking** in a decision-making process. Crisis management is normal for an operational police manager; typically his or her prior experience and analysis of facts at hand will determine the individual's perceptual judgmental effectiveness. A realization does exist that there may be some correlation between inherent intellectual qualities and judgmental actions.

Positive Judgment Actions related to leadership personality is best achieved by capitalizing on the distinctive knowledge approach of the middle manager's personal concept. Despite its vulnerability to errors of the sort identified in this chapter, it is noted that introspection provides data about the person that cannot readily be obtained in any other way and is thus virtually indispensable in a managerial personality analysis, especially when the concern is with a mid-level police manager's effectiveness. If one takes personal concept seriously as reflecting a qualitative difference between the person's job persona and his or her non-positional personality, then there is no way of differentiating these affective states accurately by other methods. To discount an introspective analysis altogether as a source of information about a person's leadership personality would be to reduce the individual to a somewhat inarticulate entity and thus the assessment would lose an enormous wealth of information about his or her inner experience and judgmental reasoning.

Chapter Nine

GOAL-ORIENTED JOB LEADERSHIP

The concept of Goal-Oriented Job Leadership or Objective Focused Management is somewhat dated. The concept was most popular in the 1950s through the 1970s. However, in looking at the total scope of mid-level police leadership, it was concluded that no subject would be complete without a comprehensive consideration of Goal-Oriented Motivation as a practical part of management. Goal-oriented leadership in the area of law enforcement is traditionally reactionary to prior events or occurrences. A consideration of objective-focused management should remain a key aim of leadership as it seeks to project the performance needs of the organization into the future. The modern term of "community oriented policing," for example, is a form of objective management concept.

Goal-oriented job leadership, as referred to in this text, is a form of a target-focused directional rationale, to ensure that appropriate tasks and obligations are fulfilled. The term previously used to describe and discuss goal-oriented job leadership in management of years past was Management By Objective (MBO). Goal-oriented job leadership is procedures in which managers in a law enforcement organization, through coordinated efforts and specified objectives, harmonize their efforts to accomplish essential tasks. The focus is usually on the future, since traditionally, a goal is perceived as a condition to be accomplished in a projected time frame. The main concern is centered on what the organization will achieve, as well as how it will be achieved. Goals or objectives are traditionally perceived as concepts of purpose and guidelines that have been formalized into the organization's process of leadership. Goals can be either short-term or extendedly ranged depending on the perceptual need of the identified objectives. Goals are sometimes universal to an agency to serve the need of the entire organization. Likewise, they are sometimes specific or individualized to a particular concern or person.

Goal-oriented leadership facilitates the source of focused ambitions from the commonplace objectives of the organization. After goals are developed or selected and assumed by a police organizational component, it is possible to structure the processes, behaviors, and requirements for achieving the desired objectives. Subsequent to the procedural methods of accomplishing a task via a goal-oriented process, there must be a consideration for the resources required, the performance time frame, the interrelations to the objectives, parameters of the operation, and the essential assessment measures of the agency on an ongoing basis.

Organizational goals or objectives can originate at any level of a law enforcement infrastructure. Traditionally, focal objectives should be developed for the overall aspirations of the police organization. It should be developed from the universal aims of the law enforcement agency and must be consistent with the ideology, policies, and the purpose of management. A mid-level police manager must be acutely aware of the purpose and objectives of the organization and its aims, when developing his or her leadership action plan goals, to be interactive within the overall operational ambitions of the agency. As discussed previously in this text, a mid-level police manager has the unique perspective of sharing knowledge of both the managerial hierarchy and the functional-level employees to some degree. This perspective allows the manager to formulate goal-oriented leadership strategies that are most conducive to the effective job performance of him/herself and subordinates.

Management by Objective for a mid-level police manager is critical to the focused goals to determine the purpose of his or her job performance. Goal-oriented leadership for a middle police manager can be concluded to be an alternative method of describing his or her task obligations. A managerial leader must be aware of the methods and the overall goals of the organization as translated into the job targets for subordinates. The adaptation of universal organizational objectives into functional terms for subordinates must be a component of a leader's efforts to be effective. An understanding of the **means-results** process is therefore essential in the determination of functional-level objectives.

Remember, goals should not be considered as alternatives for focus projections but rather as a foundation for establishing them. The managerial-focused objectives for the organization in general are the most difficult of the universal objectives within the organization. The commonplace goals within the organization by necessity are rooted on the premise of forthcoming expectations and a clear interpretation within the organization's structure. The organization's strong points as well as those lesser in strength must be considered regarding the development of goals or objectives and what is the primary aim of each. There have been a number of approaches fostered for developing appropriate and effective leadership goals for law enforcement, such as:

1. Assessing the projected aims of the organization in coordination with the changes in the social structure of the city, town, or community. Such a process should encompass an evaluation of the service to be provided and the leadership focus of the law enforcement agency.
2. A comprehensive analysis of the organization's strengths, weaknesses, resources, and other logistical factors must occur. By so doing, a portrait of the agency and the principal objectives needed to resolve the problems facing the organization should be revealed. This also aids managerial leadership in devising procedures and processes to utilize available opportunities to deal with issues confronting the organization.

ESTABLISHING GOAL-ORIENTED LEADERSHIP STRATEGIES

Leadership-oriented goals are the basis for developing organizational plans. A main concern in a managerial analysis of goal advancement is whether or not functional objectives will be achieved. Articulation of goals and objectives document the expectations regarding leadership and subordinate personnel interactions. The relationship interactions frame the tasks to be accomplished, the acceptable level of performance quality, and the time frame in which the objective is to be achieved. Appropriately, established objectives also provide those involved with a measurable and tangible basis for developing a workable plan of action. They further integrate action projections, individual job performances, and overall organizational activity.

A primary strategy focus of leadership-oriented goal setting is to provide an information feedback and assessment instrument to gauge job performances. It also supports managerial efforts to coordinate activities and facilitates a time frame adherence to achieve successful task results. Further, appropriately identified goals and objectives focus awareness on guidelines essential to management of organizational functions and provides a basis for job-associated appreciations based on empirical information.

The formulation of objectives and goals via law enforcement management depicts a **process-results** assessment, which is said to be an effort to be inclusive of requirements into defined actions. Leadership-oriented goals or management by objectives are traditionally based on the aforementioned concept. It assumes that a **process-results** form of goal setting will occur with precision and accuracy. The results epitomize a circumstance that is most desired, a mission to be accomplished, and is easily assessed in terms of organizational goals and objectives. Thus, a disruption of the leadership-oriented goal process once implemented could result in problems ensuring task accomplishment and managerial effectiveness. Therefore, mid-level police managers must recognize that commitment, effort, and the support of top management are critical. There is a quintessential need for middle management's consensus agreement on a goal focus purpose that is necessary for interactive cooperation. The aforestated is required for task achievement and the use of established objectives as criteria for performance assessments.

THE RANGE AND NATURE OF MANAGERIAL LEADERSHIP GOALS

The Goal-oriented job tasks for mid-level police managers should reflect the **resource-results** that were discussed earlier in the chapter. It is critical that established goals and objectives are *easily understood, comprehensive* with some degree of *brevity,* and non-equivocating. Being *easily understood* is essential because of the various levels of management and personal perceptions that must interact to the objective. *Brevity* is a requirement in that communication between elements can be better achieved if the information is in a concise format. The conciseness of the information must also be *comprehensive* to ensure sufficient data to meet the knowledge needs of each element. There must be an assurance that doubtful or double-meanings are not commonplace in the absence of clarifying explanations.

Development of effective managerial task objectives should also be consistent with operational policies, procedures, and plans of action for the managerial element. It is essential that the task goals are accurate, reasonably learnable, somewhat interesting, and as challenging as may be possible. It is important to note each of the criteria cited for establishing objectives suggest areas of performance, as well as specify some degree of necessary quantity, quality, and time frame for the action. The requirement of this delineation is apparent, as it reflects the assessment criterion. The aforementioned has plain implications for both gauging and evaluating performances.

It is not easy to contemplate the establishment of a middle-level managerial objective that would encompass each of the job's responsibilities and task expectations. The sheer job requirements of a manager's task obligations are too complex for assessment by a simple Set of Goal-Oriented Objectives. However, whenever a comprehensive set of goal criterion is established, it should make up the principal job description of the management position being considered. Also, the possibility of their accomplishment must be evaluated in terms of what is known regarding the complete job demands. If there is any perceptual conflict between organizational goals and other job mandates, the mandates of the job must be adjusted.

When contemplating the development of a goal-oriented leadership focus for mid-level police managers, it is important to consider two major factors. First is the inclusion of appropriate Task Performance Ambitions relative to those goals and actions that are interrelated to the position and assignment duties. Second, Personal Established Ambitions are associated with expanding the individual skills, task knowledge, or capability for future growth and development. Quintessential to the consideration and articulation of the goal-oriented leadership focus is the fact that it allows an evaluation of the objectives that are being applied and the specific aspects that are being promulgated.

Performance Ambitions. Task Performance Ambitions are developed specifically from the job assessment itself, referring to the principal areas of obligation and behavioral actions of the individual. Included in task performance ambition areas are the maintaining of repetitive activities considered common within the organization. Also encompassed are the process of problem solving, the procedures for creative thinking, and the development of innovative ideas and the results achieved. Some of these Performance Ambitions can be viewed as special or non-common activities to the manager's job tasks. It must also be noted that what may be typical for one similar level manager's task performances may not be common for another. For example, a task behavior to accomplish an objective that is considered a special project for a mid-level manager may be commonplace for an executive leader in the organization.

It is important to note that a mid-level police manager does not have the authority to influence universal organizational objectives or plans of action in which he or she has no discretion. Traditionally, by its nature police organizations impose limitations on individuals. The infrastructure of a law enforcement agency delineates acceptable areas of impact/input and decision making for managers. In the current era of specialization and defined focus of operation, the tendency is to restrict decisions and actions to the areas articulated for the identified job position. Therefore, executive leadership, as do mid-level managers need to identify and clearly articulate areas in which a subordinate has discretion. By so doing, it will ensure that the subordinate is aware of what the decision restrictions are. The aforementioned is essential, because when someone develops expectations of participation and influence that is not legitimate or reinforced, non-productive consequences are likely to occur.

Personal Established Ambitions. Initially, it is essential to emphasize that Personal Established Ambitions should be focused on contemporary concerns and/or deficiencies in the areas of technical skills, interpersonal relations, or alterations in job tasks. The essential nature of these ambitions or objectives is based on their potential as a method of confronting and dealing with obsolescence under an increasing advancement of knowledge. However, if at any point the mid-level manager's superior feels that the individual's Personal Established Ambitions interferes with the unit's or organization's goals, it should be made known to the individual. Personally developed goals or ambitions are essential for structuring and correcting deficiencies.

It is essential to ensure that a complete and comprehensive assessment of the importance of developing Personal Established Ambitions be identified. Thus, we should conclude this section by discussing the essentiality of identifying concerns that managers must address when considering leadership-oriented goals. Leaders involved in establishing managerial or performance objectives must consistently be aware of problems affecting their subordinates, as individuals, or mismatches in assigned tasks. The managerial leader is in a critically important position and must recognize the causal factors or concerns affecting their subordinates. An effective leader should realize that interactive coworkers are in a good position to judge the performance competence of the leader or his/her subordinates. Therefore, if a colleague is complaining about the behavior or task accomplishment of another worker, then an assessment of the goals and/or performance should occur. Also, an analysis of the reason(s) for not accomplishing the developed goals and objectives frequently reveal problem areas that should be considered when setting either personal or organizationally established ambitions.

Individually Established Ambitions. In a comprehensive evaluation of Individually Established Ambitions there are several areas that should be assessed. Three of the areas of proficiency that must be addressed when establishing personal goals/objectives for an individual leader or managerial position are: (1) Enhancing interpersonal performance ability. A leader must be able to maintain a reasonably effective work relationship with others; (2) Enhanced task performance ability. A leader must strive to be proficient in all areas of job behaviors; and (3) Pre-plan, such as establishing standards or developing performance strategies for task accomplishments.

A position manager at any level of the organization regarding Leader-Oriented Goals must always strive for self-improvement and for Individual Established Ambition achievement. The leader or manager should rely on the determination that the action plan or strategy for goal and/or objective-based leadership has been carried out. Therefore, it is clear from the information aforestated that leader-oriented goal setting for mid-level police managers is critical. No matter the term used, the process of Leader-Oriented

Goal setting or Management by Objective affects task accomplishments of positional leadership.

The relatively simple task of being a leader, in years past, has become increasing more difficult with each passing year. For example, during the Stone Age, a leader simply made known what he wanted and subordinate persons responded. Ancillary concerns were not an issue, nor was a need to provide employee work motivations. However, as time passed and life and circumstances became more complicated, the need to assign tasks and provide leadership from a planned approach became a necessity. And, even though Community Policing is a different twist to an old theme, it has brought with it some new dimensions and concerns that must be addressed.

Thus, the mid-level police managers of today must endeavor to exert every possible managerial tool for performance effectiveness. Elsewhere in this text, areas such as Obtaining Followership and Leadership Standards and Standardization are addressed and must be considered with Goal-Oriented Leadership if a mid-level police manager's overall job performance is to be effective. Therefore, it is evident that assessment of Goal-Oriented Leadership must be provided for both the objectives and the way in which the results are obtained. In the absence of the aforementioned, a critical chance to communicate expectations of desired objectives will be lost. It should be clearly understood that goals and objectives have obvious ties to plans of action and anticipated results for a mid-level police manager.

It is evident that a mid-level police manager is guided by his or her role in the organization and that the objectives set-forth for subordinates must coordinate with the overall goals and objectives of the organization. The Goal-Oriented Leadership process of most police organizations are framed in a Management By Objective (MBO) program. Thus, a comprehensive understanding of MBO as a process and the benefits it offers management at all levels of the organization should thoroughly examined. To accurately discuss and articulate Goal-Oriented Leadership in a police organization we must comprehensively consider the MBO process. The strategic planning that is essential to an effective MBO program will be clearly set forth and defined, relative to the need to establish goals and objectives which are paramount to an effective Goal-Oriented Leadership process. Effective job performances by subordinate employees are the ultimate test of whether or not a planned course of action is the most conducive method of measuring Goal-Oriented Leadership. The behavioral actions and attainments toward establishing goals and objectives should tell us how effective is our leadership efforts. Therefore, the text will next comprehensively explore Leader-Oriented Goals and Objectives or what is most commonly referred to as Management By Objective (MBO).

LEADER-ORIENTED GOALS AND OBJECTIVES (MANAGEMENT BY OBJECTIVES)

It does not matter whether we refer to Directional Leadership as "Goal-Oriented Job Leadership" or the more traditional articulation of "Management By Objective," it should be recognized that most of the sort-after results are more closely akin to the concept of being the perceptual *floating finish line* or *carrot at the end of the stick.* The idea must be toward focus and aim that include some functional pattern of action articulating to subordinates a planned method of task achievements that tells our followers where to go, how our efforts are going to obtain results, and how it will be known when the objective is reached. **Management by Objectives** (MBO) is an encyclopedic managerial method, based on tangible and quantitative group of aspirations which was first identified in the 1954 writings by Peter Drucker as a criteria of enhancing leadership directing of subordinates. Organizational Objectives (MBO) has a multiplicity of titles and formats that management at all levels of an agency or businesses will use to identify motivational goals to focus the efforts of subordinates. Most business agencies have been assimilated and used some forms of management by objectives to achieve better productivity from workers. The aforementioned statement is a clear indication that it is difficult, if not impossible, to find any type of organization that has not used some variation of the MBO process to orient functional workers. It would appear from this author's informational readings, virtually every book reviewed on the subject of organizational management has some mention or recommended use of MBO as a controlling and directing tool to enhance productivity. The foundational concept conjectures that by setting objectives, management forms an interactive participation between functional subordinates and managerial leadership to work toward a set of goals that will best achieve the organizations purpose.

It should be recalled that the primary focus criteria that was articulated regarding an MBO process execution, which makes it effective both for organizational leadership and functional participation, is the emphasis it places on establishing a goal-oriented leadership strategy. The fact Management by Objective for a mid-level police manager has proven to be most effective is that it's both *measurable* and *participative* between the leader and his or her subordinates. The importance of these terms will be explored in more detail as they relate to an organization's effectiveness later in this chapter. The theocracy of strategic objectives has been formatted into what has been termed as *leader-oriented goal setting.* The foundational concept, as previously noted, is the cooperative participation of subordinates and managers in the development of plainly focused goals, to effectively achieve employee productivity and the organization's accomplishment of objectives. Traditionally, managers at all levels of the agency and functional workers theorize collectively to project achievement parameters that are designed to assure the accomplishment of organizational success of its primary purpose. During the aforementioned process, the inaction between management and functional personnel should result in the best possible methods of overall organizational goal accomplishment. It is readily recognized that leadership or management has the ultimate say so and responsibility for the focused objectives that will purposefully be used. If for whatever reason these agreed upon goals are not satisfactory to the management, then collective interaction of objectives development will quickly become downwardly focused or managerially directed and controlled. Should this become the case, it is recommended that the differences be articulated and each element clearly understand why the planned goal focus is mandated, thus, all components can then adjust their expectations to the uniform targets.

Some theorists have conjectured that most *objectively focused management* is often utilized more or less as a measure to direct or manipulate the functional workers as a motivational tool to elevate production toward desired results. Whether acknowledged or not, most researchers in the area of Management Studies should note that Management By Objective, no matter how interjected it is, is by far the most widely and prevalently utilized planning method among police organizations. In the mid-1960s, when police management books began to appear in ever increasing numbers, MBO was originally delineated as a comparatively basic performance evaluation procedure; however, as goal-oriented verbiage became more a part of law enforcement, the process evolved into a more complex focus and directing instrument. Thus, MBO eventually developed into an essential and comprehensive management system for effective policing organizations. Also, during the past several decades, written texts in the field of Police Leadership have generally been in agreement that Management By Objectives can and has provided a fundamental base for setting forth law enforcement goal activities in a coordinated manner. It is recognized that a number of viewpoint problems can develop and even though differing attitudes are possible, there exist a number of alternatives for resolving the issues between management and functional employees.

Management By Objectives in this text has also been referred to as Leader-Oriented Goal Setting with the primary focus on a mid-level police manager's process results. This relates to setting tangible measures of efficiency and effectiveness for each leadership position and the timely transformation of these gauging methods into obtainable goals and objectives. As Management By Objective in law enforcement evolved into an in-depth leadership control methodology, a sublevel doctrine of objective-focused strategy emerged. This sublevel doctrine or systematic view was structured on a criteria of conjectured assumptions about workers and the sources of their motivation as set forth previously in this text regarding the early writings of Abraham Maslow. Maslow, along with others management theorists, such as Douglas McGregor, around the middle of the twentieth century, conjectured that most workers were motivated by needs and possessed a desire to productively perform, thus they were viewed as individuals who could accomplish tasks if appropriately directed and provided the opportunity. However, as stated by a significant number of management consultants and theorists of this era, there is a barrier that exists between the theorctical manifestation of Goal-Oriented Motivation (Management by Objectives) and the practical application of implementing a Result-Producing Process. Recent indications, since the late 1960s seem to foster the development of Management By Objective as a systematized process that involves a primary managerial procedure that clearly delineates MBO activities in a reasonable and compatible leadership focus. Some of the criteria have been identified as the development of comprehensively inclusive organizational objectives and tactical planning, resolute action to overcome dilemmas and decision making, performance evaluations, resource management and leadership training, and augmentation. But, like most efficient and effective practices, endorsers of the concept quickly point out that when Management By Objectives is applied as a comprehensive leadership process, it is most likely to become an integral part of the mid-level police manager's task behaviors.

ADVANTAGES OF MBO FOR A
MID-LEVEL POLICE MANAGER

Mid-level police managers who are proponents of Management By Objectives claim a significant number of advantages and positive productive results. It is readily understandable that at the organization's top, there typically is driving force to introduce the MBO process as a continuing, yet new directional focus of management, each year becomes the new basic foundation of MBO. MBO has been set forth as a single focused process as well as layered procedural tasks set up to define the ultimate organizational goals and objectives that are to be achieved. Some theorists have conjectured that have implemented several layers of achievement-focused leadership into a Management By Objective, which often causes confusion, a degree of dissatisfaction, and failed functional results. Some management leaders believe that it may take as much as three to five years for even a moderate-sized police organization to evolve a full functional MBO system that links together such performance areas as planning, directing/control, behavioral appraisal, and a workable employee recognition system. Law enforcement organizations that are proponents of MBO believe that effective functional performances and increased motivation, through the use of a realistic process of focused-oriented goal setting is ideally suited for the military structure of most police agencies. To better explain the previously stated conjecture and a reason why many in law enforcement are proponents of MBO, the text will identify several positive aspects of goal-oriented leadership.

First, top level police managers often feel more secure in openly stating and forecasting projected goal results, as well as in planning future activities. Its recognized that his/her view, planning objectives and action projections are a continuous process. To accomplish this, a leader must focus on the positive aspects that managers should used when setting goals, such as: (1) Clarifying common objectives for the comprehension of all subordinates; (2) Setting goals high enough to challenge each individual subordinate; (3) Utilizing results previously achieved as a foundation for utilizing creative efforts to develop imaginative interaction; (4) Conjoining responsibilities and interactive behaviors into a performance flow that is most conducive to efficient functional tasks; (5) Disperse job assignments and workloads to individuals with the consideration of being most appropriate for overall attainment of goals; (6) Openly project as tactfully as possible that the ultimate goal is to achieve the organization's mission while interacting positively with employee motivation; (7) Develop his or her element's operation and individual employee expectations in a manner that are most conducive to the basis goals and objectives that coincide with the organization's purposeful accomplishment; (8) Allows the leader to formulate a structure of responsible that separates task obligations and establishes a format that emphasizes the contribution of each employee, thus, assuring that each feels that he or she is a vital part of accomplishing the desired results; (9) Permits the inter-dispersing of relatively easily achieved objectives to enhance employee confidence and motivation to continue his or her progression toward the established goals; (10) Allows the goal-setting manager to create procedures and performance guides to accomplish desired results and to establish alternative actions should a modification be required; (11) Putting into place performance requirements the emphasizes methods of behavioral actions rather than having to clarify misunderstood areas of expectation; (12) Seeks to allow and even request employee positive participatory input as to methods that may enhance or readily assure the achievement of the goal and objective, but with the understanding that ultimate decisions and responsibility lies with leadership; (13) A positive police manager is highly motivate to input his or her personal concepts and those of upper management that interrelate with functional employee contribution to appropriately effect the accomplishment of the organization's goals and objectives; (14) Readily consider the new task behaviors and /or problem concerns identified by subordinates; (15) Utilize a comprehensive analysis assessment of what action he or she as the managerial leader will direct functional employees to undertake and the possible consequences or accomplishments; (16) An effective police manager will introduce innovative concepts from both inside and outside the organization, as well as emphasize to subordinates that such consideration may at time be helpful to task accomplishment; (17) A manager will often recognize that conceived obstacles to MBO, if comprehensively analyzed with the idea of resolving the problem, may at times produce and enhance course of action toward objective achievement; (18) To allow within the parameters of goal achievement subordinates to focus on objective factors of opportunity while progressing toward the organization's overall desired results. The targeting of intermediary focus will often time enhance the employee's knowledge as well as foster the attainment of established goals and objectives; (19) An effective leader who is considered a goal-oriented motivator and will positively induce conducive subordinate performances when goals and objectives are accomplished and will not fail to correct behavior that is inappropriate or insufficient whenever they are not aligned with the objectives attempting to be achieved as a result of non-productive actions; and (20) Positive MBO leaders will readily move forward from actions and projected efforts that have fail to produce desired results in the past, he or she will typically show a willingness to change a course of action or method that has shown to be unfeasible, or impossible.

Second, an effective manager who is a proponent of MBO as the most appropriate method of Objective-Focused Management will assure that his/her subordinates acquire a knowledge of the leader's expectations and the unwavering desire to achieve the organization's goals and objective. In most police organizations, Management By Objectives has been proven to be successful in motivating managerial leadership in gauging subordinates performance behaviors toward accomplishment of organizational goals and objectives. However, comprehensive assessments have indicated that concerns frequently develop in the absence of meticulous and carefully set-forth and implemented plans. Upper-Level Objective-Focused Management of the organization should articulate a very active endorsement of the MBO process. All agency members should perceive that objectives planned and utilized will be applied, as indicated and feedback should result from performance accomplishments and will serve as the basis for implementing functional objectives in a future period. Management By Objective in virtually every law enforcement organization is perceived as a dynamic procedure that has the capability for altering the focus and goals of the agency.

Third, in most police organizations a mid-level police manager has the obligation to set the objectives for his/her area of responsibility. Thus, he or she is tasked to assure that his/her element's objectives coincide with the overall mission and goals of the police agency, this obligation provides and increased incentive to ensure that the functional objectives set for subordinates provide for employee motivation and is achievable. The Management By Objectives goals set-forth for subordinates by an effective police manager should be target specific and pertinent to the unit's success as part of the organization's overall mission. The managerial leader must be comprehensively aware of the organization's objectives and that the individual goals and objectives of functional employees under his/her direction will effectively influence and support each other's effective performance. The inter-laced performance behaviors are critical to all levels and components of the organization. However, to be comprehensive in our discussion of Management By Objective, the author must point out that some studies have said that even though an initial view of MBO as a part of an organizational setting appears that it is and would be an ideal fit for a goal-oriented organization, such as a police agency, there are some aspects of MBO that despite its widespread use indicates that Goal-Oriented Leadership effectiveness may be somewhat limited. The concept and the perceptual view of MBO have most organizations accepting it on what may be its potential. Some studies have indicated that because total success or the fact that all objectives are seldom, if ever, achieved. Thus, actual proof of the effectiveness of MBO is lacking because it is very difficult to prove a casual effect between a multidimensional leadership methods, such as an objectively directed management and ultimate task performance results. So as not to distort the author's intent, it is important at this juncture to interject the old saying, "**In order to get to the moon we have to reach for the stars.**" Consequently, some managerial theorists have focused their contention on the fact that success of MBO as a leadership technique should be based on measuring employee attitudes toward goal-oriented motivation. It is recognized that Subordinate Motivation Research is somewhat deficient because it merely conjectures rather than proves that goal-oriented leadership effect on actual job performance by functional employees. But from the growing number of organization using MBO, it is a clear indication that the leadership technique works as a tool, to as nearly as possible accomplish desired results. Most knowledgeable managerial leaders have long recognized that to a large degree, Management By Objective as a leadership tool for directing the functional aspects of others is an evolving process that like many other areas associated with the behaviors of human beings is basically accomplished through trial and error. The basic concept of setting a target upon which to focus efforts should be specific, tangible, and that its attainment is under the effective control or influence of those setting the goals. These limitations would at first glance appear to favor the concept that MBO is not provable as an effective management tool; likewise it appears that we would be incapable of precisely defining the *Channeled-Results* of establishing goals and objectives. But to suggest that such an approach is only effective if it is measurably attainable and that the benefits of the collateral accomplishment while working toward the set-forth objectives *should not* be considered as a portion of the overall success of the efforts toward a goal-oriented objective is unthinkable. When we consider the derived benefits from the motivational aspect and functional collaboration that is engendered within the organization by a Management By Objective process, the police organization has already achieve success before any consideration of the results of attempted goal-oriented attainment. Recognizing that virtually all law enforcement agencies function well in the planning aspects of its operation, however, because of the nature of police functioning, it must not be overlooked that such organizations are tied to its past successes or failures while required to anticipate and project the needs of the future. For the aforestated reasons, the author maintains that while a comprehensive consideration of job behaviors, along with the close observance and the computation of results may be the best gauge for determining how successful MBO is as a management tool, the identifying of responsibilities, the planned action to achieve organizational objectives, and the collateral benefits should be the true focus of Goal-Oriented Leadership.

Fourth, it is generally agreed that Management By Objectives will be most effective in any organizational setting if subordinates at all level of the agency agrees on clearly defined goals and the purposeful method of gauging effective job performances, as well as the determination of what will be considered successful results. Some will readily agree that focused-results; meaningful contribution in setting goals and objectives; and the availability of an effective measuring process are positive indications. However, the main question becomes, can mean-result objectives be developed for the individuals and each operational component of the organization? To get a better grasp of the aforementioned and how organizational management should measure MBO our analysis must closely examine the specific requirements of the goals and what method will be used to gauge effectiveness. A practical view indicates that the most reliable measures is the actual information in which the managerial goals that are attempting to be achieved and what criterion of effectiveness will ultimately be used to measure results. The author believes that if the established goals are readily accepted, but not easily attained that they will in most cases stimulate a greater degree of enhanced functional performances by employees than will goals and objectives that are less challenging. Goal setting is typically accepted to be effective at both the management and functional levels of the organization. Establishing a Goal-Oriented Leadership Strategy where both managerial leaders and functional workers actively participate in setting the organizational objectives is believed to enhance the job performance at all levels of the agency. The clear indication of the prior statements will be demonstrated when the use of challenging yet attainable objectives, as prescribed by most Management By Objectives advocates, is shown to enhance the overall job performance effectiveness throughout the organization. But the key to success, as indicated is persuading employees to accept difficult objectives. It is at this juncture that research theorists and staunch endorsers of the Management By Objectives ideology and goal-setting-oriented leadership differ in concept. Management By Objective proponents steadfastly maintain that participation by both managerial leaders and functional level employees in developing and setting organizational goals and objectives is necessary for personal commitment. Whereas the research theorists expound the conjecture that goals and objectives established for the organization by management and subordinates do not indicate that enhanced performances necessarily is based on the participation of either of these components. The contention for this disparity lies in the expectation of self-motivation that is generated by participatory involvement that should be fostered by input into the direction and focus of the organization. The conceptual belief, which was prevalent in the past, has assumed that most, if not all, functional-level subordinates are desirous to elevate their individual personal directional leadership status. The afore concept indicates that we should accept the prior notion that all subordinates and employees are desirous to achieve a higher degree of performance efficiency and that what is generally considered positive incentives of accomplishment or gratifying attainments is the stimulating focus for all levels of the organization. Some will still argue that goal-oriented motivation, if achieved via the aforementioned methods, is gratifying and meets the basic criteria of MBO, but that for the concept to be ideal, it must be measurable and visibly quantitative before it can truly be considered as an effective Goal-Focused Management concept. It is generally recognized that any widely used managerial technique such as the MBO process will surely generate a theoretical discussions about its inter-related strengths and weaknesses. Many managerial leaders who may be closely gauged by their successes and failures based on tangible results of subordinate job performances and established objective achievements will shy away from stating *leader-oriented goal setting,* as they tend to be viewed by others as realistic expectations. Thus, anything but a total and complete accomplishment of stated goals and objectives could be viewed as a leadership failure. However, as previously stated, the author believe that by setting a focus or achievement goal for which to aim and obtaining an effort from both management and functional employees is the best way to achieve success in a police or any organization. For example, the basic *goal of law enforcement is prevent crime and apprehend offenders.* The goal as stated has a built in variant that success will not be achieved, because if crimes are prevented then there will be no offenders to apprehend. But by a coordinated effort throughout the organization, there may be a reduction in the number of crimes committed and the number of malefactors taken into custody, so the traditional verbiage is to say that offenses will be reduced by $\underline{X}$ percentage, which in reality cannot be assured because of the external factors that effect criminal behavior are constantly changing. The prior statement presupposes that management and functional employees have conferred and reached a consensus that the goals and objectives established for the agency will foster performance effectiveness within the organization and that the agreed upon consensus will motivate dedicated efforts, along with the satisfaction of overall process-results.

KEY AREAS OF FOCUS FOR EFFECTIVE MBO

It should be clear that Management By Objective (MBO) is quintessential to an effective operation where planning strategies and the efficient use of resources is a key component of a police organization's functioning. To simply state that the implementation of an MBO practice and procedure is inadequate because it can be shown that the single most essential guiding focus of the organization is its Strategic Planning and demonstrated efforts to achieve established goals and objectives. The developed and implemented directional focus toward the set-forth goals controls the basic job performances of all levels of the organization and it also sets up parameters for the focused use of resources that are usually somewhat limited. The Management By Objectives focus is the key element in the purposeful directing and controlling the functional work performed by employees, as well as the motivation and regulation of the external interactive forces that influence and/or impact a police organization's operation. It is recognized that MBO, as an effective managerial technique, is the foundational component in the organization's employees' purposeful use of good judgment, integrity, initiative, courage, patience, and flexibility in their task performances toward attempting to foster organizational attainment of its goals and objectives. It is plain that without the Strategic Planning that permeates MBO, an effective management process and the directional controls necessary would be wholly ineffective. Strategic planning in the development of a course of action for success in a law enforcement process is formulated at three distinct-levels, (1) *conceptual,* (2) *practical,* and (3) *functional.* First, *Conceptual Strategic Planning* in preparation for implementation of a goal oriented leadership process refers to a mentally conceived plan of action designed to achieve desired results. Second, a *Practical Strategic Planning* procedure is the preparation for actions that are capable of being used without elaboration, it is generally considered adaptable and measurable. Even though, as previously discussed, the absolute measurability of a Management By Objective technique is not the most appropriate gauge of leadership effectiveness. And, third, *Functional Strategic Planning* is the developing of a goal-oriented plan of action that is workable, to wit: the normal or characteristic actions of functional employees performances in the work environment.

A mid-level police manager must utilize a number of criteria in the formulating or design of his or her strategy for action to enhance subordinates chances of successful task accomplishments in a goal-oriented motivational process. The approach must be viewed as *objectively focused and achievable* by both management and functional workers. Self-delusion by managerial leadership has no place in a MBO process where an honest dispassionate view of the strengths and weaknesses of a mid-level police manager's behavioral skills to effectively perform is analyzed. It is essential that the manager's goal-oriented leadership skills are set forth in a manner that will be perceived as positive aspects of the behavior qualities of an effective leader who utilizes input from subordinates to achieve the overall goal and objectives of the organization. The **KISS** (Keep It Simple Stupid) principal of developing and implementing is the most effective and desirous method of planning or projecting a MBO Strategy or expectations of behavior from others. *Keeping it simple and focused* has proven to be most effective. It is easier for mid-level police managers to remember and put into practice and it is more recognizable and understandable to subordinates and functional workers, who must clearly understand managerial actions to assure that the goal and objectives are clearly articulated and task performances fulfill. A mid-level police manager's efforts and behavioral attitudes should be concentrated where the directional impact and results will be the most effective. The planned and delivered actions must be directed toward a method of attaining the planned functional objectives, in a manner that will most effectively motivate subordinates, as well as, the resolution of whatever problems and issues that may manifest themselves as a hindrance whether unanticipated or expected.

The leader initiating a Management By Objective process must focus on *result-bearing efforts.* The key to implementation and success in an MBO process depends on the mid-level police manager's ability to demonstrate the proper leader-oriented, goal-setting skills of leadership. The managerial skills of leadership must be projected in a manner that reflects an ability and willingness to commit oneself to an ideal or practice that will effectively deal with problems or concerns that are not conducive to organizational accomplishment of its goals and objectives. Too often managerial leadership concludes that if they project an idea or strategy that will allow coping with a problem, that this will or should be sufficient. However, it has been demonstrated in several MBO processes that if management leaders can set forth a concept or practice to resolve issues or problems and not just cope with them, it is most likely to be concluded that the Management By Objective approach will be successful. There are numerous key areas of focus that a mid-level police manager should be aware and utilize when developing and establishing an MBO process for subordinates that coincide with the goals and objectives of the organization. Some of the key areas of MBO focus, as observed and noted by the author are:

First Key: *Establish a participatory **Leader-Oriented Goal Setting** effort to develop an MBO focus to assure that all levels of agency's leadership and functional employees purposefully desire to perform job tasks toward the accomplishment of the goals and objectives of the organization.* It is an accepted concept that organizational leaders at all levels should be desirous of their responsibility for task accomplishment and conclusive attainment, in a properly established objectively focused management process. A recognized fact is that a "chain is only as strong as its weakest link," and that an "automobile does not travel very well with one flat tire" is a similar concept that if a component or unit fails to accept or perform appropriately as an element of a Management By Objective process, the overall effective accomplishment goal oriented leadership will fail.

Second Key: *There must be a clearly articulated desire and demonstration of effort by managers at all levels of the organization to share authority in developing a **Goal-Oriented Strategy** for his/her component.* All organizational leadership is assessed the obligation and expectation of analyzing objectives that effective their component and to share concerns with upper management. Thus, for a truly effective MBO process, to work top-level leaders should be willing to allow the necessary authority input into planning strategy to accomplish the agency's overall goals and objectives. The manager's first task is to set-forth the participatory strategy with the input from subordinates that was considered in the formulating of the interactive objectives of his or her functional employees. He or she has to make sure the goal-oriented focus interacts positively with the organizational goals and objectives. The mid-level police manager is responsible for coordinated compatibility and development of his or her element's focused strategy with other agency components within the ultimate Objective Focused Leadership of the organization.

Third Key: *The implementation of a **Objective-Focused Management** process that structures the formulation of a well thought-out process that will assure the proper accomplishment of a functionally conceived MBO (means-results) plan of action.* Traditional goal-oriented motivational planning tend to be more conceptual than implemental from a practical standpoint. This occurs because managers like most people find it easier to imagine things than to conceive of the actual steps necessary to functionally make operational. Thus, managers attempting to develop a goal-oriented motivation process are most likely to focus insufficiently on the end-result rather the beginning or the initial start of a managerial leadership process. But unless the process-results are supported by concrete actions to be carried out by functional employees toward specified organizational goals and objectives, from start to finish, it is unlikely that a Management By Objective strategic plan will succeed. However, if any type of relative success is to be achieved, a manager has to ensure that there is sufficient forward thinking and foresight planning that will lead to effective motivational leadership of subordinates to accomplish a productive Objectively-Focused Management. The Objectively Focused Management or MBO should include primary approaches to interval direction, established parameters of performance, previously gathered knowledge, and logical inferences.

Fourth Key: ***Goal-Oriented Motivation*** *is a prerequisite for the successful planning and accomplishment of an effective Management By Objective process, which requires the participatory willingness to appropriately perform by capable subordinates.* As with most managerial practices, it is recognized that a Management By Objective cannot succeed in the absence of mid-level managers and functional workers that are both desirous and have the performance capability to undertake the tasks of added responsibility of assuring that the duties related to organizational goal oriented objectives are accomplished. However, to ensure appropriate tasks accomplishments toward an effective MBO, each of the planned functional tasks should be simplified into specific performance objectives, both short term and long term. This should occur at each level of management that must be involved in the strategic planning to set goal-oriented objectives for the components that promulgate the overall accomplishment of the *Channeled-Results* of the organization's focused attainments. The organization's top manager is the individual who has been given the ultimate responsibility and obligation for determining which objective are best suited to meet the needs of the organization and what managerial methods or procedures it takes to achieve those goals and objectives. This projects him/her as the logical individual to establish the leadership's motivational planning and process to garner the performance functioning of subordinates at all levels of the organization, his or her ability to pull together information to set attainable objectives, to set-forth planned strategies, as well as structure the overall procedural process to implement a functional plan to achieve objectives. He or she should be the catalyst to ensue that all of the necessary functions for effective accomplishment of established goals and objectives are developed and implemented. The degree and focus for Managerial Leadership toward directing subordinate performances so that goal attainments serves as a motivational tool of management must be structured to meet of the overall goal and objectives of the organization and achieve the desire for self-actualization of subordinates. To assure that these factors are closely aligned often involves a process in which managers at all levels will have to set purposeful targets and construct Channeled-Results that ultimately lead to attainment of organizational objectives.

Fifth Key: *Organizational management must assure that a **Goal-Oriented Leadership Environment** is pervasive and positively endorsed throughout the managerial structure of the agency, as well as, favorably accepted by functional level employees.* Different organizations, even police departments, have problems that usually vary in degree and type, thus, by necessity they will have differing objectives or at-least alternative focuses from responding to the identified concerns. Also, the issue of available resources will greatly affect the manner and what approach a particular police organization will utilize in setting its goals and objectives. Therefore, organizational management must have an awareness of the effect of external influences, the type and pervasiveness of problems with which their agency is usually confronted and the willingness of subordinates to follow the leadership's directed focus to achieved desired goals and objectives. An effective organizational leader will recognize that more often than not, setting goals and objectives will represent a change in the environment and the traditional norms of an organization, thereby, necessitating that his or her leadership style, focus, and procedural methods may have to be altered for an effective Management By Objective process to succeed. And, since Management By Objectives is itself a change and is likely to be altered as the different influences and problems shift, managers at all levels of the agency should agree that positive alterations are necessary if performance is to be enhanced and move toward established accomplishment of goals and objectives. Most persons aware of the needs and aims of management will readily recognize that efforts directed toward an individual accomplishment instead of toward an interactive role in achieving the organization's goals and objectives or a concept that is opposed to change can limit the success of an MBO program before it gets off the ground. Some endorsers of the MBO process have indicated that setting goals and objectives within an organization can be viewed as somewhat personal, since each element or component in the agency has its own set of objectives that should positively interact with the ultimate effort toward achieving the overall organizational *Channeled-Results.* As a final note in discussing this Key Area of Focus to MBO in the setting of organizational goals and objectives, it should be indicated that what managerial leadership is doing through the use of a participatory process, as noted earlier in this chapter, is determining what is feasible and most desirable in terms of the capabilities and potentialities for achieving desired results and enhancing the effectiveness of the organization's leadership.

Sixth Key: *Assuring that a climate within the organization exists where the* **Establishment of a Goal-Oriented Planning Strategy** *is predictable and solicits input from all levels of the organization.* Traditionally, in all police operations, top-level management engages in the Establishment of a Goal-Oriented Strategic Plan that encompasses the entire organization, while middle management assumes the performance obligation of intermediate goal setting and functional-level subordinates carries out the developed plan to achieve the determined goals and objectives. As previously articulated, strategic planning is the process of determining how to pursue the organization's goals and objectives with the resources expected to be available, while allowing for the effects of other influences. Police organizations are usually not as balance concerning the unpredictability of the day-to-day changes necessary because the variation of factors that are too unstable and not conducive to a static MBO process. The accomplishment of a planned strategy by a private organization is usually considered a successful goal achievement. However, a planned strategy by a police department is recognized by most authorities in law enforcement as only a target in which to focus, because no specific objective should be strictly used as a performance gauge. To be productive and perform as expected, strategic planning most start at the top level of the organizational edifice and progress downward throughout the agency. If this practice were not adhered to, then the means-results flow toward the accomplishment of goals and objectives would be ineffective. It is the obligation of organizational leadership to establish a goal-oriented strategy that will focus the effort of the entire agency. In public law enforcement, society expects and requires the organization's leadership to clearly articulate his or her agency's purpose and operational doctrine; develop and identify performance priorities; and document the planned process-results of the stated goals and objectives. It goes without saying that any successive strategic mid-levels planning cannot realistically be made until after top management has set-forth the goals and objectives for the entire organization, because an intermediate strategic planning process will determine and focus on an effort to ensure that the overall goals and objectives of the organization are accomplished. Subordinate components must be a contribution and compliment to the top level of management.

Seventh Key: *True **Goal-Oriented Job Leadership** can only effectively occur in a non-threatening or input soliciting environment.* Police Managers at all levels of an organization who purposely display a non-arbitrary, and input soliciting style of leadership have a better chance to the generating the employee confidence so necessary for participatory worker involvement is actual goal and objective setting for the agency. Strategic planning in a climate of **Goal-Oriented Job Leadership** is the process of determining how specific tasks can best be accomplished utilizing available resources in an allotted time-frame. Each level of managerial level of projecting desired objectives to be accomplished is vital to the organization's success and is interdependent on the other components of the organization. An area not greatly discussed but yet one that is critical to an effective form of strategic planning or MBO process is time. Time is a vital variable in distinguishing between strategic and functional level performance planning. A noteworthy commitment by organizational leadership to a Management By Objective process is absolutely essential to the success of a **Goal-Oriented Job Leadership** program, fundamentally because objective setting begins at the managerial summit of an organization and permeates the subordinate level of the agency. Also, it has been well established in management that managerial leaders tend to be very influential guides for subordinate-level leaders.

SYNOPSIS

The task obligation and role the each organizational leader should be articulated by his or her job performance toward the established mission of the manager's individual unit and the overall accomplishments of the agency's projected results. The strategic planning efforts of the Mid-Level Police Manager's job should be defined by the contribution her and his subordinate component makes toward the ultimate goals and objectives of the department, the projected process-results that a leader sets for his or her unit must consider the need for the planned action to be a Goal-Oriented Motivation. An appropriately planned and implemented Goal-Oriented Motivation will serve to not only stimulate the efforts of subordinate in their work performance, but also it will significantly contribute to the Channeled-Results of the organization.

The upper levels of management must, of course, exercise the power to approve or disapprove these projected plans of action to be implemented by subordinate leaders to assure that these efforts coordinate with the performance behaviors of other organizational elements and is a positive contribution to the accomplishment of the agency's established goals and objectives. Each managerial leader must be aware that his or her performance obligation is part of a manager's responsibility; indeed, it is his or her primary requirement. The prior statement refers to each managerial leader's obligation to participate in the development and establishing of the goals and objectives of the entire organization. Top management establishing an environment where all member of the organization, especially intermediate leadership recognizes and actually considers that his or her input and task performance is a significant contribution to the success of the organization has shown to be quintessential. Inasmuch as the text and this chapter have purposefully focused on Mid-Level Police Management and the need to utilize **Goal-Oriented Job Leadership** as the process of accomplishing a program of Management By Objective, it is clear that managerial leaders at all levels of the organization have a responsibility for result attainment. Primarily, a manager's leadership focus should reflect the objective needs of the entire police organization, rather than merely what his or her direct superior or the leader personally wants. Each unit manager must commit him/herself to both his or her unit and the department's goals with positive action toward attainment of each. The individual leader must know and understand the ultimate organization's goals and objectives, plus, specifically what is expected of him or her and why; also, what accomplishment he or she will be the gauged against and by what method of measurement that will be used. There should always, as near as possible, be total agreement within the entire organization's management and hopefully with each unit and functional level worker. This can be achieved only when each level of management contributes to the strategic planning and the attainment of as much functional participatory input as possible, to what goals and objectives are actively and responsibly defined by the organization. Some of the most effective managers have each of their subordinates' leaders articulate a documented plan that defines objectives of his or her unit and articulates how it envision these accomplishments will positively interact with the overall strategic Management By

Objective process established for the entire organization. By so doing, a leader can then set down the performance standards, which he or she believes are most conducive to the MBO program being implemented. Also, such an effort helps to establish teamwork, and harmonize the Goal-Oriented Motivation of the individuals within the organization's goals and objectives. Management By Objectives and Goal-Oriented Motivation make the achievement of the organization's goals and objectives the focus of all levels of management. Implementing Goal-Oriented Motivation as a prime element of MBO inspires both managers and functional employees to action, not because they are being directed to do something, but because they perceive a positive incentive in the objective task. The doctrine of MBO has shown to be one of, if not, the most significant concept in managerial leadership for all levels of organizational direction, control, and task accomplishment. It is clear that Management By Objectives, the positives gained from Goal-Oriented Job Leadership, and the Channeled-Results obtained from formulating a strategy planning-focused process may properly be called the principal doctrine of effective managerial direction and control. MBO, as Goal-Oriented Leadership, is foundationally based on an analysis of the specific needs of all levels of an organization's management leaders and the obstacles that will be encountered. Finally, it applies to every managerial leader, whatever his or her level and position within the agency's edifice, as well as insuring that the functional performance of employees while coordinating the personal need of workers with the goals and objectives of the organization.

Chapter Ten

PERFORMANCE INITIATIVE

The term performance initiative may appear to be a new dimensional characteristic in association with operational police management. However, it is a term meaning basically the same as managerial initiative, innovation, or being a self-starter. The correlation and/or synonymous nature of these terms relative to this dimensional trait will be additionally clarified later in this chapter. But before the text gets into defining terms and establishing their influence on managerial behavior, it is important that some concept is gained of where this leadership characteristic originates. It is basically a "job performance concept," referring to the fact that a manager should develop and implement new or modified programs if his or her operation is to remain effective. Most job situations will require adjustments in methods from time to time to remain effective (and police work is no different). People and situations quickly adapt to the routine or traditional methods, much the same as the human body does to medication. Therefore, job performance actions rapidly become ineffective in dealing with a behavior problem.

Thus, there is generally a need for performance modifications through the initiation of new ideas and actions relative to the situation. A performance initiative is an innovative trend for department leadership to break away from the traditional conceptual view of police agencies, which are known to be conservative and very slow to change. However, modern times have produced subordinates that are less disciplined, more prone to ask why, and a clientele (offenders) that are mentally superior and more innovative than their predecessors.

The most effective approach will be to not suddenly make a number of radical changes over a very short period of time, especially realizing the orthodox nature of an organization such as a police department. The nontraditional changes should be made in a manner that attempts not to be disruptive. However, if a situation calls for immediate radical changes, an effective operational manager must respond appropriately. But if the situation does not require an immediate innovative action, a police manager must avoid getting the impression that the new approach to the job will be a total abolishment of the established procedure. Typically, top-level police managers that are unfamiliar with a new operating philosophy or technique will be hesitant until it has proven itself. An operational police manager must remember that innovative actions of any form that originate below the top management level will traditionally be initially viewed cautiously. The primary fear will be that it is an abdication of the established structure and a loss of control by management in the traditional sense. The chapter on "Communication" clearly indicates that information flows more freely and positively in a downward pattern in law enforcement agencies. This is a result of a police department's general pyramidal structure that is fashioned for complete and accurate information to be channeled down the chain of command. Affirmative performance initiative can be very positive for an operational police manager's organizational growth and development, but if misperceived, it can label him or her as a **radical** and be a detriment to intradepartment advancement.

But before we become more entwined into the functional aspects and beneficial outcomes of a **performance initiative** by an operational police manager, it is important that a comprehensive definition be set forth. A performance initiative by an operational-level police manager is defined as "job behavioral activity that actively influences functional occurrences toward effective goal achievement and which postulates the individual as an innovative self-starter." In other words, it is the initiation of appropriate actions rather than the clinging to a passive approach of a follower, who will traditionally await direction or adhere to outdated patterns. Principally, it is a demonstrated ability to take necessary action to accomplish goals and objectives beyond what is basically required, as well as the origination of creative and effective programs by taking that extra step. From this elongated definition and explanation of what is meant by performance initiative, it is clear that the text is referring to this dimensional trait in terms of being more than just **initiative**, **innovation**, and/or a **self-starter**. The text is concerned also with this leadership characteristic as a **creative management** tool that is essential for effective managerial performance.

When upper management evaluates an operational police manager in terms of performance initiative, it generally considers this dimensional trait as a measure of the individual's demonstrated activity, which refers to whether or not the person needs prodding for action and is alert to opportunities to improve job performance and work output. The traditional inquiries are:

OPERATIONAL LEADER "C" HAS FAILED TO DEMONSTRATE <u>PERFORMANCE INITIATIVE</u> WHICH IS AN ESSENTIAL TRAIT CHARACTERISTIC.

1. Does the positional leader need pressuring to finish assignments in a timely manner?
2. Does the positional leader take action to achieve an objective that is considered beyond what is normally expected?
3. Does the positional leader request additional tasks and/or demonstrate innovative ingenuity?

What has been said to this juncture has been an attempt to adequately introduce the concept of performance initiative as a viable and essential characteristic of operational managerial leadership. But the real essence of the information presented maintains that management is made up of a number of interrelated activities, such as decision making, training, planning, organizing, and many others, that must be aggressively and positively approached if a positional leader is to be effective. However, before desired effectiveness is achieved, it becomes paramount for the individual to explore how an operational police manager can improve personal job behaviors in the performance initiative dimensional characteristic.

REQUIRED INNOVATION
AND AGGRESSIVENESS OF ACTIONS

The two primary factors that most affect an operational police manager's creativity or adaptability during on-the-job performances are the individual's **degree of innovation** and the **channeling of aggressiveness**, both of which are considered important to effective leadership behavior. An analysis of the top managers of any organization will generally reveal a high degree of these overt tendencies. However, to simplify our discussion concerning the components of performance initiative, this text will combine these factors and hereafter refer to them collectively as **behavior initiative**. The men and women who seem to advance to the top of modern-day police departments are the ones who display a noteworthy amount of behavior initiative and whom are generally effective in making things happen. These **result-achievers** will typically demonstrate a focus on affirmative job performance actions that seems to distance them from **competitors**. Most notable among these qualities are:

1. **A Practice of Extra Effort and the Demonstrating of a Zest or Zeal for Meticulous Goal Achievement**. A behavioral initiative that exhibits these qualities will reveal themselves in an energetic display of assignment accomplishment. It will usually give the appearance of dynamic enthusiasm for the overall job and the individual's contribution to the department's mission. In the traditional sense, this does not imply that the person is a wildly happy or an indefatigable worker. The individual will not appear vastly different from any other worker or equivalent status. The difference will be in the person's approach to the job and his or her specific assignment, as well as the individual's itinerant observation for opportunities to improve what may be done and the tendency not to be content with the status quo. Typically, the person displays an innate ability to isolate the essential components of a multifaceted task and focus personal knowledge, influence, and leadership ability to get the job accomplished. The above definitive descriptors appear to be an acquired habit and/or skill among those who advance as leaders in most police departments.

2. **The Ability to Discern What Is Important from the Insignificant Aspects of an Assignment**. The capability to judge the more significant demands for action is nothing other than an ability to prioritize the events that an effective positional leader will handle. The demands on most people's time, especially those in leadership positions, is such that a prioritized response to job requirements is mandatory. An effective operational police manager or result-achiever will cultivate the skill of differentiating between essential things that need to be accomplished and the things that can be del-

egated, delayed, or dismissed. As with a positional leader going through **incoming communiques** or a candidate handling an **in-basket in an assessment center testing process**, each item should be reviewed prior to any action. This should be accomplished, because the last item reviewed may affect how the previous ones must be handled. An operational police manager, as with other positions of leadership in the organization, must acquire the ability to perceive the entire picture, meaning that the individual must train him- or herself to ascertain the total problem or concern before taking any action. This will include not only availability of time and resources but also the effect the item's handling will have on the overall operation. An operational manager, like functional leadership, should have a productivity focus if he or she is to be effective and/or aspire to ascend the hierarchy ladder within the organization. It should be pointed out that not only is prioritizing work a must for the ascending leaders of an organization, but it is a necessity for any individual responsible for accomplishing a number of tasks in a specific time frame. Prioritization, like most other performance traits detailed in this text, is a practiced skill that can be enhanced and improved upon. Remember, the greater the effect on a leader's operation and the more critical the time allotment for handling a concern, the higher the priority rating the item should receive.

3. **Responsiveness in Seeking and Utilization of the Concepts of Others (Participatory Management Whenever Possible).** The effective result-achiever realizes that a type of collective brainstorming is the best way to arrive at the most practical ideas for dealing with a problem. The individual should also realize that because of the external influences, it is not always possible to utilize a participatory style of leadership. But, at the same time, it is recognized that no particular individual in the department will have all good ideas all the time. The adage "that two heads are better than one" certainly applies in this situation. The individual should assure that he or she fosters an atmosphere that will allow others, subordinates and peers, to express their ideas on the accomplishment of goals and objectives. These individuals must have the perception that their suggestions will be given **due consideration** and that, if implemented, deserved accolades will be appropriately disseminated. A practice of actively seeking the input of others is a recognition by a positional leader that he or she is not a "know-it-all" genius who can operate in isolation. The fact that the individual gathers and uses information from a number of sources is actually a positive, as it is reflective of a personal leadership ability to utilize all available resources. There's an environmental attitude that is a creative byproduct in functional-level subordinates who realize that their suggested operational ideas will be used to improve their working conditions and productivity. The realization of hav-

ing those recommendations acted upon is an immeasurable subordinate motivator. The real leadership accomplishment in this situation by the positional leader or result-achiever is the confidence of subordinates that they can generate and/or apply new concepts in their assignment for improved effectiveness. This kind of behavioral initiative by a positional leader is generally contagious when performance effectiveness becomes obvious.

4. **A Tenacity of Purpose of Goal Achievement and an Elusion of Inept Influences**. The previous quality raised the awareness of a need for "participatory management" whenever possible. However, at the same time, the individual has to be able to distinguish when an adamant approach to directed activity is required. A tenacious behavioral initiative does not imply a lack of concern for the self-actualizing needs of others but rather a realization that at times circumstances and the situation will not afford an opportunity for external influences before a decision is made or implemented. A **tenacity of purpose** also implies a patience on the part of an operational police manager to wade through the trivial matters and bureaucratic delays that will often incarnate his or her job. The positional leader's tolerance in dealing with people or meticulously working toward objective achievement should not be confused with submissiveness, because the truly behavioral initiative individual will not hesitate to affirmatively take direct action when needed to handle a situation. This should be generally apparent in aspiring or accomplished leaders in their refusals to vacillate when firmness is needed, and the willingness to display tactful patience as required makes the attribute of the individual's intellectual capability and comprehension very evident.

5. **A Mental and Operational Ability to Circumvent Barriers to Goal Accomplishment**. The true result-achiever has heightened personal ability to bypass the many obstacles that may present themselves. The individual develops an ability to scrutinize barriers to effective objective achievement and determine methods for eliminating them or their effect on the task's completion. An effective behavior initiative leader can often rotate an obstacle into an advantageous adjunct to desired goals. It has been said that this particular skill is more conducive to reflecting an operational manager's desire and enthusiasm for the leadership position than any other job factor. The zestful result-achiever will get a positive charge from being able to confront and successfully deal with barriers that have stumped others. As a leader becomes more experienced and practiced in dealing with obstacles that hinder goal achievement, the individual will be able to anticipate and take steps to avoid them before it becomes a problem. This, too, is a practiced skill that can be improved through experience and concentrated effort.

These qualities all call for an operational police manager to display a predisposition for **required innovation** and **aggressiveness of action**. None of the qualities are thought to be an inherent aspect of personality and therefore are not innate to any particular individual. They are trait characteristics developed through experience and practice. Any person said to be predisposed toward leadership can, through acquired knowledge and an expenditure of effort, fine-tune personal behavior initiative into effectiveness as a positional leader. Most organizational leaders will readily admit that an operational manager will need to develop and utilize such behavior if the person is to be effective in a modern-day police department.

In concluding this section on "Required Innovation and Aggressiveness of Actions," it must be said that most operational police managers' expenditures of time and effort are noteworthy. Their operational proficiency has to be so finely tuned and functional that the extraordinary event or unexpected incident is handled with the apparent same ease as the so-called routine one, basically because in police work nothing can or should be considered strictly routine. Thus, when dealing with the volatile extremes of human emotions, as does operational law enforcement, there are very few static situations. Most successful operational police leaders display an exceptional zestful enthusiasm for their position, which translates into a great deal of psychological and physical output of energy. In other words, they are usually very dedicated and hardworking members of the police organization. Another factor that should be considered when an individual becomes a manager or positional leader at any level is that the person no longer stops working when his or her shift ends. This becomes clearly focused when we realize that every time the individual gives consideration to handling a personnel or operational problem while not at work, the person is performing as a responsible leader. And, it is only natural to give some contemplation to a specific or a perceived difficult job-related problem that has to be faced during the quiet reflective times, such as the drive home or the interval between laying down and the onset of sleep.

With what has been discussed in this chapter, it is clear that a controlled degree of aggressiveness and innovation is necessary in order to be an effective operational manager in a police organization; also, the aggressive innovation must be properly channeled and focused to achieve maximum results in meeting objectives. Further, it should be realized that pride and self-confidence are factors in an operational manager's over job performance initiative.

PARAMETERS OF INNOVATIVE ACTIONS

The apparent need for innovative actions on the part of an operational police manager is clearly delineated by the nature of the duties; so too are

"John has found a sure way of initiating action."

AN EFFECTIVE OPERATIONAL LEADER NEED NOT UTILIZE EXTERNAL STIM-
ULUS TO MOTIVATE JOB PERFORMANCE ACTION IN SUBORDINATES.

the requirements to set limitations within which innovation or deviations from the norm are acceptable. Police departments as a general rule have long been known for their conservative approach and traditional patterns of behavior in dealing with problems. Also, when considering parameters we must take into account that police departments are in business of enforcing criminal and civil laws, which by necessity are very rigid and precise in definition and application. Therefore, it is not difficult to understand why uncontrolled innovative actions on the part of positional leaders in a police organization are not commonplace as a way of life. The text is not attempting to imply that innovation is a stranger in police organizations but rather to point out some of the traditional negative influences experienced by positional leaders. It should be delineated that the concerns identified above are not exclusive to police departments but exist in most rigidly controlled and/ or regulated organizations.

In strictly controlled or tightly regulated operational settings such as a police department, innovative decision making in dealing with concerns are generally not encouraged and likewise they are not discouraged. Innovative decisions that are untested or tried have to be scrutinized as to their legality, economic effectiveness, and correlations with other operations. The organization simply does not provide a creative mechanism for expression and use of non-traditional ideology. Most upper level managers in larger police departments recognize the value of initiative and creative actions that go beyond what is merely required. However, it is difficult to "throw off the yoke" of established precedential methods that are tried and proven, especially when every decision that the individual makes in an operational situation has the potential effect that most police concerns do. The process and desire for innovative thinking or creative execution is highly promoted in administrative or staff assignments. Improved efficiency and accountability is viewed as a plus in the paperwork aspect of law enforcement, but in a society and field of employment where the per capita rate of litigation against the organization and its leadership is almost the same among workers and as against clientele. Human resource managers are especially vulnerable to this type of legal action. This trend does not reflect any particular thing that the organization or its leaders are doing but rather that a tightly controlled public operation is a much easier legal target than a loosely regulated entity.

The formulation of specific parameters that can be established to cultivate innovative aggressiveness of an operational police manager ostensibly is not possible. In fact, this apparently is not possible in any system where performance activity of workers are strictly organized and controlled with precise parameter guidelines. If independent or innovative action permitted based on personal perceptual opinions and differences in enforcement activity, behavioral performances would vary as greatly as the personalities of the individuals rendering them. Therefore, most police organizations will establish procedures with basic guidelines for as many situations and variations as can be perceived. An operational police manager is then directed to adhere as closely as possible to the documented procedures, and if a situation does not fit established precedent, then the actions must be comprehensively recorded. The recorded information will be evaluated as to being proper or improper and how to establish a criteria for a future-like occurrence. Thus, the parameters are set by the individual's application of established procedures to a situation being dealt with. No operational police manager is expected or desired to be a robot with little imagination and no creative drive or ambition. But in police work, unlike an architect where the person can let his or her imagination run wild and then test each concept to determine if it works, if an operational manager, functional leader, or line personnel employed that concept of operation, it could well result in an injury and possibly even a loss of life. Performance initiative is not a foreign concept to operational management; it's merely a process that is typically tempered by a need for tight controls at all levels of a police organization.

Parameters of innovative actions are further restricted by the fact that no preconceived notion or predisposition can be determined for dealing with the various human emotion, whether an employee or a police clientele. A centralized control of innovative ideals and/or an across-the-board standardization of reactive policies tends to be vastly overdone in most police organizations, but this does not mean that the controls hinder effectiveness. To the contrary, it improves the department's operation, even though a creative atmosphere is inhibited. Thus, the most obvious way to address the issue of police managerial innovative action is to say that scrutiny and restrictive controls forces the individual to be reserved in deviating from precedential practices. In other words, aggressive innovation is to be approached with caution and guarded efforts so as not to violate or circumvent any established departmental directives.

WHAT ARE THE MEASURES
OF PERFORMANCE INITIATIVE?

Identifying specific occurrences or behaviors that can be unequivocally used as an appraisal of performance initiative in an operational police manager is as difficult a task as establishing static parameters of innovative actions. However, because of the current trend toward establishing criteria for measuring the performance behavior of modern police personnel on the basis of tangible results, we have identified some managerial behaviors that are traditional to positional leaders. These same behaviors tend to enhance an operational manager's performance through increased emphasis. But if these measures are to be used and have some positive effect, it is important that an operational manager get a clear understanding of the identified criteria and that he or she advance a positive performance behavior in regards to proposed measures. An increased emphasis in these areas will be important, as they may help the individual elevate personal work output and improve operational processes.

Social scientists have disagreed as to whether performance initiative can adequately be measured in an operational manager. The points of contention are: (1) that much of an operational leader's behavior is **situational adaptivity**; and (2) that actions or recommendations to improve his or her operation's productivity is an **expected consequence of the job**. Therefore, viewing these contentions from a purely pragmatical standpoint, there may be some credence to the argument, because if a person performs a task that he or she is required and expected to do as a part of the individual's normal duty obligations, can that truly be considered performance initiative? That's an interesting question, as is the expectation of **mental adjustments** to problem solving. But if we consider innovative actions and extra effort as a natural consequence or expected behavior of an operational police manager, then performance initiative becomes less significant as a leadership trait. Also, the appropriately defining and establishing of measurable criteria will be virtually impossible. However, the author does not subscribe to the theory that "performance initiative is a natural course of managerial action that cannot be measured." An alternate theory conjectured by other social scientists contends that performance initiative is an evaluative characteristic of operational leadership. This latter contention, favored by the author, sets forth that some **situational adaptive behavior** and **innovative actions** are required and/or expected of an operational manager, but that "there is a point where extra effort and creative accomplishments goes beyond what is merely called for, to become **self-initiated activity**." When this occurs, performance initiative becomes a viable and measurable trait of leadership.

Utilizing the latter-stated social scientist view of performance initiative, the author has developed the following list of behavioral measures from an upper-management perspective. The following list, though comprehensive, is not absolute for all police organizations.

1. Does the operational manager's research and knowledge acquisition allow the individual to be prepared to respond readily to most questions or concerns regarding his or her operation? Accomplishment is obtained through anticipation of problems/concerns and the obtaining of needed information to appropriately respond.
2. Does the operational manager display a positive perception of **cost-effective** use of resources and manpower? Does he project changes in operational influences and prepare for these adjustments?
3. Has the operational manager developed safeguards to deal with unexpected crisis situations? The person should avoid always being a **reactive manager**; prior planning is more productive.
4. Does the operational manager show a willingness to go beyond what is obvious in dealing with subordinates' behavior? In other words, does the individual react only to the symptomatic behavior without seeking the possible underlying cause, to prevent future occurrences?
5. Does the individual frequently check the progress of subordinates' job performances with an eye toward successful goal achievement? Do the **work standards** established promulgate effectiveness and efficiency?
6. Are there frequent crisis occurrences in the manager's operation that are caused by a lack of teamwork between the element's subordi-

nates? Have operational situations reached a critical phase because of managerial inaction or inappropriate action?

7. Does the operational manager meet **due dates** consistently, handling operational as well as administrative matters in the allotted time frame and thus promoting smoother interaction with other elements?

8. Does the operational manager appear to be in full control of his or her operation at all times, not only possessing some knowledge of most operational occurrences but also having a notable influence on the outcome, through managerial input, if necessary?

9. Does the operational manager have an efficient **appraisal process** that is tied to an effective training program for subordinates? Areas of deficiency in workers need to be determined, as well as a method of eliminating them.

10. Has the operational manager made **provisions for** and/or **assured that** adequate leadership and responsible authority will be available during his or her absence? A **chain of responsibility** should be set up to achieve goals and objectives when managerial presence is not possible.

Even though these measures are clearly considered a part of the overall functioning of an effective operational police manager, it should be evident that a non-industrious or a weak performing positional leader could function adequately without going the extra step that most of the identified measures delineated. Therefore, the ten appraisal areas identified become key functions in which an operational police manager or any positional leader can be evaluated as to personal performance initiative. Thus, an operational police manager who wishes to strengthen a personal display of this dimensional trait characteristic should assure that the questions are answered affirmatively about his or her performance. Like so many of the other traits discussed in this text, Performance initiative is improved through special effort and consistent practice.

Performance initiative, as may be apparent, relative to the previously stated information has its basic derivation from **managerial motivation**. Managerial motivation, in reference to an operational police manager's performance behavior, reflects the inducement of subordinates to perform effectively. It also has reference to the influences that a manager can stimulate desired performances in a positional leader as well as subordinates toward operational achievement. The motivation of workers has been well-documented as being primarily linked to the individual needs of subordinates. The **needs factor**, beginning with the **basic need** through the **self-actualization need**, is discussed in some detail in the chapter on "Obtaining Followership" (leadership). The department's mission accomplishment through the efforts of an operational police manager is to motivate subordinates to perform productively. A police manager's **innovative resourcefulness** enters into this phase of the performance process. A positional leader motivates subordinates in a manner that will assure that their personal needs as well as organizational goals and objectives are achieved. The **innovativeness of job performance** and/or the **self-motivated efforts** on the part of an effective operational police manager surfaces as the individual attempts to deal with the diverse factors that inspire different people, principally because typically appropriate job performance in no two subordinates will be induced by exactly the same incentive motivators. And, it is a well-documented contention that employee need fulfillment is directly associated with personal motivation to meet organizational objectives. Creativity and adaptability is necessary, because often certain needs requirements of a subordinate is unknown even to the individual. But until the unknown need is filled, the employee's motivation is lacking and so may be the positional leader's effectiveness in the performance initiative. In other words, an operational manager must be able to understand his or her subordinates in order to be able to detect when satisfaction is not being achieved by a perceived need objective and to adapt or develop tangible or psychological influences that will motivate each individual subordinate.

Therefore, an abridgement of what has been stated about performance initiative is that it's not merely being a **self-starter** or an **extra effort** performer as a positional leader. It is also an idea person, one that is innovative and creative, within established parameters in developing ways or methods to improve his or her element's operational performance, as well as being a **comprehensively aware leader** whose knowledge of the psychological influences and the incentives that motivate subordinates is effectively used. An effective performance initiative police manager is a positive combination of all of these factors. The simplest way to define an operational police manager under this dimensional trait characteristic is to say that **the individual is a high energy, self-motivated, confident and assured leader with the personal courage to be creative or to try new things, within limits, in an effort to be as effective at goal achievement as possible**.

SYNOPSIS

Performance initiative is not a dimensional trait traditionally thought of as being associated with managerial leadership. Initiative as a characteristic has long been identified with leadership assessment to gauge a person's job motivation and functional efforts. However, when the term performance is added as part of the nomenclature of this dimensional trait, it is no longer orthodox as a measurement of managerial ability and behavior in this area. Terms like innovation, creativity, and motivation then become a part of a comprehensive definition.

We now recognize that performance initiative in an operational police manager as a desired trait characteristic is very difficult, and not all social scientists agree that it can be effectively gauged. The point of contention is whether or not displayed performance initiative is a plus in leadership behavior or merely a carrying out of what is expected of a positional leader.

Our contention in this text is that a non-industrious or adequately performing leader can meet expectations, but that an operational manager displaying the ten identified areas of evaluation is apparently more positively motivated and effective. Performance initiative, as perceived and utilized in its proper perspective, has a positive motivational effect on subordinates that generally translates into increased productivity and higher morale. Therefore, it is essential for functioning operational police managers to be aware of the elements and measures of performance initiative. This knowledge should then be transposed into positive action that will enhance personal managerial performance and overall effectiveness as a positional leader.

Chapter Eleven

THE DYNAMICS OF A SECONDARY LEADER'S ROLE IN THE ORGANIZATION

Leadership is a dynamic process, in that it is the influencing of subordinates to work toward the achievement of an objective. The need for management and control of human and material resources in an organizational setting is ever-changing, thus requiring managerial leadership to be dynamic (adaptable) to the events or situations confronted. In this text, as with other books addressing the concept of leadership and management and as they relate to a mid-level leader, the terms are used interchangeably. In actuality, leadership is a function of management; however, since they both refer to the controlling and directing of organizational resources, the synonymous use is very appropriate. *In this section we are concerned with not only the components and aspects of managerial leadership but with the required knowledge needs, organizational role, and development of subordinates.*

In addressing functional mid-level police management there are a number of traditionally required knowledge areas that are associated with operational secondary leadership. Generally, those areas that an effective leader or manager are required to know are concerned with the management and handling of subordinates. However, there are other areas where specific knowledge needs are essential to basic managerial functioning in modern policing, where legal actions are a primary motivator. This sue-prone motivation encompasses not only components external to the police organization but it also involves the current subordinate mentality of seeking legal remedies for every imagined wrong. Therefore, recognizing the previously stated tendency, it is essential for an individual who has direct management responsibility for job performances involving the behavioral control of others, to have some basic knowledge beyond the traditional concepts. From what has been discussed to this point, it is apparently critical for the modern-day police mid-level manager to have a basic knowledge of: (1) the operational or technical skills of his or her subordinates; and (2) the behavioral limits of midlevel managerial actions or interactions with subordinates. During the discussion of the areas of required job knowledge that are perceived as being very necessary to the effective and efficient performance of an operational police mid-level manager, the text will cover role responsibility, functioning, subordinate development, plus some practical knowledge areas that are considered critical.

Previously, it has been discussed how the personal factors contribute to the effectiveness of a functional police mid-level manager. But it must be remembered that the personal characteristics of a positional leader do not operate in a vacuum. The positional leader's perception of what his or her organizational role is has a lot to do with job performance as a mid-level manager. Every individual has some kind of a self-perception of the way that he or she should act in a given position of leadership; this personal view is generally referred to as a role concept. Those persons surrounding the projected position also have a role perceptual view of how the individual in that position should act or perform. These role expectations are important to the functional-level police mid-level manager's performance because an awareness of what is expected by self and others will enable the individual to meet the organizational requirements.

Organizational role expectations of positional leader such as operational police mid-level managers are usually formalized into written directives as position guides or job descriptions. These *position guides* and *job descriptions* are generally formulated from the actions of prior and/or incumbent leaders in the identified position. A mid-level leader's role expectations are divided into two fundamental categories: the **Responsibility** (obligation) and the **Function** (technical).

Responsibility

The functional police mid-level manager's responsibilities reflect the core essence of what his or her role expectations are in the organization. The five performance responsibilities identified should put this discussion into perspective. These role responsibilities refer to:

A mid-level manager is a member of management. The functional police mid-level manager must recognize that as a positional leader he or she is a member of the leadership team of the organization. The method of leadership and the performance of subordinates must coincide with the overall goals and objectives of the organization. A police mid-level manager should operate the unit or element as an essential part

of the overall organization, with the realization that he or she is personally responsible for its operational makeup and performance. Typically,
the overall organization's documented formalized structure will establish
the basic makeup of each unit or component. However, an awareness of
organizational concepts and basic principles reflect an important part in
managerial development and effectiveness of performance.

A functional law enforcement mid-level manager is principally responsible for overseeing the job performance of subordinates. The mid-
level manager must assure the performance of achievements of his/her
element or unit toward the organization's goals and objectives by getting
things done through subordinates. Operational mid-level managers should also have a comprehensive knowledge of their functional position in
the management chain and what authority this status entails. Further, as a
positional leader the functional police mid-level manager must be aware
that an organizational leadership role refers to *the process of directing and controlling subordinates and materials resources toward goal accomplishment and that
a basic managerial obligation, as a member of the hierarchy, is the responsibility of
leading in compliance with the dictates of upper organizational management.*

A mid-level manager should be a loyal company employee.
The functional police mid-level manager should be loyal to the organization and its goals and objectives. As a member of the management team,
a functional mid-level manager should support the decisions of his or her
superiors. It must be remembered that each employee of the police
agency has an obligation to be loyal to upper management and the organization as a whole. This holds true especially for positional leaders such
as operational mid-level managers. They were supposedly selected or
promoted for their ability to get the job done and their willingness to support the dictates of the organization. Thus, operational police mid-level
managers, by virtue of their position, have a duty to perform within the
guidelines and practices of the organization toward goal accomplishment.

Like the functional level officer and primary supervisor, a mid-level
manager in a police operation should attempt to perform personal duties
as objectively and impartially as possible without stepping outside of the
expected role as a loyal member of the organization's management. By
this, the author is referring to the need for the line police leader to possess the courage to advance a feedback suggestion or recommendations
made by subordinates that will improve the element's operation or overall goal accomplishment even though it may not be initially popular.
However, once upper management makes a decision, even though personally the mid-level manager may not agree, the decision should be
supported and endorsed just as if he or she was in total agreement.

It is considered a fact that a mid-level manager cannot be a totally effective positional leader if he or she is considered *bias to the views of upper management or subordinates.* There tends to be less respect for positional authority concerning rank or command responsibility, and thus the mid-level manager will not be effective and efficient in all instances as a leader. Some professional organizations have long recognized the closer that mid-level leaders are aligned to the worker level views of duties performed, the less productive they are as managers. The mid-level manager who functions as a secondary leader/supervisor in public law enforcement, like the crew leader in general industry, is an extremely difficult and often impossible position for maintenance of a managerial detachment and objectivity duties, the positional leader (mid-level manager) is required to perform the same functional tasks as subordinates. Therefore, for functional-level mid-level managers of a public police operation to be totally effective as positional leaders, they must be positionally situated in the organizational structure (referring to duties and authority) and attitudinally loyal to the organization.

The line mid-level manager is a key person in the organization. To simply state that the functional mid-level managers are important to the success of an organization is almost an understatement. It can be shown that it is the second most essential position in the hierarchical edifice for an organization to achieve its goals and objectives, because it is at this functional managerial level that control over basic work is performed. It is the mid-level manager as a primary managerial leader who directs, controls, motivates, and regulates the efforts of the functional-level employees who make up the actual base upon which an organization is built and performs.

The functional-level police mid-level manager's responsibilities as the key to management's success include good judgment, integrity, initiative, courage, patience, flexibility, and many other leadership qualities. The duty tasks of a functional police mid-level manager listed below clearly delineate the individual as an essential member of the management team regarding organizational goal accomplishment.

A functional mid-level manager of a public law enforcement operation is responsible:

1. To upper management for the efficient and effective performance of his or her subordinates in accordance with established organizational guidelines.

2. For exercising the command authority consistent with his or her position in the organization.
3. For having knowledge of organizational directives, such as the rules, guidelines, policies, and procedures affecting his or her operation and/or subordinates.
4. For understanding and transmitting to subordinates all directives of upper management intended for their use in performing assigned duties.
5. For adherence to an exemplary standard of personal conduct and duty performance as an example for subordinates.
6. To avoid actions that may be perceived as being in violation of a subordinate's moral or legal rights during his or her performance of duty.

The operational functions listed above are but a few of the responsibilities associated with functional mid-level management. The identified duties clearly illustrate the important role that the functional mid-level manager plays in a police organization's operation.

An operational police mid-level manager serves as a buffer between management and functional level workers. The word *buffer* may not be the most appropriate term to describe the role responsibility of an operational police mid-level manager. Terms such as **translator**, **transmitter**, or **go-between** may be more appropriate as to the fact that operational mid-level management works closely with each element and thus has a better comprehension of both their respective motivational needs and efforts. However, because most of the traditional concepts of the adversary management-worker relationship that still exist and the fact that both entities have to be effective if the organization is to achieve its goals and objectives, the functional police mid-level manager does serve as a cushion between the two elements.

The term *buffer* as used in the context of a secondary manager's role responsibility means a person who shields both management and operational level subordinates from the routine of each component's respective functions. This does not imply that directives or recommendations will be filtered by the mid-level manager but rather that information relayed will be formatted in a form that is most understandable and acceptable to the respective level for which it is intended. The aforementioned areas of role responsibilities and the basic skills of leadership are essential knowledge requirements for a functional mid-level manager, if the leader is to function effectively within a public police organization.

"I am right about the way it should be done."

"No, you're wrong, it should be done my way."

A MID-LEVEL MANAGER MUST BE ABLE TO HANDLE DISPUTES BETWEEN SUBORDI-NATES AND BETWEEN UPPER AND LOWER LEADERSHIP.

Operational Actions

Operational mid-level police leadership, as previously defined, means the handling and management of functional-level personnel and material resources. This does not imply that a mid-level manager needs to possess great technical skills in the areas that are being supervised. Operational midlevel managers are not employed as technically skilled craftspersons but as first-level leaders. This may seem to be somewhat of a contradiction, especially in light of the fact that most police organizations tend to promote the best workers or most skilled employees. It is generally agreed that there is a need to recognize and reward the efforts of an organization's best employees. Also, the subordinate's work habits and performance are clear indications of the person's pro-organizational attitude and motivation. It is readily admitted that these qualities are important to a mid-level manager's makeup, but they're not all inclusive and should be considered in conjunction with other trait characteristics for effective handling of personnel.

The type of secondary manager who is expected to have greater skills than subordinates is considered a *Functional Patrol Leader*. However, as has been articulated, police mid-level managers/supervisors are traditionally not as effective and efficient as functional secondary police leaders, because the individual can concentrate solely on the job of managing people and resources. The functional police mid-level manager does not need to be expertly skilled in the technical area that is being managed. The mid-level leader does however need to have a working knowledge of the fundamentals of the operation as well as the desired results. The mid-level manager should maintain a basic and current knowledge of any changes in practices, techniques, and procedures concerning the operation being supervised. The operational police mid-level manager is also expected to have comprehensive organizational knowledge of overall goal-achievement expectations. Also, the leader should have a fundamental awareness of the interpersonal and scientific knowledge skills of personnel management in the handling of subordinates.

The operational knowledge requirements that a functional police mid-level manager is expected to be aware of during daily operation are listed below. The identified knowledge areas are not exclusive to an operational police mid-level manager, but they are considered critical to the effectiveness of a positional leader. The required operational knowledge areas are:

An ability to formulate a plan of action. The modern-day police mid-level manager, whether in public policing or some other industry, must be able to project the available resources, human and material, toward accomplishing the organization's goals and objectives. From this projection and evaluation the mid-level manager is expected to develop an operational plan for subordinates. The knowledge required for a mid-level leader to be effective as a planner was presented in the chapter regarding *Decision Making*. The police mid-level manager must also have a working knowledge of *how to obtain* and *how much* information to acquire before developing a workable plan. The secondary manager must further demonstrate an ability to analyze and interpret the collected information as to what is the most effective and efficient use of the allotted resources to achieve desired results.

Additionally, the functional-level police mid-level manager as a planner must be able to conceptualize the future of his or her operation and then forecast coming needs and adjustments. Also, the mid-level manager has to develop the management skills necessary to be able to anticipate problems and make decisions to resolve them prior to the situation occurring. He also needs to be aware of possible personnel changes or adjustments that will affect his or her element's operation, through transfers or promotions, etc., and formulate strategies that will compensate for these modifications.

In essence, a primary function of a functional mid-level manager in a police operation is the anticipation and planning of the performance activities of subordinates.

An ability to provide training for subordinates. An effective functional police mid-level manager should have the ability through personal efforts to provide necessary training for subordinates. Whether the training is initial orientation or on-the-job training, such as in-service training for incumbent subordinates, the more accomplished mid-level managers will assure that their personnel are adequately trained. A mid-level leader must realize that training is a never-ending process, especially in public policing where court decisions, laws, and procedural techniques change almost daily. The effective police mid-level manager must maintain a current knowledge of these changes and develop the skills necessary to train subordinates for improved efficiency of their performance. A line police mid-level manager must be aware of the techniques of effective teaching and the personal traits needed, such as patience and clarity of presentation during their instruction efforts.

Effective mid-level managers are motivated to enhance the development and performance of their subordinates through continuous on-the-job training.

An ability to control subordinates. Police mid-level managers must have the knowledge and ability to control the performance behavior of subordinates if they are to be effective. A mid-level manager should learn to use appropriate managerial control techniques to direct subordinates toward a successful conclusion of their performance objective. There must be a thorough awareness of the rules, regulations, policies, and procedures of the organization to assure that the dictates to subordinates will be in compliance with established directives. An effective mid-level manager knows the value of disciplinary actions, both positive and negative, to re-enforce desired behavior in subordinates. It is realistic to anticipate that some errors of performance or misbehavior by subordinates will occur. Therefore, a primary measure of a competent functional mid-level manager is the ability to deal with these performance exceptions by leading and guiding the employees toward the desired organizational goals and objectives.

An efficient and effective police mid-level manager will direct or control a subordinate's job performance behavior through motivation and manipulation.

It is clear from the above information that police mid-level managers must enhance their required knowledge in the areas of the specific responsibilities and functions to be effective. There are other informational areas in the workplace that a police mid-level manager must have knowledge so as not to infringe upon any applicable employee rights or constitutional safeguards. These general information needs are categorized later on under the Essential Managerial Knowledge requirements.

TASK DELEGATION AND SUBORDINATE DEVELOPMENT

Typically, all the duties, functions, and responsibilities of an operational-level police manager cannot be effectively performed independent of some assistance. That is not to say that police managers at the operational level are incapable of performing assigned duties, but, rather, that the volume of work required to manage the on-the-job performance of functional leadership and operational subordinates is a monumental task. This is especially true when you add in the need to manage and allocate resources, plus respond to the dictates and directives of superiors. It does not require a great deal of insight

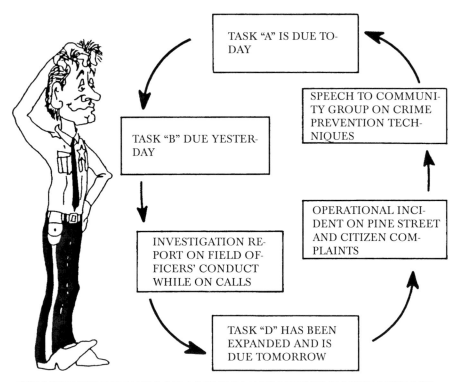

THE MULTIPLE DEMANDS ON A POLICE MANAGER'S TIME MAKES THE USE OF DELEGATION AS A LEADERSHIP TOOL MANDATORY.

to become aware of the volume of performance expectations of a modern-day operational police manager.

Therefore, in order for the individual to be effective, inasmuch as he or she cannot be in several places at one time, etc., it becomes mandatory for an operational police manager to appropriately **delegate** part of the work to others. The individuals to whom work is delegated then become responsible for that part of the designated task. Remember, a manager can delegate authority and a requirement to do the work to someone else, but the **ultimate responsibility for the task's accomplishment cannot be passed on to others**. The key here is that the delegating manager has to assure task accomplishment in a satisfactory manner.

Before further discussion of the context of leadership responsibility, plus the format and technique of effective delegation, it should be formally defined from the perspective of being a dimensional characteristic of management. **Delegation** is defined as **the knowledgeable capability to use subordinate personnel to effectively achieve assigned tasks by designating authority and accountability for decision making and performance accomplishment of a specific job. The delegated right of authority must be accomplished in a manner that is conducive to effective performance behavior and the enhancement of the subordinate's abilities**. This definition appears to set quite a task for delegation as a performance skill of an operational police manager. While it is true from a comparative perspective of other required leadership dimensions that delegation is not thought to be a quintessential skill, as a point of fact, it is no less important than any other leadership skill that's considered critical to an operational manager's performance. The interrelatedness of all the skills, one to another, is so vital that a failure in either area can and most likely will be detrimental to effective performance in several other trait characteristics.

A TOOL OF MANAGEMENT

To be effective, an operational police manager should delegate certain tasks to others. The delegation will not strip the manager of any leadership authority. To the contrary, it will simply mean that the operational manager is expanding his or her capability by attempting to get the most out of subordinates and personal time availability. As noted in the stated definition, delegation is a procedure whereby subordinates are assigned a responsibility and given the authority to accomplish the specific task. The persons provided the **delegated right of power** are held accountable for its use in achieving the established goals and objectives. Mention should also be made of the fact that those who are given authority to perform will be held responsible and/or accountable for the use or misuse of the delegated power. A positional leader, such as an operational police manager, should use his or her delegation skills the same as any other performance tool or resource. The less experienced and insecure operational managers will generally be reluctant to delegate authority and responsibility to someone else. From their perspective, many have indicated that they perceive that delegating will weaken their control over the situation and that in order to assure correctness, a formal managerial guidance must be maintained. The more effective and self-assured leaders tend not to be intimidated by the use of delegation as a managerial tool for increased productivity. They are not fearful of a loss of leadership control, nor is there a concern that the assigned person will do such a job, good or bad, that it will upstage or reflect negatively on him or her.

It should be realized that delegation should be considered no less a management tool than is an assignment roster or an account ledger. It may be true that the use of delegation is less tangible and more risky than the assignment roster or an account ledger. But the gains in personnel management, resource usage, and goal achievement is conversely greater when the **delegated rights of power** are appropriately and effectively used. The time-saving capability and broadened managerial accomplishment potential makes delegation not only an important tool of leadership but an essential trait characteristic of an operational police manager. A manager must realize that he or she can't do everything personally. No individual can be as productive as a group of persons, especially over a long period of time. The functional-level activities must be left to subordinates; overseeing and directing become the optimum terms for an operational manager. In other words, operational duties should be delegated to functional-level positional leaders, etc. The same principle of leadership philosophy should be applied to the assigning of subordinates to delegated managerial duties when an operational manager's personal guidance is not possible. The use of a capable subordinate to perform specific managerial tasks should not be viewed in terms of ersatz leadership. If appropriately handled, the delegation effort and subordinate's performance can be a positive for the assigning manager and the performing designee. The delegating manager looks good because the objective was effectively and timely achieved, and the personal leadership knowledge appears positive for selecting and utilizing such a capable subordinate. The delegated subordinate is shown in a positive perspective because he or she was able to perform the managerial task satisfactorily, thereby revealing a leadership potential and capability. The previous statements highlight the value of delegation as a tool of management. There are a number of justifications why a manager should use delegation as a leadership tool.

First, **hands-on knowledge of a situation**, such as that available to an assigned subordinate who deals with the problem daily, may be an advantageous asset to objective achievement. The person nearest to the problem or situation will often have a better feel for what will work best. Therefore, they are generally in a more favorable position as a decision maker regarding the concern. It is fact that no matter how scrupulously an operational manager monitors subordinates' performances, he or she is still one or two steps removed from the actual process and, therefore, is less knowledgeable about the intimate details of the situation. This becomes more of a factor when numerous components of a **span of control** or a **multifunctional** task is taken into consideration. The greater the manager's **span of control** (subordinates managed) and the amount of **activities accountable for** (number of projects managed), the less individual time commitment each can or will receive. From this, it is plain to see that the intimate knowledge expectations of an operational police manager can't conceivably be the same as the functional leader or the personnel performing the task. This is not to say that the manager need not have a basic or working knowledge of each project under his or her management, but the individual also need not be a performance expert in a task to effectively manage it.

Second, **the decisive reaction response interval** will be reduced by the elimination of the communication time lag that may occur when information has to be transmitted to an additional source for a decision. In some situations, an immediate responsive action is required to effectively and efficiently resolve a problem. Having to transmit sufficient information to another level and then await a decision before action is taken may not be plausible in all instances. But without a delegation of specific authority to make a decision and/or react to the situation, subordinates have to await the arrival of the operational police manager. In the interim time, because an operational manager can't possibly be at the scene in all functional situations, the problem may escalate out of control, thus creating a larger and more difficult problem to deal with. The more specialized the nature of the job, the greater is the need possibility for some amount of delegated authority to functional leadership or other subordinate personnel. This goes back to a recognition that an operational police manager cannot expect to know or do everything personally.

Third, **improved manager-subordinate relationships** will more than likely be a byproduct of effective delegation. An operational leader's demonstrated willingness to appropriately delegate responsibility and authority for action will generally create an atmosphere of trust and respect among subordinates. It will be apparent that the manager is not afraid to allow subordinates to demonstrate their abilities. The delegation will also be an **ego**

boost and focus the perception that job accomplishments have not gone unnoticed by the designee(s). Depending on how the job accomplishments have been handled, the manager's actions will show not only the designee but all subordinate members of the section or unit that the positional leader respects their judgment, values, their abilities, and trusts their capacity to make correct decisions and/or take appropriate action. Typically, a more involved perception and commitment to the achievement of organizational objectives will be reflective in the subordinates' job performances. It is a well-documented truism that most persons involved in law enforcement, no matter what level, take considerable pride in the job they do. And, a failure on the part of an operational police manager to entrust these normally above-average persons with some level of responsibility would be detrimental to their self-image as well as be a drawback to perceived positive association with the department.

The three previously cited justifications for viewing delegation as an essential tool of an effective operational police manager are but a few of its positive aspects. There are a number of additional ones that interact so closely with other dimensional trait areas that they may be considered part of the characteristic itself. In detailing some of the positive aspects of delegation from a managerial perspective, it should not be overlooked that effective execution of this trait area has boundary limits as does all leadership characteristics.

PARAMETERS OF DELEGATION

Delegation, like virtually every other facet of positional leadership, has certain parameters within which to operate for effectiveness. These limitations are contiguous to the negative side of delegation should the operational police manager fail to adhere to the scope of legitimate execution. The following areas of limitations listed will be referenced throughout this chapter, as effective delegation cannot occur without their consideration. The most prominent parameters for appropriate distribution of job responsibility and authority by an operational police manager are:

1. **Allocating Responsibility**. A manager or positional leader who has the obligation to assure the accomplishment of certain tasks can delegate a limited responsibility for achievement to others. The designee then becomes responsible to the delegating manager for his or her performance. But in no way can the designating manager **abdicate** positional leadership responsibility for task accomplishment. In other words, **a manager can delegate a performance level obligation but not the ultimate responsibility for**

task achievement. The manager remains responsible for meeting the correct and accurate objective of the project, etc.

2. **Providing Necessary Authority**. It is a simple matter to designate a subordinate to carry out a task. But doing so without also providing the individual with the authority of power to execute the delegated activity dooms its accomplishment. For example, assigning a subordinate as acting manager during your absence without first allocating the support that the leadership decisions made will be backed up is tantamount to constructing a building with no support beams. There will be no **base of force** behind the designee's actions. Past experience has shown that most people's behavioral actions are motivated by incentives, either positive or negative. If the acting leader has no authority to impose incentives, then he or she cannot effectively influence subordinates' behaviors.

3. **Delegate to a Willing Individual**. Delegating a task to a person should take into consideration the individual's desire to perform a task, delegation is an allocation of decision-making powers that constitute a latitude of action, whereas a specifically assigned job does not. The designee must be willing to accept the responsibility for performance that can be considered a **core** of delegation. An operational manager should not delegate to a subordinate who is unwilling to accept and/or carry out the responsibilities of the task. A realization must be understood that not all subordinates are willing to accept more responsibility than is absolutely necessary to do their job. An appropriate question for a manager to ask him- or herself is, will the person perceive a positive recognition of personal ability from the delegated task, or would the performance be considered negatively, as an extra work type of assignment?

4. **Providing Adequate Information to Perform**. In order for a subordinate to accomplish a delegated task in a satisfactory manner, he or she must be supplied with sufficient information. This information is traditionally thought of as a part of effective communication skills. While this is true, it is also an essential component of establishing the parameters within which delegation functions. A subordinate should never be assigned or designated to perform a task without sufficient data as to the scope of authority and the conditions under which they may be applicable. When a subordinate is unable to fully comprehend the responsibilities and authority that are being delegated, then the delegation is unworkable. There should be a complete comprehension of parameters, criteria, expectations, and ultimate objective for the delegation to be successful.

Within these parameters, an operational police manager should delegate authority for action by subordinates where: (1) there is not sufficient time for personal completion of a task, which is an excellent indicator that some job responsibility needs to be delegated; (2) an improvement in the decision made will be enhanced by the persons most knowledgeable of the concern; and (3) the delegation of authority and related responsibilities will serve as a development device for the designee. Also, it should not be overlooked that effective goal achievement is the paramount objective in any decision to delegate a task to someone else.

GENERAL RULES FOR DELEGATING TASKS

There are some generally acceptable rules associated with delegation of responsibilities within a police department's organizational setting. It should be principally noted that delegation is basically a timesaving device of leadership. With this in mind, an operational police manager should (depending on the critical nature of the problem) designate those tasks that require the largest amount of time and don't need managerial experience to handle and, then subsequently, the routine or simple task that could best be handled by the person closest to the problem. Effective designation actually expands an operational manager's capability. It extends what can be physically done on a personal basis to what can be accomplished through delegation. Appropriate delegation will afford the manager the opportunity to channel personal efforts to tasks that require direct managerial intervention and control.

One factor not touched upon as yet in this text's discussion of designating tasks is **improper delegation**. It has been effectively demonstrated many times that **improper delegation** of responsibility and authority can be more detrimental than not delegating when a leader should. It will often expand the manager's time usage in attempting to correct the miscues of an improper designee's actions. There is also a likelihood of ego or self-confidence damage to the designated subordinate who fails to live up to the expectations of the delegated position. Therefore, a great deal of care needs to be exercised when considering delegation of a task as to how to effectively establish the parameters and a determination of who to delegate to. Here are some basic rules conceived from previous experiences and documentations:

1. **Don't Relinquish Responsibility After Delegation**. An operational police manager should not abandon input and monitoring procedures once a task has been delegated. To the contrary, he or she must remember that a leader can't escape ultimate responsibility for effective task achievement. The manager should consult with the designee before and during the task's operation to assure a desire for the assignment and the performance ability to carry it out. An effective operational manager should also develop an OJ.T. (on-the-job training) method to enhance the subordinate's ability to meet the objective.

2. **Consider Eliminating the Task before Delegating It**. If the planned delegation is purely for the purpose of gaining more time for the operational manager to focus on other areas, he or she should first review the task from the perspective of whether it could be combined with another job or eliminated without adversely affecting the operation. This would avoid time on non-productive and trivial matters that don't rise to the level of considered effective use of man-hours. However, it must be noted that in police work, because of the potential life-or-death aspect of most operational decisions, very few tasks will fall completely within this basic rule.

3. **Delegate Some of the Desirable Tasks to Subordinates**. An operational police manager will generally have a tendency to maintain for personal handling those tasks that offer some measure of satisfaction, as well as the ones that are most challenging and skill developing. It is only natural for a person to do the things that he or she enjoys and delegate the tasks that are less desirable. The term **risk management** is also a factor in which items may or may not be delegated to subordinates because of the fact that a manager cannot abdicate responsibility for tasks. And more than likely, the jobs that are particularly sensitive or exceptionally challenging the individual leader will often desire to retain personal control to assure appropriate handling. By doing so, a subtask performance by the delegatee is less likely to be reflective on the delegator and, as a consequence, make the manager look bad. But it is these jobs, the ones that are most challenging, that a designee will generally profit the most from performing. These types of jobs allow the subordinate to gain in knowledge and experience while also developing the confidence that is so necessary for job performance growth.

4. **Provide Directional Guidance and a Clear Explanation of Acceptable Results**. The delegating leader must provide the delegatee with sufficient information as to expectations and parameters in which he or she must operate. For example, an operational police manager desiring a crime pattern report of a certain district for presentation to upper management should not delegate this task by simply saying, "Smith, prepare and submit a crime trend report on your patrol area." This seems clear enough, but when analyzed we find that Smith was not provided sufficient detail of what is desired. The manager failed to note the time frame that the report is to encompass, the due date of the report, any particular offenses of concern, whether the report is to be typed or handwritten, and a host of other expectations that would achieve desired results. Proper delegation seems so simple that it almost appears to be a natural or automatic occurrence, but in actuality, it is one of the most common mistakes made by leaders. Effective delegation will generally result in the task being done better by the designee. Research in the area of delegation tells us that a manager should stress the specifically

desired results and not emphasize the performance process. This will place less pressure on the delegate, who will often infuse some personal concepts with expected results and thus may enhance the overall report. If these procedures are followed, an operational manager will usually receive a more comprehensive report and better result than may be anticipated.

5. **Avoid the "One Person" Syndrome of Delegation**. Operational police managers are generally no different than positional leaders at any level of the organization. That is, for the most part, they are not quantitative **risk takers**, meaning that when they find someone who is perceived as best for the job, socially acceptable and/or who has demonstrated a past capability, the leader will generally utilize that individual at every opportunity. By doing this, the positional leader does not run as great a risk as when using someone who is unfamiliar to the job and thus may fail, which would reflect negatively on the delegator. Typically, by not taking on the challenge, the untested subordinate is not provided an opportunity to perform in order to grow and develop his or her skills. It should be remembered that one of the prime reasons to delegate is for **subordinate development**. The person who has shown time and time again that he or she can do the job needs no development time in the area. Therefore, an operational police manager should seek subordinates without a prior delegated performance record but who have demonstrated a desire and potential to do the job. We as leaders must realize that **nothing ventured, nothing gained**. Also, a very real possibility is that if only one individual has been given the experience and should that person be absent, there may be no one available with the desired experience in a critical situation. Thus, in so-called routine or non-critical situations, the manager should make a practice of exposing as many subordinates as possible to added task responsibilities to elevate their developmental growth and self-esteem. Some of the positive benefits that can be obtained from delegation for both the leader and the subordinate were explored earlier in this chapter.

6. **Allow a Work Tolerance for the Delegate**. The designating manager should not delegate the authority and responsibility to perform a task to a subordinate and then hover over every aspect of the job continually. By doing this, an operational manager has not really delegated the task and in reality is still maintaining operational or functional control. A leader must learn to trust the designated subordinate's capability of doing the job. The constant looking over a subordinate's shoulder may cause a mistake that would not have happened had the added stress or pressure of continuous managerial scrutiny not been a factor. Allowing **work tolerance** or **operating space** does not imply that managerial progress reviews or follow-up checks shouldn't occur; on the contrary, they are a very necessary part of

effective delegation. What is being stated is: **Do not delegate a task if you plan to do it yourself**.

From the context of the basic rules outlined above, it is a reasonable assumption to state that an operational police manager must be familiar with the "delegation principles" set forth in order to be effective. It's said that leadership is a paradox, because to be truly effective a person must achieve results through the directional or performance work of others. Thus, a leader capability is measured by the activities of someone else's work output. And, by doing this, the capability of subordinates to do his or her job comes into focus. A manager must realize that becoming a good delegator is a learned procedure and a practiced skill. Delegation is one of the best training tools for development of subordinates that is available to an operational police manager.

SUBORDINATE DEVELOPMENT

Development of subordinates by an operational police manager is defined **as the performance behavior implemented in an effort to enhance and/or elevate the skills of workers**. The improved subordinate performance skills can be accomplished by delegation, training, and on-the-job experience. This is also one of the primary dimensional areas used to gauge the effectiveness of an operational manager. It is a building block for subordinate confidence toward the utilization of interpersonal traits that reflect leadership skills. Delegation, without a doubt, is a major step toward subordinate development. The designated subordinate is allowed and required to perform on his or her own to display whatever abilities that the assignment calls for. It is an opportunity to explore the limits of their personal capabilities. Delegation for the most part can be classified as employee training, particularly when the operational positional leader does not overcriticize when miscues occur. Instead of being overly critical, the supportive manager will work positively with the delegates to find out where problems occurred and then point out ways to correct and/or avoid them in the future. In this context, training and development learning occur best in employees. By choosing the subordinates to be delegated a responsible task, a certain amount of trust in the person's ability, judgment, and dedication has been displayed. Therefore, it should be no major step for the manager to be willing to tolerate limited minor errors or miscues as the individual actually grows into the delegated responsibility. Remember, none of us were born as managers and positional leaders; it occurred because someone was willing to take a chance and to help us over rough areas of development.

As stated earlier, goals and objectives achievement is usually the ultimate aim of any delegation effort and a manager's choice of delegatee is typically toward that end. However, when delegation can be used as a training tool to develop and enhance a subordinate's skills, the paramount concern may not be totally on results. But make no mistake about it, **result-accomplishment** cannot be dismissed. It may take a lesser focus, but productive achievement is what it is all about. Therefore, the most effective positional leaders will not merely assign tasks through delegation and react to results, positively or negatively. He or she will tactfully guide the subordinate to competent and effective performance. This should be accomplished without being "johnny-on-the-spot" every time the delegate has to stop and think over a concern. A manager must make certain that he or she is available to answer questions and give encouragement but not allow this to be a crutch for the designee.

The exercised capability to develop a subordinate is a skill that is considered essential to the truly effective operational manager. There are a number of positive aspects to the development of subordinate personnel. Major among these pluses are:

1. Increased comprehension by subordinates through improved performance effectiveness, which will enhance employee compliance with departmental directives; and
2. The better and more productive a manager's subordinates perform, the greater the proficiency perception of the positional leader's capability by top management.

The author recognizes that these are but a couple of the numerous other positive aspects of a manager's development philosophy identified with employee enhancement through the use of delegation. But essentially anything that makes a manager's job easier and improves upper management perception of the individual is ideal. Basically, that is what positional leaders are all striving for in accomplishing task responsibilities, effectiveness of performance and recognition for the job achieved.

While it is true that aspiring operational-level employees develop in many ways, their development can be enhanced through experiences on the job, training efforts, and other formalized methods traditional to police organizations. However, past events have proven to be the greatest developmental device for the subordinate enhancement toward advancement within the organizational setting. And, managerial experience for subordinates is usually through delegation. This brings up an interesting question about delegation and subordinate development. Is delegation a **correlation** or **causation** in the development of subordinates? As formally defined, **correlation** essentially means a relationship between two or more factors, a symbiotic association; and **causation** is when an act motivates another action to occur, occasioned by. The author's research failed to focus delegation and subordinated development exclusively to either of these factors. It would appear that from the diverse learning capabilities of subordinates, either one may be suitable for the classification of delegation in relationship to the development of subordinates. This knowledge may be beneficial to an operational manager's formulation of a planned approach to subordinates' internal training. In either case, the utilization of delegation for subordinate developmental knowledge enhancement appears to be an essential tool in a manager's training process.

EMPLOYEE LEARNING AND
SELECTING DEVELOPMENTAL TASKS

It is an established fact that the acquisition of knowledge in an on-the-job training format is much more likely to occur when the subordinate is motivated to receive it. Therefore, an operational police manager should exercise

KNOWING WHICH TASKS TO DELEGATE TO WHOM CAN BE THE DIFFERENCE BETWEEN SUCCESS OR FAILURE AS A POSITIONAL LEADER.

some selectivity in choosing a subordinate for experience training through delegation. The manager can aid the development of a positive attitude in the selected employee(s) by emphasizing the benefits for the increased knowledge, etc. These reasons for learning will translate into a favorable atmosphere of self-motivation and an intellectual frame of mind that is more conducive to knowledge attainment. From what has been identified relative to **employee learning**, it should be clear that **communication** is the critical element in an operational manager's conditioning of subordinates for learning through the use of the delegation process. Communication of what the possible benefits are and requirements of the delegated task will generally remove much of the subordinate's hesitancy. A human tendency is to show reluctance toward and even fear of the unknown, as well as the frightening aspects of the assignment and make the person aware of what is needed. This will undoubtedly make the individual aware that they can successfully do the job, as well as profit by the experience. What is being said relative to **employee learning** and delegation is that confidence gained through knowledge may be an essential consideration of the designating manager.

The **selecting of development tasks** to delegate to a particular employee may take either of two courses. First, a manager may delegate to the individual's weakness in order to build strength and confidence in a specific area. However, in delegating for improvement in a specific area, the manager must assure that the tasks assigned are difficult enough to be challenging but yet simple enough to be handled. If the task is too difficult, the individual will surely fail, thereby suffering a setback in confidence of performing that job and thus an increased ineptitude in the area. Conversely, if the job is too simple and not challenging enough, the person will not profit, as concentration and expanded knowledge will not be needed. The second focal point in the **selecting of development tasks** is delegating jobs that the person has demonstrated a proficiency for handling. However, the job should be so sufficiently structured as to be challenging to offer some self-gratification for task completion. Delegating to a strong area with added challenges will enhance the subordinate's confidence and performance capability in that area. It will also make a strong point even stronger. This may serve an operational manager as well at a time when **risk management** is not a viable option that is available, because there are situations when success even in delegated tasks are an absolute must.

DELEGATION: THE ESSENCE OF
EFFECTIVE SUBORDINATE DEVELOPMENT

Delegation as a leadership characteristic is a quintessential tool of police management. The effectiveness of a functional-level police mid-level manager is dependent to a large extent on his or her willingness and ability to delegate tasks to others. A commonly recognized fact has been that the higher up the hierarchical structure a manager is, the greater the need for time management. Time management is not limited exclusively to allocation of time periods to perform essential tasks but also to the shifting of those duties that do not require your personal handling. The number of duties, functions, responsibilities and tasks typically associated with operational secondary leadership in a police operation do not allow for unilateral actions by a mid-level manager. Police leaders are required to manage not only resources, both personnel and material, but the mission accomplishment of his or her elements within the organization in a satisfactory manner. The essence of effectiveness for a police mid-level manager is his or her perceptual efficiency under heightened public scrutiny of actual performance.

Delegation relative to police leadership is the knowledge capability to use subordinate personnel to effectively accomplish assigned tasks by designating authority and accountability to make decisions for performance achievement of a specific job. The *delegate right of authority* must be accomplished in a manner that is conducive to effective job performance actions and the enhancement of the subordinate's ability. The stated comprehension definition of *delegation* clearly points to the fact that it's an essential trait characteristic of police leadership; it is no less and perhaps even more important than other skills typically attributable to managerial leadership. The delegating leader must realize that the assigning of tasks to others does not hamper or limit any of his or her leadership authority. It merely implies that the police mid-level manager has expanded personal capability to get the most accomplished in a minimal amount of time. This delegation of authority and a requirement of task performance by others does not imply an abrogation of ultimate responsibility for the job accomplishment.

A police mid-level manager should use his or her designating authority the same as any other leadership skill or tool. A less knowledgeable or more insecure secondary police manager will often be resistant to the delegation of authority or responsibility to someone. *Many have stated that they believe that allocating personal responsibilities will weaken their perceptual control over the task and the individual assigned to perform it. Plus, personal attention is needed to assure an accuracy of performance.* The more confident and self-assured leaders will generally perceive less of a threat by the use of delegation as a leadership tool for increased effectiveness. They are not apprehensive of a personally perceived loss of managerial control, nor is there a concern that the designee's performance may be such that it will reflect negatively upon him or her.

There must be a recognition that **Task Delegation** should be considered no less critical to leadership functioning than any other tool available to a police mid-level manager. While it may be true that the use of delegation as a management tool is less tangible and somewhat more chancy than most of the other leadership traits attributable to operational managers, the perceived gains in personnel development, resources utilization, and goal attainment offset the risk aspect when the designated authority is efficiently and effectively used. The timesaving efforts and expanded leadership achievement potential makes task delegation an essential trait of management, as well as a critical characteristic of an effective leader. Most mid-level leaders realize that he or she cannot accomplish every task personally. No one individual, no matter how good they may be, can accomplish a multifaceted task, as well as a number of persons in a specific time frame. Certain leadership tasks must be left to lower level subordinates. Guidance and control then becomes the optimum term for a mid-level leader. The designating of specific mid-level managerial tasks to a lower-level subordinate may be considered critical to overall effectiveness. The same managerial logic could be applied when a police mid-level manager or leader's personal attention is not feasible. The use of a knowledgeable lower-level subordinate to perform specific leadership duties should not be perceived as a less effective job performance because personal attention was not provided. If purposefully applied, the delegation effort and the delegator's actions will be favorably perceived when the task is effectively and efficiently performed in a timely manner. The designating manager will look good because the projected goal was positively achieved. Also, the individual's personal leadership awareness and knowledge appear positive for choosing and assigning such a capable designee. The delegatee is positively projected because he or she was able to perform the assigned tasks effectively, thus revealing a mid-level managerial leadership capability. The above information typifies the value of delegation as an essential tool of every secondary police leader.

There are an infinite number of reasons why an effective leader should utilize designees as an efficiency device. Some of the condonable reasons were comprehensively delineated as: (1) *hands-on knowledge of the situation* (if appropriately chosen the assigned designee may have increased knowledge of the actual circumstances); (2) *a reduction in the decisive reaction response interval* (an increased knowledge will often lessen the time frame required to gather sufficient information upon which to make a competent decision); and (3) the appropriateness and effectiveness of the delegation will *improve manager-subordinate relationships* through perceived recognition of capabilities and a willingness to share authoritative actions.

The noted areas clearly focus on the benefits of a mid-level manager's delegation of tasks that reduce their effectiveness through excessive time drainage. However, experiences in public law enforcement have shown that police personnel in general and managerial leaders in particular seem to be overly conservative, especially in the area of shared authority or risk taking in the utilization of someone perceived by them as unproved. It may be very appropriate to say that from what has been observed, the **"Good Ole Boy System"** lives and will continue to survive for some time to come. In other words, if an individual is not a personal friend (acquaintance) or has not had a positive personal encounter with a mid-level manager either personally or professionally, then the person is *persona non grata* relative to a perception of the individual's work performance, capabilities, etc. Most persons who have been in public law enforcement for a number of years can identify a time when hierarchy leadership changed and almost overnight it seems that *new stars* or *effective performers* materialize. The outgrowth of **cloning** is also very prevalent in public police leadership; the notion is to develop persons with the same philosophy and ethnocentric ideology so that personal concepts will persevere long after they leave the organization. By so doing, a leader often feels that he or she will have some continuing influence in the organization's leadership. This is another symptom of the conservative nature of public police management. The so-called **shining stars** or **productive performers** under the past administration, often as a situational consequence, are perceived as ineffective non-producers. The perception has little or nothing to do with actual or perceived performances but rather a personal like or dislike. Political catering or perspicacious sycophancy at all levels of police leadership has more to do with perceptually favorable delegation and recognition of supposed capabilities than does developed trait characteristics and/or skills.

Thus, it may seem somewhat hypocritical to talk about *Delegation* as an essential tool of effective and efficient leadership development while at the same time describing conditions that are closely akin to perceptual *nepotism* or *crony-ism* in concept and practice. The actual conditions under which some agencies operate do not alter the fact that a proper distribution of tasks can increase the performance effectiveness of everyone involved. However, like any good managerial tool there are specifically defined limits in which delegation should be executed for maximum effectiveness.

The previously cited "General Rules for Delegating Tasks" is typically a self-contradictory set of parameters for accomplishing tasks that are unable to be performed by the person responsible for their achievement. This paradoxical inclination develops because in order to be an effective performer as a leader the individual must give up some portion of his or her leadership authority. In other words, to be effective as a leader the secondary police manager must lead by allocating to someone else the power to direct and control a task's accomplishment; in other words, *to lead by not leading.* This in and of itself is not an easy concept to grasp, because effective leaders are generally products of developmental learning through doing. And, developmental learning tells us that an accomplished and efficient leader will take charge through the exertion of copious task work to meet performance expectations.

Task Delegation is and must be a *prime developmental tool* of functional police leadership. This overall view and analysis would in no way be complete and/or comprehensive without an excursion into the aspects of delegation upon employee learning and development. Concerning **Subordinate Development** and **Employee Learning**, it is clear that the traditional concept of prior circumstances or events may be the best developmental tool for use by a police mid-level manager for accentuation of employee development in concurrence with successful task accomplishment. Managerial leadership experience through practical efforts for functional level primary leaders is best accomplished via delegation. There have been a number of attempts to classify delegation relative to subordinate development. Terms such as Correlation, Causation, Manipulative Training, and Operational Learning have all been used to indicate the connection of *associative development* to *practical experiences.* The varied ways that people acquire knowledge, as well as the rate at which it is retained, imply that either classification would suitably fit the intent of developmental training. A police mid-level manager who is aware of the essentiality and benefits of the proper use of delegation as a management tool has gone a long way toward ultimate success in the **Human Aspects of Management**.

Motivation as an essential aspect of mid-level managerial leadership is not a common term used in either public or private industry, inasmuch as a performance incentive is unnecessary for organizational leaders. Traditionally, it is considered unusual for any level leader in the organization not to be self-motivated by work environment, challenging responsibilities, and the discharge of positionally assigned authority. However, an effective police mid-level manager will realize that while *self-motivation* is not typically a problem area concerning the performance of leaders, he or she will nevertheless foresee the benefits of remaining aware that no matter at what level a subordinate is positionally assigned, the individual is a human being with wants, desires, and aspirations. If asked to specifically label Developmental Motivation for a positional leader, this author would identify it by a descriptive term such as **Ego Incentive**. The human tendency to need an ego boost in coordination with learning development will notably benefit the organization as well as the designated leader.

In summation of what has been conveyed to this point, it would be appropriate to say that there is a critical need awareness of the quintessential aspects of delegation for a leader. And, that for most police mid-level managers, there is generally an insufficient amount of time for most effective managerial leaders to complete all necessary tasks personally. Therefore, selecting which tasks and appropriately assigning them to a subordinate becomes a viable option, if the leader wants to be managerially effective. Although not specifically mentioned, a primary factor that permeates the entire delegation process is the manager's ability to communicate effectively. Being aware of all the critical aspects of communication and assuring to utilize those techniques and components to effectively convey adequate information and/or expectations is basic to every characteristic of leadership. A police mid-level manager will utilize delegation opportunities to enhance the self-esteem needs of as many subordinates as possible and not become a victim of the trap of the *"Fair Haired Boy"* syndrome, which should be appropriately viewed as an antiquated leadership approach. He or she should maintain an awareness of the efficacious quality of selecting developmental tasks to be delegated so that they coincide with desired employee learning and purposeful subordinate development.

The effective mid-level leader will also realize the basic human tendency toward a *reluctance* to delegate challenging or self-gratifying tasks. However, an accomplished leader will not fall prey to the intimidation of sharing authority for task accomplishment. The individual will assess accountability for task achievement to the delegate without abrogating ultimate responsibility for accomplishing the goal or objective. Typically, this text has referred to appropriate delegation of decision-making authority as necessary *risk management,* but as it was delineated to the author by a recognized effective executive-level manager the term was nothing more than a synonym for *good leadership.* But no matter the term reference, the bottom line is that if a police mid-level manager wishes to be effective, he or she must develop and appropriately use the trait characteristic of delegation. It must be employed as efficiently as any other leadership dimension typically associated with managerial effectiveness. By viewing task delegation as explained in this text, it is obvious that mid-level managerial effectiveness rests upon a pillar of positive leadership traits and that *appropriate delegation* is as vital to the overall edifice as any other skill used to achieve goals and objectives.

A SYSTEMATIC APPROACH TO GENERAL DUTIES

In addition to whatever specific duties that are specified in his or her organization's policies and procedures, a secondary police manager should be responsive to the tasks set forth by the hierarchy leadership. The general duties and command authority over subordinate personnel shall be documented into the Standard Operation Procedures (SOPs) for the position that he or she is assigned. The functional aspects of an effective mid-level manager is much the same as a *System Approach* to leadership. The basic definition of a **system approach**, as it applies to leadership, is the blending of a collection of functional components that operate separately and combine them into a coordinated unit to achieve a common goal. A police mid-level manager in essence takes a collection of interrelated functional-level personnel and directs their efforts into a common purpose. This is termed a *system approach* to effective leadership. It is recognized that all workers may not have the same goal achievement in mind and that a leader's conceptual method of handling subordinates may need to be non-conventional. In other words, operational-level police officers may not all fit into the theoretical category of being a **Theory Y**-type employee.

An effective police mid-level managerial leader will often have to utilize the universal process of scientific management in the handling of subordinates. The scientific management process emphasizes the analytical disassembling of the functional workers unit to assess each component separately and then to affirmatively direct and control individual efforts of subordinates toward a common objective. The idea of **Scientific Management** in this conceptual form refers to the clinical application of task performances based on a step-by-step methodical procedure. A mid-level leader using a scientific approach to manage assumes that *the whole of the functional unit is equal to the sum of its parts* and that *the performance achievements of the unit can be determined or explained in terms of the actions of each part.* In contrast, a *system approach* to mid-level managerial leadership is the coordinating of work efforts toward functional achievement. A **system approach** to general midlevel managerial duties and concerns assumes that *the whole is greater than the sum of its parts.* The basic comparisons of leadership is an Analytic Process versus a **Synthetic Pattern** of concern. In other words, analytic is primarily an inward-focused process, while synthetic is the opposite or an outward-focused process. Both processes are considered positive, if the leader recognizes which approach should be used in a particular situation. The inward-focused process reflects to an employee-centered assessment, and the outward-focused process tends to be an evaluation concept of organizational achievement of goals and objectives. Many theorists believe that the latter approach (synthetic pattern) allows greater comprehension than does the analytic process.

The need to recognize various methods and to utilize a systematic approach to the general duties performed by organizational leaders is important because primary police mid-level managers do not operate independent of other elements. Elements within a police organization affect the operation of other components or entities and likewise are affected by the functioning of other units, etc. The use of a formalized systematic approach by a primary police leader is conducive to effective leadership. Also, such an approach to leadership offers a tremendous challenge for a police mid-level manager to identify interactive components within the organization. The determining of specific interactive units and how each affects his or her element's performance should make the secondary manager more effective as a leader.

It is recognized that through the use of a systematic approach to leadership, a mid-level manager should acquire an increased perspective of the total spectrum of managing subordinates. A more clinical view of systematized leadership practices do not endorse a leader's ignoring any specific aspect of organizational management. Therefore, in actuality a leader must be aware of all available resources, both human and material, as well as functional developments that influence subordinates' job performances. Finally, systematic leadership practices are said to integrate and/or combine the variety of managerial approaches into objective achievement. It should also be made clear that both functional leadership and organizational behaviors are greatly affected by a leader's systematic performance approach. A police mid-level manager's systematic approach to duty performance is typically viewed as an interdependent arrangement specific to the individual leader. In other words, a leader's approach is individual to him or her, but yet it should also be coordinated with the practices and performances of other organizational managers.

Essential Managerial Knowledge

An effective and efficient functional-level, mid-level manager in today's work environment must not only possess the technical knowledge and personnel skills or traits of a leader but must also have practiced awareness of *the basic employment rights of subordinates.* A good functional mid-level manager should understand all the legal and moral ramifications of his or her position concerning the responsibilities and liabilities for actions affecting subordinates. Functional mid-level managers should acquire a general basic knowledge of the legal parameters of mid-level managerial actions concerning subordinate employees so as to avoid becoming an unanticipated liability to the organization. This unanticipated liability is typically generated from the legal settlements of lawsuits against the organization by employees because of a perceived mid-level managerial action or inaction.

The Concept of Sexual Harassment

A few decades ago the very *concept of sexual harassment* was merely a joked-about concern; it was treated as a natural and expected interplay between men and women on the job. The laws and the rights of women have been recognized and the adverse effect of sexual harassment on females in the workplace has been addressed by the courts. Leaders and managers in all industries, including public policing, must be aware that unwelcome sexual advances in the workplace is detrimental to positive behavioral performance of workers. Employees in the workplace are protected by law against sexual discrimination. The most traditional areas cited in sexual harassment complaints are hostile work environment, dismissals, conditions of employ-

A LEADER CANNOT ALLOW INAPPROPRIATE ACTIONS IN THE WORKPLACE. IF ALLOWED, THE LEADER AND THE ORGANIZATION MAY BE GUILTY OF PERMITTING A HOSTILE WORK ENVIRONMENT THAT COULD RESULT IN A LAWSUIT AGAINST THE DEPARTMENT.

ment, disparity in wages, promotions, intimidation threats, pregnancy being treated different from other non-duty-related injuries or illnesses, hiring, and reprisals. As can be seen by the areas identified above, sexual harassment wears many faces and can be harmful to individuals as well as to organizations. The persons most targeted for sexual harassment are generally new employees, individuals in a probation status, and youthful naive workers. Also, employees who have recently lost a mate through divorce or death seem to be in a high-risk category for unwelcome sexual overtures.

Traditionally, and certain most frequently, females are the target of sexual harassment, but it must not be overlooked that it also occurs to male workers as well. An article by Arthur Hayes said the courts define sexual harassment as:

1. *Unwelcome Sexual Advances.* A worker who is repeatedly propositioned by a mid-level manager or coworker to establish an intimate relationship, on or off the job, could sue for sexual harassment.
2. *Coercion Tactics.* A worker whose mid-level manager asks for a liaison or sexual favor with the stated or unstated understanding that a favor will be gained or a negative reaction may occur.
3. *Recognized Favoritism.* The legal system has indicated that an employee may be held liable if an employee who submits to sexual favors is rewarded while other employees are denied the same benefits.
4. *Indirect or Circuitous Harassment.* Employees who observe sexual harassment on the job but who are not so approached. This is said by the courts that an environment of sexual harassment was created.
5. *Overt Physical Actions.* This refers to gestures, languages, etc., where this may also constitute harassment and create a hostile work environment.
6. *Visual Display Harassment.* The display of written material, photos, printed material, or writing on bathroom walls about an individual may all be considered sexual harassment.

Behavior that may be considered by some as friendly interaction may be perceived by others as sexual harassment. Therefore, the courts have defined it in the categories mentioned above. It must also be made clear that intent is not needed to support an allegation of sexual harassment. There only needs to be the perception that the mid-level manager created a hostile work environment using one of these areas.

Sexual Harassment: Essential Information

Sexual harassment, according to equal employment guidelines, is defined as perceived actions toward an employee of unwelcome insinuations of a sexual nature, whether verbal or physical, occurring in a workplace environment. A police mid-level manager must be aware that personal comments by him or her to a subordinate of the opposite sex may be interpreted as harassment, if gender is implied in terms of exploitation or job affecting. The knowledgeable mid-level manager should also know that sexual harassment does not only occur in a leader-subordinate situation but in a peer setting as well. The liability for peer sexual harassment comes into play when a mid-level manager has been informed of the unwelcome insinuations and fails to take action to stop and/or prevent future occurrences.

There are two essential information areas to remember when considering possible sexual harassment liability: (1) the test of whether sexual harassment actually happened is that the employee perceived some act of conduct of a sexual nature that occurred and that the employee's job was affected; and (2) in almost all judgments in sexual harassment cases today, the unwelcome actions must be linked, directly or indirectly, to the terms and conditions of employment. These areas were articulated in more detail in the previous section. The essential thing to remember is that action must be taken to prevent or halt reported cases of sexual harassment.

An effective functional-level police mid-level manager in a work setting should be aware that according to equal employment opportunity guidelines, **prevention is considered the best weapon against sexual harassment complaints**. The actions that a police mid-level manager can take to prevent or eliminate sexual harassment in his or her operation are as follows:

1. Establishing a policy against sexual harassment in his or her operation and assuring that the policy is clearly communicated to and understood by each subordinate.
2. Assuring that each subordinate is aware of the procedure for making a sexual harassment complaint known to the mid-level leader immediately above the offending person.
3. Assuring that all sexual harassment complaints that come to the mid-level manager's notice are immediately reported to the organization's leadership and that the appropriate investigative actions are taken to determine the facts.
4. Assuring that appropriate recommendations of corrective action, positive or negative, are taken to deal with and/or prevent future occurrences.

The above documented information concerning the limits of sexual harassment complaints and the methods that an operational police mid-level manager can employ to adequately deal with the problem are not all inclusive. An effective secondary manager is expected to use good common sense and judgment in the handling of these situations.

Sexual harassment is much more prevalent in business and organizational settings than may be realized or reported. The overt forms of sexual harassment practices of the past have given way to more subtle and calculated efforts. Like ethnic and racial bias, sexual harassment seems to be on the increase. Also, there is still a great deal that is not understood by lay persons relative to sexual harassment. There still exists sexist attitudes, unclear definitions, perceptual misunderstandings and court decisions that are ambiguous. As previously noted, sexual harassment is typically undesired sexual behavior or innuendos by one person to another. The unwanted attention must be in some way that a person's job status or work environment is negatively affected. Whereas sexual harassment usually involves persons of the opposite sex, it can also be directed toward individuals of the same gender, if the harassment produces a hostile work environment because of a sexual life-style preference. The increasing numbers of known persons with alternate life-style preferences, relative to gender, have produced some cases of sexual harassment. But generally, it involves males and females, with the female most often being the target of the harassment.

Title VII of the 1964 Civil Rights Act governs sexual harassment and protects both men and women. The law as written includes but is not confined to undesirable innuendos, physical contact, gestures, jokes, language, or demonstrations that are sexually suggestive and intimidating relative to the job climate and/or offensive to the worker. When sexual harassment is claimed, an organization's leadership is obligated to investigate and correct such practices, if they are found to be actual. A public policing agency must assure that any claim of unlawful behavior such as brutality, dishonesty, ethnic bias, and sexual harassment is not tolerated by its personnel. A public police organization and its managers and leaders are obligated to implement policies and procedures designed to discourage sexual harassment in the workplace before it occurs. Precedent law has indicated that a *lack of knowledge of such activity is not a valid legal defense* in sexual harassment cases. General research information is that unwanted sexual propositions, promises, and work-related threats or lewd comments are the most prevalent types of sexual harassment reported. Sexual gestures, jokes, and unwanted touching are the second most frequent forms of harassment that leaders should be aware of. A police mid-level manager must be aware that personal perceptions and individual sensibilities can vary greatly from one person to another. Thus, organizational leaders must be attentive because, like beauty, sexual harassment is in the eye of the beholder, or in this case, the offended person. An effective leader who observes an act, comment, joke, etc., that may be perceived as sexual harassment should take immediate steps to halt such behavior and not merely wait for a complaint from the offended person. By waiting the leader and the organization may be judged liable for inaction in a court of law. Documented zero tolerance by an organization is the best preventative defense in sexual harassment situations.

WORKPLACE DISCRIMINATION

Each mid-level managerial leader within a police organization must be especially aware of workplace discrimination that prevents or hinders equal employment. Discriminatory practices in general society and subsequently in the workplace are typically a consequence of stereotypical prejudice. Prejudice is generally defined as a bias attitude or a negative prejudgment of a situation, group of people, or a person. The prejudgment is usually a stereotyping that is not based on observed facts but rather on a convenient grouping of people, etc., that are different from personal self. Some management theorists argue that a prejudice of bias in and of itself is not harmful; it only becomes hurtful if a negative action results therefrom. This author disagrees and believes that prejudice or bias is harmful because the attitude that results therefrom is a perceptual negativism that is manifested in stereotypical behavior based on unfounded concepts. It is believed that prejudice cannot exist without the exercise of discriminatory behavior against a person, group, or situation in one form or another.

Discrimination in the workplace is harmful to the mid-level leader who allows it to exist within his or her unit/element. Prejudicial or discriminatory practices typically are based on race, gender, religious beliefs, or ethnic origin. A police mid-level manager should be aware that he or she may display bias or prejudice without a conscious desire to do so. Personal bias or prejudice may cause the leader to select a person for a desired assignment because of friendship, sameness, or personal comfort, rather than actual ability to perform. This is discriminatory. The person that was selected was not chosen for performance ability or through a fair selection process but rather through the **"good ol' boy"** process with noticeable bias. The discriminatory areas most identified as visibly common in a workplace are: (1) hiring, (2) job assignment selection, (3) compensation, (4) promotion opportunities, and (5) job performance evaluations. A classic example of each of these discriminatory practices common to functional and mid-level leadership are:

1. **Hiring**. The concept that because someone or something is different from the leader, he, she or it cannot or will not fit in. Also, that the selector simply does not wish to be around the individual.
2. **Job Assignment Selection**. The most desirable task or hours of assignments are given to persons based on the leader's personal likes or dislikes. A choice preference made on stereotypical concepts.
3. **Compensation**. Placing person in assignment that is less monetarily rewarding because of personal like or dislike about the person. Until recently, this was a common practice that was condoned regarding black Americans and females. Functional leadership generally affects this through task assignment or merit assessments.
4. **Promotions Opportunities**. A majority of the promotion processes are dominated by the "good ol' boy" syndrome, even at a work simulation processes (assessment center) that uses in-house assessors or evaluators that have attitudes of bias against a group, etc. We need only look at the makeup of the population to observe the disparity of minorities and females in leadership positions in most police organizations. The comparison of percentage makeup should be gauged by the demographic composition of the community it serves.
5. **Job Performance Evaluations**. Evaluations by functional mid-level managers usually reflect personal likes or dislikes rather than actual performance behaviors. Even in a situation of non-bias rating, leadership theorists recognize that job performance evaluations are usually slanted toward leniency rather than actual behaviors. It is not uncommon for a person being discriminated against having to overcome deliberate barriers and having to achieve higher than normal achievement goals just to be considered an equal performer to preferred subordinates.

An effective police mid-level manager realizes that, whether intended or not, discrimination in the work place is illegal. Therefore, proof of such actions could result in a sanction by civil court for violation of the civil rights act of 1964 and/or 1983. Besides, bias actions are generally wasteful of vital human resources and could negatively affect the capability and efficiency of a leader.

The Changing Work Force

A mid-level managerial leader must be aware of the changing nature of the work force that he or she has to manage. The work ethic of a few decades ago and the majority of workers coming from a military background, when discipline and strict compliance with directions was paramount, are no more. The modern work force is more diverse as to makeup and less inclined to react favorably to *old iron-fist approach to leadership.* A recognition of the multicultural nature of the modern work force and the requirement for more interactive leadership tactics are essential if a police mid-level manager is to be successful. Differences in cultural behaviors of various minority groups may be somewhat alien from the traditional majority members. This does not mean that the cultural differences are wrong but rather that they are not the same. An effective police mid-level manager must be prepared and willing to accept and positively deal with these differences. For example, a firm handshake or eye contact during an interview or interaction is considered normal in a traditional police atmosphere. However, in other cultures, being reserved in shaking a hand and being submissive (not making eye contact) when directly addressing a superior is expected. Therefore, a leader, a functional mid-level manager should not be quick to prejudge the performance ability of a subordinate based upon different cultural traits or a reserved approach to interactions with a superior.

The efficient and effective line police mid-level manager dealing with a multicultural mix of personnel must realize that for individuals reared in U.S. society, an apparent independent approach to dealing with problems and not expecting help with personal concerns that one can handle him/herself is commonplace. However, to other cultures, especially some Asian type behavioral concepts, the American approach to problem solving seems somewhat cold and standoffish. Thus, the interactions between line leaders and subordinates may at times seem awkward and uncomfortable. The operational mid-level police manager should not be seeking sameness or "yes men" but rather workers who can perform as needed and who may bring some new and innovative approaches to dealing with some common problems.

A police mid-level manager must strive to achieve a harmonious working relationship with all subordinates, no matter what the cultural differences. The leader should attempt to create a workplace atmosphere that has a **win-win situation** for subordinates and not one that says all subordinates must fit the exact same mold or be the same as the leader to be considered satisfactory. Studies as far back as the Hawthorne research show that workers perform tasks and are more satisfied if the workplace atmosphere is positive and the leadership recognizes the efforts of the functional-level employees.

Today's leaders can anticipate complaints of discrimination both directly expressed and perceptually perceived. The effective police leader will be attentive to the complaint and react to resolve it as soon as possible. In addition to superior-subordinate discrimination, there also exists subordinate-to-subordinate workplace discriminatory practices. In either situation, the leader must be prepared to listen to or be very attentive to expressed or recognized problems. It should be verbalized to the parties concerned, to assure correctness and to let everyone involved know, that the leader recognizes the concerns and plans to resolutely address it. In attempting to resolve the problem, it may be appropriate to have those involved recommend solutions. This will not only involve them in the decision making but may also more clearly articulate the problem and the need to resolve it. As with all problem-solving attempts, a leader needs to assure that all of the facts related to the problem are known and considered before a decision on resolution is made. Once the functional police mid-level manager conceptualizes a plan to effectively deal with the discriminatory actions, he or she should react affirmatively to stop or alter the unacceptable behavior. The actions taken may need to be direct and forceful or indirect or circumspect. Either way, the problem must be effectively and noticeably dealt with. Once the actions have been initiated, the leader must implement a follow-up review to assure that the problem has been addressed and resolved.

Another area that fits under work force discrimination is most noticeable in the area of pay and assignments which is based on sexism or gender stereotyping. Sexism is the term traditionally associated with discriminatory practices in the workplace based on sex. Sexism related to the workplace is not limited to the female members of our society. In fact, both men and women encounter discrimination when they pursue careers that have been traditionally held by the opposite sex. This typecasting of individuals, both male and female, injures persons who dare to be different and seek employment in job areas typically held by opposite sex members. A traditional perception of the roles held by men in a societal work force is an assumption that they are aggressive and unemotional. Conversely, a traditional concept of women in the work force is that they are more emotional and better suited for clerically skilled jobs associated with hand dexterity. The stereotyping of both men and women are unfair and tends to limit which jobs that an organization will fairly allow them to pursue.

There is little doubt that the changing fact of the work force in our society will demand a re-affirmation of eliminating gender bias by police mid-level managers. No longer do women enter the work force seeking just a job to supplement their husband's income. They are seeking careers and requiring equal opportunities to compete for assignments and promotions. No longer is their self-worth measured in terms of their attractiveness to males or the success of a husband and the ability to run a household. Traditionally, women were raised to be passive, supportive of others, emotionally less restrained than males, and less adventurous or inclined to seek leadership roles. We now know that the aforementioned concepts have dissipated and the modern females are now encouraged to become career women and to attempt to move away from the traditional female-dominated occupations of being salesclerks, waitresses and clerical workers. There is nothing wrong with these positions; it is merely being acknowledged that in the past they were female-dominated jobs and lower paid than the male-dominated jobs at the time.

The male role in the work force has traditionally been more toward a dominant, strong, and unemotional reaction, in much the same manner as the perceptual role in society. It is recognized that males still hold the majority of leadership positions in the workplace in our society. But vast numbers of women entering the work force during the past decade have forced a change in the traditional concept of the male vs. female roles in the workplace. The *domestic roles* of some males are not the stereotypical weak male dominated by a strong *tomboy*-type female. Leaders in all job categories, including police work, have had to rethink their focus of a male-dominated work force. The traditional pattern of treating women as emotional or less competitive elements in the work force has given way to recognize and treat them as colleagues and equals in the workplace.

Police leaders, as have mid-level managers in other industries, are required to view women's roles and pay status in the work force in terms of comparable worth. The concept of comparable pay for comparable worth was mandated under the Civil Rights Act of 1984. It basically means that different jobs requiring comparable skill level or performance ability should receive pay at the same rate. It must also be recognized that there has been a revolution in what was traditionally thought to be male or female jobs. The masculine, more physically demanding jobs are no longer exclusive to males. Likewise, clerical and other traditionally female tasks are being performed more and more by males. The modern-day, police mid-level manager should not view the changing work force as any trend to role reversal but rather to acknowledge that the face of the work force is now changing to include both male and female. This transition is no different than the changes required by the entrance of large numbers of minorities into policing. No longer is the task of policing society the exclusive job of the white male. Police officers today are multiracial and gender inclusive.

The Rights of Employees

There are very few, if any, specific documented laws or court decisions that outline specific employee rights in a work environment in all situations.

But as may be apparent in cases of civil litigation, a **judged wrong** need not have been previously documented into law for an individual or organization to be held liable for a tort sanction. Almost daily, precedent-establishing cases or settlements are developed, which enact new laws, because an employee felt that an organization or a superior violated what was perceived as an individual right.

As previously noted, there are few, if any, specific laws detailing employees' rights, but general informational guidelines do exist, such as the text written by Outten and Kinigstein which states, "The role of the law in employment relations has become more intrusive in five distinct areas: (1) providing economic protection to employees through minimum wage/maximum hours laws, pension plan oversights, etc.; (2) barring or restricting discrimination on the basis of race, sex, age, handicap, national origin and, in some states, on the basis of marital status, sexual preference and classification; (3) seeking to ensure a safe and healthful workplace; (4) recognizing and protecting employees' privacy rights; and (5) seeking to mandate fairness by, for example, recognizing the right to a hearing in discharge and disciplinary matters involving public employees, upholding the primacy of grievance procedures established under collective bargaining agreements, and requiring disclosure of the identity of toxic chemicals in the workplace." The information presented by Outten and Kinigstein provides some general limits that a mid-level leader, such as a secondary manager, can use when dealing with subordinates.

An Employee Bill of Rights-A Proposal by David W. Ewing was adapted as a basic guide in this text for the police mid-level manager's use in determining the *do's* and *don'ts* concerning subordinate rights. The proposed subordinate rights that a functional mid-level manager should not violate are:

1. The right to vote a criticism about organizational management's actions without negative reprisal actions or discrimination against the employee.
2. The right of personal actions by workers external to the organization, so long as those behaviors do not affect the employee's on-the-job performance or violate legitimate and recognized conditions of employment without adverse measures against the subordinate.
3. The right of an employee to not comply with organizational directives that are contrary to commonly accepted norms of morality and law without punitive sanctions.
4. The right of an employee to expect that conversations, test results, and job actions that he or she perceives as private will remain confidential in the absence of a legal revelation waiver.

5. The same basic due process rights against unreasonable search and seizure apply to property under the employee's charge in the workplace as in his or her private life, with the exceptions as prescribed by law.
6. The right to expect former mid-level managers to not make subjective or derogatory statements concerning the prior employee to perspective superiors and/or employers.
7. The right to be adequately and appropriately informed as to the reason and nature of perceived negative job actions taken against the employee by mid-level managers.
8. The right of access to the organization's formal appeal process for a fair and impartial review of an employee's grievance request.

The above adapted employees' rights outline serves as an excellent parameter guide for a functional police mid-level manager's knowledge. An acute awareness of these areas, as the principle source of most employee-generated lawsuits against organizations, will enable a mid-level leader to function more effectively. It is realized that the suggested areas are not absolute or all inclusive, but it can be shown that a leader operating within the scope of these parameters are less likely to be the cause of an employee-generated legal action against the organization. It is apparent from the dynamic knowledge requirements of a functional police mid-level manager as revealed in this chapter that the job of a functional police leader is not a simple matter. The more efficient and effective functional police mid-level managers will possess not only the personality traits of a good leader but also the operational or technical skills of the job actions being supervised. Most knowledgeable police leadership realize that it is no longer just the person with the greatest technical skills that should be considered as the best positional leader or mid-level manager. It is the person with superior ability to direct or control the efforts of subordinates and who has the practical knowledge of the parameters within which an effective mid-level manager should function.

Employee Job Wants

Previously, in this text, leadership styles, management theories, and employee motivation were discussed. However, it is concluded that employees' job wants is a separate criteria that needs to be addressed under THE DYNAMICS OF A SECONDARY LEADER'S ROLE IN THE ORGANIZATION. In the considering of job wants as a workplace motivator, they become a required knowledge need of a police mid-level manager. It is essential for a leader to recognize that subordinates have varying needs and goals that inspire their work performance. These needs are continually influencing the functional-level worker's behavior. Inasmuch as each subordinate worker is an individual, it must be remembered that employees do not have the same formula of wants, needs, strengths, and weaknesses. Financial gain as an incentive seems to be a motivator of limited duration for most but not all functional workers. Some functional-level employees are motivated by challenges and task variety for expanded job knowledge and performance ability. A functional secondary leader must recognize the differences in subordinates, but this recognition does not always imply that a mid-level manager can determine which job want will be dominant at a given time. Just as line workers vary from one another, so too does the motivating wants of subordinates shift as time and situations change. It becomes critical for a midlevel manager to ascertain what a subordinate wants from the job. The overt sought after attainments, etc., may change from day to day, but the foundational or basic job wants of workers tend to remain relatively consistent. Therefore, a critical task knowledge requirement of an effective mid-level police leader will be a perceptual awareness of subordinates' job wants.

Several studies, including Lindahi Lawrence's research using line mid-level managers to rank order things workers may want from their jobs, have been conducted. Lawrence's research was documented in a magazine article, entitled "What Makes a Good Job?" coincided with several other studies on the subject. Essentially, the studies asserted that employment security, pay, promotional opportunities, and workplace environment as the most desired aspects of a job. However, queries of workers revealed that recognition, appreciation, knowledge of how they contribute to the finished product, and a leadership understanding of their operational problems were their desired motivators. The two groups' research results were almost in total reverse order of ranking when compared. Thus, an effective mid-level manager will not rely on his/her perception of subordinates' job needs. A good leader should involve subordinates in decision-making processes, if the situation permits, and will also obtain through observations and inquiries the motivating factors (needs and wants) of employees.

Traditional concepts, such as pay, benefits, and job security, have been shown in recent times to be not as influential as job wants. It is extremely important that a police mid-level manager realize the great discrepancy that exists between what organizational leaders think functional workers want and what employees actually want from a job. Mid-level managers and line supervisors as leaders must know their subordinates and understand what influences them as a job want. As previous studies have shown, leaders tend not to accurately perceive the wants of functional employees. Questioning in the absence of observations and/or other information-gathering factors may not correctly provide the answers. Perceptual trust and rapport may distort information, and often material needs will be expressed because of our monetarily focused, pluralistic society. The multifaceted aspects of society from a pluralistic perspective will generally focus on finances as the number one priority because it's expected, and in this capitalistic society one never wants to chance not monetarily advancing. This occurs even when functional workers actually desire recognition of work performance and appreciation for task accomplishments as a priority job want. The first three needs (Basic, Safety, and Social) as articulated by Abraham Maslow are quickly satisfied with the acquisition of acceptable employment. Therefore, the **Recognition** and **Self-Esteem** needs become primary when the foundational job requirements are satisfied. The police mid-level manager should be aware of the aforementioned and strive to create an organizational environment and opportunity to satisfy subordinates' job wants.

SYNOPSIS

An essential factor to recall from the discussion of delegation as a necessary and essential dimensional skill of a police manager is leadership limitations. An operational police manager must realize that no positional leader will possess all the leadership traits or the performance time to manage in a vacuum. Yet, no one can provide him or her with an absolute performance formula for task delegation that works in every situation. Therefore, if a manager's leadership is to be effective, he or she must learn to properly delegate authority and responsibility to others. This delegation is a sharing of power, not an abdication of ultimate responsibility for the satisfactory task achievement.

Remember that delegation by a manager is not an indication of weakness or an inability to do the job. It is a realization that the number of tasks required of an operational police manager is not conducive to an egocentric type handling approach. It is basically a way of allocating appropriate personnel and management in a manner that is most productive toward assignment fulfillment. Proper delegation also affords the positional leader an opportunity to develop subordinates for their self-enhancement while at the same time fostering a positive commitment to the department. As noted, functional motivation is important to employee performance and concern for the organizational objectives. The learning desire of employees is affected by their mental perception of the delegated task that was assigned. And, the operational manager's influence, on the positive or negative environmental atmosphere, is affected by the information that he or she communicates about the task. Proper task execution depends on the fact that a manager select the right assignment for the specific individual. This should be based on a consideration that enhanced knowledge growth and development are paramount.

But in the final analysis, it must be stated that the **delegation dimensional trait characteristic** is a skill that must be learned by a manager. Like the other positive trait characteristics of an effective leader, it is not inherent but rather a developed skill. An operational police manager who plans to be proficient and skillful in the use of delegation must acquire experience in its use through practice. Thus, a recognition of the critical nature of delegation to managerial effectiveness should be a primary focus of an operational police manager.

Chapter Twelve

COMMUNICATION

If there is one dimensional trait characteristic that should be considered unfailingly essential to effective operational leadership it is communication. Communication, as the text will explain later in this chapter is "the tie that binds" virtually every leadership characteristic with operational task accomplishment. It is almost an understatement to say that one of the most critical capabilities that an operational police manager must possess is the ability to make him- or herself clearly understood by others in the organization. This applies not only to subordinates but to peers and superiors as well. The art of sending and/or receiving messages cannot be overdeveloped, as the exchange of ideas, directives, and meanings are essential. Basically, what this text is referring to is a bilevel of communication, where information flows both up and down the chain of command through the positional leader. This up-and-down flow of information seems like a natural process, but as will be noted later in this chapter, most formal organizations', such as a police department, communication edifice are focused primarily on a downward flow of data. However, if an operational positional leader cannot efficiently communicate in all directions, his or her efforts will not achieve desired results.

During the contextual discussion of communication from an operational police manager's perspective, this text will focus on both **sending** (verbal, documentation and body language) and **receiving** (listening and reading) messages. The primary methods considered most important by social scientists through which individuals communicate are talking, writing, listening, reading, and gestures. Through one of these methods a person usually sends or receives a message from another person. It would be a mistake for a positional leader to take either aspect or component of communication for granted, because it is a skill that permeates his or her capability as a manager. Note should be made that communication skill can be improved through a conscious effort and practice. While admittedly the enhancement of communication skills is not as difficult as some of the other dimensional trait characteristics, it should not be taken lightly, because improper or poor communication skills can be very detrimental economically and wasteful of resources (human and logistical).

Communication as a dimensional trait characteristic of an operational police manager is defined as the displayed capability to send and receive information effectively, as well as making certain that adequate information is presented and obtained for practical use by the recipients. It is well known that no member of a service-oriented firm or an organization, such as the police, can operate in virtual communication isolation. Therefore, it is not practical to assume that an operational positional manager can function effectively in a vacuum. The requirement for an efficient and effective exchange of information is essential to assure coordinated efforts in the achievement of desired results. There are numerous reasons that could be expressed as to why communications is a critical component of an operational police manager's makeup. But for expediency and to avoid elongation of the obvious, this text will cite the two more notable from which most of the others are generated in an organizational setting. In an operational environment of a police department, the predominant reasons are:

1. The formulation of an appropriate plan of operation to meet established goals and objectives necessitates a comprehensive interchange of communication between the various levels of hierarchical responsibility and authority within the organizational sphere; and
2. The implementation of a preoperational plan is predicated on the positional leader's ability to communicate to subordinates the projected course of action and the expectations of goal accomplishment.

An efficient operational manager must be cognizant that the productive performance and the meeting of expectations by subordinates can only be effectively achieved as a result of appropriate communicative exchanges. The success of an operational manager is dependent in large measure on the effectiveness of the individual's subordinates, as has been noted previously, and also through the coordinated effort of not only his or her subordinates but also the cooperative interaction with other departmental elements. The emphasized back-and-forth flow of information is required to achieve the already stated results. Traditionally, the basic duties and functions of each organizational position is generally detailed in some form of directive; however, without some type of formal leadership through communication efforts, seldom will desired results be adequately achieved. The other dimensional trait characteristics have all pointed to the fact that the operational positional leader, whether a first-line controller or the functional manager, has a profound and significant impact on an organization's objective accomplishment. Upper organizational echelon generally establishes overall goals and objectives that influences progressive functional actions through directional communication. This informational flow is usually filtered through the operational manager to the functional level. Such procedures are common in all organizations and are typically referred to as **formal communication**. In researching the communication processes of various organizations, the author found that basically all are predicated on a primarily gravitational or downward flow of communication. In other words, the top leadership of an organization wants to assure that their communicative directives are transmitted and received at all levels. Also, it's an adequacy of information exchange that is necessary to inform subordinates exactly what is required and to promote cooperative efforts with other elements to achieve overall departmental objectives. It is then a truism to state that **communication may be the single most important thread that links all components of an organization**. Top organizational leadership's concept of the relationship of operational management and effectiveness of subordinates' performances has become increasingly apparent in the work place. There's an apparent recognition that subordinates cannot be expected to perform effectively until adequate instructions and/or information has been communicated by operational leadership. This has established a realization of the importance and essentiality of effective communication as a dimensional trait characteristic of operational police management.

Job satisfaction, as emphasized throughout this text, is a prime concern of an operational manager, as it has a direct effect on subordinates' performances and ultimately task accomplishment. An effective communicative effort will not only explain and clarify what is to be done but also how its accomplishment will help achieve desired results. It has been shown in numerous "worker productivity studies" that most employees display a noticeable enhancement in job satisfaction and an increased work output when they are aware of how their function fits into the finished product. For example, **a factory line worker may feel his job is unimportant and therefore he does not take pride in personal functions. Such attitudes can result in low productivity and decreased job satisfaction, etc. However, when this same employee is shown the finished product and an explanation of how the mechanical fitting he installs is essential to a successful end result, the pride in what he is doing will generally improve as will job performance and other work-related behaviors**. From the example cited it is clear that without a comprehensive awareness of why a subordinate is required to perform specific tasks toward accomplishment of the overall organizational mission, there can and probably will be a decline in motivation and self-initiated effort on the part of the operational-level employee. This is especially true in police work, where the ultimate results and sought-after goals are not easily quantifiable. However, based on the accepted validity of previous studies, it is clear that effective communication on the part of an operational police manager is paramount to the performance accuracy and subordinates' overall job satisfaction.

However, most police administrators tend to assess the effectiveness of communication in themselves and in others from a subjective perspective of whether information is formally passed down the chain of command. This is far too narrow a view of communication in an organizational setting, especially when it is considered that absolutely no function of a police department operates without some form of effective communication. When the basic nature of police work, plus the variance of situations handled and the behavioral actions reacted too, are considered, it is plain that the critical framework and essentiality of effective communication in law enforcement is a must. This means that all phases of affirmative communication are necessary. The phases being referred to are **sending**, **receiving**, **feedback**, and **clarification of information**. There are of course other facets that the text will examine later in this chapter, along with the phases above identified. Thus, being able to communicate efficiently through an appropriate technique is of extreme importance to an operational police manager in a work situation. Everything stated thus far in this chapter points to the fact that communication is critical to positional leaders for passing on assignment information and for the clarification of data for each individual concerned.

Another important aspect of the need for effectiveness of communication by an operational police manager should be explored before the text concludes its introductory analysis of the importance to positional leadership. Although briefly touched upon, the need for cooperative actions and requirements of communication to achieve the desired coordination should be more emphatically stressed. The need for **teamwork** in law enforcement, both within and external to the organization, is a must before there can be effectiveness of objective achievement. The hazards of police work and the mobility of crime during the last couple of decades necessitate interactive cooperation if any effectiveness is to be achieved. Teamwork is generally predicated on effective communication and may be considered a prime foundation of efficient and productive law enforcement. Since interactive coordination between separate components usually requires a focal point of communication to avoid confusion, it is usually the operational police manager who is that focal point and may be required to communicate with virtually every social and economic level of society. Therefore, it is not difficult to see why the communicative skills of an operational positional leader in a police department may in some respects be primarily the most critical trait characteristic. An efficient operational manager will transmit or translate information to control, direct, and coordinate the performance of his or her personnel with the activities of other elements, the objective being the attainment of overall goals of the organization. As indicated, a positional leader generally operates within the structured communicational system of the organization. But he or she is expected to be effective and achieve desired results through subordinates' efforts by way of a formalized effective dispersal, translation, and receiving of information. Traditionally, this is referred to as **effective communication** in order to provide a more comprehensive and insightful perspective. It is now appropriate to discuss transmittal of information from an operational police manager's perspective of communicative skill requirements.

TRANSMITTING INFORMATION

The sending of messages is a misnomer in terms of terminology for what it means to the functioning of an operational leader, because transmitting information does not only apply to original concepts, ideas, or decisions coming from the leader. It also includes the information that is received from other sources that are translated and then transmitted to the appropriate element. There is no easy path to operational communication, because frequently it presents concepts and decisions that require interpreting before it can be put into action by others. Therefore, a close adherence to the basic rules of communication will be needed. But operational communication is concerned with all the detail factors that are an integral part of an information exchange process. Thus, the contextual concentration of this text will begin to look at the sending aspect of information exchange and a discussion of effective verbal communication techniques.

Verbal Communication

When attempting to communicate verbally with subordinates, peers, superiors, etc., the useful things for an operational manager to keep in mind is his or her listeners. The manager should remember that an inherent barrier to any effective communication is **listener comprehension**. Therefore, the knowledge level of the audience concerning the issue being discussed must be given consideration. For example, if the positional leader is talking about an operational problem to a superior, he or she should attempt to speak in layman terms so that what's being said is clearly understood. This example

AN INABILITY TO EFFECTIVELY COMMUNICATE CAN BE DETRIMENTAL TO AN OPERATIONAL LEADER IN A POLICE ORGANIZATION.

assumes that the upper echelon leader is not as familiar with the technical aspects and terminology as someone who works with it daily. There are other aspects of verbal communication that can be detrimental to effectiveness. Two of the more notable ones have to do with verbal conversation and ego aspect of disaffecting listeners. The author is referring to talking in a manner that the listeners perceive as (1) being talked down to or (2) that the verbalizer is communicating at too simple a level. Either situation implies that the communicator perceives that the audience's intellectual process has a simple capability. Neither of these may be true in an operational police manager's communication attempts, but remember, like so many other things, the test of effectiveness is in the **eye of the beholder**. In other words, what a person as a leader intends to communicate matters little if the listeners do not understand or tune the communicator out for offended reasons.

There are certain specific problems associated with listening that this text will address prior to terminating the discussion on verbal communication. An effective police manager or communicator should keep in mind the problem of listening, as well as certain things about his or her audience. To wit, **the individuals' capabilities, knowledge, academic level, specific awareness of the topic material** and many other factors will influence listening. The positional leader as a communicator should then assure that the presentation of the message that is attempting to be transmitted is in a logical sequence, contains comprehensive language, and is concise enough not to lose the interest of the listeners. The presenting communicator (operational police manager) must choose personal words carefully, clarify each area of confusion, and summarize the presentation, assuring to highlight the important or critical areas. Paramount to his or her communication efforts should be an attempt to make certain that essential points and meaning of the information-sharing effort is clearly understood by the listeners.

If the operational manager is presenting a verbal presentation, whether formal or informal, the structure of the material should be in three parts: a **start**, a **middle**, and a **finish**. Most generally, the middle, or body, of the presentation will contain the majority of essential pertinent facts. However, in this text's discussion of a manager's verbal communication skill, there is less concern with the oral presentation's content and will therefore concentrate on interactive operational sharing of information.

There are several verbal practices traditionally used in oral communication that are considered essential for enhancement of an operational manager's effectiveness in transmitting information. The ones provided in this text are but a few of the attributes that are thought to be important in any form of verbal or oral communication. But in most textbooks' contents in reference to the essentials of good communication skills, the categories generally found will be: (1) **factual**, (2) **clarity**, (3) **concise**, (4) **comprehensive**, (5) **accuracy**, and (6) **timeliness**. However, for purposes of concentrating on effective verbal information exchange at this point, the text will limit its discussed attributes to the Basic **A,B,C's of Communication**. The A,B,C's of effective communication are:

1. **Accuracy of Information Transmittal**. An effective operational manager/communicator must assure that the information transmitted **through** or by him or her as a positional leader is factual. It is generally recognized that as information passes from one hierarchy level to the next or from one person to the other, there is some filtration. A positional leader must realize that the information received for transmittal to others is first perceived by him or her relative to a personal understanding. The perceived information is then translated into a self-comprehension and language to be transmitted to subordinates, etc. During the above described filtering process, some factual information, such as originally intended, by the communication source can become confused or lost. The altering of information to be passed on is usually not an intentional consequence by a positional leader, but if the individual fails to recognize the possibilities and specifically guard against them, then distortion can easily occur. Therefore, information transmitted through an operational police manager must be factual as received and not confused with personal opinions and conclusions of the positional leader. Generally, this can be accomplished through the use of precise language without the

embellishments that appear to be human nature. Accuracy of oral execution in communication does not apply to information transferred via the positional leader, it also applies to decisions and directives originated by the manager. In other words, to achieve the desired effectiveness and/or results, the operational police manager must assure that all of his or her verbal communications are precise and correct. An operational manager can accomplish this by thinking over what is to be said before speaking and considering what the listeners will perceive from what has been stated.

2. **Brevity of Information Presented**. Verbal or oral communication on the part of an operational police manager should be as brief and concise as possible. The brevity of presentation should not be done at the sacrifice of any factual data that is pertinent to satisfactory task accomplishment. Lengthy orations tend to be wordy, circuitously factual, unnecessarily confusing, and time consuming. However, to say that verbal communications should be brief does not imply that information presented can be less than complete. The operational police manager must exercise extreme care in his or her efforts to be brief and/or concise so as not to exclude accuracy, completeness, and clarity when communicating. Each of us can identify someone who we perceive as a **talker**, referring to the fact that the person appears to talk too much, too long, and unnecessarily. This tends to be irritating or boring, which is why we may oftentimes "tune the person out," meaning that the individual is at times listened to but not heard by his or her audience. The intellectual mind sort of blanks out what the person is saying. This often happens during long and redundant verbal communicative efforts. Therefore, to be an efficient and effective communicator, an operational police manager must avoid the pitfalls of excessive oral dialogue. Brevity of the information presented can be accomplished by a manager's consideration of the information needed by the listeners to effectively perform and his or her avoidance of the temptation to embellish or be circuitous in presenting required information. Be aware that it is a natural human tendency to add a little of his or her rationale into data presented and couple this filtration with the listener's propensity to interject self-perceptions into what is being stated. It becomes clear why the adage "what you think was stated by what you heard is not what was meant by what you think the individual said" is more often than not very true.

3. **Clarity of Presentation and Meaning Is Essential**. A verbal information exchange should be made in such a way that it is easy for the listener to comprehend. The use of a simple or common language in a logical sequence and pace will assure that the information can be easily understood by others. The true value in effective communication of any type depends in large measure upon how clearly it is presented. It does little good to present

accurate and useful information to others if it is offered in a manner or language that is not effectively comprehended by recipients. A clear verbal exchange by the police manager to subordinates, peers, superiors, or others will reflect positively upon the positional leader as being competent and effective. Decisions, directives, or objective information that is illegibly presented in regards to a listener's clarity of comprehension wastes organizational resources. The wasted resources (human and material) is typically the product of a misconception of the information offered. Thus, less than desired results and other such miscues that require the use of additional resources (time and material) may be needed to achieve a satisfactory outcome. An operational police manager can usually avoid a lack of clarity by: (A) regulating the speed of the verbal transmission so as to not talk too fast for effective understanding; (B) assuring that the language and terminology used is common to the listeners (whenever possible using plain and simple wording); (C) keeping the amount of information presented at one time to a minimum (the greater the volume the more likely there will be some confusion); and (D) making certain that the communicator's words don't say one thing while his or her body language implies something else.

4. **Completeness in Regard to Sufficiency of Information**. Law enforcement in modern society dictates that an operational-level employee or primary leader needs as much information as possible to be effective. The ebb and flow of human emotions or actions makes it essential for functional personnel to have sufficient information to adapt to changing situations. The verbal exchange or presentation of information should be as complete as possible, because the smallest essential detail omitted could be critical to the effective disposition of an incident. Necessary details or information added at a later time because it was left out of the original presentation causes the recipients to reassess planned actions and at times to undo processes that have been initiated. However, if the information exchange is as complete as possible at the time it becomes available, it will make for better use of resources. Timeliness of information is a consideration under the aspect of completeness. Remember, that in order for communicative efforts to be effective, it should be received in time to allow proper actions. A positional leader can improve his or her performance in this aspect of verbal communication by reviewing the information to be transmitted prior to speaking. There should be notes or key phrases written to assure that essential and pertinent facts are not overlooked. The information should also be presented as soon as practical in consideration with the task concerned and the effective use of the data by the recipients.

5. **Courtesy Is an Asset to Communicative Acceptance**. Consideration for the opinions and perceptions of the audience can be a prime factor

in the effectiveness of verbal communication by an operational police man-ager. Negative perceptions of a demeaning or inflammatory nature by the recipient blunts the desired results of effectiveness of a positional leader's communication efforts. There are a number of actions that a positional leader can take while attempting to orally communicate what would be considered **discourteous** or **detrimental**. **First**, the manager can be obtrusively coun-termanding, to wit: negatively contradict the comments or suggestions of the audience when the ideas, etc., do not correspond with his or hers. **Second**, each individual or group has certain phrases or terms that they perceive as offensive; the use of those inflammatory remarks will alienate a leader's lis-teners through this blatant demonstration of disrespect. **Third**, when address-ing subordinates concerning inappropriate performance or behaviors, the operational manager should avoid generalities of action. He or she must at-tempt to be specific as to what the problem is and how to correct it; the na-ture of the concern will dictate how specific the manager should get, realiz-ing, of course, that individual subordinate problems should almost never be addressed in his or her peer group setting. **Fourth**, a positional leader must avoid appearing to disparage a subordinate or to talk down to listeners be-cause they lack intimate knowledge of the situation being addressed. The communicator/positional leader should talk in layman's terms, projecting an aura that the recipients have the mental capability to understand what is be-ing stated. **Fifth**, a presenter's display of a non-positive attitude or disposition toward the subject or audience is a definite turnoff to the people that a man-ager is attempting to reach. Remember, courtesy is just as much a projection of attitudinal behavior as the overt things that a verbal communicator does and says. And, that the perception of the individual speaking will affect **how well** or **even if** the desired informational exchange is accepted by the lis-teners.

From our discussion of the basic A,B,C's of verbal communication, it is easy to see why communicative skills from an oral perspective are essential to an operational police manager. Next, the text will focus its discussion on documented or written communication as a component of transmitting infor-mation.

Documented or Written Communication

Verbal communication skills are very difficult to master and execute be-cause of the immediacy of the effort. However, official writings by an oper-ational positional leader are equally as difficult, though in a different context. It often leaves the most lasting impression of the manager's ability and is a communication skill that can be effectively acquired. Like most skills, the major areas of concern are: (1) sufficiency of data; (2) clarity of documentation; (3) legibility of writing; (4) conciseness of comments; (5) accuracy of information; and (6) timeliness of submissions. When writing formal correspondence in a business setting, an operational police manager should avoid trying to impress others with his or her written skills. The operational leader should assure that personal written communiques are stated as simply as possible, because difficult-to-read documentation can be confusing and very time consuming to effectively comprehend. A leader must also remember that **what is clear to the writer of the communique may not be as understandable to the reader**. Also, various words and phrases may have different conceptual meaning to another person.

The positional leader must be aware that the best assessor of written communications, whether formal or informal, will be the receiver or reader. A properly prepared and contextually documented communique will be revealing of informational data to the reader. Also, it must be made clear that most written information exchanges in an organizational setting, such as a police department, should be formatted in a formal style. Further, the communique will need to be structured in a fashion that projects continuity of information, clearly comprehensible language and format, a legibility of written symbols, concisely accurate data, a sufficient amount of used content, and a timeliness of submission. A written communique that contains all of the above identified qualities will not only fulfill its purpose but reflect very favorably on the manager preparing it. Along with the areas noted, the positional leader must make certain that the written communication is not in conflict with any established departmental policies or procedures. Imagine the confusion, embarrassment, and negative perception that would be created should an operational police manager issue a written communication that conflicts with an already established and documented organizational policy. It is a perceived standard for a formally written communique in a highly structured organization to focus the reader's attention toward the material content and its useful aspects of objective achievement.

There are numerous factors set forth in various texts on preparation of formal writings and some of the more notable aspects of effectiveness. Some of these component aspects usually considered essential to effective formal written communications are:

1. **Offering a synopsis sentence at the start of a lengthy written communique**. This often aids in focusing the attention of the reader to the purpose intended. The person is less likely to become lost or confused at what is being written about. It also aids the writer to stick closer to the essential points and eliminate the tendency to ramble on with adjectival information.

2. **Utilizing concise and/or underlining sentences or phrases will**

serve to emphasize desired material. This method will make more noticeable the pertinent areas that the operational manager wishes to highlight in his or her written communique.

3. **Use phrases and wording that are commonplace to the organization and the recipients for easy comprehension**. The tendency for an individual is, no matter what his or her personal status, to attempt to write at a higher-than-normal level. This generally makes for poor written communication, because the recipient often cannot follow the continuity of the communique. If at all possible, avoid the use of ambiguous terms when expressing an idea or directive. Remember, the person's personal perception of the terms may be entirely different from the individual charged with following or utilizing the information.

4. **When actions are recommended, as opposed to being directed by the operational police manager, they should be clearly distinguished and prioritized**. An effective police manager recommending resolutive actions to a concern will generally offer more than one possible alternative to deal with the problem. However, in suggesting such recommended alternatives, the positional leader should assure that they are set apart and clearly distinguishable from the discussion thesis of the proposal. Also, never should a number of alternatives be offered without being prioritized and specific documentation presented as to the one primarily endorsed by the writer.

As stated, these are but a few of the tips and/or suggestions that a positional leader can gather from researching enhanced skills in formal writing practices. Like the verbal communicative skills that can be enhanced through practice and effort, so can writing. It too is a vital component of this essential dimensional trait characteristic. A police manager should be especially aware that carefully worded, easy-to-comprehend written communiques are most essential in directives, instructions, official reports, and business correspondence. The positional leader must strive to not only make them easy to read and comprehend but almost an impossibility to misunderstand. The effective operational police manager should be able to communicate equally well in both written and verbal forms.

The author is aware of no guide or format that covers every written communicative situation that a positional leader will encounter. However, there are a number of concerns that an operational police manager should consider regarding effective written communications. These considerations should be based on response to the following influences:

1. Basic purpose of the written communique.
2. Achievement of expectations as an ultimate result.
3. The knowledge level of the recipients regarding the concern.

4. The basic action sought from the communique.
5. Sufficiency of available resources to support content of the communique.
6. Sufficiency of facts and/or useful information.
7. Availability of viable alternatives.
8. Requirements of support material (graphs, films, etc.) needed.
9. Clarity of intent, overtly stated.
10. Easily comprehendible by the recipient(s).
11. Composition to the knowledge level of the recipient(s) about the subject.
12. Critical points or factors emphasized.
13. Written composition to make for interesting and informative reading.
14. An obvious continuity of information.
15. Ideas, opinions, and recommendations clearly identified as to their area of applicability.
16. Conciseness and/or brevity maintained as much as possible.
17. Summation for lengthy writings to aid rapid idea conception, if needed.
18. Sentence edifice, comprehensively brief with commonly used terminology.
19. Initial comments should immediately focus reader attention.
20. Grammatical correctness in word usage, punctuation, and spelling.
21. Factual information, accurate and sequentially presented.
22. Avoidance of unusual metaphors and abbreviations.
23. Written communiques to be timely submitted; allowing for comprehension, meeting due dates, etc.
24. Written communiques properly addressed and appropriately routed.
25. Clear statement of whether or not a reply is required; if so, when it will be desired or needed.

As is readily observed, if a person assures that each of these concerns is addressed in a written communication, it will be effective. This text does recognize that because of the nature and brevity of some written communications by an operational police manager, it is not practical to assume that each of the points will be reflected in all documentation. However, in our contextual discussion of the written aspects of transmitting information as a component of communication, it is perceived that the text has not only shown the importance of written communication but also some very vital techniques whereby a positional leader can enhance his or her skill in this area.

The final area of transmitting information relative to a positional leader is perhaps the most critical, because words and written documentation will not always be believed, but displays of body language or physical gestures usually will.

Body Language or Physical Gestures

The various body postures, movement, physical gestures, and facial expressions are as effective a transmitter of communicated messages as verbal and/or written presentations. The basic difference between body language or physical gestures (**body communication**) and the verbal or written forms (**conventional communication**) of information exchange is that the latter is usually intentional. In other words, conventional communication is usually preplanned and utilized to convey an intentional or purposeful message, while body communication is most often unintentionally transmitted, typically without the communicator even knowing that a message has been projected. The more notable of these body communications that are readily noticeable are: (1) eye-to-eye contact while listening or talking to someone; (2) voice control through volume, pitch, and/or inflections; (3) physical gestures, actual movement of body parts; and (4) facial expressions, the contortions of various facial muscles that project internal feelings.

Most social scientists and scholars in the area of human information exchange recognize and emphasize the importance of body communication in the work place. An operational positional leader must be aware that his or her seeming inconsequential gestures or movements could notably affect subordinates' perceptions. An effective police manager will become familiar with the various bodily gestures and facial expressions that will project the desired messages. He or she should then utilize individual body communication efforts in conjunction with conventional methods to convey and emphasize the information desired. Along with bodily movements and gestures, it should also be stressed that the positional propinquity of the body has a direct influence on message sending and/or reception. People (human beings), as a general rule, consider the area directly adjacent to his or her body (approximately 15 to 18 inches) as **personal space**. Anyone coming within that interpersonal space noticeably affects the person who is being approached. If the approach is anticipated and desired in a caring emotional sense, then the pleasure sensations are heightened from a communicative perspective. But if the encroachment into the perceived personal space was not anticipated or desired, then the individual being approached generally experiences an uneasiness and will often retreat a step as a defense mechanism to regain his or her separation distance. The uneasiness caused by the invasion of personal space and the individual's automatic internal defensive reaction will hinder effective communication. Therefore, it is easy to see how a manager's use or misuse of a subordinate's personal space can have a direct influence on communicative effectiveness.

Significant to remember relative to body communication is that inter-personal space encroachment, movement, and gestures of the positional leader should not be allowed to distract from the informational exchange efforts. In other words, if a police manager's gestures distract the attention of his or her audience while presenting information, then the person's body communication becomes a negative factor. Effective communicators realize that it is natural for most people to utilize their hands and some body motion while talking. However, productive leaders have learned to control and/or limit these movements. In fact, appropriate body language is often used by polished speakers to enhance their communication efforts during a presen-tation. The raising and lowering of the voice during speaking efforts can prove very effective when emphasizing a point. A subtle leaning forward toward an individual while maintaining eye contact tends to stress the per-ception that the communicator considers the point important. Likewise, a nod of the head, a smile or a wink of the eye reflects agreement with what is being stated. All of the non-conventional methods of communicating are too numerous to mention. But if the effectiveness of a police manager as a com-municator is to be a reality, then he or she must become familiar with and utilize the techniques to a personal advantage.

The nonconventional or body communication is extremely important in enhancing and/or conversely damaging communicative relationships. This is basically true, because body communication generally reveals messages that we do not intend to make known.

The saying that goes something similar to "your words say one thing but your actions say something else" is very true in body communication. The unintentional communicative expressions reveal self-perceptions, personal concepts about the topic, and even individual emotions relative to another person. Therefore, it would be justified to say that body communication is a personal commentary about an information exchange and the perceptual relationships. What may be most significant by what has been termed **unin-tentional communication** is the influence it usually exerts on enhancing or tearing down an interactive relationship. Generally, an inaccurate articula-tion of an unintentional communicational situation may project a demand or perceived necessity by the recipient to react inappropriately. Consider the universally utilized example of comparing two photographs, one showing an individual in an aesthetically approved attire and posture, while the second picture shows a person negatively dressed, etc. The caption usually read "Who would you believe?" Decisions on this basis are dictated by perceptu-al observations and not any consideration for intellectual ability. "Judging a book by its cover" may have no reality of job performance capabilities or knowledge, but it is truly an influential factor. Likewise, the perception created by a person's body language could project an undesired and unplanned message. Therefore, the importance of body communication must be a prime consideration of an operational police manager in the performance of his or her duties.

Environment as a Communicative Influence. An accession to concluding the text's discussion of body communication as an essential component of the message-transmitting process, the contextual content must consider, at least superficially, the use and advantages of environmental factors as a critical component of non-conventional communication. Surroundings or environment can be positively utilized to facilitate communication by arranging to meet in an attractive location in which the recipient(s) feel comfortable. Comfort and at easeness in their surrounding will make the audience much more pliable and receptive of the communications. Seating arrangements have an effect on the image and power projection of the positional leader. If she or he wants to control, dominate, or project power during a session with subordinates, then being seated behind a desk with papers at your disposal while the other person is seated in a chair without such paraphernalia is most certainly the power position. The desk becomes a barrier for the leader and tends to foster a perception of superiority to the manager while projecting the subordinate in an inferior position that is usually somewhat intimidating. It should be stated that separation is not always negative and is typically expected and often may be less stressful for positional leader/subordinate interaction. The same power or dominant role is assumed when the subordinate is seated and the leader is standing over him or her. A school classroom is a prime example of teachers utilizing authority control by standing up to address their students.

Conversely, if a police manager feels that the most effective form of communication for the situation is a more relaxed and informal atmosphere, there are several methods of accomplishing this without relinquishing leadership control. He or she can arrange to meet the subordinate in their office or work location; also, to arrange the seating in his or her personal office so there are no barriers to create an automatic power perception. Seating yourself on the same side of the desk and using a casual tone of voice and volume of speech are all positive atmosphere creators. Remember, the arranging of the seating should be such that the distance in between is comfortably close without encroachment on the subordinate's personal space.

To this juncture, the text has comprehensively discussed the three most common methods of transmitting information by an operational police manager. The next logical step in our progressive examination of communication as an essential dimensional trait characteristic of operational leadership is to discuss the **receiving of information**.

RECEIVING INFORMATION

Reception of information is not a difficult concept to grasp, because the five senses that man is blessed with are all information intakers. However, for purposes of dealing with operational management in a police department, the text will concentrate on information reception from a conceptual stand-point. Therefore, there will be only two basic areas in which the discussion will concentrate. Those areas are **listening skills** and **perceptional read-ing**, which the author has found to be as critical to effective communication as transmitting information.

Managerial Communication Methodology and Technique

Many researchers in the field of organizational leadership and manage-ment have indicated that in a very real sense the exchange of information is quintessential. Aside from the job responsibility, the most glaring difference between hierarchical leadership and functional personnel is mid-level lead-ership's communication methodology in both receipt and distribution of in-formation. Top management information needs and dissemination techniques principally focus around strategic planning relative to the overall organiza-tional achievement of goals and objectives. The secondary manager's com-munication efforts are generally limited to worker level subordinates. Simply stated, a mid-level police manager deals with programmable, decided upon actions that develop from precise concerns of quantity and quality job per-formance.

Communication of an informational nature at all levels of the organiza-tion involves the dissemination of data that have been adapted and formu-lated into a meaningful and understandable format for the receiver. The above is very important inasmuch as factual data not understood by the receiver is information that has not been communicated. And, without adequate and appropriate information, subordinates cannot perform effectively in achiev-ing desired results. For example, a supervisor tells subordinates, "See that pile of boxes in the middle of the room, stack them against the wall," then the leader turns and leaves the room. A very simple directive but when ana-lyzed, we find that it is very poor communication, because the leader did not specify which wall or how high the boxes are to be stacked. A skeptic would say "the subordinates should be intelligent enough to decide on a wall and know how high to safely stack the boxes." That may very well be true, but if certain wall space was to be used for other purposes or that other boxes were to be delivered for stacking, the lack of additional adjective information could notably affect how and where the crates are to be stacked. The functional-level workers in any field of employment need information that is specifically relevant to the functional aspects of their job actions. In other words, at the organization's functional level through the middle manager position, specific operational information is most needed.

The effect of communicated information relative to method and technique focuses principally on the job performed by the mid-level manager. The secondary leader typically communicates to relay information concerning decisions made or to control the actions of subordinates in getting tasks achieved. Perceptually, it is believed that communication at the mid-level police manager's position is easily adaptable or changed because of the limited number of organizational levels affected. There is also the perception that a mid-level manager's communication is limited to directing performance output, keeping superiors informed, scheduling of worker-level activities, and articulating procedural information. The theoretical concept and the innovative aspects of strategic planning associated with top management is generally thought not to be an essential focus of secondary and functional leadership.

The line mid-level manager needs to tailor the communicative delivery of information to the data to be presented and his or her personality projection. One of the biggest problems for mid-level leaders in delivering information effectively is that the data to be presented may or may not fit precisely what a subordinate needs to perform efficiently. Too much information to an already knowledgeable worker may confuse or alter a planned appropriate action. Likewise, too little information to an unknowledgeable worker will often produce unacceptable work. The aforementioned is a continuing dilemma for police mid-level managers because functional-level supervisors and police officers must also be adjusted. The above information is presented to articulate the importance and difficulty that a leader faces when attempting to transform essential data into useful knowledge for subordinates.

MANAGERIAL COMMUNICATION PROCESS

No individual member of an organization or operating element can perform effectively if it remains in isolation. There needs to be an exchange of information to assure cooperation for overall accomplishment of goals and objectives. This exchange of factual data is known as formal organizational communication. Communication is an essential part of the managerial process for a number of reasons. Most notable among those are: (1) the effective formulation of an operational plan to achieve goals and objectives requires an extensive communication exchange between the various hierarchical command levels and influences of the organization; (2) the effective execution of an operational plan depends on communication, not only for an understanding of the proposed programs, but also the coordination of efforts.

A functional-level middle manager should realize that desired performance by a subordinate can only be achieved through effective communication with the employee. The successfulness of the manager's operation is dependent upon the effectiveness of his/her individual subordinates and upon the cooperation through teamwork of each person in relationship with one another. The general duties and responsibilities of each position are usually outlined in the organization's operation manual. However, without some form of communication from organizational leadership as to direction and focus, seldom will overall goals and objectives be achieved.

Mid-level managers have a significant influence on the work performed by officers. However, upper police management exerts directional goals and objectives filtered through several levels of leadership and the operational secondary manager via a line leader to the functional-level employees. This process is known as formal communication, inasmuch as it is a structured and planned informational flow that affects the entire organization. Then it is reasonable to assume that communication is the thread that connects all elements and individuals of an organization together.

In this section of the text, we will explore the various concepts and patterns of communication from a functional mid-level manager's perspective. It will also provide some practical methods of how a mid-level manager can improve personal communication skills.

GENERAL CONSIDERATIONS

Communication in an organizational setting is said to be a multi-level component, because each layer of the agency has different expectations of direct influences. For example, the higher you go up in an organization's hierarchy, the more the communicator is reliant upon intermediates to relay his/her message to the primary work force. A principal focus on communication at the basic level of the organization may be both heard and observed. It is a very simple transaction, from one person to another, to produce a desired reaction. The stages above the primary level are based on prior experience of interaction and the transactional control of managers, etc.

The style of management or leadership communication will vary from organization to organization. For example, in one organization, the communication concept may be based on receipt and acceptance of general direction prior to action, while in another organization, it means to do what you are told because there is little or no tolerance for secondary ideas or solutions. Unfortunately, the latter autocratic style of communication is very prevalent in a number of public police organizations. The general consideration of communication can be received in a number of ways. The most obvious perceptual point of view is that informative behavioral action often results from an effective exchange of information. In other words, it is what may best be defined as good communication. Communication within an organizational setting assumes many forms and/or functional aspects. The nonverbal communication practices of the organization's leadership, such as body language, gestures, and facial expression, may be just as powerful as the spoken messages. Verbal or written communication is obviously the principal form of organizational communications, but the aspects of interpretation, reading between the lines, or perceiving the unspoken message, are just as powerful components of communication as any other. An effective mid-level manager who communicates efficiently will project an emotion that should positively influence behavioral interpretation and the perceptual idea that the leader wants to present. It must be remembered that communication between sender and receiver carries both meaning and intent relative to message content.

Whenever a miscommunication occurs relative to the meaning and intent, the fault generally lies with the sender. The error most often can be traced to the message's content, clarity, or completeness. Extensive messages (too long) have the potential of adding to loss of interest and/or confusing the receiver. Likewise, being too brief also occurs in communication. The leader must continually be cognizant of these communication concerns. Additionally, a leader's communication of statements will have a greater effect the more often it is repeated. Don't be afraid to repeat your message for clarity.

Importance of Communication

Leadership perceptions in regards to operational mid-level police management have become increasingly conscious of the importance of communication in effective duty performance. It is realized that until a subordinate has been effectively instructed in the performance of duties, he or she will be unable to function efficiently. And also, without a comprehension of why the employee is performing a certain task and its benefits to the organization, a subordinate's personal motivation is much more susceptible to decline.

A LEADER SHOULD ASSURE THAT THE EFFORTS OF SUBORDINATES ARE COORDI-
NATED AND NOT COUNTERPRODUCTIVE TO ONE ANOTHER.

Too often we tend to measure the effectiveness of communication from a
subjective perspective of how we are transmitting information. But because
of the critical nature and importance of communication to public policing, it
is essential that all facts be considered; to wit; *sending, receiving, feedback,* and
clarification.

Being able to communicate in an effective manner is of extreme importance to the functional mid-level manager. It is essential to the position's job
performance that the mid-level manager be able to pass on assignment information and understand the subordinate's perspective or feedback. As was
previously stated, communication is essential to teamwork and teamwork is
the foundation upon which a law enforcement organization is built.

The secondary manager should realize that ideas and decisions can more
readily be translated into the needed action when they are communicated to
others with some consideration given to the emotional needs of the subordinate. Good communication is not only accomplished with words but with
voice inflection and behavioral action. Often these are very important. Therefore, it is essential for a mid-level manager from time to time to review the
basics of good communication practices, since they tend to become lost in
the day-to-day activities of positional leaders.

A good police manager communicates to direct and coordinate the activity of subordinates with the actions of other employees toward the accomplishment of the overall organizational goals and objectives. The mid-level manager typically functions within a hierarchical system of communication established by the organization's management. The process is principally structured to disperse and receive information in a formalized, prescribed manner. Whisenand and Ferguson state that such a system's "degree of success is based on its doing five things:

1. Providing sufficient information to accomplish assigned tasks. This communication function may be satisfied through a variety of forms, such as periodic training, provision of technical reference manuals, daily coaching, and order.
2. Communicating clarified perceptions and expectation of responsibility. Organization charts, job descriptions, work plans, schedules, routes, performance rating, orders, and other devices may serve this function.
3. Facilitating the coordination (now and in the future) of men and materials in achieving specific objectives.
4. Making possible organizational problem solving (task oriented) and conflict resolution (interpersonal problems).
5. Furnishing general direction not only on what to achieve but also on how to achieve it."

Comprehensive Listening

Listening for an operational positional leader in a work setting is not the mere hearing of comments made by subordinates or superiors. It is comprehension and association of what is heard to operational concerns of his or her functional responsibilities. Adequate listening skills as an essential component of managerial leadership is a task that requires practice and efforts for performing. Appropriate information attainment from a listening process is not an automatic consequence. An operational police manager must actively apply him- or herself in order to develop efficient and effective comprehensive listening techniques. The beneficial aspects of positive listening makes the time spent in enhancing this skill a worthwhile investment of a manager's effort expenditure. There is often an economic loss associated with poor comprehensive listening, the same as there may be through ineffective presentation of information. The foul-ups in information exchanges often result in increased expenditures of resources (human and logistical) to undo or redo a task. In one-on-one situations with subordinates, low morale may also be a consequence because of a seeming disinterest in what the individual is attempting to convey. Poor listening skills displayed when dealing with superiors negatively reflect upon the manager's perceived capability and attitudinal interest. From this, it is not difficult to see the importance of listening skills to an effective operational police manager.

Comprehensive listening by a positional leader is undoubtedly an activity that takes a great deal of a manager's time and is deserving of more than a casual consideration. However, like any other worthwhile skill of leadership, there are influence factors that negatively impact managerial listening. It is therefore incumbent upon the leader to recognize these reverse positive factors and compensate for them. The first step to overcoming these concerns that tend to interfere with effective listening is to recognize and identify their potential influence. The following identifies some of the more pertinent interference factors, but in no way do they represent the totality of all the potential negative influences on communicative listening.

1. **Attentiveness to the Information Being Presented**. It is a truism that the attention span of most individuals are far too brief, meaning that if a communique requires more than three to five minutes time frame to absorb the information exchange, a sort of mental boredom sets in. When this intellectual disaffection of what is being stated comes into play, much of the comprehensive intent of the message will be lost. It is a natural human characteristic to seek intellectual stimulation and excitement, but more often than not job communiques are neither stimulating nor exciting. Therefore, the operational leader must intentionally focus personal attention on not only what is being said but its ultimate meaning. At first this will seem like a laborious task, but as time passes and the effort continues, it will become almost automatic. In other words, the manager will begin to do it as a matter of habit or form rather than through a forced effort.

2. **Assuring Complete Comprehension of the Information Received**. The length of a communication exchange is inconsequential if there is no real understanding of what may be expressed. In saying this, the text is not simply referring to word terminology and their dictionary definitions. It is the meaning that the speaker was trying to convey that is significant. For example, in a continuous five- or ten-minute verbal exchange, a manager could be exposed to between 250-1,000 different words, depending on the pace of the conversation. And, no matter how attentive he or she may be, it is estimated that some 15 or 20 words or phrases will be used that the recipient(s) won't comprehend in the same context as the speaker intended. The changing times of the communication age in which we live have seen the faddish birth of **contrived word usage** as a way of personal identity. With this in mind, an operational manager must be on guard to inquire as to specific meaning whenever there is the slightest doubt of total understanding. Like-

wise, an effective operational leader will attempt to regulate the speaker's pace of conversation to assure that none of the intended meaning of the information is missed. Also, by regulating the information flow, the speaker is less likely to forget pertinent areas. An operational police manager's concentration on comprehension and regulation of data intake will help keep his or her mind from drifting from the process. Human mental abilities not only exceed presentation efforts but will also summarize and anticipate what the person is going to say. This is especially true where significant technical knowledge is already known by the recipient. Therefore, it takes a concentrated effort not to allow intellectual processes to wander while information is being articulated. If the recipient allows this to happen and there is an unexpected twist to the information being presented, it may go unnoticed by the individual, which could prove detrimental to successful task achievement.

3. **Avoidance of Allowing Environmental Factors to Negatively Affect Communicative Listening**. Influence factors such as excessive noise, interruptive coming and going of personnel, physical discomfort, and numerous other interference features can be detrimental to listening efforts. Therefore, the operational leader should preplan as much as possible the place where an information exchange will take place. Distractive occurrences will not only affect the leader's ability to comprehensively listen, but it can also interfere with the speaker's ability to present information effectively. Continuity in the acquisition of information is vital to a comprehensive understanding of what has been stated and its conceptual meaning. Environmental control then is a direct responsibility of the operational police manager in the preplanned receiving of information.

4. **Preconceived Concepts or Bias Negatively Affecting a Manager's Comprehensive Listening Ability**. A simple way of stating this **influence factor** is to say that "a closed mind will hear only what it agrees with." A lack of objectivity will tend to make the listener reject communicated ideas and suggestions without a real bias to do so. Add to this the problem that often an individual will fail to perceive that he or she has a preconceived concept or bias and the negative effect on listening becomes fairly obvious. This failed realization will often blind the person to prejudicial actions as the individual will substitute rationalization for objective assessment. Thus, if a bias or prejudice toward a concept will sway an individual's ability to listen objectively, then so too will these negative perceptions influence him or her about the speaker. An effective operational police manager will not only evaluate the information received, but he or she will also assess personal concepts. This will assure that actions taken are based on relevant facts and not preconceived notions.

To be an effective communicator (from the aspect of enhanced listening ability) takes concentrated work, plus a forced effort and patience on the part of an operational police manager. However, utilization of suggested methods should result in critical and noteworthy improvement in a leader's listening skills. This is vital, because it is a managerial responsibility that consumes much of a positional leader's functional time. Comprehensive listening is the most crucial of the **receiving of information skills**, but no discussion into this area could be considered complete without a review of **reading comprehension**.

Reading Comprehension (Document Analysis)

Comprehensive reading is **an ability to interpret, learn from, and utilize information observed in written or printed form**. Basic to the legal need for accuracy and record keeping in law enforcement, it is not practical to rely on non-documented communication resources. Public scrutiny from every segment of society demands a strict accounting of police personnel time usage, resource allocations, and enforcement actions taken. Therefore, it is plain that the amount of paperwork encountered by all levels of a police department is enormous. A **hard copy** (written documentation) is generally maintained for most major directives issued within a police agency. Most assuredly, all policies, procedures, general orders, and special directives are distributed and retained in a written form. Thus, it is imperative that an operational police manager have the ability to read and comprehend if he or she is to function effectively as a positional leader in a law enforcement environment.

Traditional concepts imply that comprehensive reading by an operational police leader of duty-related material is a laborious task. This perceived difficulty or lack of enthusiasm may be based on the fact that it seems to be a never-ending task of handling similar paperwork. Often, it appears the individual could utilize a whole day's effort and still not complete all the operational paperwork that is encountered. In the chapter on "Delegation," the text discussed assigning some of the performance responsibilities to subordinates. This will undoubtedly help; however, the operational manager must first read through the material and sort out the items that can be delegated from the concerns that he or she is required to handle personally. The manager need not be a speedreader to effectively accomplish this, but the individual must know how to read for recognition and problem identification. This type of reading is somewhat faster than comprehensive reading, where a complete understanding is necessary. Some textbooks on enhanced reading skills say that **reading the first and last sentence of lengthy**

paragraphs, plus the final recommendations, will give the reader a relatively complete knowledge of what the documentation is about. This is supposedly true of most formal writings and/or textbooks. And, while the author agrees with this concept, it should be pointed out that police reports are formally written based on actual facts, meaning that there should be little or no adjectival information contained in the report. However, if a reader utilizes the first and last sentence and the recommendations approach, along with a thorough **scan type** reading of the rest of the report, this method can prove to be quite effective. An enhanced speed can then be achieved without overlooking vital factors in the report.

Whenever an operational manager reads official directives or reports, the individual should devote his or her complete attention to thoroughly understanding what the writer intended to convey. An effective leader will look for content facts to support the documentation or other tangible environmental influence factors. Note will need to be made of any additional information that may be required to improve the quality or comprehensiveness of documentation submitted by subordinates. Also, an operational police manager should constantly be on guard against giving less than a comprehensive analysis of written documentation and should continually practice the techniques that will enhance overall reading skills. The individual can often do this by increasing the amount of personal reading efforts at every opportune instance. It has been shown that the more frequently a person reads, the better he or she will be able to read. Likewise, through a conscious effort to increase speed and comprehension, an individual can noticeably improve in a short period of time. Remember, communication is a vital component of demonstrable managerial abilities, which is desirable in a positional leader. A noted deficiency in this area could be detrimental to a leader's chances of advancement in a highly visible and structured environment such as a police organization.

Therefore, receiving information is essential for an operational leader's effective performance. A positional leader must realize that communicated ideas and concepts can be more readily utilized if he or she thoroughly comprehends the transmitted message. Good communication means not only the ability to convey information but also the capability to absorb vital factors. Hence, communication is often referred to as an information exchange, indicating a flow of comprehensive data in both directions. Thus, it is important that an operational police manager from time to time evaluate the basic concept of his or her usage of good communication practices. Inasmuch as these practices tend to get lost in the normal activities of job performances, it should also be remembered that an effective operational manager transmits and receives information primarily to direct and/or control the activities of subordinates. The subordinates' performance activities must be coordinated with the actions of other departmental performances in an effort to achieve overall goals and objectives. An operational police manager principally functions within the communicative hierarchical structure of a police department. The established communication edifice will generally set specific parameters on the dispersal, receipt and/or use of the information-exchange process.

All of the aforementioned information emphasized the importance of communication to an operational police leader. There has also been an identification of several pertinent aspects or methods of improving a positional leader's communicative capabilities. This enhanced communication ability is critical to a positional leader's development of a functional plan for his or her unit's operation, improved efficiency of subordinates' performances, and coordinated teamwork with other departmental elements. The position of an operational police manager within the structure of the organization makes it mandatory to examine **hierarchy communication** during the text's discussion of this dimensional trait characteristic.

HIERARCHY COMMUNICATION

Hierarchy communication applies to an operational leader's capabilities to send and receive information to all levels of the organization. Most organizational edifices within a police department demand rigid accountability of responsibility and actions relative to formal communication. These structural controls are necessary to maintain effective managerial controls, but they are somewhat restrictive of the flow of communication between the various levels of the organization. The traditional staff structure and organizational emphasis for the downward flow of functional information are usually much more accurate and formal than is the less formal upward responses of functional subordinates, primarily because most organizational systems are designed to assure that issued directives reach the targeted element. However, the feedback or response flow of communication is not so precise and well structured. Top-level echelon of most organizations normally are less concerned about responsive comments than they are regarding the downward flow of decisional communication effectiveness.

In addition to the **vertical** (downward and upward) flow of communication, there is also a **horizontal** and a **diagonal** direction in which information travels within an organization. While the vertical flow tends to be more formal in nature and was purposefully built into the system to accommodate the pyramidal hierarchical structure, the **horizontal** and **diagonal** communication flow of information are generally informal in nature and depend more on personal associations or contacts than a formalized structure.

A principal concern in formalized communication in a highly structured environment tends to be strict adherence to an established chain of command. Potentially promising careers of many managers have been irreparably damaged by simply bypassing a link in the hierarchical chain of command. Communicative effectiveness in a quasi-military edifice, such as a police organization, does not function well without a firmly adhered to **chain of responsibility**. The actual process of information exchange improves as the number of leadership filters are reduced. But in eliminating levels of bureaucracy, the span of control for positional leaders expands and concurrently a reduction in the attention a manager can give to each subordinate or assignment. It has been clearly shown that increased leadership controls and attention will enhance the probability of achievement of desired goals and objectives. Therefore, the hierarchical communication networks established within a police organizational structure are vital to the operational functioning of its managers; likewise, so is the essentiality of an operational manager's utilization of the **basic forms of communication** within a police department.

BASIC FORMS OF COMMUNICATION

Relative to the categories of communication in the work place, there are two basic forms universally known. The two basic classifications or forms are the **formal** and **informal**. Each category has specific benefits and drawbacks particular unto itself. The essentiality of both forms to an effective communication process of an organization cannot be overlooked. As the text examines each separately, the reader will readily observe the benefits of their respective application. An effective operational police manager should be totally familiar with the positive and negative aspects of each and be prepared to utilize both to his or her best advantage.

Formal Communication

The primary leadership structure of a police department will determine the parameters and flow of formal communication. Formal communication is the information exchange that is dispersal in accordance with structural departmental guidelines based on leadership responsibility and authority. It is principally true that formal communication is a direct responsibility of the department's hierarchy to assure that the edifice of the organization provides clearly defined channels of information exchanges. Research has shown that

EFFECTIVE COMMUNICATION AT ALL LEVELS OF THE ORGANIZATION IS
CRITICAL TO AN OPERATIONAL LEADER'S SUCCESS.

formal communication can also flow in an upward or lateral direction, even
though the downward flux is more traditional. It is clear that a primary emphasis of an operational manager's formal communication drift is in the downward direction. Positional leaders tend to be more concerned that the directives that they issue are received and implemented than their subordinates'
reactions about the decision.

Formalized communication in a law enforcement-type organizational setting occurs within established structural controls and procedural guidelines.
Generally, formal communication flows down the chain of command from
upper echelon to functional personnel who will carry out the directives. The
frequency of use of the formal lines of communication will tend to strength-
en the process, as will the status and power of an operational police manager and other positional leaders. An effective operational police manager will
solidify his or her positional authority by communicating with both subordinates and superiors as often as possible, thereby achieving desired results
from the formal communication process through comprehension and compliance. The operational police manager should primarily attempt to utilize

formal channels of communication within the department for organizational concerns.

Informal Communication

The traditional or formal communication lines within a police department represent only one method of information exchange. The informal communication process, sometimes known as the "grapevine" or "rumor mill," can often be as effective and necessary as a formal communication process to an operational police manager. It is also true that some informal communication processes can be detrimental to the organization's effectiveness. These negative forms of informal communication are **malicious rumors** and **unfounded gossip**, as well as partial or incomplete information exchanges. Informal communication typically develops through a chain of contacts and can be favorable, if properly utilized by an operations leader to provide positive assistance to the formal communication process. The informal informational flow generally follows a pattern and usually occurs as a result of personal associations outside of the formal departmental chain of command. The capability of an informal process to move information rapidly can at times be advantageous to organizational leadership. It has often proven to be the most effective way of obtaining reliable feedback information from functional-level personnel about directives, etc. Traditionally, hierarchical leadership's ability to tap into the informal process is severely limited; the number of persons and/or command levels that the information tends to filter through will affect the data received. An operational police manager is in a good posture, because he or she may have only one or two intervening steps between his or her position and functional personnel. This provides an opportunity to receive information from the informal communication process because of the span of contacts with subordinates, peers, and superiors.

As emphasized, communications whether formal or informal occur in all directions of contacts within the police department. The various directional forms of communication is of value to all command levels of an organization. Therefore, effective leadership should carefully maintain the **formal communication system** to assure its effectiveness and continuous use, because failure to do so will likely weaken the process and diminish the authority status of the operational police manager and other hierarchical organizational leaders. It becomes blatantly obvious that operational productivity and effectiveness will not occur unless there is an adherence to the requirements of both formal and informal communication concepts. An operational police manager will usually be ineffective as a communicator if he or she fails to recognize and utilize both processes to a personal advantage. The hierarchical position of an operational police manager is challenging not only because of the insulation levels between functional personnel and the intimate knowledge of line concerns not shared by superiors but also because there are certain inherent **department obstacles to communication** that he or she must be aware of and cope with.

DEPARTMENT OBSTACLES TO COMMUNICATION

The various systems of communication within a police department create some concerns or obstacles that are inherent to a highly structured process. These obstacles to effective communication will affect an operational manager's successfulness in attempting to disperse required functional information. An effective operational police leader should be aware that if the listed obstacles can be mastered, an efficient and viable communication process will be achieved. Some of the barriers influencing a department's communication process are identified in the following text.

The more notable of the obstacles to effective organizational communication referred to are filteration, misrepresentation, appropriate attentiveness, common vernacular, timeliness, and appropriately dispatched.

Filtration. The fact that directives filter through a number of authority levels in a chain of authority will alter the information based on personal perceptions, communication ability, environmental factors, and numerous other influences that are specific to the individuals. An operational police manager should transmit directive information in a very concise, simple, and specific terminology so that it does not require interpreting.

Misrepresentation. The phrase that goes something like, "he speaks from his personal point of view, but I listen from my perspective" may be very applicable to this obstacle. Quite simply, it means that what a person meant by what he or she stated may not be what the recipient understood the person to mean by what was heard. The operational leader communicating the information must request immediate response from subordinates in most cases of technically complicated messages. This should assure that the information exchange is clearly comprehended; if not, clarification can be provided.

Appropriate Attentiveness. A knowledge of the importance of adequate listening by the recipient of information will enhance understanding of what is being transmitted. A capability to listen appropriately is a learned skill. Too often, a positional leader is so intellectually distracted by other projects that he or she has underway or will implement in the future, that only part of what's being communicated is actually comprehended. An operational manager must be alert to listen skillfully and be observant to detect through responses when a message has been misinterpreted. A positional leader should assure that he or she is in a position to be clearly heard and observed by those whom the communication is directed to. And, the individual must assure that the recipients' reactions and questions display a clear understanding that they are correctly receiving the information.

Common Vernacular. The terminology used must be common to the police organization and the recipients. It should also be simple so as not to be misunderstood by whomever in the organization receives the communication. In other words, keep it simple enough that the person is capable of understanding it. This will tend to eliminate distortions through misunderstandings from one responsibility level in the department to the next. This is applicable to all methods of intradepartmental communications. An operational-level manager must adjust personal vernacular to accommodate the receiving audience to assure comprehension. A leader should also avoid the use of metaphors or terms that are not totally familiar to the recipients. An effective positional leader should make personal communiques as understandable and concise as possible. Further, an operational police manager should remember that simply because he or she is an accomplished speaker does not necessarily indicate proficiency as a communicator.

Timeliness. The necessity for presentation of information in a timely manner is well documented in law enforcement. Information released too soon or too late for effective use by the recipient is tantamount to a failure to provide adequate data. A leader must recognize that for information to be most productive and appropriately used, it must be received in a time frame that is adequately conducive for its effective application. It should be apparent that timeliness of information is a major obstacle in a department's communication process. The operational positional leader should assess the information as to what the requirements for use are. Also, the leader must determine who needs it and when the information will be most effective to disseminate. A police manager must assure that communiques are timed and issued in a manner to coincide sequentially with operational functions so that subordinates' performances will be distorted.

Appropriately Dispatched. Information routed to an inappropriate location or individual will unnecessarily delay its effective use. This often results in added economic expenditures because of timing problems and needless confusion. Indirect routing also results in an increase in the number of filtering elements that become involved, which enhances the chances of distortion. An operational police manager should ascertain the routing of the communication he or she is to transmit from its informational content and purpose. The individual must then direct the information through proper channels toward the desired recipient in as concise a manner as possible.

The discussed departmental obstacles to communication can be effectively dealt with by an operational manager by the use of the methods and practices detailed in the contextual discussion of the individual obstacles. A police manager should be aware of the need to limit as many of the external concerns that influence communication as possible.

ENHANCING COMMUNICATION SKILLS

The information contained in this chapter has reflected the recognized importance of communication as one of the most vital dimensional trait characteristics of an effective operational manager. However, as the text concludes its discussion on communication, it is essential that an assessment of possible ways to enhance effectiveness be considered. There have been no established universally accepted methods of evaluating communicative effectiveness from an operational leader's perspective, but there are some generally known parameters that can be utilized. Initially, there should be a sense of freedom to express ideas among subordinates. In other words, do the subordinates give the impression of being hesitant to complain or make suggestions toward changes? Further, do subordinate personnel and functional-level employees appear knowledgeable about their role and position in the department? And, finally, are there a protracted number of inquiries or inappropriate actions that occur each time a decision is communicated by the operational leader? The collective responses to the concerns mentioned will provide an operational police manager with a comprehensive evaluation of individual communicative effectiveness within the organization.

An operational police manager must recognize that communication is a critical component of his or her efficient performance of duty; also, that communicative effectiveness requires continuous attention to remain useful and efficient. Enhanced communication may produce results not just in terms of improved subordinate job performances but also in their attitudinal approach and overall perspective of the organization. There are several influences that an operational police manager can utilize to enhance personal communicative behavioral skills to elevate performance effectiveness.

1. **Prioritizing the Flow of Information**. Establishing a sequence by which information exchanges will be distributed and their relative importance.

2. **Forecasting Future Communicative Needs and a Method of Implementation**. Appropriately scheduling and preplanning the communication efforts required to improve overall effectiveness.

3. **A Concentrated Effort to Coordinate Operational Activities with Other Departmental Components**. Assuring an effective rapport

with those whom an operational police manager will communicate can increase the efficiency of information distribution.

4. **An Ability to Perceive the Communication in the Manner that the Recipient Will.** The ability to project one's self into the recipient's position will enhance an operational leader's communication capability, because the leader will often recognize a requirement for additional information or the clarity to accomplish desired results.

It is recognized from all that has been presented relative to an operational police manager's role and position in the organization that the individual is considered the key to proper communication. Through the methods and operational practices presented during this chapter's contextual content, a positional leader should be able to enhance personal communicative skills. However, the individual must realize that an operational manager is basically a translator and/or transmitter between the department's hierarchy and the functional-level leaders and personnel. An assurance of an appropriate and accurate flow of information both up and down the chain of command is a direct responsibility of an operational manager. The effectiveness with which he or she accomplishes this task will determine the overall efficiency of the organization in achieving established goals and objectives.

Positional Communication

Positional communication as it applies to a mid-level manager refers to a personal ability to receive and send information upward, downward, and laterally in the organization. The basic hierarchical structure of a police organization inhibits the smooth flow of information from one level to the next. The downward flow of information is much more precise and smooth, as most hierarchical systems are designed to assure that decisional information from management is received by the target elements. The upward flow of information is not as precise and well coordinated, as managers tend to worry less about adequate feedback systems than they do about subordinates' communication feedback systems.

Another major concern of positional communication in a hierarchical structure such as a law enforcement agency is the prohibitions against bypassing an element in the "chain of command." It is a **"no-no"** in quasi-military systems such as public policing to bypass an element in the chain of responsibility without an extraordinary reason. A manager who skips a supervisor to communicate decisions directly to functional-level personnel on a consistent basis will soon relegate that primary leader to little more than a figurehead. While it is true that reduced levels of bureaucracy improve overall communication and a broader base of control is created, this broader base of control can be more detrimental to the manager's effective performance than the improved informational flow. Concerning upward communication the old adage holds true: bypassing your boss may be a mortal sin in an organizational setting.

For our comprehensive look at **positional communication** and the functional mid-level manager, we are referring to **Vertical** and **Horizontal** communication in a public police operation. But before we take an individual look at the directional flow of communication, the various forms of intra-organizational communication need to be addressed.

LEVELS OF COMMUNICATION

Effective communication within an organization's setting is both a multi-level and a multifaceted process involving each strata of the agency. It has been said that through efficient communication efforts an organization's leadership attempts to develop and implement desired behaviors by subordinates. Primary to the *Levels of Communication* within an organization is the interchange of information between the secondary leader and line supervisor/subordinates. At this level, the communications are usually very basic and involve a little of the interplay that can lead to confusion. This level involves the development of an understanding between the middle manager and the primary supervisor/workers. The second level of communication generally involves mid-level leaders and upper management of the organizational layers. It could be an operational leader and his/her superior or a higher level manager and his or her superior. The strata of the organization is not the overriding issue in second-level communication. Informational content and intent is considered most critical, because it involves an individual having multiple responsibilities to someone else whose effectiveness is gauged by the performance of others. The highest level of communication, of course, is that involving the top manager to subordinate leaders. The top manager has ultimate responsibility for the organization's accomplishment of its goals and objectives. This form of communication is generally that of a visionary and conceptualizer on the part of top manager toward the conveying and/or convincing subordinates. It is not surprising that the higher up the organizational ladder a communication interchange occurs, the greater the need to sell or *convince* the receiver through presented actions.

From the very top of the organization's layer to the primary level of communication, it is incumbent upon the sender to reduce or eliminate confusion. Other authors in the area of organizational leadership indicate that principally confusion occurs when the receiver cannot differentiate between factual information and inference data. If for some reason a leader, during communication, makes an inference, he or she should assure that the receiving party recognize it as a premise as opposed to it being a fact. The failure to eliminate or avoid confusion will only multiply the error or misinformation as it travels down the organization's chain of command. Specific traits determine articulation of facts from statements of inference. Articulations of factual data must be based on a specific awareness of what is being conveyed. Stated premises can be visionary, based on logical conclusions, having a perceptual foundation in prior experiences. There is virtually no limit to inferences because they involve imagination and probability.

A police manager must recognize that effective communication in an organization, especially public policing, involves both transmitting data and receiving feedback. The process of information traveling down the chain of command typically is not a problem since most organizations are established with a formal downward flow of information. The manager must work hard to assure and maintain a viable and consistent reaction to information from subordinates. Effective and efficient establishment of a feedback process has to start with an environmental climate that lets subordinates know that their ideas and utterances will not be overlooked. An effective leader is generally confident enough in his/her ability and positional role to solicit feedback by encouraging subordinates to do so. The leader must be careful not to challenge feedback that he or she doesn't agree with, inasmuch as this has a tendency to stifle the upward flow of information. There should be a willingness to deal openly with issues articulated during feedback sessions. Remember that organizational communication can be both formal and informal. Typically, downward communication is formal and feedback communication is informal, unless the organization's leadership makes it a formal process. The more effective and efficient organizations seek to formalize both exposure and feedback communication. As previously stated, the different directions of organizational communication are:

1. **Downward**: Directives or orders from superiors down the chain of command to subordinates (usually formal).
2. **Upward**: Feedback or response information from subordinates back up the chain of authority (can be formal or informal).
3. **Horizontal**: Peer level sharing of information (can be formal or informal).
4. **Diagonal**: Communication with superiors or subordinates not in the individual's chain of command (usually informal, as staff principles not lines of authority apply).

Now that we have examined the various facets of information distribution as it applies to the mid-level manager, it is important at this time to relate these elements to the basic concept of effective communication.

Concepts of Communication

There is no easy road to effective organizational communication because it often presents ideas and decisions that need to be interpreted and put into action by others. Thus a strict technique and rule approach to communication will not necessarily be considered effective in all instances. However, effective communication is concerned with more than good ideas and well thought out decisions by the organization's leadership. It is structured on a concern for many detail factors that are an integral part of the communication process, including the comprehension of the sender and receiver.

Melnicoe and Mennig, in their book *Elements of Police Supervision,* provide some sound concepts for effective communication for an operational police leader in a quasi-military organization. Their concepts, referred to as **"Principles of Effective Communication,"** are:

1. **Clarity**: The primary element in effective communication at any level is clarity, being clear in what is relayed. Whether the communication is in verbal or written form, the presentation must be clear or it will not be understood.
2. **Consistency**: Consistency is considered an extremely important part of any effective communication process. Consistency down the chain of command demands that communicated decisions reflect the same focus, even though it has filtered through several levels of responsibility.
3. **Adequacy**: This infers that the communicator provides sufficient information and detail so that the receiver knows and understands what is expected. And the knowledge that has been gained will enable him or her to function efficiently and effectively.
4. **Timing**: Being timely is important to every aspect of life, but nowhere in the organizational setting is this more true than in the communication process. Ill-timed communications can be counterproductive if given too soon or too late. But well-timed, appropriate information can be the difference between message acceptance and the effectiveness of subordinates.
5. **Distribution**: The communicator must be aware of the audience that he or she is attempting to reach, so that the message can be structured and directed to assure that it reaches the ones intended. The commu-

nication effort is not effective if it never gets to the subordinates or elements that require it for appropriate action.

As can be gathered from Melnicoe and Mennig's concepts of communication, productive and efficient communication cannot occur without adherence and compliance with these concepts when exchanging information. The functional mid-level manager will be ineffective as a communicator without assuring that each concept is addressed in his or her communication efforts. The distribution and assignment of functional-level police supervisors/personnel make effective communication by the mid-level manager critical to their efficient performance.

Assessing and Improving Communication Effectiveness

The information provided in this text has attested to the importance of communication as one of the most vital components of an organization's effective operations. But before we close our discussion on communication, it is important that a brief analysis or evaluation of its effectiveness be conducted. There are no traditionally clear-cut methods of assessing communication effectiveness from a leadership's perspective, but there are some general guideline questions that can be used.

First, is there a sense of freedom of expression among subordinates? In other words, are your subordinates always agreeable to your suggestions or comments, apparently too frightened to complain or suggest changes? Second, do your subordinates appear knowledgeable about their role and position in the organization? And, do they respond readily to directives, both oral or written? Third, is there an endless line of questions or inappropriate actions each time a decision is communicated by you? The collective response to these questions will provide the mid-level manager with a comprehensive assessment of his or her communication effectiveness with subordinates.

The secondary manager must realize that communication is an essential part of a leader's efficient duty performance and requires continuous attention to remain viable and effective. It can yield results not only in terms of increased subordinate performance but also in terms of their attitude and overall outlook on the organization.

Some elements that a functional mid-level police manager can add to his or her communicative behavior to improve its effectiveness are:

1. **Setting Priorities**: Establishing a sequence by which information will be distributed and the relative importance of each.
2. **Planning**: The proper scheduling and prior planning of communication efforts can improve its effectiveness immeasurably.

3. **Smooth Relationship**: Having an effective rapport and the confidence of those who the manager is to communicate with increases the efficiency of the information's distribution.
4. **Objectivity**: The ability to project one's self into the receiver's shoes will enhance the sender's communication efforts, as he or she will recognize the need for additional information/clarity to achieve appropriate understanding.

Through the techniques and practices as outlined in this text, a functional mid-level police manager can improve personal communication skills and, thus, will increase his or her overall effectiveness as a positional leader in the organization.

Communicative effectiveness can be as simple as the self-confidence of the sender to articulate and assure his or her message is appropriately received. Leaders at all levels of the organization should use personal communication skills to enhance both their professional and authoritative image within the organization. This is accomplished through a projection of a positive self-esteem and an articulated, straightforward approach to communication. In other words, "say what you mean, and mean what you say" is a quality that is easily discernible by others in the organization. The respect and perception of others will enable the police manager to cash in on the rewards of utilizing powerful communication skills.

A secondary police manager must learn to inspire, influence, and obtain enthusiastic support of others through communication. Utilize arbitration skills and communicative plans of action to influence the behavior of others to accept or consider your points of view. An effective leader as a communicator must learn to present ideas to superiors and subordinates in a manner that will generate the respect and support so necessary for behavioral effectiveness. The leader should also be supportive of organizational policies and procedures in all of his worker communication efforts. Remember, as previously stated, leaders at all levels of the organization are members of the management team and should react accordingly. Communication skills include an ability to convey sufficient information in a concise and persuasive manner. Additionally, an effective leader will develop the communication skills to negotiate action to resolve adversarial encounters. Also, a leader must be competent in recognizing the barriers to communication and in developing an unobstructed path through these common obstacles (identified earlier) and short-circuiting them.

The expression *"the right tool for the right job"* is synonymous with utilizing appropriate communication styles, etc., to efficiently and effectively accomplish tasks. A mid-level leader must recognize how a few inadvertent comments by him or her can seriously affect or destroy the message he or she is trying to convey. Voice, volume, physical gestures, and body language all will positively or negatively affect a leader's communication. The enhanced capability to communicate ideas and planned actions in a persuasive manner and to utilize that skill to motivate and influence others is a quintessential trait of an effective leader. A self-assured and appropriate display by an effectively communicating leader will increase his or her organizational respect. It should make the secondary police manager more confident, as well as increasing his or her bottom line effectiveness as a leader within the organization. Police mid-level managers need to be acutely aware of the need for their behavioral effectiveness, inasmuch as they do not always exert direct or performance controls over operational personnel in field situations, due to the nature of the tasks performed.

SYNOPSIS

Communication may very well be the single most essential of all the dimensional trait characteristics of an operational police manager. To comprehensively discuss communication from an operational manager's perspective, the contextual content must focus on both sending (verbal, documentation, and body language) and receiving (listening and reading) messages. Communication is formally defined as the displayed capability to send and receive messages effectively. An efficient operational leader must be cognizant that the productive performance and meeting of expectations by subordinates can only be effectively achieved as a result of appropriate communication. The transmission of information is a misnomer in terms of transmittal of data does not apply to information relaying but also dispersing original concepts, ideas, or decisions coming from the leader. If an operational police manager is making a verbal presentation, whether formal or informal, the structure of the material should be in three parts: **start**, **middle**, and **finish**. Typically, the essentials of good communication skills that make up an effective presentation are: (1) factual, (2) clarity, (3) concise, (4) comprehension, (5) accuracy, and (6) timeliness. However, the author recommends the use of the **A,B,C's of Communication** for effectiveness in verbal information exchanges. The A,B,C's of effective communication is an acronym for accuracy, brevity, clarity, completeness, and courtesy.

An operational police manager should assure that personal written communiques are stated as simply as possible, because difficult-to-read documentation can be confusing and very time consuming. He or she must be aware that the best assessor of written communications, whether formal or informal, will be the recipient or reader. There is no specific guide or format that will cover every written communicative situation that a positional leader will encounter. A positional manager should be aware that the various body postures, movements, physical gestures, and facial expressions are as effective a transmitter of communication as a verbal and/or written presentation. Consequently, reception of information should not be a difficult concept to grasp, because the five senses with which man is blessed are all informational intakes. Receiving information for an operational manager is principally through listening and perception reading.

Hierarchical communication within a police department applies to sending and receiving information to all levels of the organization. It also applies to the various directional flows of both formal and informal communication. Further, to be an effective communicator, an operational leader must be aware of and overcome the obstacles to effective communication within the organizational setting. Enhanced communication skills can be accomplished through a series of behavioral techniques designed to elevate job performance effectiveness.

Chapter Thirteen

DEVELOPING A LEADERSHIP VISION THAT ENHANCES A MID-LEVEL MANAGER'S EFFECTIVENESS

Achieving effectiveness by a middle-level police manager comes from being responsive to a developed vision. The vision being referred to is an illuminated self-motivation that fosters organizational task accomplishment. Initially, a manager should consider essentialness of the need for personal vision enlightenment and the requirement for it to be established as a top priority achievement goal. A manager's vision effectiveness is articulated via his or her personal commitment to each of the areas identified and set forth in the developed performance vision.

To comprehensively discuss the development, relationship, and effectiveness of a Leadership Vision for Mid-Level Management, we must first set forth its designed purpose, its focus aim for task accomplishments, and performance efforts provided.

PURPOSE OF A LEADERSHIP VISION. Managerial Leadership Visions come from the performance behaviors associated with development and the principal aspects of accomplishments in a work environment. Defining leadership vision for a mid-level police manager means creating a foresightness that fosters effective management of subordinates personnel and effectiveness of organizational service to the public. Thus, it is clear that developing a managerial projection and ideal focus is critical to effective patterns of job performance by a mid-level police manager. The leadership vision sets forth a manager's values and what he or she anticipates will be accomplished under his or her direction.

ASPECTS OF A LEADERSHIP VISION TO BE CONSIDERED DURING ITS DEVELOPMENT

Creating a managerial leadership vision particular to you as a mid-level police manager and your organizational goals and objectives is essential. By being specific in the developing and scope of a leadership vision, a manager is better able to facilitate effectiveness and the focus of task accomplishment. In other words, "the smaller the bite, the more manageable the chew."

Recognize and control a leadership vision's positive interactors, detractors, and those who wait for success or failure before reacting, for or against. A mid-level police manager who is able to identify positive interactors to his/her vision will be able to utilize their support in promoting a vision's concept and objectives to others in the organization. The overall effectiveness in the empowering of middle-manager effectiveness through a leadership vision and directed actions may depend on selling the projected concepts to subordinates and the organization. Very few things in existence can exist in the absence of some type of support or backing.

Detractors to a manager's leadership vision for the performance effectiveness of subordinates are as predictable as "rain in the spring." Adversarial views and attacks tend to strengthen most successful things in life. Reacting to challenges often helps us to identify flaws or areas of weakness. And, in some cases when an idea or concept is not sound, the challenge may cause it to be redeveloped and/or refocused. Therefore, when a mid-level police manager creates a leadership vision, he or she should consider what areas that adversaries will identify and attack. Thus, if questionable areas can be identified and addressed prior to the initial presentation of the leader's vision, the idea focus and potential effectiveness of the concept will be greatly empowered toward success. Those waiting for success or failure before committing will generally make up the largest portion of those interested in a particular Leadership Vision by a manager. Thus, a manager must not only develop and set forth an effective and feasible leadership vision, but he or she must also be efficient in the presentation of the concept to others. Often the success or failure of an idea, projection, or concept is based on its initial accomplishments, setbacks, and the knowledge expanded to others in the organization.

Displaying the fortitude to create and set forth the development of a leadership vision is quintessential to the projective planning of middle-level management. It is common for persons at various levels of an organization to conceptualize ideas of positive performance behaviors of others. The fear of failure is a very strong influence in each of our lives, which often means the status quo prevails. A mid-level police manager must have the courage to not only creatively think in terms of how to influence the behavior of subordinates, but to also display a willingness to set forth and implement his or her vision. Ideas that are unexpressed or implemented are meaningless and for all practical purposes never existed. If new ideas are never set forth or tried, a manager's performance will never improve or enhance his or her effectiveness as a leader.

An appropriately conceived leadership vision by mid-level police management makes a positive impact on others. An effective police manager wants to build a performance pattern from a created vision that not only performs desired tasks but also is positively perceived by subordinates and the organization. Also, Integrity and Mastery of the Vision Concept are quintessential aspects of an effective leadership vision. Integrity is a willingness to carry forth vision, even against all odds. Mastery is a commitment to knowledge, especially about how to effectively perform productively.

Developing a creative leadership vision is the decision that a police manager makes to enhance effectiveness as a leader. His or her most foundational choice is to establish a project function of personal choice. Frequently, the future is the result of a person's present demeanor and/or reaction to current events. A managerial leader will typically have a concept of a focus which he or she wishes to achieve and the kind of task accomplishments that are desired. The action or vision focus is generally aimed at pursuing that goal.

An option that may be considered a reliant choice is to focus behaviors and choices on anticipated outcomes of someone else's development. Many managers seek direction from the organization in the formation of a performance vision for his or her element. They adopt the set forth values and the already established parameter of the operation that becomes the beacon they follow. Choosing the alternative of utilizing the organization's already pre-established vision and values ensures a smoother interaction with the overall goals and objective of the organization. However, it may somewhat limit the creative ability to perform in the future, better and more efficiently than in the past.

The author suggests utilizing some autonomy in creating a **vision focus** for subordinates, ensuring that whatever innovative ideas or processes implemented are in harmony with the goals and objectives of the organization. In other words, a task need not be performed the same way all the time if a new or innovative method will more efficiently and effectively accomplish desired results. However, methodology and results must not negatively impact what is to be achieved by the organization. A "rule of thumb" is that if it does not aid in accomplishment of goals and objectives, then it should not be attempted.

Exercising autonomy as a manager in creating a performance vision or work focus for an element means controlling your own performance destiny.

The recognized benefit to exercising autonomy in creating a performance vision is that your subordinates' work behaviors can be more conducive to meeting your expectations. Also, if a leader chooses to use someone else's work plan and it does not work, he or she is still held accountable for the performance results related to subordinate actions.

Many non-creative leaders will opt to use the vision and work plan of another and thus attempt to claim it is not their fault the effort did not work; it is the blame of the ineffective vision plan. An attempt at avoidance of autonomy in creating a performance vision or work plan for subordinates is to choose **dependency** as a method of not being responsible and held accountable for our managerial actions and/or the performance results of subordinates. Simply put, dependency is a choice of innocence, while autonomy is a choice of accountability. Remember, a leader is creative in his or her vision and work planning for subordinates, inasmuch as he or she is acting on their own choice. Therefore, he or she is attempting to define the individualized work performance of subordinates for the present and into the future.

The primary step to a mid-level police manager is being autonomous in developing a leadership vision that enhances his or her managerial effectiveness in articulating what he or she wishes to create for their element or subordinates. The basic concept is that we define and set forth a desired future that subordinate actions will be committed to achieve. Generally, if the creative vision is well founded and appropriately focused on the goals, objectives, and needs of the organization, it is viewed as good for a managerial leader, his or her subordinates, and the effectiveness of the tasks to be accomplished. It can be said that creating a vision of leadership is a middle-level police manager's essential act of management.

If the middle-level police manager conceives of changing performance directions, unit goals of structures to better achieve ultimate success as an element of the overall organization, it is critical that he or she discusses with others his or her creative vision. Because no matter how well thought-out one person's ideas, he or she often overlooks a detail that can significantly impact ultimate success. A managerial leader should document the creative vision, then discuss it with others as much as he or she can, and as soon as possible before implementation of action. Appropriate communication occurring before implementation action and prior adequate clarification of plans behaviors are approved will save time and effort. Also, the mindset of subordinates will not have to be altered and refocused once the created vision results are made operational.

The creditability of the manager is always in question when new or creative ideas for planned actions are set forth. The implementation of an autonomous vision focus that has been given due consideration is a must. The manager should use language that describes reality rather than masking reality. The concept of articulating a properly conceived leadership vision means that a leader should be not only open about events and plans, but also ensures that his or her performance visions are clear to others.

To this point we have talked about a leadership vision and possible benefits derived therefrom, but what if a manager does not have a performance vision for his or her subordinates? Then it is reasonable to conclude that the manager does not have optimism and is not a forward thinker in terms of task accomplishments and achieving goals and objectives. However, it is not conceivable that a person in a leadership position has not given some thought to the future and related projected behaviors. A vision exists within each of us, even if some have not been expressed or set forth in some manner. Typically, a reluctance to articulate a leadership vision by a manager is a lessened desire to take responsibility for personal actions, behaviors of subordinates, and for the organization. An expressive leadership vision by a middle-level police manager is an expression of hope. And, if he or she has no hope, then it is difficult and may be impossible to create a work vision.

HOW TO DEVELOP A LEADERSHIP VISION

There is nothing new or unique about displaying a performance vision for subordinates or an organizational unit. A creative vision is basically a philosophy about how a manager or leader will direct the task accomplishment of subordinates. Most police organizations have a mission statement and a vision for the overall accomplishment of its goals and objectives. However, it is not unusual for lower-level managers and leaders to utilize the overall organization's vision and fail to realize the importance of developing a performance standard and direction for his or her subordinates.

Many times as managers we tend to think of the end objectives of the organization and not the more basic accomplishments needing to be done by sub-elements in order to make the final attainments possible. For example, if one of the beam supports for a tall structure is not installed or inappropriately set into place, then the building is weakened and may fall. Thus, the vision structure of a middle-level unit is critical to the success and overall accomplishment of the goals and objectives of the organization. Just think of the middle-level unit as one of the support beams for the building.

Now that some information has been set forth regarding the importance of middle-level task accomplishments, and we have discussed to some degree what is a leadership vision, this text should now address how to develop a leadership vision. Some managers formulate performance visions or work projections for subordinates as a normal course for other managerial tasks. It matters not whether they call the leadership vision a *"work credo,"* *"established core values,"* or *"guiding principals of performance,"* the reality is that a work projection has been set into place.

Each middle-level police manager should realize that his or her origination of work goals and objectives for each subordinate is an essential step toward the overall success of the organization. The common pattern of utilizing top management's vision of each element of the organization is not always suitable for lower level performance objectives of the organization. The act of creating and communicating a leadership vision for subordinates is conducive to effective management. When we begin to think about how to establish a leadership vision, it must be kept in mind that the process begins at the top and then each succeeding step required is developed from the performance level beneath it.

It is the job of each middle-level police manager to create a performance vision for his or her unit. The leadership projection of a middle manager and the people above his or her level become input for the *work credo* of subordinates and the unit.

There are three basic stages a middle-level police manager should consider when formulating his or her leadership vision. First, a leader must forget about outperforming other elements; his or her main concern is to enhance the performance behaviors of his or her subordinates and unit. The leadership vision set forth should express the contribution or task performances related to organizational success. An attempt at individual greatness or recognition is an act of self-service and an expression of personal interest. Remember, if there is justice in the world (the organization), rewards for good work will be forthcoming. If a leader is rewarded for making a performance vision happen, he or she should accept the recognition gracefully, but know that is not why the *guiding principles of work performance* was pursued.

The second stage of developing a leadership vision is to not limit your considerations to what may only seem practical at the time. Remember, creativity and innovation have long been associated with visionary thinking. For the most part, as derived from traditional teaching, our society can typically be considered pragmatic because we tend to set specific measurable objectives, and then enact performance plans or projections that set forth how tasks are going to be met and goals will be achieved based on prior methods and practices. The desire to always be practical sometimes works against the innovative creation of a performance vision. A developed performance vision or *established core values* expresses the spiritual and idealistic portion of our nature. Sometimes the most productive methodology for task accomplishments are derived from a visionary or innovative approach to the future that is not pragmatic or practical at the time. Also, following the limits of what seems practical too quickly sometimes acts as a restraint to a creative vision. A mid-level leader's purpose in creating a leadership vision is to clarify and set forth the performance behaviors that a middle manager wishes to create. A leader recognizes that a truly creative visionary approach to task accomplishment may never be fully achieved. He or she should realize that the vision is the beacon of light that generally provides direction rather than a specific destination.

The third stage in developing a performance vision for subordinates is to focus on what you want to achieve and the tasks that need to be accomplished. This may best be done by consideration of how more effectively to serve the long-term needs of the organization's clientele. The effective survival of any organization which includes a police agency depends in large measure on how well the services provided meet the need of customers, clientele, and interacts with other elements of the agency. The basic mindset put forth in other texts on the subject is for a Leadership Work Vision for a unit. Such a mindset tends to view clientele and other organizational elements as either customers or interrelated service providers. It is natural for elements of a **for profit** service agency, dissimilar to a police organization, to share a somewhat competitive interaction with other elements. In police departments, unlike private or commercial agencies, the competition is not of the nature of profit production or the number of "widgets," etc. produced. The competition within a law enforcement agency focuses on the task efficiencies and the contribution to the overall goals and objectives of the organization.

The direction focused through this competitive or collaborative uncertainty is for each function to seek a responsive answer to who its users are and then create a performance vision. Also, the unit leader should target a preferred future of how desired work behaviors of subordinates will accomplish anticipated end results.

Another prime consideration a leader must consider when developing a work plan or performance vision for subordinates is to ensure clientele is not treated any better than we treat each other. Each person/clientele requesting police service wants a unique and understanding response from the unit or organization. If defensive competition occurs within the unit, actions are cautious, judgmental with one another or other elements, and a unit cannot give its best service or desired response to clientele. A clear example of this is when management inappropriately treats a patrol officer. The officer will often display a cold indifference and unresponsiveness to clientele. Remember, the way subordinates are treated is a very good clue as to the management style of their leadership. A projected leadership plan or management style has to manage subordinates in a way that is absolutely aligned with the way that is consistent throughout the organization. An effective leader cannot use fear and punishment to improve behavior and service. If so, the employee's ultimate negative response is to take out resentment and frustration on clientele or other elements instead of rightfully aiming it at leadership.

A mid-level police manager's subordinate unit may also be considered his or her testing ground for discovering what is possible for the overall organization. One of the manager's primary purposes is to create within his or her own unit a model of how the whole organization should function.

An analytical consideration of an employee unit, both internal and external, must be considered when articulating how a leader wants subordinates to work together and with other units. It is the task of the leader and the focus set forth in his or her projected work plan/performance vision for subordinates. A leader must recognize that his or her personal values most often drives the elements of the performance vision created for subordinates.

- *A leader wants consistency between his/her projected plan and the resulting actions.* It is often counterproductive to set forth a blueprint designed to accomplish an objective and have actual behaviors not adhere to the proposed plan of action.
- *A willingness to share information and task accomplishment is a principal desire of leadership.* Cooperation and effective interaction are primary elements of success for most multi-unit organizations, such as a policing agency. Typically, guided positive interactive functioning is an essential work objective of middle police management.
- *An effective managerial leader seeks to allow disagreement as to methodology, etc. between subordinates and other elements without the fear of creating a negative working relationship.* Disagreements and discussions, if appropriately focused and handled, can lead to more efficient and effective task accomplishments. But management must create an environment where fear of non-positive reactions does not exist for an employee expressing an innovative idea to enhance results, etc.
- *Managerial leadership must be willing to commit to a long-term strategy if goals and objectives are to be achieved.* Organizational goals and objectives usually require an ongoing effort of behavior and dedication by subordinate units and personnel to obtain desired resolution of sought-after results.
- *The need to create a non-hostile and physically safe work environment is paramount to worker satisfaction and performance.* However, in law enforcement, the creation of a safe workplace refers to a non-threatening atmosphere, where ideas and alternative work strategies are allowed to be appropriately expressed. An effective and knowledgeable manage-

rial leader recognizes that subordinates performing functional daily tasks often develop conducive concepts for task accomplishments.

- *A mid-level police manager should seek a method whereby employees not only observe the results of unit operation, but also derive some sense of accomplishment therefrom.* It has been recognized that workers are more motivated and perform better when they can see the results of their work and how their labor contributed to the ultimate success of the organization.

- *A leader must learn and practice the techniques of uniformly fair treatment of all employees while still providing a unique reaction to the problem of individual subordinates.* Most workers express the desire to be treated equally fair when compared to other employees, while at the same time desiring unique consideration for personal concerns that are non-traditional to other workers. An effective mid-level police manager must balance universal fairness and the need for individualized treatment of subordinates.

- *A primary task of middle management is to clearly articulate to workers and the organization that functional workers are as important as the services they provide.* Also, that the success or failure of an organization is dependent on the behavioral performance and attitude of the base-level employee. It is essential to the morale of the workers to know that management values them and their task accomplishments.

- *A primary goal of virtually every organization is the creation and maintenance of a positive attitude among employees. Also, lessen the efforts that are inappropriately expended on non-productive tasks.* It has been realized that employees who enjoy their work and the working environment perform better and have fewer absences. Plus, the timelier that a non-productive or positive effort toward goals and objectives accomplishment is recognized the sooner the focused performance can be channeled toward a more desired result.

- *A leader strives to ensure that each subordinate recognizes how his or her job performance relates to the overall success of the organization.* The "Job One" project of the Ford Motor Corporation of years past showed the positive aspects of workers recognizing how their efforts contributed to the final product. This also relates to virtually every organization, including law enforcement. For example, when it was clearly shown that for every traffic ticket written for excessive speeding, the overall number of vehicles exceeding the speed limit reduced and speed reduction results in "X" number of fewer accidents and lives being saved. Thus, the results of an officer's efforts are shown as a contribution to the overall success of the organization goal and objective regarding lowering accidents and saving lives.

- *Achieving teamwork is a foundational goal of every managerial leader.* The need to function collectively is a matter of necessity in virtually every organization. This is particularly so in a policing agency where area of operation is so expansive, but yet they must draw together for accomplishment of organizational goals and objectives.
- *A mid-level police manager's principal task is to ensure that each subordinate under his or her leadership has a place at the table.* This, of course, refers to the need to assure the contribution of each subordinate to ensure all subsidiary personnel to his or her management is recognized for their input to the unit's task fulfillments.
- *Each person (subordinate) having a positive bearing on the success of the mission of the unit must be made to feel valued and respected.* A managerial leader must recognize the importance of self-esteem to each employee's motivation, and thus strive to enhance the personal perception of the employees that he or she directs.
- *Ensure that the tasks assigned to subordinates provide meaningful work.* Performing tasks that are purposeful for the ultimate success and productivity is valuable to both the employee and the organization.
- *A managerial leader recognizes that managers exist to serve the directional needs of subordinates.* Actual work performance is accomplished by subordinates (functional-level workers) and the task of a manager is to coordinate and guide job behaviors. Thus, a manager's primary responsibility or reason for existing is to serve the leadership of subordinates.
- *Each management leader must strive to identify and eliminate non-productive or counterproductive work by subordinates.* Frequently, tasks are performed because they are traditional to the organization, but yet have no positive impact on the overall accomplishments of goals and objectives. Therefore, it is essential that management undertake the evaluation of tasks being performed and the need for modifications as events and circumstances change over time.

The areas identified above reflect a number of the factors that must be considered when a mid-level police manager contemplates developing a performance vision for subordinates. It is up to the individual leader to know his or her own values and to decide how best to express them through the unit's work accomplishments. All of the factors that are identified, and a leader's individualized concept of personal values must focus toward the overall accomplishment of the goals and objectives of the organization.

Also, during any comprehensive analysis of the choices available in the structuring of a work vision for subordinates, it should be noted that the ultimate goal is task performances. The aforementioned is essential to increasing upper management and the functional-level workers' belief in the plan of action set forth, and to obtain a working agreement between task objectives and the actual work to be performed. Thus, it makes sense to focus and to be expressive on the positives and more acceptable aspects of the defined leadership vision. Remember that a well-articulated vision of planned work behavior and sought-after accomplishments is the best way to garner support for a task performance projection.

A well-articulated Leadership Vision teaches persons about the arena in which action will take place and the projected results desired. A properly stated *work credo* tends to speak for the leader when he or she is not around to express the components of his or her *guiding principals of work performances.*

SYNOPSIS

To conclude our brief discussion on the establishment of a leadership vision or work performance plan for subordinates by a middle-level police manager, the leader's stated purpose must be clearly articulated. Likewise, the leader must set forth the objectives, the goals for the planned performances, and perhaps even the whole of the leadership vision. A leader should reaffirm the facts that support that he or she has gone on record as supporting the performance work plan and vision concept. Also, the leader should acknowledge the contributing worth of the support that he or she received from all elements of the organization with regards to the content and projected outcome of the leader's expressed leadership vision.

It must be remembered that the objectives of goals of performances are critical, but the actual behaviors undertaken by employees are also important for effective productivity. It is not enough to set a leadership vision into place for desired results and anticipate that these will justify the methodology. The methods or activities, and the *how* of the desired results of task accomplishments are equally essential. Further, it is important that leaders seek to aid subordinates in comprehending the makeup and focus of the leadership vision or articulated work plan. leadership visions or work plans seem to best accomplish desired results when performed by well-informed and knowledgeable subordinates.

Chapter Fourteen

DEVELOPING A MANPOWER USAGE STRATEGY BY A MID-LEVEL POLICE MANAGER

The fast-paced and constant changes required in today's law enforcement organizations mandate that leaders formulate personnel management plans that are dynamic. Considering the numerous concerns that must be addressed, the restricted time frames and resources available, a managerial leader needs to effectively face up to the critical issues of management. The need to plan, allocate, and purposefully use human resources available to his or her is one of the primary concerns to be dealt with by a mid-level police manager.

The current era of rapid changes in technology, employee rights, and the complexity of the workplace environment necessitates that manpower usage strategies are less static, more short-term, and directional. Human resources strategies have been said to be, "more valuable as an instrument for eliciting thoughts and discussions, than as a procedural method for setting forth long-term goals and objectives."

Public agencies, like private businesses, are being altered to assist organizational management in recognition of, and dealing with matters that require changes. By so structuring, management is given the opportunity to effectively address and manage these changes. The plan of action changes referred to focuses on the issues of significant importance and establishes an opportunity for an effective managerial response. Also, focused planning establishes an opportunity for an effective managerial response. Also, focused planning establishes an opportunity for dialogue by management as to how to effectively address key human resource issues.

Management leadership in most major organizations has long recognized that there is a critical need to balance technology and budgets with available manpower resources. The more limited the availability of manpower resources, the greater the need to rely on technology. An example of this is the use of cameras to monitor traffic flow and violations of vehicle laws, inasmuch as the budgetary and actual availability of personnel to perform such duties is limited. However, without some enforcement capability the use of cameras are rendered somewhat useless. Thus, the need for a plan of action to utilize available manpower resources is necessary. Through this very limited example cited above, it is clear that the developing of a Manpower Usage Strategy is quintessential at all levels of organizational management.

There is no definitive sequence in which personnel strategies should be addressed by management. Manpower usage plans in terms of their use and availability can be addressed in part of the organization's overall strategic planning. If addressed as part of the overall strategic plan, the functional planning of employee resources must be considered equally with the budget, technology usage, and the product or services to be provided. Second, Human Resources Planning can be developed as a support for the other functions. However, if developed in a support mode of consideration, then it can be said that manpower resources strategies are being established separately. Human resource strategies that are planned separately tend to focus on tasks, goals, and objectives of the task functions of available manpower. The planned actions identified above effectively support strategic priorities, as long as the concerns are interrelated to the organization's ultimate objectives.

It is clear that a primary purpose of a manpower resource strategy is to direct the development of flexibility and adaptability within an organization. The requirement to put into place an effective operational strategy mandates the implementation of a manpower usage strategy, which focuses on employee-related concerns. Manpower planning or human resources strategy is more than a pattern of behaviors or planned actions related to management of employees. It is an incorporated, many-sided, and extended agenda for altering the core character of an organization.

Although manpower usage planning is a logical component of an organization's strategic plan, in actuality, it is often developed separately. No matter the way they are created, manpower usage strategies serve to translate subordinate resource concerns into plans of action. Human resource strategies project management of manpower staffing as the essence of organizational strategy. Appropriate resource planning aligns the management of employees with the overall directional leadership of the organization.

Evolution in the field of manpower usage has evolved in recent years from a limited scope or focus on personnel staffing to a much broader process, encompassing numerous people-related concerns. An enlarged definition of manpower usage strategy is said to be the *assessment of the employee resource needs during the altering factors and innovative changes required to fulfill organizational mandates.*

It is clear from the earlier writings regarding Human resources planning the focus and scope have been reduced while manpower usage strategies have been expanded. Many organizations have structured manpower allocation plans to deal with agendas for strategic changes. Most, however, have favored a more specialized and operational strategy to focus on issues such as projected manpower needs, management's chain of command, and workforce leadership. Also, many manpower usage strategies were established by and for the benefit of employee staffing behavior rather than managerial practices within the organization.

The core essence of manpower development planning or strategy for a mid-level police manager is neither a specific number of practical methods nor a related set of complexities, but rather their availability and usage by managers in establishing subordinates' work patterns. Created strategies for effective and practical use of manpower resources are organizational leadership's reaction to the changing issues confronting the agency. Quite simply stated, they are planned strategies set forth to take advantage of chances to acquire and maintain an effective range of action through the directional leadership of subordinates.

A planned action for the effective use of available subordinate resources can be considered a focused strategy when it aids organizational leadership. The strategic aid being referred to is management's ability to anticipate and direct the dynamic and fast pace of societal and workplace changes. Manpower usage strategies are the methods of coordinating the leadership of subordinates' resources with the planned goals and objectives of the organization. It should not go unnoticed that there is a comprehensive focus regarding the concerns developed from the environmental evaluation as indicated earlier in this text.

An effective law enforcement agency's operational plan or strategic objective should focus on the overall direction of the organization. This focus must be structured in a manner to address issues under whatever condition of change or anticipated/unanticipated concerns may surface. Such a strategic plan should include multiple programs and activities, principally involving multifaceted projects that extend over a number of years.

As noted earlier in this chapter, manpower usage planning should be a part of the overall organization's strategic plan. At the top level of management within a law enforcement organization, the budgetary planning, information acquisition, technology usage, and the accomplishment of overall goals and objectives must all be formulated and implemented within the same framework.

FORMULATING A MANPOWER USAGE STRATEGY

When considering the *formulation of a Manpower Usage Strategy,* a mid-level police manager must examine relevant factors (internal and external) affecting his or her unit. The examination must be done in the context of a law enforcement environment and in correlation with contemporary concerns or situations that affect the organization. The manager should then formulate a conclusion based on the organization and in turn his or her unit's mission, vision, planned objectives, performance goals, and projected actions.

As stated above, the formulation and implementation of a strategic process for a mid-level manager's unit may appear simplistic. However, a comprehensive consideration of explicit factors that influence the process and the systematic focus that should be employed indicates that the formulation of a strategic process is not always as simple as it first appears. The numerous and varied planning processes, the differing methods of managerial leaders, and the interpretation of projected needs and their planned approach complicates the formulating of any Manpower usage strategy.

One of the strategic processes set forth for formulating a manpower usage plan is to reassess mission objectives or visions, establish planned target accomplishments, create a workable plan of action, and then assign manpower resources. Thus, the planned action becomes more directed toward specific behavior as they flow through the various levels of the organization. A mid-level manager's manpower usage strategy, like that of the organization's hierarchy, is somewhat expansive and conceptual. A somewhat theoretical and broad approach to an overall strategic planning is necessary and often needed. Frequently, an interpretation of functional strategies and individual performance plans are required before they can be implemented at lower levels of the organization.

ORGANIZATIONAL STRATEGIC
MANPOWER (RESOURCES) USAGE

The interaction and/or connection between the various levels of the organization during the development of a resource usage plan are essential. This ensures that projected behavior is reactive to the concerns at each tier and produces desired employee demeanor. It is recognized that resources usage strategic at all levels of the organization must work in harmony. Although manpower resource usage strategies are frequently defined and set into place from the top-down, in reality, it is a multidirectional concept. Traditionally, strategic plans begin at the top level of police management with an overall planned focus and goals, but mid-level police managers are required to utilize the organization's projections to formulate operational and projected functional unit objectives. Usually, there are adjustments to the process and procedures where the strategies are altered until they fit into the plans of the overall organization, while accomplishing the goals and objectives of the unit.

Police-type organizations traditionally utilize a top-down approach to strategic manpower resource planning; however, many private companies emphasize a middle or bottom-up approach. The middle or bottom-up planning is utilized to adjust priorities, plans of action, goals and objectives to coincide with the budgetary request from lower-level units.

The bottom-up or middle approach to strategic planning is believed to foster a better opportunity to be responsive in a free marketplace to:

1. Frequent operational changes that may be needed;
2. Reduce centralization of many operations for a faster response to changes;
3. Focus interaction between employees and clientele, providing direct information regarding challenges and opportunities; and
4. Achieve the empowerment of workers as part of the total quality effort of the organization.

A middle or bottom-up strategic approach can be applicable to law enforcement agencies and is being used to some degree by most. It is recognized that the mere nature of the goals and objectives of a police organization can at times be counterproductive to a totally middle or bottom-up approach to strategic manpower planning.

EVOLVING MANPOWER USAGE STRATEGIES. Managers or positional leaders in a police organization are required to develop various goals and objectives which at times may be opposing or mandates the usage of the same resources. Thus, there must be an emphasis within the organization on future or projected analysis to ensure adjustments as needed. Manpower and resources in a police organization are more often than not limited; therefore, there must be a plan of action where resources are shared. Plans of action in a police organization call for long-range strategies, such as the establishing of a broader interactive relationship within the agency. These long-range strategies must provide a method whereby conflicts that arise with near-term objectives can be resolved to the overall benefit of the organization and elements involved.

Developed plans or strategies for allocation and use of resources can frequently sprout from the pattern of action employed. Exploits of behavior are frequently projected to react to separately specific planned goals or an element's functional purpose. Unit and individual work strategies and purposes are typically put into place with an absence of regards for an overall organizational plan. This occurs because managers and leaders normally think in terms of the operational success of their unit or element as primary. Thus, there is no intent to disregard overall organizational goals and objectives but rather a normal human instinct to consider self-survival or success first. Unit goals and purpose are normally thought of as near-term objectives and organizational strategies are thought of as long-term plans.

Tactical planning frequently evolves from particular conclusions rather than a blanket approach to advance projected strategies. It has been said that management hierarchy typically deals with element planning rather than an overall systematic and/or structural tactical projection of action. This, of course, does not infer that developmental calculation or actions are unplanned. Typically, they merge the positive aspects of a structured strategic approach with the realization of an actual performance behavior in an organization. This should not be considered a way of "wading through," but rather a method by which leaders can consciously cope with situations of unsystematic or unstructured forecasting.

FLEXIBILITY OF MANPOWER USAGE STRATEGIES. Some organizational resource theorists indicate that in truth many firms desire both explicit and developing plans. An overreliance of explicit strategies tends to shortcut creativity and innovative advances of overall involvement in strategic development in an organization. Also, too much emphasis on methodology will risk the loss of significance to upper organizational leadership's priorities and the effect of overt workplace evaluations.

Flexibility in today's police organization fosters an overall emergent, simplicity, informality, and mutual respect. The directional intent is on the future, anticipating and projecting situational changes that may notably affect the organization. The rapid changes in societal mores and advancing technology indicate that organizations will continually change rather rapidly. The non-static reality of in-place strategies can be viewed as historic documents. Flexibility of forecasting is a must to adjust to the anticipated changes. Although desirable, it is not possible to develop a strategic plan for the total organization each time a circumstance or event requires an adjustment in human resource projection or usage.

The essentiality of flexibility planning in relationship to strategy projections is a product of many factors influencing the allocation and usage of resources. The surrounding assessments are considered critical, because of the interactive nature of clientele and other organizational elements that are somewhat visionary. However, the exploration and viewing of actual concerns are pragmatic with its assessment directed to where it is most significant. Flexibility in strategic planning tends to be management-driven and a systematic course of action, as opposed to the more traditional and institutionalized private organizations. In the changing age in which we live, police organizations are rapidly moving toward a more line management activity. This shift in management concept means involving employees at all levels of the organization. The afore information indicates that mid-level police management's role in manpower usage strategy will continue to grow in the future of projected changes.

A manpower usage strategy for a mid-level police manager is viewed as an operational plan of action like any other duty function. Any operational or functional planning effort sequences a somewhat systematic pattern, complete with variations and adaptability. In some organizations, long-term operational planning for general resources is a required component of an extended-range functional planning process. However, manpower resources strategies are different from the method by which other organizational strategies are implemented. Manpower usage strategies needs to be an integral component of all other organizational strategies.

INTEGRATION OF MANPOWER USAGE STRATEGIES. The preferred approach to emergent manpower resources planning is for it to be an essential component of the overall organizational strategy at all levels of the organization. It can be shown that in any organization, the management of human resources is more important than some strategies and less important than others. A realization of the aforestated indicates that manpower management should be inherent in the organization. Normal strategic goals and objectives plans reflect a need for consideration of manpower usage in any future organizational structure. Manpower or human resource considerations impact workers numbers, budget allocations, and possibly several other areas.

In law enforcement organizations, when upper- and mid-level police managers recognize manpower resource concerns as critical to the accomplishment of the agency's overall objectives, such planning is integrated into the organization's strategic plan. An integrated inclusion may not always denote that individual work behavior, manpower allocation, strategy creation organizational concerns, or problems have been appropriately addressed. It does mean the middle and upper management has put forth an effort to be comprehensive and effective in the development of a strategic plan for its units and the organization.

SYNOPSIS

Manpower or human resource usage plans are quintessential to the success of an organization during the current era of rapid social changes and employee focus. The appropriate consideration and usage strategies direct the creation of a more adaptive organization structure. Properly researched and developed strategies focus on opportunities to positively affect subordinates' performances and the achievement of desired goals and objectives.

Manpower usage plans evolve from an organizational focus and migrate toward specific behavior flexibility and process traditionally identified in terms of human resources functions. Thus, the action of a mid-level police manager's manpower usage strategy tends to span the planning progress. It also forms or conforms the conceptual and long-range projections to the more contemporary and immediate concerns for the effectiveness of his or her subordinates.

Chapter Thirteen discussed the Creative Vision of a mid-level police manager needs in setting forth a plan of action for subordinates. Chapter Fourteen has focused on the strategic planning development concerning manpower or human resource usage, and Chapter Fifteen (following) will emphasize the practical aspects of Strategy Projection for a mid-level police manager's implementation of a Creative Vision and effective Manpower Usage Strategies for performance success.

Chapter Fifteen

STRATEGY PROJECTION
(PLANNING AND ORGANIZATION)

The acquisition and utilization of information by a police manager to forecast, scheme, and/or systematize obtained data into an effective operational program are primary dimensional character traits necessary for a positional leader. Productivity output and appropriateness of a leader's unit or element depend to a great extent on the availability of the various resources and the established procedures set forth by an operational police manager. These projections or forecasts are what positional leaders assume will occur in the foreseeable future and how to best apply resources to achieve desired results. The manager should consider the information received from sources throughout the department in his or her **planning** and **organizing**. This contemplation and incorporation of received data are essential, inasmuch as the leader's functional operations must intermesh with other organizational elements. An effective manager must then review the goals and objectives of the organization to assure that systematization of his or her strategy projection is in compliance with departmental expectations.

Alternative solutions for resolving whatever needs that exist should be mentally balanced by the manager in forecasting operational activities. This may be accomplished through various methods, including formalized research or personal assessment possibilities by a police manager. In either case, systematized strategic alternatives are considered to determine how to more effectively enhance quality and elevate the job performance capability of subordinates. The practical feasibility of each alternative is evaluated in terms of overall effectiveness and task accomplishment. An operational police manager should then take the strategy projection and develop a systematized plan of action by combining the current functional status with the forecasted needs. By doing this, a formalized and practical **plan of action** can be established. This **plan of focus** is then utilized to guide the organization's operational functions toward accomplishment of overall goals and objectives.

A strategy projection from the perspective of a positional leader in an organizational setting, such as a police department, generally will involve most of the influences that can conceivably have a positive effect on the accomplishment of goals and objectives. The influence factors so closely aligned with strategy projection and systematization by an operational police manager are:

1. Development of a translucently expressed purpose that exactly sets forth operational benchmarks to achieve the desired goals and objectives;
2. A comprehensive statement of the essentiality of these goals and objectives;
3. Establishing a **plan of focus** to set parameters for achievement of precise organizational objectives;
4. Delineating specific job performance criteria for subordinates and putting into place an appraisal process to assure functional behavioral quality;
5. Providing a flexibility of projected actions to accommodate possible deviations in expectations of personnel performances and availability of logistical resources; and
6. A planned correlation and coordination of the functional objectives for subordinate personnel and the unit's operation within the scope of the organization's overall mission.

As is readily discernible from the above components of projection strategy, the development of an effectively planned and organized course of action for an operational police manager is not a simple task. It is, however, a critical part of the assessment criteria typically utilized to evaluate the effectiveness of a positional leader. Therefore, if a police manager or any other person of authority aspires to be efficient, he or she must master this dimensional trait characteristic, which is an expectation of an effective positional leader.

The tendency is for organizational leadership to focus its forecasts on past performances and conditional actions to formulate strategy projections. But, as most knowledgeable managers are aware, nothing is exactly the same from day to day. Therefore, it is illogical to base future plans or systematize objectives on what happened yesterday. Literally everything in our environment, including our own personality, changes and develops with time. This text is not attempting to imply that statistical trends or past actions cannot aid in projecting certain future events within a specified tolerance. Past factors can be very useful, if utilized in conjunction with anticipated influences that become known but are not reflective in previous observations. Many police operations often fall prey to this **after-the-fact** thinking and planning. For example, many police organizations employ what may be termed "crime trackers," who plot and pinpoint prior crimes on some type of jurisdictional map. Thus, **in an area that has experienced an abundance of break-ins over the past 60 days, they may plan to combat this problem by moving in additional manpower, etc. However, during the subsequent 60 days they find that the break-ins have shifted just outside the area of their concentration**. The first conclusion arrived at is that the extra effort displaced the crime pattern. To some degree this may be accurate, if significant conspicuous actions, such as arrests and convictions, were made during the concentrated effort. However, if the activity focus shifted without notable or verifiable enforcement results, the police manager must also consider the possibility that factors or influences external to his or her executed plan played a role in the crime shift. Influences such as transit population shifts, weather conditions, and acquired mobility of the offenders may have been factors that should not be overlooked. Primarily, what's being communicated is that when a police manager develops a **plan** and **organizes** an operational strategy, the individual should perceive beyond the past and consider all possible factors. To put it simply, you should anticipate when and where to focus future operational efforts. A simple example of what is being endorsed is cited below. Keep in mind, however, that the stated scenario is somewhat limited in focus and specifically targeted so as to more precisely illustrate the contextual point of emphasis.

> A number of years ago a robbery was broadcast over the police radio describing two suspects and the original direction they took for the "hold-up" scene. Two officers patrolling several blocks away heard the pick-up broadcast. One wanted to drive to the robbery scene and start a pattern search of the surrounding streets and alleys. However, his partner reasoned that the suspect would follow a certain route to a general location. The partners disagreed, but when the No. 2 officer explained his knowledge of the area and a number of other factors including the inconspicuousness of a getaway car if left in a certain area, the other officer agreed. The officers then proceeded to the area and waited (inconspicuously, of course); sure enough, several moments later the suspects appeared and were apprehended with the weapons used and the money stolen still clearly identifiably marked.

This was no fluke or just simply good police work, which from a pragmatic standpoint it was, but it was a projection of a **strategy** based on environmental influences and correlated factors known to the officer. Now had the robbery occurred in the daylight hours, the influences may be somewhat different and the employed strategy would not have been applicable. As noted, this is a simplification of the message that the text is attempting to relay, which essentially infers that using past practices based on statistical patterns may not be adequate in and of themselves. **Goal setting**, whether for the organization, an operational element or individual subordinates, should include a recognition of the need for primary objective achievement, as well as a continuity of development that considers probable changes and environmental influences.

A positional leader, no matter at what level of the organizational strata, attempts to define the department's overall objectives from his or her perspective in developing a projected plan of action. This defining of ultimate goals and missions is necessary so that his or her planning and organizing fits positively into the overall achievement format. Also, it prevents proposed actions from being too broad or too limited to accomplish desired results. Also, through strategy projection efforts, an operational police manager can affirmatively demonstrate **innovative actions**, **creative thinking**, and **logical inferences**, which are all considered positive and essential dimensional character traits of an effective positional leader. However, in order for the text to properly delve into this dimensional trait characteristic as a unified topic, it may be more prudent to discuss the two most recognizable constituent components separately. By doing this, the author concludes that the reader can better grasp the importance of each and thereby associate the essentiality of this trait characteristic to positional leadership.

As identified in the title of this chapter, the two constituent components of an operational police manager's strategy projection are **planning** and **organizing**. Planning is basically a process where a positional leader establishes objectives and/or operational activities for subordinates that are designed to accomplish a desired goal. Organizing is simply the systematizing or establishment of a functional procedure whereby the **planned action** can be implemented to achieve operational goals and objectives. Thus, strategy projection, i.e., **planning** and **organization** as a leadership tool is essential to the effectiveness of a police manager in the development of a course of action for mission achievement. The consummation of effective achievement is typically through the appropriate and efficient use of human and material resources resulting from organizational goal setting by departmental managers. The recognition of the importance of organizational goal setting as a forecasted and systematically arranged entity is generally revealed in a stated specific objective. It matters not whether the organization is a private manufacturing firm producing a product or a police agency having a social responsibility to provide a public service, there must be an expressed aim or basic purpose of action that coincides with a statement of primary goals and objectives for the organization. The statement should be designed to answer

"I think I have everything that I'll need."

"It looks as if your information was correct. Our new Positional leader is a proponent of Planning and Organization."

STRATEGY PROJECTION SHOULD BE A POSITIVE CHARACTERISTIC TRAIT OF AN OPERATIONAL LEADER, RATHER THAN A CONSEQUENCE OF THE POSITION.

what the organization is attempting to achieve and whether it has the ambitious endeavor to achieve the expressly desired results.

Planning is principally the process whereby operational goals and objectives are established to assure achievement of desired results, while **organizing** is articulated as the means of developing a performance process whereby the operational functions established during the planning stage can be carried out. Therefore, **Planning** and **Organizing** are leadership requirements of operational middle management that develops courses of actions for functional-level subordinates to accomplish established goals and objectives. This is generally consummated through the proper assigning of personnel and the appropriate use of material resources. However, in order to take a more comprehensive and effective look at Planning and Organizing as a practical secondary leadership process, it is necessary to review each separately.

PLANNING

As indicated in our introduction of the character traits of planning and organizing, planning is an essential and very difficult operational function of positional leadership. The difficulty lies in forecasting and developing a course of action for subordinates to follow. The fact that a positional leader is only as effective as his or her subordinates is true, and likewise, the productivity performance of workers are dependent upon the operational plan of the manager. Therefore, it is evident that there is an interdependency and that each phase has to be effective if goals and objectives are to be met. A police manager must realize that **planning** from an operational perspective is the thinking through of alternative actions considered necessary to achieve task results. It involves the use of logical inferences and a prudence in developing a course of action that will prove efficient and effective in accomplishing goals and objectives. Managerial planning, which is often referred to as the **blueprint of effectiveness**, should be established with certain concepts in mind. First, the manager must consider the reason for the ultimate goal and overall departmental objective that should be achieved. Consideration of these factors as influences on an operational plan adds realism toward meeting mission objectives. Second, a positional leader must determine what alternatives are available for use in obtaining the desired purpose, plus meeting the goals and objectives of proposed operational actions. Third, the police manager should choose the most productive and efficient course of action to accomplish what is needed or desired from the activity of subordinates.

Operational managerial planning or forecasting as an integral component of organizational leadership concerns the expectancy and readiness to perform anticipated functional requirements by a manager's subordinates and/or unit. There should also be a comprehensive assessment of the various choices of possible actions prior to deciding on the one thought to be more conducive to positive results, especially as an essential leadership tool for effective managerial forecasting in the directing and controlling of human and material resources. This refers to the availability of required subordinate personnel and logistics, as needed, to effectively achieve desired results. Additionally, police managers should not overlook the positive effect that appropriate planning or forecasting of needs will have toward enhancement of subordinates' task gratification. The improved job satisfaction is generally a result of the **elimination of wasted work efforts** by erroneous task planning and the establishment of a structured procedure that clarifies desired results and methods of achievement. Perhaps a more precise and comprehensive definition of planning at this point would focus the perceived importance of forecasting as a leadership tool.

Spriegel, Schulz, and Spriegel state, "Planning is the act or process of interpreting the facts of a situation, determining a line of action to be taken in the light of all of the facts and the objectives sought, detailing the steps to be taken in keeping with the action determined, the making of provision to carry through the plan to a successful conclusion, and the establishing of checks to see how close performance comes to the plan." This clinical definition of planning from an operational mid-level police manager's perspective clearly sets forth the desired direction of action for an operational level leader.

Functional police managers at all levels of the organization should be aware that in order to be effective in the administrative handling of personnel and material resources, a positional leader must use some form of preplanning or important things will often be neglected. The preplanning done by a police supervisor or primary manager is a prerequisite for efficient and effective subordinate performance. Many leadership theorists have indicated that the effective techniques of planning by a first line supervisor or manager is not inherent but developed over time through practice and effort.

The effective police mid-level manager should plan the activity of his or her element so that the subordinates' performances coincide with the efforts of others in the organization. Also, effective planning at the middle police manager's level is not an automatic chain of events. The functional-level, mid-level manager plans must be based on as complete information as possible. And to obtain this thorough knowledge, the leader must know the capabilities of his personnel and the material and performance limitations of available resources. To a great degree, planning is the most critical administrative task performed by a functional-level police mid-level manager, inasmuch as manpower availability, performance activity, and in-service training are all traditional and primary tasks.

Considering all of the situational concerns and various interactions that occur relative to an operational manager in a police organization, it is imperative that he or she establish some type of preplan or a "things-to-do" list. The development of a preplan will help insure that necessary things are accomplished and that essential functions aren't overlooked. A "seat-of-the-pants" philosophy or a pure crisis leader will often bypass vital areas that would enhance an element's operation. This occurs simply because a thing was not thought through due to time pressures or an inadequate assessment opportunity. A forecasting of essential components of effective operation in terms of manpower or logistical acquisition and use is an absolute prerequisite for efficiency as an operational police manager. A number of experts and social scientists in the area of managerial leadership have inferred that an effective technique of strategy projection by an operational manager is a talent that can be developed. A productive positional leader from an operational perspective must format a structured course of action for subordinates to assure maximum performance productivity and coordination of efforts with other organizational elements. As noted, strategy projection is not an inherent trait of a positional leader, nor is the development of preplanned activity for subordinates. While it is true that planning as a necessary component of operational leadership is an organizational expectation of a police manager, it is still not an autocratic occurrence but one that is achieved through knowledgeable awareness and special effort on the part of a police manager. An operational police manager's forecast of projected strategy must be based on a thorough knowledge of the influences and other pertinent factors. These factors include performance capabilities of subordinates, availability of both human and material resources, and the environmental impact of external pressures.

The previous information relative to planning of forecasting clearly illustrates the perceived importance of it as a major dimensional trait characteristic of an operational police manager. But before this text considers its discussion of planning too complete or comprehensive, the **process of planning** must be highlighted. A planning process may parallel a basic decision-making procedure but will differ in several important respects.

The Process of Planning

The process of planning or forecasting the activities of an operational element has several very distinct and well-defined steps. As with most sequential progression processes, they can be syndicated into what appears to be a collective procedure. However, for our purposes of obtaining a clear and understandable concept of the planning process, each step will be examined individually.

1. **Ascertain and Focus on the Objective**. It has almost become a constant component to analyze a managerial process by beginning with identification and clarification of the basic concerns. Essentially, an efficient preplan is not possible without the focus of concern being comprehensively interpreted. The clarification must concentrate on the overall goals and objectives that are to be accomplished. With a specific understanding of desired results and a knowledge of what it will take to fulfill the objective, an operational police manager can project a strategy to effectively achieve aspirations. A formulated format has been set forth earlier in this text. And, a determination of what is a problem or concern was clinically detailed in the chapter on "Decision Making" as was a suitable method for ascertaining a planning focus as well. Therefore, it is recommended that the same procedural processes be utilized.

This determination of goal focus involves both the general and specific objective results desired. The decision of directed actions must include an awareness of the role of each department element that interacts with the

planned-for unit or operation. The ascertainment of objectives should be such that it provides information to prevent elements working at cross-purposes or infringing on the duty responsibilities of others in the organization. An avoidance of a duplication of subordinate performance efforts is also a by-product of effective objective identification and preplanned focus. Once the primary goals and objectives have been affirmatively developed and a comprehension of the methods to achieve them, the second step in the process can be undertaken, which is an **analysis of the objectives**.

2. **An Analysis of the Facts and Objectives**. As with decision making, the analyzation of the identified concerns is merely an extension of the initial phase of recognition of the problem and determining appropriate action. This stage of the process of planning must continue as an assessment of the various objectives to be achieved as they exist (now and in the future). Again, it should be emphasized that the most comprehensive and effective method of analyzing objectives to develop a preplan can be obtained from the analytical phase in the chapter on "Decision Making." But there are some very pertinent concerns at this juncture that an operational police manager should address when formulating a plan of action. Some of these questions are:

A. What are the major influences that affect an objective?
B. What resources are available for managerial use?
C. What factors can accurately be forecasted from the known information?
D. What control factors should be used to assure achievement of goals and objectives?

The progression of the above questions clearly indicates that the sequentially accumulated answers will provide sufficient information for a well-planned strategy of action.

An operational police manager must be aware that the assumptions drawn and planned actions will only be as good as the information obtained. In other words, **faulty data in, faulty results out**. Therefore, a positional leader should attempt to ascertain that the information received and utilized is as accurate as possible. Remember, only to the extent that pertinent information is valid will the strategy projection be logical and effective. Of the information sought in the previous questions, a leader should realize that it may be difficult to obtain adequate information, especially where the future availability of resources and time frame allocations are concerned. An operational police manager must take into account such limiting factors but should not allow them to adversely affect development of an appropriately practical plan of action.

3. **Assimilate the Influence Factors Obtained**. Once essential information relative to the factors that will have a bearing on the conclusions and ultimately the forecasted strategy has been accumulated, it must be interpreted, just as critical pieces of a puzzle need to be fitted together in order to form a complete picture. As with most fact-gathering endeavors, the acquisition of essential information is generally not in an orderly or properly sequenced format. The data must be sorted and integrated into a usable form. Also, it is highly unusual for the data to be specific and in clear clinical language that can be readily utilized to formulate a positive plan of action. The collected facts often need to be assimilated into an understandable information package. Referring to the taking of useful bits of information and data from various sources and piecing together pertinent influence factors for consideration, an interpreted recognition of the factual data needed will determine if vital information is still missing. The same rationale that is set forth in the section "Developing Alternative Resolutions" in the chapter on "Decision Making" is applicable in the planning process.

The operational police manager should be aware that the greater the amount of information evaluated and assimilated, the more comprehensive and effective will be the projected strategy. The interpreting individual should not overlook the cause-and-effect phenomenon of integrating data into a workable plan. Likewise, the sequence of events and time frame commitment is a critical aspect in **making a true assessment and developing a workable plan of action**. It is clear that the obtaining of factual data and the interpretation of pertinent information should continue until a comprehensive and functional plan has been developed.

4. **Development of an Effective Plan**. A thorough comprehension and use of the data collected, once assimilated, can lead to an effective projection of a strategy to deal with the concerns. The operational police manager must maintain a focus on the desired results of his or her element's objective accomplishment. The formulated plan developed through analysis and selected from among available alternatives must be both effective and interact positively with other programs toward overall departmental goals. Therefore, the more information that a positional leader has at his or her disposal, the greater the likelihood of a plan that will meet necessary requirements. The formulation of a final plan that is both effective and efficient is nothing more than the weighing of all the influence factors against the available data and desired results. Thus, a commonsense analysis and a positive conclusive assessment should manifest itself into a plan of action encompassing all pieces of the puzzle, thereby producing a feasible and workable planning effort.

At this juncture of a planning process, contextually speaking, a decision on a final **plan of action** to accommodate a concern is generally based on a selection between alternatives. As in the chapter on "Decision Making," the leader is advised to view the alternatives based on certain criteria and influence factors before deciding which one would be best. A decisive selection of an alternative is not always very easy, because often there are a number of choices that would adequately handle the problem. But because there may be effects that are not readily visible, a manager must perceive and focus beyond the immediate and obvious before making a decision. He or she must consider all the information that is available, project future reactions and then make as logical and sound a decision as possible in the operational planning of subordinates' activities.

Principally, planning as a tool of operational management is one of the primary dimensional trait characteristics that a positional leader in a police organization is measured by. The lack of an abundance of human and material resource availability to the public sector in this day of tight budgetary constraints makes their efficient use critical. As indicated, this is not a new concept to law enforcement but rather one that has taken on renewed emphasis in the last decade or so. Now that a comprehensive picture of the importance and processes of operational planning have been explored, it is appropriate at this point to detail the use of a projected strategy. By use of a **planning effort**, the text is referring to the systematization of subordinates' actions, or, in other words, **organizing** as an effective tool of operational management.

Organizational police leaders from the secondary level up have no real option but to anticipate and project future needs. They should attempt to structure operational performances to adequately deal with both short- and long-range goals. It is generally recognized that future projections are based on past experiences and expectations of things to come. This method has shown some success in the past, but it cannot be perceived as an infallible method of determining strategy projections or actual need requirements. In other words, planning for the future is at best a calculated best guess. The aforementioned is not meant as a negative view of strategic planning. In fact, the opposite is more actual, because if a manager at any level of the police organization fails to plan work activity and/or performance requirements for self or subordinates, he or she may be destined to failure as an effective leader. Operational planning can be considered an essential and necessary function of a mid-level leader. Police mid-level managers are therefore required to be skilled in forecasting actions and making decisions based on future expectations. Future subordinate performances to meet task expectations or needs do not just happen; they are usually a consequence of leadership strategy. Strategic planning, like decision making, is considered risky for the planner. The planner or leader exposes his or her perceptual performance ability to evaluation by superiors, peers, and subordinates. Failure to be relatively accurate in projecting future needs and planned actions leaves the leader open to second-guessing or criticism by others. However, it can easily be seen that a leader who fails to plan is much more likely to be ineffective in having subordinates meet future needs. The ability to strategically plan for the future and much of its success rests on the leader or planner's comprehension of the information considered. Long- or short-range future planning is basically an analytical consideration of prior information and events as to commitment of resources, both human and material, to meet the projected need. Strategic planning has been said to be **an application of some scientific methods to determine performance needs and making work decisions**. But some well-known management theorists, such as Peter Drucker, appear to disagree with this assessment. Drucker, in his book, *Management,* indicates that planning was *the application of thought, analysis, visionary innovation and logical inferences.* Drucker also indicated in the text that *strategic planning is a responsibility rather than a method or technique.*

Planning of any sort is projecting rather than forecasting. By this, it is meant that planning is basically the evaluation of present and past circumstances and the projecting of future needs from the assessed data. Forecasting or prognosticating the future resource needs of an organizational element is unacceptable as a sound leadership practice. However, it cannot be overlooked that forecasting and prognostication, when done in conjunction with analytical thought and review of prior data, become synonymous with strategic projecting. Therefore, it should be acknowledged that predicting future needs or performance action from past data are not merely guesses as to what will or will not occur in the time that is to come. But rather, it is the assessment of prior circumstances and the making of present decisions to positively interact with anticipated future needs and events. Managerial theorists generally indicate that leadership decisions only exist in the present. In essence, *mid-level managers can make decisions that may or may not affect the future, but they cannot make future decisions in the present.*

Planning as a generalized dimensional trait is typically associated with secondary police management. It is the formulation of projected courses of actions that meet expected requirements. Projections as associated with perceived future goals and objectives should be articulated by identifying both **purpose** and **direction**. The *purpose* and *direction* being referred to are the future organizational need projections that have been clinically assessed and articulated. An effective secondary leader will first determine what needs to be accomplished and the perceptual best method to achieve the objective (purpose). The primary leader should then ascertain how best to present or articulate this information to subordinates who are expected to implement

ORGANIZATIONAL GOALS AND OBJECTIVES

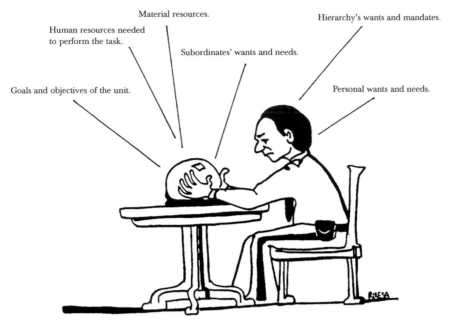

Material resources.

Human resources needed
to perform the task.

Hierarchy's wants and mandates.

Subordinates' wants and needs.

Goals and objectives of the unit.

Personal wants and needs.

STRATEGY PROJECTION IS AN ESSENTIAL PART OF A MID-LEVEL LEADER'S DUTIES. ALL FACTORS MUST BE CONSIDERED.

actions, toward goal attainment (direction). Directions by police mid-level managers, as it relates to planning, refer to both information data needed to accomplish the task and the focal objective that is trying to be reached.

It has often been said that "the only certainty about the future is its uncertainty." Recognizing the reality of this statement will aid a secondary leader in developing strategic actions that are adaptable to changing dynamics of objectives. Strategy projection in its truest sense is the putting into place of processes that will cope with the uncertainty of future events; in other words, to implement transactions for dealing with the uncertainty of the future by developing projected courses of actions to attain desirable results. Some basic techniques for planning with uncertainty of the future in mind by a secondary leader are:

1. Becoming experienced through hands-on efforts before attempting to plan a task achievement in the future.
2. Incorporating the actual task performers into the planning efforts.
3. Being creative in developing strategies to deal with perceived future performance needs (goals and objectives).

4. Assuring that the plans developed have the flexibility needed to adjust to unanticipated events or shifts in the organizational focus.
5. Developing and articulating a plan in the purest sense is a how-to-do-it guide, to assure understanding by those who are to implement it.

These techniques are not represented as a cure-all for planning the use of resources to deal with the uncertainty of the future. But consideration of the suggested factors should help a police mid-level manager develop plans that are more durable and effective in dealing with the uncertainty of the future.

A statement like *the only certainty of the future is its uncertainty* may appear to be a gloomy prospect for police organizations and their leaders. But it does represent a truism theme in the modern operational existence for organizations and their work leaders. Law enforcement organizations like most other public and private entities, are forced to cope with the uncertainty of tomorrow through projected efforts today. Therefore, police organizations' leaders at all levels are challenged to strategically plan actions that are both efficient and effective in a climate of perceived expectations but unknown realities of the circumstances and events to come. There may be degrees of uncertainty that a police mid-level manager has to consider in much the same manner as he or she has to evaluate the job performances of subordinates. In other words, there may be unknowns regarding shifting trends in society or subordinates' attitudes, each of which is usually preceded by indicators that allow adaptive changes before dramatic situations. However, there can be sudden unexpected changes in the budgetary stability of the organization or subordinates' reactions to a situation that is totally unanticipated. In either case the mid-level police leader must be prepared to implement whatever changes that may be needed to achieve desired goals and objectives by his/her unit in the face of the change.

Some leaders, like organizations, are better at adapting and effectively dealing with uncertainties that occur than others. There are definitive categories that articulate the methods these entities utilize to respond to unanticipated changes:

1. There are the **Evaluative Leaders**, who are particularly cautious in planning their actions. They tend to carefully assess planned strategy and focus on methods and techniques that are conservative. This type of leader tends to be less innovative or creative and is unlikely to project a strategy that will not deviate far from the established norm of operation, even in the event of unanticipated actions or changes. Fear of failure is a trait aspect of this type of leader.

2. The **Adventurous Leader** will be creative and innovative in his or her strategy planning for task performance for subordinates. This individual tends to be less fearful of failure because of the uncertainty of change than he or she is of ineffectiveness due to inadequate actions. This type of leader is notably aggressive in his or her personal approach to task accomplishment. The adventurous leader also believes that it is better to make things happen than to wait for them to occur before taking action. There is the belief that uncertainty can be controlled to a degree by aggressive and forceful action, and that the control obtained by aggressive action will make the unexpected less damaging or less destructive to task accomplishment.

3. The **Responsive Leader** differs greatly from the aggressive approach to strategy planning, by believing that it is more cost effective and efficient to be reactive to uncertainty. This type of leader considers the Adventurous Leader wasteful because of the possible failures of innovative actions that may have to be changed when something unexpected occurs. Responsive leaders tend to be slow to develop and implement new ideas or actions. This type of individual can be considered conservative, as is the Evaluative Leader. The Responsive Leader's actions to deal with uncertainty or unexpected actions are usually after the occurrence of an unanticipated change. When challenged, these type of leaders will acknowledge their actions are after the fact but will quickly point out that their approach is less wasteful of resources used in dealing with a known, even though it is a corrective mode. There is almost no justification to dramatically change strategy actions because of uncertainty, as it would be under an Adventurous Leader and to some degree under an Evaluative Leader.

4. The **Guardian Leader** is usually the protector of the *status quo* form of strategy planning, meaning that this type of leader prefers to attempt to keep planned action in a narrow focus to avoid far-reaching unanticipated deviations. In private industry, such an approach may mean that an organization limits its diversity of product production so that variations and unexpected changes can be better gauged. However, in public policing, a functional mid-level leader who restricts subordinate personnel in their job performance to the status quo may be more detrimental than is the dealing with the unexpected. Police work is a field that is not as attractive as private industry in terms of financial gain, recognition, and other like incentives. It is also an employment field where the person can draw criticism for doing his/her job properly and for not doing the job properly. *The potential for living your life and performing your job in a fishbowl-type existence cause many to abandon a public*

policing career. There is also the aspect that law enforcement deals with the behavior of other people as a behavior-controlling entity. Also, there is a definite uncertainty to the actions of people when confronted by a police officer who could notably affect their lives in the course of doing his or her job. Thus, attempting to limit or control this type of individual in a job, where the unexpected is the expected, may in the long run be far more destructive than their having to deal with unanticipated changes. The unanticipated changes being referred to are the deviations of job expectations and/or varying performance requirements caused by our changing society. Therefore, the guardian type leader in public policing should not attempt to limit the focus or parameters of subordinates' duties, if he or she chooses this type of leadership approach to cope with job uncertainties. The status quo efforts should focus on rules and regulations, operational policy compliance and other guidelines that are unlikely to be dependent upon the actions of clientele.

As can be seen, there may be no best way or leadership approach to deal with the uncertainty in job actions. Police actions in planning or projecting future strategies should consider that functional-level performance must be focused on the fact that operational workers are expected to deal with the unexpected within preset parameters.

Planning as an element of leadership in an organization is one of the most important aspects of duty performance. Even though strategic planning is more characteristic of a leadership position, everyone in the workplace is a planner. The Chief of Police or CEO sets the overall goals and objectives for the organization and articulates the mission plan to achieve them. The managers at all level of the organization develop strategy action plans for subordinates to achieve desired results in their area of command responsibility. The functional workers or police officers devise the best method to do assigned tasks within the limits established by his or her immediate supervisor and/or mid-level manager. The focal method devised is essentially a plan of action to do the job expected with the least amount of inappropriate behaviors. Remember, planning is basically a specific focus effort that is intended to consistently accomplish desired results. For the organization and its functional mid-level leaders, planning centers around achieving the overall goals and objectives of the agency. And, for the functional-level workers or operational police officers, the planning focus is to achieve desired job performance. Strategic planning is said to be the achievement of certain end results through a projected action that's considered the means to accomplishing the objective (end result). Quite simply, the *objective is the target of the effort* and the *planned action is the ammunition or means utilized* to get there.

ORGANIZING

Planning will choose and forecast the action that is to be taken, but from that point on the resources must be formatted and arranged in a conducively interactive structure. Remember, that for a preconceived plan (no matter how good) to accomplish its objective, it will be the organized reactive use of the resources that ultimately must achieve the desired results. Therefore, organizing as a leadership trait is essential to the achievement of a common purpose, which constitutes a systematic or more effective method of getting something accomplished. It is no secret that when a number of persons interact to achieve some activity, there must be some individual leadership to take charge and arrange specific tasks or responsibilities toward a desired conclusion. The basic procedural process for organizing functional operational activity should be through coordinated efforts that are acceptable for directing the integrated relationship of tasks and clarifying specific lines of authority and/or responsibility. The proportional allocation of work and the proper channeling of information or task responsibility is a specific result of a police manager's organizing effort.

An important conclusion of researchers in the field of managerial performances indicates that attempts at accomplishment of goals and objectives by an organization may be useless until there is a clearly defined purpose and a systematized method of attainment. Human and material resources are organized to achieve a specific task result or organizational mission. The greater the distinctive knowledge of a specific goal that a positional leader has, then the more comprehensively aware of the desired results he or she may be. Thus, a practical organizing effort should consider such influences as: (1) the need for specialization; (2) establishment of clear lines of authority; and (3) responsibility, environmental factors, resource availability, and several other prime components that may positively or negatively affect the results. The organization of operational activity does not occur in a vacuum. Like operational planning, the performance efforts of other elements must be considered and coordinated toward ultimate objective accomplishment. An operational manager should remember that up to this juncture of actual task performance, organized concepts and preparations must be somewhat flexible to accommodate unforeseen changes. An organization's ultimate mission may be an inflexible ambition, but progressional goals and objectives cannot be static. Frequently, revisions and/or new focuses are required to meet changing conditions. There are any number of factors that may cause adaptations in systematized formats, such as improved functional methods, an increase or decrease in resources, changes in experience level of personnel, public laws, and many others. Therefore, an operational police manager organizing efforts should not be so rigid or fixed as to disallow the adjustments that may be necessary for reaction to changing influences. There are certain **essential considerations** that should be perceived as vital to include in a comprehensive assessment of managerial organizing at this point in the text's contextual discussion of strategy projection.

Essential Consideration. These essential considerations are closely aligned with task responsibility and overall job authority. A positional leader in a highly structured organization, such as a police department, will often find his or her duties cumbersome and difficult to manage. The operational police manager must then take estimation of work load, patterns, and projected objectives. By doing this, the individual will be better able to consider a planned and organized structure as a guide to a formalized, systematic method of task accomplishment. Responsible leaders should not overlook the fact that highly competent personnel can sometimes make poorly organized operations function adequately, but that an appropriately planned and

EFFECTIVE STRATEGY PROJECTION IS A <u>BENCHMARK</u> OF AN EFFICIENT OPERATIONAL POLICE LEADER.

properly organized work edifice will accomplish results far more efficiently and effectively.

There are a number of difficult essential or basic considerations in organizing an operational plan of action, although these could be better clarified and more specifically labeled for directing a focus of the systematization of tasks to be accomplished. However, the basic approach to task achievement will not change. Therefore, this text will only address the three major considerations, as they typify the basis from which formalized organizational strategies of work generally originate. **First**, the overall functional task to be performed must be given initial and due consideration. It is at the juncture that the basic aim and direction of the organizing effort may be formed. Without a basic focus or objective, the police manager would not be able to properly channel his or her subordinates' performances for desired results. **Second**, the specific or specialized details required to effectively accomplish the task must be considered. Within every operational function, there are levels or plateaus of achievement that serve as benchmarks to assure ultimate goal attainment. The positional leader should acquaint him- or herself with the specific operational details and the need for specialized knowledge in the more intricate situations, because no matter how well planned, an **edifice for execution** cannot be formulated without such basic information. **Third**, the environmental influences, time frame, and other affecting factors must be given consideration. The identified influences, as well as many others, will have a bearing on what the operational positional leader establishes as a method for functioning. The carrying out of any plan of action to achieve an ultimate goal involves not only the accomplishment of desired results but also performance practices within a specifically detailed framework and, as it has already been stated, the parameters of law enforcement operation are far more limited than private industry.

Organizing as a formalized component of strategy projection for an operational police manager is an expectation by virtue of his or her positional leadership role. The positional leadership role requires a concerned effort on the part of the police manager to direct and so arrange the performance activities of assigned resources (human and logistical) to coordinate with the primary mission of the organization. These knowledgeably structured exertions of a positional leader are positive aspects for establishing both general and specific duties or responsibilities of his or her assigned personnel. An operational police manager must thoroughly comprehend the functional characteristics of administrative organization from a managerial perspective. An effective positional leader should also have some knowledge of the parameters within which his or her organizing authority exists. This is in reference to the fundamental controls usually maintained by the organization's hierarchical structure to set policy and other operational procedures. This should, however, not be confused with the power that an individual exerts over the functional performance of subordinates' personnel. It simply implies a need for personal awareness of the upper echelon's authority that typically dictates the positional leader's limitations of action. Traditionally, this awareness will assist an effective positional leader in his or her personal actions to arrange and/or systematize an operational preplan into an efficiently functioning process. The development of a productive organizing method by an operational police manager is essential to effectiveness of resource usage. The established method is affected by the successfulness of the task and the interactive manner in which it is performed. As noted previously, employee satisfaction tends to rise when they are functioning in a well-organized system where objectives are clearly defined and within foreseeable reach. Remember that a subordinate's satisfaction will be tempered and/or influenced by the person's basic **hierarchy of needs**, which influences the individual's personal perception and organizational attitude. Therefore, for the primary goals and objectives of a police department to be attained, the actions and performances of operational personnel must be organized and in coordination with the other organizational elements. As a final note before concluding our contextual discussion on the specific focus of organizing, it should be emphasized that the arranging and systematizing of preplanned work for subordinates is a continuous and ongoing process.

Organizing as a leadership requirement of an operational mid-level police manager concerns the effort to structure the performance activity of subordinates or elements to coordinate with the overall objectives of the organization. The organizing efforts also help in the formatting of duties, responsibilities, and assignments of his subordinates into a goal achievement in as efficient and effective a manner as possible. The effective functional mid-level police manager must understand the characteristics of administrative organizing from a management outlook. The mid-level manager should be acutely aware that while he or she does not usually control the fundamental hierarchical structure of the element, foundational leadership does dictate its functioning and performance. This basic knowledge will aid the effective mid-level manager in his efforts to organize an operational pre-plan into a workable and efficient function.

The achievement of an effective organizing pattern by an operational midlevel police manager is critical to efficient subordinate performance. It affects not only the manner in which they work but also the effectiveness of their job accomplishment. Personnel functioning in a well-organized framework where goal accomplishment is clearly defined and attainable will generally reflect a high degree of job satisfaction. The inherent characteristics of subordinate performance and the perception of each toward the organization also have some influence upon this job satisfaction and attitude. Therefore, for the goals and objectives of an organization to be reached, the activity and performance of each employee must be organized and coordinated into a smooth interaction.

Organizing as a major component of "Managerial Planning and Organizing" is not all inclusive but rather one of the principal vehicles for effective performance as a functional-level mid-level manager.

Planning and organizing are two inseparable tasks of the effective functional-level, mid-level manager. A mid-level manager must be able to analyze all available data and formulate a smooth and efficient performance plan, and also, to be able to take that plan and organize an operational structure or procedure that will attain goal accomplishment in an organizationally coordinated and effective manner.

Before concluding our look into the management requirements of a mid-level leader, we must identify the basic steps that a middle manager can use to aid this process.

Step 1. Identify the goals and objectives that he or she wishes subordinates to attain.

Step 2. Review all available data or information that pertain to the goal attainment.

Step 3. Make a decision on a course of action that will achieve the desired goal or objective.

Step 4. Relay appropriate information and directions to subordinates, assuring their comprehension.

Step 5. Monitor progress of the task or project on a continual basis.

Step 6. Upon completion of the task or project, conduct follow-ups to check and/or reinforce results.

Effective use of material and personnel resources are as necessary to management as is good leadership skills. Therefore, it is a logical assumption that *managerial controls* are essential if the functional-level, mid-level manager is to perform effectively and be able to get the job done in an efficiently desired manner.

Organizing or Coordination of Efforts

Organizing is a managerial tool or effort to achieve a desired result, which often focuses on the prioritizing of work around such considerations as command authority, division of work and assignment responsibility. In this text, the discussion of organizing as a leadership tool refers to the use of functional controls and limits of performance actions. Any discussion of planning and organizing ultimately focuses of the effectiveness (end results) and how it was achieved. Thus, it becomes imperative to concentrate on objective achievement through the organizing effectiveness of police mid-level managers. The end result, product, or service is important but so is the aspect of how it was achieved. The prime measures of a leader's effectiveness in organizing work efforts is gauged by not only end results but also coordination with other organizational elements and the efficient use of available resources. The police mid-level manager must be concerned with the outcome of personal leadership efforts, as well as the effectiveness of the entire organization in achievement of its goals and objectives.

Work organization as a separate leadership term is not easily identified or discussed without the inclusion of planning as a prime preparatory term. However, if organizing is viewed in its most basic intent of managerial action, then the aspect of *performance control* becomes the prime focus. And, when utilizing *performance control* as the definitive component of work organizing, there is a clearer ability to delineate and separate from strategic planning. The primary thing to consider about organizing as a managerial work control is that it can be neither totally objective nor non-committal. A leader involved in organizing or setting work standards is concerned with overall mission accomplishment and therefore cannot objectively consider or assess performance controls developed external to achievement of organizational goals and objectives. Leadership controls in an organizational setting are primarily focused on goal establishment and developing priorities. The police supervisor and mid-level leader, like leadership in other fields of employment, must realize that operational-level workers need guidance and performance parameters. If functional workers were allowed to deviate at will from established procedures, a leader would quickly find him/herself attempting to manage a number of individual efforts all going in separate directions. To be most effective in work performance, there needs to be leadership direction and coordination toward achieving a desired end result. In an organizational environment, there needs to be a performance criteria for the individuals and for the element. This should allow mutual participation and effectiveness of both individuals and the organizational element toward ultimate objective achievement.

Organization of work behaviors and the control of subordinates' actions are needed to focus efforts on the end results. The means to which a worker achieves desired results are often as important as the outcome of the labor itself. The *Ends Justifies the Means* is not a practical management approach in the application of performance methods. If the performance efforts are too costly or laborious, then the effort is wasteful of organizational resources. To avoid waste, the secondary police manager should coordinate subordinate actions and the efficiency with which their efforts produce desired results. The mid-level manager should remember that both the leader and subordinates exist to contribute to the accomplishment of organizational goals and objectives.

To assess the effectiveness of job performance actions of functional-level police officers toward ultimate task accomplishment, a leader must assure that needed controls over strategized work are implemented. The aforementioned controls reflect that the necessity for the managerial parameters to be used are both measurable and meaningful. Seven specific managerial controls were identified by Peter F. Drucker in his book, *Management.* They were:

1. **Economical**—cost effective
2. **Meaningful**—aimed at achieving desired results
3. **Appropriateness**—adequate or sufficient
4. **Congruency**—compatible with ultimate goals and objectives
5. **Timeliness**—meaningfully timed
6. **Simple**—uncomplicated and easily understood
7. **Operational**—functional toward ultimate achievement

All of the above articulated controls should be considered by a police mid-level manager in his or her organizing of the work efforts for subordinates.

Organizing as a leadership objective has in some cases been articulated as the development of a relationship process between authority and responsibility. The work-structuring process identifies who does what and who has responsibility for the task to be accomplished. Additionally, the work procedures established by a secondary leader during the process should be convertible into a productive task achievement. In most well-managed police organizations, an effectively developed process comes after strategy projection. In other words, *organizing* follows *planning.* Performed work and its coordination with other efforts cannot be accurately or clinically defined in the absence of an awareness of the organization's overall goals and objectives. Furthermore, planning and organizing determines the resources needed for task accomplishment. The traditional view of planning and organizing reflects a rigidly structured and systematized process that may be outdated in today's environment of rapid changes, advancing complexity of needs, and a requirement to be flexible enough to adapt to changing social demands. Technology and work attitude demand a consideration of contingency changes as needed. Most effective organizations are adaptive and changeable to accommodate sudden influence alterations. They also tend to be more interesting and challenging to functional workers, which frequently is an added incentive to most intellectually aggressive police officers.

A police mid-level leader as a planner and organizer of subordinates' task behaviors should display a concern for synchronized performances and objective achievement. The efforts of functional-level police officers can become counterproductive when labors are not coordinated or fail to achieve a desired result. Therefore, the mid-level manager must assure that the aforementioned objectives are accomplished. The leader is further expected to assure that the purpose of the task expectations are identified to functional-level workers and that a sense of leadership stability is reflected in his or her managerial approach. The enlightened police officers of today demand that leadership reflect the skills associated with planning and organization, if a mid-level manager is to efficiently and effectively perform as a leader. There is nothing mystical about a mid-level police manager's effectiveness as a leader; it is simply a matter of appropriate performance execution within established parameters. The secondary police manager need only be aware of the importance of the process and then assure that personal efforts toward strategy projection are purposeful and effective. The associative pattern of inseparably linking **planning** and **organizing** as one component in assessing the leadership skills of a leader is essential, because strategy projection and event management at times appear to be synonymous. Remember, **planning and organizing** essentially develop and clarify task priorities and operational standards. Together, they establish courses of actions for the organization, its leaders, and subordinates toward accomplishment of specific goals and objectives. Under the concept of **planning and organization**, a mid-level manager determines the appropriate assignment of subordinates and allocation of resources to assure task accomplishment.

The Scope of Strategy Projection and Action

The total scope of *planning* and *organizing* may assist the aspiring secondary leader to better comprehend their conceptual distinction and importance to the organization. Planning and organizing as a self-contained managerial strategy is a cluster of decisions and behaviors implemented to formulate actions. The strategy, when put into action, should provide an interactive relationship between the organization and the achievement of its goals and objectives. The knowledge of expected functional behaviors will assist functional police mid-level managers in projecting the effectiveness of planned actions. Through this recognition and direction of actions by secondary leaders in an organizational setting, a clearly defined strategy can be enacted. As noted earlier in this chapter, planned actions must be considered in light of available resources, in relationship to overall goal attainment. Planning and organizing as a total strategy process to achieve a specific objective have three basic components. The components has been identified as *deployed resources, unique capability,* and *coordinated resources.*

Deployed Resources has to do with an organization's distribution of its human and material assets toward achievement of its goals and objectives. Because mid-level leaders and primary supervisors are generally positioned at the focal point of job performance, actions by subordinates are most noticeable in the deployment of resources. The organization's hierarchy usually decides the size of the work force units and the available resources allocated to resolve a problem. But it is the secondary leader that on a day-to-day basis will be assigned the responsibility for assuring the appropriate handling of a specific concern. Therefore, it is the foundational leader who takes allocated resources, both human and material, and deploys them in a manner that is most conducive to achieving goals and objectives. Thus, the deployment of resources is chiefly in the hands of the mid-level manager and line supervisors.

Unique Capability refers to the fact that a mid-level manager is in a distinct position to be exposed to concerns and problems associated with *leadership's responsibility* and *functional level task performance by operational personnel.* Such a position of exposure typifies his or her knowledge of what is needed to be effective at the operational level and provides an awareness of the availability of resources, both human and material, that has been allocated. A secondary leader's ability to appropriately function in a leadership role reflects a personal competence in managing logistics and channeling resources toward accomplishment of goals and objectives. In addition the line mid-level manager must consider, in relationship to available resources, what to do concerning the managerial issues of *providing adequate services, the organizational focus,* and *functional personnel task achievement.* The above listed component areas of strategy projection and implementing actions by an operational mid-level police manager is not unique in and of itself. However, inasmuch as a secondary leader has to balance all three in order to be effective demonstrates a competence that is necessary and unique to a functional-level, mid-level manager.

Coordination of Behaviors is the performance interaction of organizational entities that are essentially orchestrated by the operational mid-level police manager. The combined efforts of the coordinated elements is greater than the sum of each component's individual performance output. The coordinated behaviors that accomplish goals and objectives are as much a practical requirement of secondary leadership as is subordinates' task assignments.

The primary effort of a functional mid-level police leader is essentially the development of action plans that are formulated and structured into the operational behaviors to be implemented by subordinates. The formulation of functional-level strategies by an operational mid-level police manager is a significant organizational undertaking because they commit resources, both human and material, to a dedicated course of action. The adopted strategies also affect and influence the actions of other organizational elements, thus adding to the impact of the secondary leader's planned actions.

A public police organization with its multifaceted functions will typically assure that operational-level strategies coincide with interrelated performance tasks of primary-level workers. For example, Unit A may have a task that requires its performance strategies to be formulated around the activity of a highly dense populated area, while Unit B's plan of action focuses on a sparse residential, almost rural, location of the city. The basic strategy of each unit will be different, yet they must be compatible in their interrelated areas of responsibility toward accomplishment of overall organizational goals and objectives. The finished product of leadership planning is implementation, and arguably the putting into action of a decided upon strategy is the most difficult aspect of the process.

An operational mid-level police manager must remember that the ability to influence subordinates and others to implement a strategy the leader has developed is an area that gauges the effectiveness of leadership. Leadership in putting strategy into action includes areas already identified, such as persuading, inspiration, influencing changes, manipulating task performances, etc. A secondary leader attempting to implement a decided upon action may have *to explain the planned action and consequences, make demands on others, construct a coordinated effort, and persuade some individuals of the feasibility of the strategic behavior.* If possible, the mid-level leader should include those who are to implement the plan in the strategy development process. This will aid in their acceptance and commitment to making the decided upon action achieve desired results.

UNIFICATION OF COMPONENTS

Planning and organizing as components of strategy projection are two inseparable tasks of an operational manager in a police organization. The effective positional leader should be able to assess all pertinent information and then formulate a smooth and efficient operational plan. There must be some form of assurance via a checks-and-balances process to make certain that the preplan or formatted procedure will attain the desired departmental objectives as effectively as possible. If a managerial control of resources is viewed in the same frame of reference that may be perceived for a person's handling of machinery, then it becomes obvious that the responsibility of operational management is to convert available resources into task accomplishment. It should be noted that the conversion of these resources by a positional leader is expected to be achieved as economically as possible. Economic usage of resources is a prime assessment of the capabilities of an operational manager. Control over the type, quality, and quantity of available resources is often not within the scope of the operational manager. However, the effective planning and use of accessible logistical and human resources for productive performance in goal achievement is within the individual's vista of influence.

The basic perception of expectations for effectiveness is typically the same no matter what level of resource availability is allotted to an operational manager. The top echelon of leadership of the department expects and desires effective productivity and goal achievement. It is then apparent that the department hierarchy look to the strategy projection (planning and organizing) efforts of a leader as the principal element in attainment of goals and objectives. This does not imply that the department or its leaders supply inadequate resources to its operational leaders. It simply means that the best return on investment of resources is an expectation, which in this case would be efficient productivity from allotted resources because of a strategy projection's contribution to the effective accomplishment of departmental goals and objectives. This is a major consideration for the essential importance of preplanning and organizing by most top-level leaders in all industries. Planning and organizing must then be recognized as one of the key dimensional trait characteristics of an operational police manager. An analysis of what has been covered thus far in this chapter reveals that indeed strategy projection is the focal point for task accomplishment within the framework of available resources and the other effective influence factors or resources. Please note that the effective and efficient use of all available resources is an essential and natural part of operational management, and that affirmative leadership skills cannot be adequately displayed by a positional leader without effective resource control.

As a final note, much of the planning and organizing of subordinates' performances, plus the specific use of logistics, should be accomplished outside of the actual functioning unit. This means that forecasts and projected strategies should generally be made at a position of leadership above the operational or functional level. However, most of the responsibility and knowledge requirements for appropriate planning and execution are still direct duty obligations of an operational manager. Primarily, as a function of the individual's leadership position, a police operational manager must make decisions on the actual use and dispersing of both logistical and human resources. The most effective operational manager will also track his or her unit's use of resources by means of charting. This will allow the preplanned and systematized handling of available resources to be better comprehended and coordinated with other departmental operations. Therefore, it is very apparent that strategy projection as a dimensional trait characteristic of an operational police manager is essential, especially if the individual is to function effectively and be capable of getting desired results in as efficient a manner as possible.

SYNOPSIS

Strategy projection is a forecast of what an operational positional leader in a police department perceives will occur and how best to utilize available resources to achieve desired results. The police manager should mentally balance the possible resolutive alternatives in forecasting operational activity. A manager can formalize a practical **plan of focus** through the combining of current functional status with the projection of future needs. A **preplan** and **organizing effort** will generally include most of the positive influences on the accomplishment of goals and objectives. Forecasts for development of operational planning and organizing must be based on projections, as well as the trends of past experiences.

All positional leaders in an organization attempt to define the overall mission from a personal perspective in developing an operational plan of action. Effective projections of an operational police manager can positively demonstrate innovative actions, creative thinking, and logical inferences. To more effectively focus on strategy projection as a trait characteristic, it would be better to discuss the two most recognizable constituent components separately. The two elements referred to by the author are planning and organizing. Planning is essentially defined as the process whereby operational objectives and functional use of resources are developed to achieve a desired result. Organizing is the primary method of systematization established by an operational manager to carry out planned actions to accomplish functional goals and objectives. Effective managers must be able to assess information and formulate an efficient operational plan of action for the data considered. Thus, planning and organizing as a component of strategy projection are two inseparable tasks of an operational police manager.

Chapter Sixteen

SUBORDINATES' APPRAISAL PROCESS

The definition of a *Subordinate's Appraisal* is the process of evaluating the *performance worth of the individual* to the organization. However, in order to gain a better perspective of what an appraisal or evaluation is from the standpoint of the organization, there must be an understanding of its basic importance as well as the general intentions of the process. The basic importance of an employee appraisal process is that the actual job performances be evaluated and that each ratee be advised of improved task behaviors and worth to the organization. The intentions of an employee's performance appraisal is typically to: (1) determine the best qualified employee for promotional advancement; (2) determine which workers are the greater asset to the organization, during times of restructuring, etc.; (3) determine which workers are in need of additional in-service or on-the-job training; (4) determine who is qualified for a merit rate pay increase; (5) improve employee morale, through feedback to the subordinates as to the perception of their work performance; and (6) improve overall productivity.

One factor typically overlooked when there is an analysis of subordinate appraisals has been the fact that evaluation can and should be a reward process. The reward element of subordinate appraisals concerns the recognition that comes with a positive evaluation. Most effective organizations are continually looking for ways to reward their outstanding performers. Merit raises and favorable assignments are desirable, but these are somewhat limited by budgetary restraints and available positions. Public policing like every other industry has the concern of being able to retain its most talented people. The lure of private industry, where financial rewards are much greater than public service, often outdistance public policing's attractive feature of job security.

Recognizing that it is running a distant second in initially obtaining the choice candidates coming out of colleges and universities makes law enforcement seek to project a positive work environment, in addition to job satisfaction and security, for new hires. One way of identifying an organization's best and most productive performers, as a lure for prospective new employees, as well as the need to satisfy incumbents, is through the use of an effective appraisal process, and, second, to assure that appropriate accolades are accorded effective employees. Many leaders have questioned what method is best and most appropriate for identifying an organization's better performers. The traditional response from most leadership theorists has been that a well-designed and implemented evaluation process is preferred. The question then becomes since each individual has strengths and weaknesses in different areas, how does an organization clinically determine which instrument or trait characteristics are the most appropriate measure of job performance? The answer is, of course, that no one instrument or set of trait characteristics is best for all organizations. However, an effective job analysis of the position to be evaluated will identify the trait areas to be measured. The analysis should also provide an indication of which instrument will be best for the acquisition and gauging of the workers' performance worth to the organization. Elsewhere in this section, the author has identified evaluation instruments and trait characteristics which are most common and/or generally considered (arguably) best.

Essentially, the process (whichever one that's used) must be carried out efficiently and effectively. Also, the employees being appraised must perceive the police organization's leadership to be fair and objective in its use of the evaluation tool. The reward system derived from the evaluation process is essential to employee morale. It has the potential to elevate morale, productivity, and teamwork within the organization. A functional police mid-level manager nurtures the process and adapts the chosen instrument to meet the need of his or her element. An effective secondary leader also utilizes the process to obtain optimum subordinates' performance and as a positive reward incentive for employees.

Effective operational leaders have begun to realize that *performance appraisals* can no longer be considered just a control process. A well-designed and administered performance appraisal is a human resources tool, which provides a foundation for assuring equitable job evaluations for all employees. An effective reward system or process, beyond financial and/or assignments, cannot be successfully undertaken in the absence of a credible job assessment process. As noted in this chapter, an evaluation process determines or measures the individual's worth to the organization. Without an appropriately designed and utilized process, the organization's management cannot determine which employees are more valuable and contributory to the overall successful achievement of goals and objectives. Whether or not it is admitted or realized, most factors influencing incumbent subordinates' assignments, incentive acquisition, and interagency development begin with a performance appraisal process. The functional police mid-level manager must understand the *Performance Appraisal Cycles* as identified by R. M. Hodgetts. Hodgetts identified four steps to a Performance Appraisal Cycle as:

1. **Development of a performance standard,** which needs to be specific as to work expectations.
2. **An established technique of determining worker performances** that are desired and within the scope of achieving tasks.
3. **Setting a standard by which job performances can be measured.** Job behaviors must be checked against some pre-established criteria to gauge performance acceptability.
4. **Rating the performance evaluation** has to do with making the comparison of job behaviors against the task actions of other employees to determine a performance ranking.

It should be made clear that no matter what the process or trait characteristics decided upon and used, the mid-level manager has to determine those to be rewarded and the employees needing to upgrade their performances. Also not to be overlooked is the leader's obligation to determine the level of performance that is below acceptable, adequate, and superior for the position being evaluated. Performance evaluations are a major tool of the efficient and effective functional police mid-level manager.

General Information

The principal idea of appraising subordinates is nearly as old as the employer-employee concept. Evaluations of personnel typically occur in some form or another in every organization. Most organizations evaluate its employee as a basic and natural course or extension of its delegated management authority. The methods utilized will range from a general haphazard observation of employee performance to a very structured and scientific process of objective assessment and documentation. The current appraisal processes, while generally considered as adequate for most merit rating evaluations, may be far from being perfect in terms of assessing the concept of individual differences and establishing an organization-wide standard of satisfactory job performance.

As previously stated, for the first functional police mid-level manager, a formalized subordinate-appraising program is an essential means of motivating better performances, improving the morale, and identifying specific training needs. It can also be effective in determining the virtuousness of the operational policies and procedures concerning the unit or section's operation. Appraisals are a principal element to the functional mid-level police manager in the motivation and improvement of subordinate performance. As noted in previous chapters, the determination of the effectiveness and efficiency of a line supervisor or middle manager is how well subordinates perform.

A fundamental method, if not the primary one, that a mid-level manager can use to motivate subordinates to be more efficient is to discuss their performance as assessed in an employee appraisal in a helpful and constructive manner. An appropriate counseling or interview session will generally provide a sound basis for individual improvement, especially where the secondary leader is effective in connecting the subordinate's goals to the objectives of the organization. However, first for a functional police mid-level manager to be able to evaluate the performance activities, desirable or undesirable, of subordinates, he or she must appraise the individuals in terms of the specific quality of their functioning. There are some secondary benefits to an operational mid-level manager's appropriate use of a formalized appraisal process. First, as the mid-level police manager improves as a performance assessor, there will be an increase in the ability to develop the subordinate. Second, the mid-level manager is able to increase personal worth to the organization by providing positional leadership that fosters good communication, effective employee relations, and increased job productivity.

What Is the Importance of Evaluating Employees?

Traditionally, organizational management or a functional worker's secondary leader should be able to review the person's personnel folder or work file and obtain an accurate overview of the officer's work performance history. The traditional practice of evaluating subordinates, as defined earlier, is an attempt to systematically evaluate employees by specifically established organizational standards. The principal reasons for appraising employees in accordance with documented organizational standards are:

1. **To Document Performance**. A specific incident or quality of work in one or more areas will tend to alter some leaders' overall view of a subordinate's performance. When this occurs, it is unlikely that a mid-level manager's perception will be based on complete information. The accurate documentation of employees' job performance actions are essential to the organization in deciding:
   A. One employee's worth to the organization versus another worker in times of reduced manpower and increased productivity needs.

"I hate evaluation time. I always feel that the commander is waiting for one of his subordinates to make a mistake and it might be me."

EMPLOYEE EVALUATIONS SHOULD NOT BE VIEWED AS A NEGATIVE BY FUNCTIONAL-LEVEL WORKERS.

B. If an employee should receive a merit increase in salary. For those organizations utilizing a "Performance Worth Rating" system, the employees receiving a satisfactory evaluation will get a raise, while those whose performance is substandard will not.

C. Justification of personnel actions that are considered negative by the subordinate. It is unlikely that the employee will be convinced that the police organization's personnel actions, such as promotion, demotion, transfers, etc., are not based on favoritism or other influences in the absence of a perceived objective and practical evaluation system.

2. **To Identify Specific Training Needs**. A formal subordinate appraising system that utilizes job-related standards will reveal areas where employees need in-service or on-the-job training to increase efficiency. By identifying these weaknesses, a mid-level manager can concentrate training efforts in the areas that are most needed.

3. **To Assure Uniformity of Appraisals**. It is unlikely that police leaders throughout the organization should utilize the same benchmarks for evaluations in the absence of a formalized appraisal system without specific standards. The personal traits of each supervisor or manager, whether conscious or unconscious, will affect the ratings, making it virtually impossible to make a clear comparison between employees rated by different leaders. A formalized and systematic subordinate appraisal process would provide common measuring standards by which each employee can be assessed.

4. **To Improve Employee Efficiency**. A subordinate performance appraisal that is effectively used by a functional-level, mid-level manager should motivate employees' job efforts. Aside from the obvious benefits of pointing out areas of unacceptable behaviors, the appraisal system can be a positive motivator as it will show the employees that their affirmative efforts have not gone unnoticed.

By having documented appraisal information relative *to a subordinate's job behaviors,* a mid-level manager is in a better position to make recommendations concerning the employee's career advancement, etc. A police middle manager and the organization's upper management will have a greater assurance that the recommendations are objective and sound. An effective appraisal process can also serve as a checkup on the effectiveness of the manager's leadership practices. Also, a systematic process encourages the secondary police manager to take a personal interest in assigned subordinates and, thus, can have a humanizing effect on line supervision by identifying positional responsibility for the performances of employees. Ideally, an effectively articulated appraisal process will encourage mutual understanding, pride in unit operation, and cohesiveness of overall performances.

LEGAL CONSIDERATIONS

Performance appraisal processes are typically considered an essential aspect of an organization's productivity and quality control. It must be remembered that although public police do not produce a tangible product, the performance output and the quality of the services provided are essential. Traditionalists believe that appraisals, if properly utilized, are a positive form of personnel management. However, several recent surveys by management researchers indicate that frequently **Performance Appraisals** are a source of employee dissatisfaction. This author believes that *performance ap-*

praisals of subordinates can and will be positively and effectively perceived, especially when using a process that is appropriately and objectively utilized to appraise all employees who are subject to the appraisal rating. As previously noted, basic performance appraisals are a process of assessing an employee's work behavior as a primary method of making objective and fair personnel decisions.

Legal actions that challenge the objectivity and the applicability of performance rating systems are a common practice in modern-day society. Leaders at all levels of the police organization, who appraise subordinates, must ask themselves if the utilized appraisal process is legally defensible. Functional mid-level managers should assure that the criteria or traits being assessed are applicable to the job performance being rated and the process generally applies to all workers rated by the process. A *trait characteristic rating system* is the process most criticized by functional-level employees in a police organization. A trait characteristic process is subjective and generally based more on perceptual personality than on actual job performance. It should also be noted that the **Trait Appraisal Characteristic Process** is the one most used today, especially in public law enforcement. The Trait Appraisal Characteristic procedure is also the one that is most likely to be challenged by functional-level employees.

Work Simulation or Behaviorally Focused Appraisal processes are more defensible, if challenged by employees. The basic premise of a *work behavior appraisal* is that actual performance actions in the position are assessed and rated. The ratings are based on tangible behaviors that can be gauged and compared to other employees performing the same or very similar tasks. Most police organizations who utilize such a process develop them based on a job analysis of incumbents in the position(s). The appraisal process is based on objectively viewed court behaviors. The evaluation process is usually specifically documented with well-articulated parameters for the appraisers. Further, if the rating results are discussed with the ratee as to specific areas of behavior, the appraisal is considered appropriate and defensible.

There are primary areas of concern that organizational leaders should address relative to possible legal challenges to a Performance Appraisal Process. Organizational leaders must assure that:

1. A clear rationale and need for the appraisal process exists.
2. There is a visible relatedness of the appraisal process to the tasks being performed by the ratee(s).
3. The reliability of showing the objectivity of the rater(s) can be shown.
4. The appraisal process must utilize traits and/or dimensions that are both tangible and measurable.

5. The performance appraisal process must specifically be documented and articulated to all affected personnel.

An effective and legally defensible performance rating process tends to make functional-level employees more productive and provides a method of organizations to recognize the accomplishments of workers. Management's desire to equate certain dimensional areas and functional employees' on-the-job behaviors can be coordinated in a performance appraisal process. The objectives reflected in a job analysis, the synthesis of work performed versus desired goals, productivity assessments, job relatedness, and worker-level employee reward or recognition can all be acknowledged under a properly developed and implemented performance appraisal.

Commonly Used Appraisal Systems

The behavioral standards that are traditionally considered as desirable in employees' job performances are generally included in a systematic *subordinate appraisal* by the organization. It will usually be designed to meet the particular needs of the organization toward overall goal and objective achievement. Most generally, the appraisal process will not only contain those personal characteristics that are observable and distinguishable, but they also will be structured in such a way that an objective evaluation of the employee's work can be obtained. Thus, to establish a satisfactory job performance appraisal system, a police organization must assure that traits or behaviors to be assessed are recognizable, measurable, and general to its operation. Therefore, the basic characteristics upon which an effective subordinate appraisal process is based are:

1. **Recognizable**. In order to be useful in appraising identified traits, the characteristics must clearly be acknowledged as being distinguishable from one another. The traits must also easily be identifiable as being important to the accomplishment of the element's goals and objectives.
2. **Measurable**. The traits' characteristics and/or standard utilized in the appraisal instrument should be gaugeable in terms of overall accomplishment of goals and objectives. If no scale of measurement can be articulated for the standards used, then no acceptable procedure can be established.
3. **General**. The traits or standards used in the appraisal form should be pertinent to and universal throughout the police organization. They must be considered as important trait characteristics to effective and

efficient job performances by employees. Also, the traits' characteristics identified should not be distinguishable as being external to on-the-job performance by employees.

It should be discernible from the critical information presented previously what the basic characteristics are upon which an effective *subordinate appraisal* process should be built. It is easy to see that the articulated focus should be on job performance. There are a number of different employee appraisal processes currently in use, most of which concentrate their perspective on attempts to be objective or to justify the mid-level manager's observations. A few still rely on the outdated method of subjective rating by primary and secondary leaders based on personal opinion and conjecture not supported by measurable information. However, in most traditional police operations, subordinate appraisal methods fall into two broad categories. Those categories are **Comparative and Scale Rating**.

Comparative Evaluation Process

In a comparative or ranking method of evaluating functional subordinates, the mid-level manager assesses the employee's job performance against that of other employees of equal status and duties. In this method, employees performing like duties compete against one another for appraisal ratings. Traditionally, the process calls for the evaluating leader to arrange his subordinates in a rank order, usually from superior to unacceptable job performance, thereby establishing an acceptable level of performance about midway of the ranked subordinates. Those employees above the perceptible midpoint are said to be performing acceptably, while those below the line are proclaimed as needing to improve job performance. This performance appraisal method offers certain advantages, because it is usually simple to understand and use, and it is almost a natural process for a functional-level mid-level manager to positionally rank the assigned subordinates by job performance capability and functioning. The principal flaw in the use of this system is that it assumes accuracy in the differences between ranked positions. Thus, to assure fairness and a correct positional rating of each subordinate, the secondary police supervisor or rater needs to rely on accuracy and complete performance information that is tied to some type of value measure.

The author believes that some type of **Forced Choice** combined with the **Comparative** appraisal process is best for use by a functional mid-level police manager. A forced choice rating process will reduce personal biases when setting a system into place which gives the rater certain category choices within which to place the appraised subordinate. Each category choice has a value assessment, thus creating an overall hierarchical score that can be compared to the rating of other subordinates. Primary to a **Comparative-Forced Choice Appraisal** is the fact that the police mid-level manager will be required to justify their rating. By document it is meant the rater will have to provide a definite statement concerning the why of the rating and how improvement in performance can be obtained.

1. **Cause**. Articulating a specific example of behavior that justifies the leader's forced choice placement.
2. **Improvement Method**. Providing a statement of how the worker can improve job performance in a particular trait area.

Note: *Each trait appraised under the* **Comparative-Forced Choice Process** *should have at least five category choices from which the manager can choose: two negative, one adequate or average, and two positive.*

The forced choice rating process reportedly has been used by the military to evaluate officers for many years and is easily validated. A comparative-forced choice system is the most difficult appraisal process to implement, because it breaks with traditional rating concepts and it must be specifically designed for the organization.

A Scale Rating Process

This type of appraisal rating process is usually referred to as a numerical assessment and is the most common form of evaluation used, not only in law enforcement but in virtually every other industry. The point value assessment system dominates the majority of appraisal processes. Its most distinguishing feature is the use of a numerical scale. The scale will generally begin at *zero for poor* or unacceptable and advance upward to a *numerical point for good* or some other semantic term meaning positive performance. The leader/assessor will generally indicate how much or how little each of the traits being rated is exhibited by the subordinate being appraised. The rater will then indicate the employee's assessed job rating on a numerical scale.

All appraisal trait characteristics utilized in a numerical rating process should be identifiable in a successful job performance of an employee to allow the secondary manager to assess the individual factors and compute the overall rating score. The numerical rating process initially became popular because of its simplicity of design, ease of use, and it appeared to function well when comparing a large number of subordinates. The major criticism that has been levied against this type of evaluation process concerned its susceptibility to biases and technical mistakes.

APPRAISAL PROCESS SUMMARY

A comprehensive and completely objective measure of job performance should be the ultimate goal of all forms of employee appraisal systems. There are many types of jobs, of which functional level policing is one, where totally objective managerial rating is used to assess personnel during normal evaluation periods. However, in situations where negative personnel action will result from an employee's assessment or evaluation, it is recommended that documented specifics of job performances be used by the leader to justify the appraisal. When developing an effective subordinate performance appraisal, it requires that some factors or standards be used to assess the individuals' job behaviors. Those standards typically are of two general type processes: *comparative* or *monocratic*. The employee performance in a comparative process will be gauged in comparison with peer-level jobs or tasks, while the monocratic process requires that the employee be assessed in terms of a predetermined set of behavioral standards. Therefore, the type of appraisal process utilized by an organization will depend principally on the primary purpose of the evaluation and the kind of job being performed. Also, another important consideration when determining the assessment process that will work best for a particular organization is the extent to which the appraisal form itself is consistent with the demands of the job being performed.

It would be idealistic for a police organization to have a different appraisal device for each job classification, but this is not practical for most agencies. Therefore, as a concession between the idealistic and the practical, most organizations will utilize the same trait variations for different authority levels and functional responsibility. There will also generally be a variance in the value factor of each trait characteristic evaluated. These compromise variations of the basic appraisal instrument will usually be limited to one or two, depending on the size of the organization. An example of job responsibilities within a police operation which would necessitate a variance in the evaluation forms are: (1) the tasks of functional-level police officers and (2) the job behaviors of clerical staff. It is clear that the measurable work expectations and performance trait characteristics between the two positions differ greatly. Therefore, the evaluation measures must also vary. However, in the final analysis, the number of variations utilized by a police organization will depend largely upon the amount of differences between the types of jobs being rated.

Obstacles to Effective Appraisals

The obstacles that are considered traditional or common to most rating processes generally occur in a functional police mid-level manager's evaluation of subordinates. These obstacles to effective appraisals of subordinates are referred to as **common rating errors**. Most generally, it should be recognized that no process of appraising employees is going to be perfect, because the evaluation instrument itself and its use in tabulating a subordinate's overall assessment is done by human beings. There are certain failures in human beings as a species that limit their ascension to the level of perfection required when doing a totally objective performance appraisal. Traits such as personal bias, prejudices, or individual preferences will inevitably find their way into an assessment process. The very nature of the duties being performed by functional-level police employees and the kinship of primary and secondary managerial responsibility will often determine the type of appraisal obstacles that are common to the organization. For example, in a public police organization, most functional mid-level managers are promoted from within the ranks and generally will perceive an initial close kinship to the plight of the basic functional-level officer. This kinship comes from an acute awareness of the job and the specific problems encountered by the functional-level police officer. The errors generally associated with appraisals by first-line police supervisors and mid-level managers in a public policing operation are: (1) **leniency**, (2) **halo**, (3) **psychological fixation**, and (4) **trait enlargement**.

Common Appraisal Errors

The tendency is for functional-level leaders and managers in any industry, particularly in law enforcement, to appraise the subordinate and not the job performance. However, if the performance appraisal process is to be of any real value to the organization, each employee must be evaluated on actual job behaviors and not on any preconceived opinion of the appraiser. The following is a discussion of some of the appraisal obstacles common to functional-level performance evaluations.

> **Leniency**: This may be by far the most common of all rating errors made during performance ratings. A tendency to be lenient is the most common rating error whereby the rater appraises the subordinate more positively than their job performance would indicate. It is also closely associated with the leader's kinship with subordinates related to the day-to-day contact, prejudice, personal knowledge of the employees' duties, leadership traits, and biases. The leader also may not want to deny a subordinate's chances for promotional advancement or a merit pay increase; thus, he or she tend to be lenient in performance ratings.

Halo: The Halo Effect as an appraisal error is similar to leniency inasmuch as the functional-level mid-level manager's tendency is to overrate the subordinate's overall job performance. The subordinate's enhanced rating is usually based on a single factor or a positively perceived trait characteristic rather than the totality of job performance. The principles of the *Halo Effect* can also work in the reverse, meaning that a negatively perceived trait characteristic or factor can sway the rating manager's appraisal of the employee toward the adverse end of the rating scale. The negative *Halo Effect* tends to magnify every deficiency and weakness of the subordinate's performance actions.

Psychological Fixation: This type of rating obstacle to effective appraisals in a police organization usually revolves around the ideal of the *Superiority Complex*–in other words, **playing god**. The position of public officer essentially means controlling the behavior of others and is not easily standardized into a specific behavior or performance action, because behavior control of others can be through preventative measures by the officer's mere presence, or it might be through more direct or tangible actions. But the principle is the same, because public police are cloaked with more than the ordinary authority over private citizens. Thus, when a functional-level, mid-level manager is promoted from within the ranks, some will be overwhelmed initially by the perceived power. A newly promoted leader, during this time of *enlarged self-image,* will relish the responsibility and may wield the power recklessly over subordinates. The reverse of this can also be a reality for some newly promoted leaders, who tend to shy away from the use of power and accepting responsibility. The *power wielding* primary or secondary manager is inclined to be very autocratic and rigid, demanding perfection in the performance of subordinates. However, a *shy away* leader will lean toward leniency and tend to overlook defects in subordinates' performances. It should be noted that these **Psychological Fixations** are usually temporary, because, as most primary leaders or secondary managers become more comfortable in their role, the methods in which they handle responsibility, such as appraisals, will change.

Trait Enlargement. This reflects the tendency of a mid-level manager to place significantly more weight on one trait over others–for example, an employee who is aggressive in attempting to handle as many job actions as possible but who is deficient in properly completing tasks. The leader may be impressed by the police officer's zeal in aggressively pursuing job activity and overlook the subordinate's tendency to fail to follow through. This type of rating or assessment practice is not exclusive to first line leaders; it is a tendency that seems to permeate the organization. An example of this can be found in a public police organization that has a *weight control program,* not for a true *wellness concept,* but rather how an officer looks in their uniform. In the above example, an officer's job performance, no matter how good, tends to be overlooked if he or she does not present a positive image as determined by a subjective leader. Thus, it becomes clear that physical appearance is the dominant trait characteristic in this organization and that police officers will be gauged primarily in that area.

There are a number of other obstructions to effective appraisals by functional-level managers that are common in most evaluation processes, Some of the more common rating errors not previously identified are: (1) **Recency**–too much emphasis given to a recent behavior or incident; (2) **Central Tendency**–a supervisor/manager's desire to play it safe and rate everyone toward the middle or average; (3) **Prejudices**–ratings influenced by the leader's bias of race, gender, religion, etc.; and (4) **Incomplete or Faulty Data**–rating a job performance in areas that have not been observed, or on opinions formed by faulty assumptions or incomplete information.

It is the opinion of this author that the best way for a functional-level midlevel manager to avoid these appraisal obstacles is to provide adequate documentation to justify or explain each rating given. The appraisal process and assessment instrument will be considered utopian when leaders several levels above the primary or secondary manager, who did the evaluation, can review it with complete agreement and understanding of the why of each rating. In order to achieve this relative perfection, the secondary leader, after completing the appraisal, should review it from the perspective of a third uninvolved person to see if it generates any questions as to *why.* If it does not, then it may generally be considered a good appraisal. However, if it does, then the questions generated need to be addressed before the appraisal process can be considered complete.

Elements of an Effective Appraisal Process

If a performance appraisal process is going to be an effective tool of police management in increased productivity and job efficiency, it must be structured and designed to meet the specific needs of the organization. The basic concept of appraising may be the same in various organizations, but because the job responsibilities and emphasis are different the method of evaluation will have to differ also. The differences being referred to are the structural components of the evaluation process and not the overall goal objective. The foundational components of an effective **Appraisal Process** are: (1) a clearly documented organizational policy regarding the process; (2) a credible and provable job-related evaluation instrument; and (3) an interactive exchange between the ratee and the rater concerning the rating given.

Clearly Documented Organizational Policy

To insure that an organization-wide program will work effectively, it must be well documented and understood throughout the organization. For example, every public police organization has certain behavioral and job performance standards that they expect of employees, but subordinates cannot realistically be held accountable for the violations of these standards if they do not know of their existence. The supervisory and/or management personnel of an organization must make every effort to articulate and disseminate to all employees of the department the behavioral and performance standards they are expected to meet. The specific process for evaluating their job performance and the task expectations should also be articulated, with an emphasis on the possible consequences (positive or negative) of an employee's unsatisfactory rating. It should be recognized that an attempt to appraise a subordinate under articulated behavioral or job performance expectation standards will be counterproductive in the sense that an appraiser would have to make allowances in certain areas or specific situations. The net result is a waste of the appraiser's time, inasmuch as an accurate accounting of the employee's worth to the organization will not have been obtained.

A principal responsibility of a positional leader, especially a functional mid-level manager, is to assure that personnel under their control are informed of matters and operational guidelines affecting them. Therefore, the basic responsibility for articulating the organization's policy for personnel appraisals is a principal function of a mid-level manager.

Creditable Evaluation Instrument

A performance appraisal instrument's greatest value to the organization is that it requires the functional-level police supervisor and secondary manager to look at the job behavior of each subordinate individually. This individual assessment fosters improved performances and job productivity. The job trait characteristics to be assessed during an appraisal process should be comprehensive in the analysis of the employee's behavior and performance as it relates to the task expectations. Much too frequently, when a particular trait or standard is not included on the rating instrument, the rater will overlook the employee's job performance in that area even though the area may be important to the overall evaluation of the person. Therefore, it is essential that a performance evaluation instrument be as comprehensive and job-related as possible.

It has been previously stated that there is no universal appraisal instrument or process that will be ideal for every organization or situation. Specific processes or measures must be designed individually based on organizational needs, goals, and objectives. However, most public police departments are essentially the same in their overall goals and objectives. However, there are enough critical differences from agency to agency to warrant individualizing appraisal processes. Therefore, this author believes the following discussed rating trait characteristics are generic to public law enforcement and should be included in most police agencies' appraisal instruments. The identified trait characteristics or dimensions are:

1. **Image**. Does the officer present a favorable appearance? This trait characteristic measures whether or not the police officer is well groomed, neat and clean, and in general how he or she maintains the appearance of themselves and their uniform. As stated by this author in a previous text, *Appearance makes the man or rather the authority figure,* referring to an officer's image and how it affects a subordinate's job performance.

2. **Job Participation**. This dimension trait measures the officer's habits toward the job and personal dependability. Elements of this trait are: (a) habitual absence, (b) promptness in task performance, (c) dependability in meeting job actions, and (d) habitual lateness. Essentially, what this trait characteristic appraises is the demonstrated desire of the officer to fulfill the assignments, not permitting minor discomforts or personal interest to interfere with job performance.

3. **Job Temperament**. Does the worker project an image of tactfulness and good self-control? This trait attempts to gauge an intangible characteristic having to do with the officer's opinions and motivations, projected through the assignment acceptance and level of job-related performance.

4. **Effectiveness of Job Performance**. This trait characteristic is used to determine if the employee executes and completes duty requirements in a timely and dependable manner. Individual areas of concern under this dimension are: (a) whether or not the work is done haphazardly; (b) the level of experience needed; (c) the level of leadership required; and (d) whether the subordinate is able to adjust and handle difficult or changing situations.

5. **Interactive Collaboration**. This reflects an officer's demonstrated ability to perform as a team member with others, as well as how well the officer works with other agencies or organizational personnel in accomplishing assigned duties and goals. The characteristics of cooperation and teamwork are essential in most operations, but specifically so in line policing functioning because of the nature of the duties and the potential danger to the officers.

6. **Care of Material Resources**. This trait is universal to all good evaluations, without regard to the specifics of the industry. In the current era of tight budgets and strictly controlled resources, an employee must demonstrate a regard for the care and use of organizational equipment.

7. **Internal Motivated Behavior**. This trait characteristic gauges a worker's demonstrated activity as to whether or not he or she is a self-starter who is alert to opportunities to improve job performance and work output. Ask yourself such questions as: (a) does the employee need prodding to finish assignments? (b) does the employee take action to achieve an objective that is considered beyond what is required? and (c) does the employee request additional tasks and demonstrate ingenuity?

8. **Task Knowledge**. This trait characteristic evaluates the employee's technical knowledge and skills to perform the assigned job. It is fairly clear that no matter what the rating level of the trait characteristics, the bottom line will be, Does the individual have the capability to do the job? Essentially, as a trait in an appraisal process, job knowledge measures the employee's demonstrated working knowledge of assigned duties, related policies, practices and procedures, equipment used, and responsibilities of the position.

9. **Adaptability**. This is a worker's ability to personally recognize and acknowledge unacceptable self-performances, thus reflecting the capability to accept constructive critiques of work and responding to the critiques in a positive manner to correct noted deficiencies.

10. **Communication Skills**. This is an evaluation of the individual's demonstrated ability to communicate clearly, both in written and oral form; also, the ability to listen, interpret, and extract essential relevant data from information presented.

The trait characteristics identified above are recommended as appraisal measures that should be included in an effective functional-level police rating form. The organization should undertake the validation of all traits utilized in its rating form to assure that they are job related. A comprehensive validation process would also determine the value factor that each trait should carry and the level of performance that is acceptable. It would also set limits for ratings by primary or secondary managers and establish standards that are universally applicable throughout the organization. This in turn will assure that appraisals completed on employees will be reasonably reliable, consistent, job-related, and accurate. The basic purpose of a validation process to develop an appropriate evaluation instrument will assure that the results of an appraisal are not unduly influenced by the subjectivity of the rater. Remember, subjectivity may not be considered *best evidence* in a legal action brought by an employee over a personnel action influenced by a primary or secondary leader's evaluation.

Interactive Employee's Response

An appraisal process has failed to accomplish one of its primary and most fundamental objectives if it does not positively influence a subordinate's performance. The most essential aspect of a subordinate appraisal process is the information exchanged during the follow-up interview. It is at this point that a mid-level manager is given the opportunity for a comprehensive insight into the employee's actions for improvement in subordinates' job performance and productivity. The performance instrument should also provide the documentation of the areas of needed improvement by the employee.

Whenever an employee's appraisal has been executed, the rater should follow up the identified areas of **needed improvement** by counselling the subordinate in an effort to correct the perceived shortcoming. However, prior to a formal substandard appraisal, an effective functional primary or mid-level manager should have conferred with the employee during the rating period in an attempt to elevate the subordinate's performance. It is important to note, at this juncture, that a mid-level manager should continually review the job performance of subordinates during the evaluation period in an effort to improve and/or enhance the areas of deficiencies. Most major police organizations have policies that require annual job performance appraisals of its functional-level employees. These appraisal processes usually include periodically scheduled reviews during the rating period.

During the interaction or follow-up counseling phase of the appraisal process, the employee should be afforded the opportunity to respond to the evaluation that he or she received. The subordinate's response opportunity should be in both oral and written form. The oral response opportunity should occur during a continual review process and the follow-up opportunity should be afforded the employee as he or she reviews the evaluation instrument prior to endorsing acknowledgment of its content. Traditionally, formal appraisal instruments will contain a specific section for the employee's written response. The functional police leader and upper organizational management should review the response comments with interest and concern, because these comments will often provide a valuable insight into the employee's perception, desires, motivation, and attitude, which may provide the key to improved job performance and productivity by subordinates.

Improving Job Performance

A foundational focus and concern of an effective evaluation process is to improve the job performance of those employees appraised. This is accomplished through the direct efforts of the functional-level, mid-level manager during the review sessions or follow-up interview encounters. The secondary leader should warn and counsel the employee, as needed, during the review sessions, about an unacceptable pattern of performance prior to the issuance of a substandard evaluation. During the counseling sessions, the mid-level manager's principal aim should be to upgrade the subordinate's job performance. To aid the employee in improving personal efficiency, the secondary manager should provide the subordinate with specific courses of actions that will raise the job performance to an acceptable level. An effective mid-level manager will also not omit praising the good job performance of subordinates. Offering praise and recognition for outstanding task behaviors will raise the morale of not only that employee but his or her peers as well. Employees are far more willing to function at a high level of achievement when they are aware that their efforts will be recognized and rewarded by organizational management.

Therefore, improving job performance through a formal appraisal process is based upon two primary primacies: (1) the improvement of substandard performances of employees, and (2) the morale factor of keeping the efficient and productive employees' performances at an acceptable level.

The concept of improving job performance is basically the restructuring of a task to increase the positive behavior of subordinate personnel through evaluation and information. An appraisal process should highlight areas of job enrichment, as well as identify performance behaviors that a subordinate can improve. Task enrichment may be a more appropriate term than is *Improving Job Performance*. It basically means increasing the challenge that a functional-level worker deals with in accomplishing an assigned job. The workplace focus of modern police organizations seems to be shifting to a greater degree of specialization, inasmuch as law enforcement clientele are specializing. And, as previously discussed, operational-level police officers tend to be more interested in new and greater job challenges as a motivator than they are in traditionally perceived material rewards. By the use of the term Improved Job Performance, it is meant increased mental aptitude challenges and a more enhanced focused requirement as opposed to merely increased expectations of productivity. Complexity of task behavior tends to be more conducive to job enrichment for police officers than increasing the number of simple jobs to be performed.

Functional-level police officers tend to be inspired by the same job wants and desired accomplishments as middle managers in the organization. Research has shown that these job wants and/or task enrichments focus on planning, decision making, and a perceptual contribution toward achievement of goals and objectives. An increase in the responsibility delegated to subordinates also has the potential of improving job performance and behaviors.

One factor often overlooked is what the worker thinks of his or her leader's performance behavior. Thus, a self-appraisal analysis is essential for the effective mid-level manager. Articulating a self-evaluation and providing some specific example(s) to support the personal rating will make a leader assess personal performance more objectively. What is sought in any type of evaluation or rating is a recognition of both strong and weak areas of performance and subsequently an improvement in the things that can be enhanced.

In assessing personal job performance, it is necessary to take an additional look at some of the trait areas that may be considered critical. There are a number of foundational trait areas that have been articulated by some management theorists that a secondary police leader should be aware of regarding personal task enrichment or improving job performance. The trait areas that need to be considered when developing a self-appraisal focus are:

1. **Independence**. The allowance of individuals or subordinates within their areas of functioning to have more latitude in scheduling tasks and utilizing discretion in actions to achieve the desired objective. This does not mean the need to alter expectations of desired results. It simply allows the subordinates to achieve goals and objectives through procedures they have determined.
2. **Clarifying Job Expectations**. This refers to the ability of a police primary and secondary leader to express the aims of a task in a manner that will be meaningful to subordinates. Frequently, organizational leaders do not recognize that the perceptual view of workers *versus* management is not the same concerning the organization's goals and objectives. An effective mid-level manager will not only clarify the

task expectations of the functional-level workers but will also provide subordinates with an identifiable perception of how the individuals' efforts fit into the organization's overall achievement of its goals and objectives.

3. **Proper Utilization of Resources (Human & Material).** A leader needs to be aware of the skills required to perform tasks efficiently and effectively, as well as knowing the material resources necessary. The mid-level police manager needs to utilize task assignment to not only achieve results but also to enrich and enhance subordinate job knowledge and motivation. The talents of subordinates can improve, if the varying skills needed to perform different tasks are disseminated in a manner that will improve their capabilities.

4. **Subordinate Interaction.** The degree of decision-making input by subordinates will greatly enhance performance attitude of the workers. Effective leaders at all levels of the organization should, whenever possible, allow and seek the involvement of subordinate workers in the decision-making process. Subordinate interaction improves the chances of successful task accomplishment and enhances their job performances. The allowance of subordinates to have input in their job expectations and task performance procedures has been shown to be a prime motivator of workers. Therefore, communication feedback by subordinates is an essential job enhancement dimension.

5. **Recognition of Job Importance.** Man, as a thinking animal, has a need to achieve and perceive that what he/she is doing has some significance. For example, line workers in an automobile factory exhibited a marked production increase after being shown the finished product and how significant their contribution was to the overall process. We all need to feel worthwhile and that our labors are meaningful. Employees' appraisals can be principal means of demonstrating recognition of work performed. Thus, it is only common sense to recognize that improved job performance or task enhancement will follow a realization of work acknowledgment.

Each leader must be willing to do a self-analysis regarding his or her performance before assessing the work of others. It should be remembered that many of the duties performed by subordinates are the *results of* or *directly affected by* the actions of the immediate mid-level manager. The police mid-level leader must also recognize that personal traits and desires of subordinates will influence job behaviors and performance outcome. Further, a secondary leader needs to remember that appraisals as a tool of management can be invaluable, if properly used. The appraisal phase of the basic assessment of an employee's worth to the organization is the stage at which information is gathered regarding performance behaviors. This information is used to tell both the organization and the employee whether the action of the worker was effective and efficient in accomplishing his or her goal expectations. It also provides a focus for future actions to enhance behavior output.

In concluding this text's discussion on *subordinates' appraisal processes,* it is important to re-emphasize that an evaluation program is particularly valuable as a means of motivating greater efficiency and effectiveness of job performance by subordinates.

SYNOPSIS

An objective measure of job performance is the ultimate goal of all forms of subordinate-appraisal systems. There are very few, if any, jobs in which a mid-level police managers should not be totally objective measures when assessing the performance of subordinates. In those cases where measurable job performances cannot be readily discerned, a subjective leadership rating is used to assess personnel during a normal evaluation periods. However, in situations where negative personnel action will result from a Subordinate's Appraisal Process, it is recommended that documented specifics of behavior be used by the appraiser justify the rating. When developing a subordinate performance evaluation tool, it requires that some factors or standards be used to assess the individual's job behavior. Those standards typically are of two general types: comparative or monocratic. The employee performance in a comparative process will be gauged in comparison with peer-level jobs, etc., while the monocratic process requires that the employee be assessed in terms of a predetermined set of standards. Therefore, the type of appraisal process utilized by a typical police organization will depend principally on the primary purpose of the evaluation and the kind of job being performed. Also, another important consideration when determining the evaluation process that will work best for a particular organization is the extent to which the appraisal process itself is consistent with the demands of the job being performed. It would be idealistic for a police agency to have a different appraisal device for each job, but this is not practical for most organizations. Therefore, as a concession between the idealistic and the practical, most police agencies will utilize the same trait variations for different authority levels and functional responsibility. There will also generally be a variance in the weight factor of each trait assigned. These compromised variations of the basic appraisal instrument/process will usually be limited to a varying number, depending on the size of the organization. Examples, of job responsibilities within a law enforcement operation, which may necessitate a variance in the evaluation process, are the functional-level police officers and the managerial staff. It is clear that the measurable work expectations and performance traits between the two positions differ greatly. Therefore, the assessment measures must also vary. However, in the final analysis the number of variations utilized by an organization will depend largely upon the amount of differences between the types of jobs being rated. A primary focus and concern of an appraisal process is to improve the job performance of those employees being evaluated. This is accomplished through the direct efforts of the appraising leader during the review sessions or follow-up interview encounters. The appraising leader should also inform the counseled employee during, as needed, the review sessions about an unacceptable performance prior to the issuance of a substandard evaluation. During the counseling sessions, the managerial leader's primary aim should be to upgrade the subordinate's job performance. To aid the employee in improving efficiency, the evaluating manager should provide the subordinate with specific courses of actions that will elevate the individual's performance to an acceptable level. An effective supervisor will also not omit praising the good job performance of subordinates. Offering praise and recognition for outstanding work will raise the morale of not only that employee but his or her peers, as well. Employees are far more willing to function at a high level of achievement when they feel that their efforts will be recognized and rewarded by company management. Therefore, improving job performance through an appraisal process is based upon two primary factors, the first being that the improvement of a substandard performance of employees and the second being the morale factor of keeping the efficient and productive employee's performance at an acceptable level. In concluding our discussion on **Subordinate's Appraisal Processes**, it is important to reemphasize that an appraisal program is particularly valuable as a means of motivating greater efficiency and job effectiveness.

Chapter Seventeen

OVERALL PERFORMANCE EFFECTIVENESS (APPLICATION OF DIMENSIONAL TRAIT CHARACTERISTICS)

Operational management as an effective leadership component of a police department cannot be categorized under any one trait or characteristic that is inherent. Proper and efficient management is a series of interrelated skills that are learned and practiced by a person promoted or assigned to a position of operational leadership. But before it can be fully understood as to the detailed essence of operational management from its individual component parts, a comprehensive clarification must be reemphasized as well as the role and importance of operational leadership in a police department. Operational leadership is defined in the dictionary as the process whereby a person in authority directs or controls the behavior and performance of functional resources and/or subordinates' activities. This definition, while accurate and concise, falls a little short when attempting to project a true picture of what is operational management in a police organization. Operational police management includes the guidance of subordinate personnel toward the achievement of departmental goals and objectives by directing and controlling performances and the utilization of resources within prescribed guidelines of functional parameters. It encompasses all elements of the organization and involves such components as the analysis of problems, decision making, planning, organizing, and many other demonstrable skills.

However, for a comprehensive analysis of operational management in a police organization, the text has concentrated primarily on the functional aspects of a primary manager and on the trait characteristics of the measurable skills considered essential for effective duty performance. Thus, in order to initiate an intimate discussion of the component of operational police management, a comprehensive review must be taken of the **areas of responsibilities** for a functioning police manager.

WORK STANDARDS AND
SETTING PERFORMANCE SCHEDULES

Generally, it is a consideration that operational-level police personnel job requirements and basic work objectives are determined by the factors that the individuals encounter on duty and/or the number of directional dictates handled. While there is no denying that there is some truth in the previous statement, it also must be pointed out that the current era of high productivity needs, coupled with a steadily decreasing resource availability in the public sector, has forced a requirement for strong and positive operational management and hierarchical control. Therefore, to obtain a realistic and understandable perspective concept as to what is effective operational management in a police organization, this chapter will identify and discuss various features of work scheduling and performance standards individually.

It should be pointed out that there is no formal systematic or chronological format in which the following component areas are identified or discussed. Each operational police manager or potential positional leader will need to analyze his or her work situation and available resources to determine what will work best. However, it is the author's and many other experts' in the field opinion that each of the listed component areas are important and should be entrenched into the daily performance of each operational police manager.

1. **Establish an alternative time frame for pro-active job performance with consideration for current and projected work load**. By this, the text is inferring that an operational police manager should temper individual setting of performance objectives for subordinate personnel in accordance with a realistic schedule of achievement. It does no good to establish goals and objectives that are unattainable by subordinates, because the priority work load (call-for-services or upper echelon dictates) are too great to allow adequate time for accomplishment. The unrealistic projecting of schedules and performance measures will only serve to reflect negatively upon the subordinates' work output, as well as the planning of needs and allocation of resources by the leader. Remember, the skill capability of an operational police manager and his or her subordinates' performance is on display.

2. **Establish and make known to subordinates specific job requirements and criteria that they and/or functional-level subordinates will be held accountable for prior to their actual job performance**. It has been a practice of some autocratic police managers and positional leaders to make assignments without informing the subordinates of what is specifically desired or necessary to meet objectives. The axiom of "I cannot tell you what I want, but I'll know it when I see it," is totally unacceptable in an effective

and efficient operational police manager. However, even in today's enlightened society, the above is still a truism in some police operations. Decreasing resources and manpower availability in all public sectors, especially law enforcement, makes the time that is wasted doing a job unacceptably a luxury that police departments cannot afford. Operational police leadership personnel are no different from other managers or positional leaders who fail to adequately plan their activity. They have to become proficient at pressure management and are generally considered "crisis managers." And, while it is not a negative to be able to adapt and function well in urgent situations as they may develop, it is a negative, however, if the **urgent situation** or **crisis** arose because the positional leader failed to establish specific requirements or plan performance actions that would have handled the incident before it became a potential problem. Operational police personnel, whether functional or administrative, will generally move from situation to situation, handling them in a perceived-need priority. This normally occurs without much consideration for specific job requirements to accomplish organizational objectives, if the expectations are not made known by the operational manager. An operational manager should not confuse or perceive the establishment of job requirements for subordinates with the fearsome phrase "setting quotas." Here, the author is concerned with the planned usage of allocated resources by operational police personnel, basically toward pro-activity policing functions that will positively affect requested services and/or the overall achievement of goals and objectives of the department.

3. **Allocate work assignments as objectively as possible**. The operational police manager, by way of the chain of command, should whenever possible assure that work load requirements and assignments are allocated as equitably as accomplishment of departmental goals and objectives will allow. It is realized that task obligations will vary from assignment to assignment but that generally the requirement of pre-planned pro-activity performances should be basically the same for all functional personnel. The expectations criteria will of course be exclusive of operational personnel whose assignment precludes their achieving the standardized requirements, except through extraordinary means or efforts. The equitable disbursement of special assignments or duties, whether they are perceived positively or negatively, will provide subordinates with a sense of confidence in the operational manager's fairness. The more unbias that an operational manager is perceived by his or her subordinates, the greater the likelihood that most assignments will be accepted and performed well.

4. **Stay knowledgeably informed of department performance needs and adjust subordinates' work schedules or requirements as needed**. The ever-changing picture of crime pattern and the unpredictability of em-

ployees' behavior makes it essential that the modern-day operational police manager stay up-to-date on the influences affecting his or her operation and the progress of tasks allocated to subordinate personnel. This is accomplished by a conscious effort to stay abreast of the current departmental directive, as well as the strengths and weaknesses of subordinates. This knowledge assemblage should then be utilized to validate the positional leader's current operational plan(s) for mission accomplishment and to adapt work schedules as performance requirements of subordinates' activities toward goal and acquisition. Adaptability in the face of new or additional information is a hallmark of an effective and efficient police manager. The individual should utilize every avenue available to accomplish assigned tasks and to accommodate the welfare and self-esteem of subordinates. The more effective operational police managers tend to have established patterns or time frames to review work output of subordinates and performance progress toward overall goal accomplishments.

5. **Develop alternatives whenever possible to accommodate courses of actions that are likely to require adjustments**. Police actions like most things in life are subject to change depending on circumstances and occurrences. Thus, it's not practical to assume that just because a plan is developed today or yesterday that it will be effective tomorrow. Time and events will dictate needed alternatives to planned courses of actions that an efficient and progressive thinking operational police manager should anticipate. It is not possible for a police manager or anyone else to totally or accurately predict all future operational needs or crime patterns in their area of assignment on a daily basis. However, an operational police manager should be able to look at the demographics, residential stability, and historical crime paradigm of his or her assigned area and from this be able to establish subordinates' directional goals, with appropriate alternatives to handle shifting enforcement needs. Previous concentrations concerning police enforcement needs and functional personnel job performance requirements have shown that malefactors' behavior seemed to be affected by changes in a number of environmental, social, and economical influences. Therefore, it is not practical to assume that an operational manager can preplan functional performance schedules which are not subject to change on a frequent basis. The need to establish long-range schedules is essential to setting performance directions for subordinates, but these future objective requirements can become self-defeating if they are static. An effective positional leader should regularly review work schedules and performance requirements to assure that they are consistently achieving the objectives for which they were established. Also, a positional leader must assure that anychange in the requirements or scheduling of work should be communicated to the workers who must carry out the task.

As can be discerned from the previous information relative to establishing performance schedules and job requirements as an essential component of what may be considered a primary responsibility of an operational police manager, a second area of concern is the relaying of a comprehensive picture of what effective operational management is in a police department. This is perceived as essential, because it involves assuring that each subordinate is made aware of what performance expectations are required to meet the objective. This refers to the operational police manager's staff responsibilities for training, as well.

PROVIDING CREDITABLE AND SUFFICIENT TRAINING

The assuring that all new and incumbent personnel under his or her direct and indirect functional management are totally aware of their duties and responsibilities is a principal task of an operational police manager. This is generally accomplished through timely and purposeful training, either as on-the-job daily activity or a specifically structured and conducted process. As you may be aware, formal training of public law enforcement personnel is provided as a standardized process in most police academies or similar setting. However, as most operational-level personnel will acknowledge, academy training is essential and adequate, but it is only the first step in a functional officer's development. This author can perceive of no other profession where on-the-job-training (OJT) experience is as essential as in law enforcement. Thus, it is the responsibility of the operational manager to assure that procedures are in place for new personnel to receive adequate training. The established training provided should transform these novice law enforcement trainees into fully functional and performing police personnel. Likewise, an operational manager is required to be aware of any deficient knowledge areas in subordinate leadership personnel and to make sure that the **in-service training** needed to correct those concerns are provided. Considering the above stated information concerning a police manager's orientation and training duties, the following are all areas that may be said to be primary to an operational positional leader's responsibility.

1. **Develop a clear plan for articulating the basic duty expectations of subordinates**. An effective operational police manager should through the use of the department's formally structured communicative process, or by an individually established method, clearly define and outline primary duty expectations to subordinates. This process is formally referred to as an orientation, but in reality, it is a training responsibility. This introductory information process is generally provided to newly hired or transferred per-

sonnel by functional-level leadership. However, the information that is in the orientation session must also be known and utilized by incumbent personnel. Therefore, an operational police manager should assure that the orientation information changes or remains current with departmental operating procedures and is maintained in a structured format for ongoing **in-service training**. In order to be truly effective, an operational police manager must pre-plan via functional leadership what information is to be provided to subordinate personnel and then establish a schedule where and when such training sessions are to be conducted on a regular or routine basis. By setting a consistent and frequent pattern of training, the operational leader will assure that valuable operating information is provided subordinate personnel in a timely fashion. This tends to enhance the overall performance operation of the manager's element and reduce personal liability claims of managerial training neglect in litigation involving a subordinate's actions or inaction.

2. **Establish non-extensive tests to verify subordinates' knowledge of departmental directives and indicate training needs to increase employee cognition where required.** It is a common perception that departmental directives exceeding one-half page or more in length are seldom read by the majority of personnel and of the ones that do read them a significant percentage will not get a clear understanding of what is meant. This awareness makes it obligatory that an operational police manager devise a method and a consistent pattern of assuring that informational content and the basic intended meaning of issued directives are clearly comprehended by subordinates. A leader cannot expect adequate compliance and overall objective achievement if subordinate personnel fail to follow issued directives. The determination of subordinates' knowledge concerning departmental directives may be accomplished by simply asking questions or observation as to whether operational dictates are complied with. The author recommends an operational police manager assures that the functional leaders under his or her direction discuss or summarize the contextual implication of new directives with all subordinate personnel. This type of knowledge dissemination assures that each member perceives the same information and that the desired performances by subordinates will be reflective of the dictates set forth by the operational policies or departmental directives. The question-and-answer mode of testing subordinates' knowledge of department policies should be conducted informally, but frequently, by a leader. There should also be some penalty attached for not having knowledge in an area that is considered critical or essential to the subordinates' job performance. These penalties need not or possibly should not be purely punitive in nature but rather should require extra work effort by the subordinate to familiarize him- or herself with the directive's content. Requiring a formally written or

"Fred, what do you suggest we do?"

"I don't know Jim, the leader has always said to await his arrival before taking drastic actions."

EFFECTIVE LEADERSHIP PRACTICES WILL ACCOMPLISH DESIRED RESULTS, EVEN IN THE ABSENCE OF THE OPERATIONAL LEADER.

oral report on the directive to be presented before peers has proven to be an effective inducement. Remember, the more knowledge that operational employees have, the better they perform and the better their performance, the more efficient a functional leader will appear. Thereby, in sequence, the greater the perceived effectiveness of the operational manager.

3. **Cross-training subordinates where possible or necessary**. An operational-level police manager should assure functional training for their personnel in job areas not specific to the individuals' primary duties. This is especially true in situations involving small specialized units. While it is generally accepted that the expertise of a specialist cannot be duplicated without adequate knowledge and skills, a unit or specialized element can continue to operate on a limited basis if members within that element are cross-trained in each other's jobs. This may become necessary in the event of illness, injury, vacations, and a number of other reasons. In operational police work, cross-training of functional personnel is typically not a problem, because an effectively trained patrol officer can be switched from patrol vehicle to patrol vehicle without loss of effectiveness. However, in specialized units where each subordinate has a different duty function, cross-training can become critical. Cross-training, as referred to in this text, does not only apply to an exchange of specific job skills or knowledge. It does relate to a leader's development of an operational system whereby each subordinate has the functional capability or flexibility to perform other corresponding jobs. This interrelated knowledge and performance capability will assure that the unit or element can continue to operate effectively when specific or key personnel are absent. **Anticipation of future needs and planning for them is a vital com-**

ponent of an effective police manager's responsibility, as has been discussed earlier in this text.

4. **Assure the maintenance of an up-to-date departmental directive file and standard operating procedures (SOP) as ready references for subordinate personnel**. Apart from the availability of such material as a training source, the information provided will be handy for positional leadership's reference and guidance when necessary. The advantage of an operational police manager's assuring the maintenance of an accurate depository of functional departmental directives can also be realized by his or her subordinates. The persons needing guidance or refresher information to properly perform a job will be aware of a ready reference upon which they can rely. Subordinates will also perceive that their manager's maintenance of such an informational repository means that he or she has an up-to-date knowledge of SOP's, directives, etc. This perception by subordinates enhances the manager's credibility as the formal hierarchy leader. Most subordinates tend to feel that the formal leader of a unit or element should have adequate operational knowledge about the performance requirements of functional personnel. This perception is enhanced and solidified when subordinates can readily see that the positional leader maintains current and accurate operational documentation and frequently refers to them for information when necessary to assure preciseness of individual actions.

5. **Direct training type leadership in an effort to focus subordinats' goals and actions towad the organization's overall mission**. An operational police manager, through direct or indirect training efforts, should attempt to stimulate and focus subordinates' performances toward the unit's goal accomplishment. It goes without saying that a unit's goals should correspond to the department's principal objectives. This type of specific training effort on the part of operational leadership is needed because most functional-level personnel job performances tend to correlate with Maslow's "Hierarchy of Needs Theory." Thus, to coordinate the employee's personal need fulfillment with department objectives may require a special effort. This can be accomplished by development of subordinates through delegation of authority or assigning duties that will increase the person's job knowledge and performance. Necessary in-service training may also be effectively enhanced through direct efforts, such as explaining and outlining for the subordinates' comprehension as to how increasing their personal skills and performance will better enable need fulfillment. Realistically, there is no specific formula or method that can be outlined that will fit every situation of channeling subordinate development efforts toward accomplishment of organizational objectives. Factors such as individual capabilities and perceived personal need objectives will all weigh heavily on the manager's motivational training

efforts. Therefore, an operational police manager should view each subordinate dealt with individually as to the training required for job motivation and personal need fulfillment. The manager must then attempt to combine those collective training needs into a generic effort to benefit all of his or her subordinates. This should be accomplished without losing sight of the individual action needed for each subaltern employee.

6. **Establish a feedback system, both formal and informal, so that subordinates will keep the operational manager aware of changing conditions, clientele temperament, etc**. A feedback system where functional personnel perceive comfort in informing his or her immediate positional leader that a certain course of action is ineffective would be ideal. Theoretically, this would be ideal in situations and matters where there is time for deliberation and adjustments. But from a realistic perspective, without a special effort as part of the positional leader's training posture, an operational manager should not expect subordinates to readily suggest any functional changes. Inasmuch as such suggestions may be perceived as a criticism of the leader's operational plan, an operational police manager and/or primary functional leadership must project an image of knowledge and confidence in order to be effective in giving directions in a crisis situation. However, at the same time, he or she must make the functional subordinates aware that when situations or circumstances allow, their suggestions and observations are perceived as valuable. Positional leaders typically accomplish this monumental task by implanting into the minds of subordinates that they are knowledgeable of everyday activity; also, that they know basically what's going on and how to deal with it while at the same time revealing that as a positional leader he or she lacks the specific insight or perspective that the personnel handling a certain assignment on a daily basis will have. An effectively operating feedback system enables functional-level employees to feel that they are more a part of the organization. And, it gives them an awareness that their perceptions and ideals are valuable in accomplishing the department's objectives. Remember that workers perform better and more satisfied when they can see how their efforts fit into the overall organizational picture. Thus, an implementation of a formal feedback system into the manager's training efforts is a necessity.

The in-service or day-to-day training provided by a functional police leader is a necessity and must be structured to encompass the areas identified and previously discussed. It would not be possible to adequately fulfill all the descriptive informational requirements as dictated by an operational police manager without a clear reference and discussion of the functional needs of the position. It is evident that a manager's failure to adequately plan and assure execution of appropriate in-service or day-to-day training would be pernicious to his or her leadership position.

The information provided makes it clear that the establishing of work standards, setting performance schedules, and meeting training needs are principal elements to obtaining a true perspective of **"what effective operational police management is."** But primary to a comprehensive view of operational police leadership is an understanding of the **need for** and **how to maintain** quality control of work performances.

ASSURING THE QUALITY OF JOB PERFORMANCES

Achieving a level of work output from a quantitative standpoint is a major measure of a police manager's ability but so too is the quality of the job that is accomplished, because the effectiveness of what is done will often determine the amount of work that is needed. This is best illustrated in the analogy of pulling up a weed but failing to pull out all of its roots, which means that in a few days or weeks the individual will again have to remove the weed because it has grown back. Now, had the individual performed an appropriate job the first time by removing the roots as well, then the effort of repeating the weed's removal could have been avoided.

Previously, in this text we examined some aspects of quality control as a by-product of the job performance control component of effective police management. However, our view of quality control at this point will be structured emphasis which requires work accuracy, as well as an accentuation that desired job performance is essential to a realistic awareness of what the duties and functions are of an operational police manager. To comprehensively discuss how a manager can assure the quality of job performance by subordinates, the process will be set apart in topic areas.

1. **Develop a system where subordinates can assure quality job performance**. An operational manager's need to set into place a method that promulgates the accuracy and correctness with which subordinates have performed assigned tasks. It is generally known that a need exists for the positional leader to establish a format where he or she can routinely check on the performance behavior of subordinates. This was discussed in more detail in Chapter Five of this text, as it is obviously an essential component of effective managerial behavior in a job performance control characteristic. However, there exists a requirement that an internal operational system needs to be established whereby a check of a subordinate's quality of performance can be assessed while the task is in progress. Most leaders in the field of law enforcement will agree that the vast majority of functional-level personnel wants and attempts to do a credible job. This is due in part to the type of person who generally qualifies for the position. The ideal police candidate has

some degree of each of the following traits: (a) career oriented, (b) aggressively self-confident, (c) above average moral standards, (d) a degree of honesty, (e) integrity, and (f) tenacity. Therefore, a person possessing some of each of the above-mentioned qualities will tend, by personality (to some degree), to be a perfectionist, thus enhancing their ability to perform. Hence, an operational police manager's attempts to meet the needs and desires of subordinate personnel in order to fulfill their personal requirements for correctness should set standards and checkpoints for individual self-comparisons. This can be accomplished through specific quantitative goal setting, time frame allotments for completion of phases of the task and quality control standards.

2. **Anticipate review of significant job performances to assure correctness and satisfactory task accomplishment**. An effective operational manager will review assigned tasks as a function of his or her job performance. This process is typically referred to as leadership control and was explored in more detail earlier in this text as an essential component of efficient police managerial behavior. However, in the frame of reference set forth by the term **anticipated** in this section's heading, the text refers to the operational manager's subordinates' expectations that there will be a review of their work. Desired results can be achieved if a functional-level employee expects that his or her performance of assigned tasks will be critically reviewed by positional leadership to insure accuracy of job behavior. Improved performance usually can be anticipated even though the subordinate may know that such a managerial review of significant assignments' progress will occur and serve to prevent serious errors of deviation from desired objectives. The subordinates cannot help but be aware that such a review is an analysis or assessment of performance capability and that the conclusive opinion formed by operational leadership will reflect upon their appraisals. Thus, establishing a pattern of regular and consistent reviews of subordinates' work performances will serve to elevate the employee's task accomplishments. Even at those times when it is not practical to assess performances for corrective actions, the expectations of a review will improve subordinates' work output and reduce the need for definitive corrective actions by functional leadership, etc. Therefore, an anticipated review by subordinates may at times be just as significant as an actual assessment.

3. **Develop patterns or methods of performances that provide sufficient information for job accomplishment**. There are generally always standards and guidelines desired by the delegating person as to expected results. However, with the difficulties associated with semantic and terminology comprehension, can a leader ever be sure that directions given without specific criteria will be followed as desired? For example, as a positional

leader a manager may be very strict and traditionally provide close attention to meeting **due dates, requiring the submission of grammatically correct** and **clerically accurate paperwork**. Therefore, by prior communication of this to subordinates they will know not to submit work to him or her that is deficient in either of these areas. In a similar manner, an operational police manager should establish requirements for what will be acceptable and what will not. In situations of specific job performances and overall work methods, an established pattern must be articulated to subordinates if a realistic expectation of quality task accomplishment can be anticipated at those times when it is impossible to return work for correction of miscues.

4. **Develop a rapport or charismatic approach that will allow performance criticism or corrective actions to be perceived positively**. There is an overall repudiation by subordinates and people in general to being criticized or corrected. Thus, an operational police manager must have established a rapport or behavior pattern that will allow the subordinates to see beyond the negative of work rejection to the effort of overall goal attainment. The problem is that functional-level employees must trust and believe that their primary and secondary leaders have their best interest at heart; also, that the superiors actually understand and care about their needs and desires. An operational manager must then be able to intertwine this perception of subordinates' interest into a need to accomplish the unit's goals and objectives. This is not difficult when the subordinates' "Hierarchy of Needs" correlate with the goal accomplishment of the unit and the organization. The difficulty develops when these needs or desires do not seem to fit well into the unit's methods of goal achievement. An operational police manager must then closely examine each subordinate's needs on an individual basis and then devise a compromise that will achieve departmental objectives while at the same time moving the individual employee toward personal need fulfillment. At first glance, this may sound impossible, but in actuality it is simply a matter of appropriate accolades, assignment, and/or providing the right opportunities; for example, an employee wishing recognition, but his present assignment does not allow for media or public exposure. A recommended transfer or an honest commitment that the operational manager will put extra effort into obtaining the desired assignment when the opportunity develops will boost the individual's personal morale and performance efforts. This morale boost and enhanced performance productivity will admittedly be in an effort to keep his superior's favor to fulfill the pledge. Of course, this type of trust is built over time by an operational manager living up to past commitments and not promising things that cannot be delivered. The previous statement sums up in a concise manner how an effective positional leader can develop the kind of interaction with subordinates that will allow for crit-

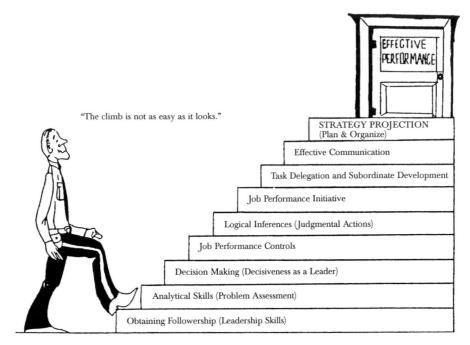

"The climb is not as easy as it looks."

EFFECTIVE PERFORMANCE

STRATEGY PROJECTION
(Plan & Organize)

Effective Communication

Task Delegation and Subordinate Development

Job Performance Initiative

Logical Inferences (Judgmental Actions)

Job Performance Controls

Decision Making (Decisiveness as a Leader)

Analytical Skills (Problem Assessment)

Obtaining Followership (Leadership Skills)

A POSITIONAL LEADER MUST SUCCESSFULLY MASTER THE BASIC "SKILL AREAS" TO ACHIEVE EFFECTIVENESS AS A MANAGER.

icism or corrective action not to always be perceived as a negative overture. The form and manner in which the action is instituted will have a lot to do with the subordinate's attitude. This is not to imply that all corrective actions need to be a soft sell; sometimes a firm or hard approach is necessary and should be used by a positional leader. But it must be remembered that the employee who is being corrected and others who are knowledgeable (e.g., coworkers) should not perceive the action taken as inappropriate or objectionable.

EFFECTIVELY TRANSMITTING AND/OR TRANSLATING INFORMATION

A truly effective operational police manager should be continually aware that he or she is responsible for the accomplishment of unit objectives by subordinates and the use of positional authority to achieve the desired results. As an operational leader, the police manager must also realize an accountability for knowledge of departmental directives affecting his or her operation; also, for the comprehension and transmitting of that information to subordinates. An operational position manager is considered the middle person between the department's upper echelon and the functional-level leadership and workers. Terminology, such as transmitter and translator, has been used by some authors to aptly describe an operational manner relative to his or her position in the organization's informational chain. The operational-level police manager works directly with both functional staff elements and is therefore, in a more conducive position to understand their basic purpose or informational intent. It is a recognized fact that a police organization cannot be perceived as functioning efficiently if either upper management or line personnel are ineffective. Also, the fact should be recognized that the department's functional-level work force and staff hierarchy each operate on a different stratum of informational need. Thus, a comprehensive understanding clarifies the necessity for a go-between. The communication from the upper echelon to the functional level often needs to be formulated into specific information as to individual responsibilities and requirements of line personnel. While communication from functional personnel needs to be transmitted in a manner that is reflective of what is best for the overall operation, the basic problem appears to be that upper echelon tends to think in terms of organizational goals and objectives, whereas a line employee generally focuses on individual performance achievement. Both are positive aspects of overall mission accomplishment; it becomes a matter of exposure and accountability. The effective and knowledgeable operational police manager will comprehend the need difference of the two components and relay information to the respective level in a manner that is conducive for their needs. The information relayed must be understandable to that level without altering the message's basic intent. In other words, the information transmitted should be comprehensively phrased without changing the initial transmitter's intended meaning. The operational manager in many organizations has been referred to as the **"buffer"** between staff leadership and the functional work force. Buffer, as used in the context of an operation leader's role responsibility, means the person's shielding both hierarchical leadership and functional-level employee from the routines of each element's respective operation. The name of **communicator**, which would be more practically termed transmitter or translator, is a primary role responsibility and a basic skill of what we describe as positive leadership ability. The truly effective operational police manager will maintain the balance between superiors and subordinates (direct or indirectly contacted), as well as interact efficiently when dealing with either group. However, to gain the desired perspective of an operational police manager as an informational transmitter, we must separate liaison duties that he or she performs relative to the two entities.

1. **Make sure that subordinates are aware and comprehend departmental directives and plans of operation that effect their element.** Generally, it has been shown that organizational directives that are traditionally issued in memorandums or written orders will be read and comprehended by only a small portion of the operational force, especially if the directive exceeds more than one or two paragraphs. Seldom will an operational order that requires explanation of policies or procedures to achieve its purpose be that limited in content. Departmental directives and procedures are generally written for the **middle of the perceived intellectual level** of all organizational personnel. This means that typically persons at both ends of the knowledge scale are not effectively informed. The person at the low intellectual end of the scale is not effectively informed. The person at the low intellectual end of the scale will tend to not fully understand the directive and thus may miss vitally needed information, while the personnel with exceptional mental abilities will fast become bored because the information presentation does not stimulate intellectual effort. These individuals often show a tendency to skim over the material and also will miss the intent of specific portions of the directives. Therefore, it is a requirement of a competent operational police manager to assure that the pertinent components of all written directives affecting subordinate personnel are interpreted and relayed by functional leadership in a comprehensive manner. This also holds true for verbal directives traveling down the chain of command for functional implementation, because as previously noted, the information needs to be translated into a fashion that the individual officer can utilize, to meet personal obligations in conjunction with the leader's attempts to accomplish overall organizational goals.

Operational plans likewise need to be simplified and presented in a manner that is conducive to the comprehension and use of all functional personnel that a positional manager commands. The efficient and effective operational manager will use some of the methods detailed previously in the chapter to assure that their subordinates are kept adequately informed of departmental policies, procedures, and operating plans. The justification for functional-level personnel being kept knowledgeably by an operational manager can be seen when we recognize that the effectiveness of a positional leader is determined by how well subordinate employees perform.

2. **Develop a procedure and process of keeping immediate superiors informed of his or her element's operation (to wit: operational plans, goal accomplishments, functioning problems, and other actions taken within established positional authority).** It is detrimental to an operational police manager's survival in a structured organizational environment like law enforcement not to keep the agency's hierarchy or his/her im-

mediate superior informed of functional activities. A forwarding of the stated information should include his or her personal actions relative to the use of positional authority in matters relevant to the unit's operation, etc. This text is not attempting to infer that every matter handled, situation addressed, or decision made by an operational police manager should be reported to superiors. However, all actions that affect the overall goal accomplishment of a manager's elements and matters (personnel or operational) that could have an impact on other components of the department should be reported. The establishment of an effective process while still appearing to be a strong self-sufficient manager is accomplished by initially contacting the immediate superior to determine what matters he or she requires knowledge of, etc. Second, an operational police manager should access each individual situation reacted to relative to its effect on the unit's accomplishment of established objectives, thus assuring that all matters of an extreme or controversial nature are brought to a superior's attention. Third, that personnel actions that can or will adversely affect a subordinate's economic status, job tenure, or work performance are included in the established prerequisites for notification of departmental hierarchy. These are but a few very obvious situations and/or circumstances where an operational police manager needs to keep upper management informed.

A police department, more than any other public agency, is answerable to scrutiny as to its actions or inactions regarding the community's interest. There is no other public agency, excluding penitentiaries, by court decree, where a person can deprive another person of his or her freedom and under certain circumstances be sanctioned to take an individual's life as a part of established duties. This alone puts an immeasurable burden on police personnel and department leadership to assure appropriate behavior during the accomplishment of the agency's objectives. Add to the above-stated reasons the fact that over the last decade the number of lawsuits by employees of police departments against the employer has increased dramatically and the requirements for such an established procedure become quite evident.

As previously indicated, an operational manager should when first assigned a specific positional leadership determine through inquiries what the parameters of his or her actions are and what to notify superiors about. The individual should inform subordinates of what situations and circumstances that he or she wants to be notified of. And, finally, as a general rule of thumb an operational police manager should:

1. Adhere to departmental directives concerning notifications;
2. Notify superiors of any matter that may be documented in the media (electronic or printed);

3. Inform higher-ups of all matters that are extremely unusual to normal operational occurrences; and

4. Contact superiors on all personnel matters that may be subject to challenge in court because of a negative effect on a subordinate status (performance or economic). This should also be extended to include positive personnel matters that elevate a subordinate's morale or job performance.

It is easy to tell from the shotgun manner in which these issues have been discussed that relative to this managerial task, a specifically established process that covers every contingency cannot be developed. The very nature of police work and dealing with the various extremes of human behavior precludes the development of more than a general procedure from which the manager can use innate judgment for required action.

The following statement is a **notable commentary** of the contextual need to keep superiors informed of certain actions or situations. Inasmuch as there are matters requiring a decision or recommendation by a police manager, the immediate superior of the positional leader should not be expected to make the decision for the manager involved. In other words, an operational manager should not inquire of supervisors what personal recommendations or actions should be made. A firm decisive commitment is required. Now, should a situation develop where the manager concludes that the advice or thinking of a superior is needed, then he or she should phrase the inquiry as follows: **"Sir or Madame, the situation is . . . and my recommended course of action is . . . I would be interested in your wisdom and insight on this matter as to whether there is a concern or factor that I may have overlooked."** By phrasing an inquiry this way, the manager has indicated his or her decisiveness and willingness to make a decision, but also that he or she is intelligent enough to know that an added insight might improve the decision. More often than not, if the decision was objectively based on fact, the superior will add very little for consideration. It is suggested, however, that this type of inquiry should not be made too often, because it will look as if the manager is unsure and perceives that personal actions should be checked through the boss before implementation. Predeveloped procedures for keeping the boss informed will go a long way toward establishing the effectiveness of an operational police manager.

3. **Be overtly supportive of upper management decisions when communicating with subordinates**. Based on the close working relationship with functional-level personnel, an operational police manager will find it easy to shift the requirements of negative actions onto upper management. For example, a positional leader directing a non-popular course of action by

saying, "You are required to do it this way because my boss or his boss wants it that way." An appropriate leadership approach is to simply say, "This is the way that the task will be performed," or "The effort will better suit the department's overall mission if the task is performed this way, so that is the action to be taken." The reality may be that the task is being done a particular way because that's the way a leader's superior wants, but as a member of the management team an effective operational manager cannot make such statements without damaging his or her credibility as a positional leader. If an operational manager establishes a pattern of these types of comments, then the individual will be viewed by functional personnel as a part of us rather than a positional leader responsible for getting them to do the job. The author, while not subscribing to the **Theory X** perception of employee behavior, does conclude that a feeling us versus **them** does exist between the functional level and the department's hierarchy. Maslow's "Hierarchy of Needs" theory more closely approximates the behavior of most worker-level employees. Even the needs theory sets the pattern for a natural separation of management and labor. Thus, an operational police manager must realize that a personal positional leadership role makes him or her one of the bosses, a member of the management team.

Positional leadership, whether at the top of the department or at the operational and/or functional level, means accepting responsibility for the actions of subordinates and getting objectives accomplished through the work of others. The manager who tries to shift that responsibility to superiors soon will lose the respect of both higher-ups and subordinates. An operational manager who has lost respect soon loses his or her effectiveness as a positional leader. This loss of respect is due to the individual's obvious lack of courage to accept responsibility to get the job done based on his or her own authority and the willingness to assume the negative aspects of positional duties.

To be efficient and effective as a police manager, the individual need not be totally aware of what upper management's objectives for the department may be, but he or she must abide by their decisions and directives to achieve them. And, the leader must communicate managerial policies and directives in a supportive manner. The individual must not relay the decision in a manner that separates or indicates the resolution was made without his or her full endorsement. This is accomplished by stating specifically what the decision is and pointing out, when appropriate, how the change or actions will benefit his or her element and the department as a whole. This is not to imply that an operational police manager or any positional leader should take credit for someone else's idea. But likewise, they should not attempt to divorce themselves from implementation of departmental operational procedures that are unpopular.

Most worker-level employees are susceptible to the influences of their positional leaders (direct or indirect), whether the impression is positive or negative. An operational police manager's affect is magnified when the individual appears to side with functional-level personnel against upper management. This is especially true when the policy or procedure reflects a change that initially is perceived as negative to functional-level need satisfaction. The message conveyed by an operational police manager need not only be by verbal acclamation, it can also be communicated through **body language** or a **tone of voice**. Therefore, when conveying a departmental operating procedure or policy directive, a positional police leader must be aware of all the factors of effective communication and assure that personal actions reflect appropriate endorsement.

Remember, an operational police manager while engaged in or performing positional duties should never attempt to step outside of his or her assigned role. A pattern of this behavior will only increase the difficulty encountered in performing assigned tasks through the work efforts of subordinate personnel.

4. **Displaying an objective image when communicating or dealing with all subordinates is essential.** As noted in a prior statement, if an operational manager's subordinates perceive that he or she is biased against or favors one person over another, that individual's effectiveness and credibility will be damaged. The individuals that conclude that they are not in favor with the positional leader will assume a defensive or protective posture, thus reducing the chances that what the manager states will be positively received. It is a natural concept to feel that if a person does not positively regard you, then whatever he or she implements will not be to your benefit. This innate perception and consequential reaction is detrimental to unit morale and overall effectiveness. An important personal requirement in all workers is a basic need to be recognized and to have his or her efforts appreciated. It is a known fact that employees who are happy with their work environment, leadership, and other aspects of their job tend to be more motivated. And the more motivated an employee is toward job accomplishment, the greater the positive aspects of the individual's productivity and overall work performance.

An efficient and effective operational manager must assure that not only should the assignments given out be distributed objectively but also that his or her verbiage and demeanor reflect impartiality at all times. Obviously, if there is an indication of partiality, then the perception will be a perceived inequity of assigned work despite the actual objectiveness of assignments. The military experiences of two world wars and two (so-called) police actions have shown us that some separation of leadership and workers is necessary for the response and respect for authority that is essential for effective productivity in critical life-or-death situations. Likewise, the mentioned military events have indicated that a total association gap between operational leadership and the work force can be counterproductive. Therefore, a controlled involvement and socialization between an operational police manager and subordinates must be established. This personal interaction must be perceived by each individual as being equally applicable to the whole group. It is a realization that managers are not robots and as such will have likes and dislikes or favorites among his or her subordinates. The essential trick is for the manager not to show it when communicating with any member of his or her element and to transcend personal preferences for effective mission accomplishment. The most complimentary statement that I have ever heard about an operational manager was, **"I know I am not among his favorites, but I can say that he is fair and does not differentiate when it comes to work performance requirements."**

Therefore, an effective and efficient operational police manager must be aware that the perception of subordinates concerning his or her objectivity is just as important as the display and exercise of impartiality. It cannot be stated or emphasized too often that a positional leader is only as effective and productive as subordinates' performances.

5. **Effective operational management will curtail and/or dispel rumors or grapevine information that is untrue and damaging the departmental functioning**. The "grapevine" or "rumor mill" of the department, which organizationally is better known and referred to as **informal communication**, can either be positive or negative to departmental operation. Its plus or minus to the department is mainly dependent upon what information is being disseminated through the process. Most upper-level leaders view the grapevine network as detrimental to effective departmental communication because of the frequency and speed with which information and facts get distorted and disseminated. However, efficient operational police managers can better see the positives that can be obtained from this unstoppable form of departmental communication. Their recognition of the sometimes positive value of the process is attributable to their close association with the personnel who use the informal communication system the most: the functional-level leaders and workers. An operational manager should realize that the system basically exists as an informal link between peer-level personnel and because of the basic communicative nature of human beings. It is a natural and/or inherent desire of employees to receive and pass on perceived unknown or interesting organizational information (real or imaginary). An effective positional leader knows how to use the informal system to receive information not officially distributed and to forward advice or

knowledge that would not always be well received through the formal process.

Just as important as it may be for an operation's manager to utilize the informal system to positively affect communication, it is his or her duty to interject clarity or attempt to put a stop to unfounded or untrue information being disseminated on the "grapevine." It is basically a truism that a lie or scandalous rumor will spread quicker and get more attention than a positive, less spectacular situation about someone or some event. An effective operational police manager, because of personal day-to-day contact with functional-level leadership and personnel, where informal communication is most prevalent, will have access to most rumor information in the system. However, as a proponent of effectively accurate organizational communication and a realization of management's responsibilities, the manager should intervene to correct the misleading or inaccurate information encountered. It is important to note that the manager's intervention and clarification in halting the incorrect information should be accomplished with a great deal of tact and finesse. This approach should be used so as not to damage personal access or unduly influence communication opportunities in the future. An additional concern to the communicative functions of an operational police manager is the staff hierarchy's expectations, which typically calls for the individual to immediately react to put a halt to unfounded or distorted rumor information that might be detrimental to the department and/or its personnel.

As specified and disclosed in the foregoing information regarding a police manager's communicative responsibilities and duties, it is clear that it is an essential component of the makeup of an effective positional leader of operational personnel.

DISCIPLINE AS AN ESSENTIAL FUNCTION

It is a responsibility of an operational police manager to utilize disciplinary action as a functional tool of his or her positional leadership in the organization in order to enforce established employee behavioral requirements. Discipline by a positional leader, whether staff or line, should be viewed as a training device through the use of actions to reinforce appropriate behavior and/or performance. It should never be viewed or used as a purely punitive action to execute punishment for an employee's deviation from the expected norms of the organization. Punitive or punishment actions taken for this purpose is an attempt at retribution for an employee's perceived error or misconduct—in other words, a basic revenge motivation for the disciplinary action. Many positional leaders now realize that penalties administered during their anger or frustration over a subordinate's miscue is for self-gratification, a way of relieving personal hostility over the incident. It is generally a pretext to say that it is for corrective measures; this factor has not gone unnoticed by subordinate personnel. Aware leaders also know that measures taken during a reactive mode is not for training purposes to teach or prevent future like behavior but rather to negatively impact the individual. For the above-mentioned reasons, many parents or authority figures have gotten away from administering immediate physical punishment for upsetting action of siblings, etc., in favor of waiting until anger subsides and deliberation over appropriate action can take place. The author recommends that positional leaders at all levels of the organization should use this approach toward administering disciplinary action.

One of the primary factors that an operational police manager should consider when contemplating what disciplinary recommendation to make may be what is the **best** and least **detrimental action** that can be taken to prevent future like errors or misconduct by the person. The essential point the text is attempting to transmit is that a leader should avoid the overkill approach. Relatively speaking, **why kill a fly with a sledgehammer when a fly-swatter is just as effective and less damaging to whatever the fly has landed on**? The principle applies to disciplinary action, overreaction, and unnecessary heavy-handed punitive measures that can damage morale and alienate a positional leader from subordinates. The damaged morale and disaffection of an operational police manager by subordinates will result in low productivity and substandard performances. All of this could lead to additional negative discipline that will only generate less affirmative behavior by workers, and the cycle will persist until the manager is rendered ineffective as an efficient and productive leader relative to the employees involved or knowledgeable of the events.

It should be noted that the author endorses that the disciplinary action taken should be perceived as the **best** and **least detrimental** for resolution of the problem. The key word here is **best**, because at times, the most effective training measures may call for a heavy-handed disciplinary action. What the author is attempting to convey is that efficient disciplinary practices in a police organization can either be in a **positive** or **negative** form, depending upon which will more effectively foster compliance with established departmental requirements of behavior or performance. As previously stated, **positive discipline** is an affirmative action that is considered favorable to the employee but yet at the same time provides the reinforcement to correct misconduct of deficiencies. It is principally a condition of affirmative training to alter inappropriate and/or to maintain constructively perceived organizational behaviors or performances. This type of discipline, when appropriately applied, is most effective in cases where disciplinary training measures are necessary to deal with error or deviant behavior caused by lack of knowledge, misjudgment, and some form of carelessness. Obviously, it cannot be pinpointed as to when it should be used or under what circumstances the discipline will be most applicable. Factors such as the number of prior incidents, seriousness of the miscue, and the individual's personality will often impact the positional leader's decision. **Negative discipline** is the corrective or training measures employed to correct a misconduct, etc., through the use of actions that will impact the subordinate in a non-positive manner. Negative discipline, by its very nature, is used to be injurious to the employee in some form. By injurious, we are not referring to actual physical damage or pain but how it may negatively impact the employee's economics, future opportunities, or status perception by other department members. The important factor is that negative discipline is a thing to be avoided in much the same manner as a person would avoid walking through fire so as not to get burned. In other words, the unpleasant effects of negative discipline make it a thing to be evaded through appropriate behavior and performances. When the term **discipline** is used, the average person will tend to more naturally associate it with a negative action. Therefore, the concept of "negative discipline" conforms to the more traditional view of a **disciplinary action** taken by an operational police manager. The range of action for negative discipline extends from a warning to a forced loss of employment.

In most police organizations, the operational managers are allowed to execute up to a verbal or written reprimand without superior or upper management approval. But actions such as position transfers, economic sanctions, etc., where causation records will need to be maintained in the employee's permanent file, may need the endorsement from top echelon because of the potential effect and/or consequences to the person and the department. But the essential thing for a positional police manager to remember is that no matter the nature of the discipline used, it should be implemented with the perception of being a training tool to correct whatever inappropriate behavior is under consideration.

As has been stated by the author in a previous context, unlike the misconception of who is primarily responsible for finding a cure for an employee's personal problem, it is clearly the responsibility of the operational police manager and/or functional leader to enforce the guidelines of the organization. These guidelines are usually set forth in written directives, such as procedures, policies, or various types of documented orders. The requirements of enforcing compliance or assuring objectives are met then become a prime function of the primary positional manager or operational-level leader. There are certain criteria and standards of operation that an effective operational manager will observe when administering appropriate discipline. Principal among these objectives are:

1. **Assure that established departmental directives for administering discipline is invoked uniformly**. The general concept of discipline, whether positive or negative, is that it should be appropriate, timely, and specific to the misbehavior. In addition, it should be dealt with in much the same manner as **work assignments**; that is, it should be applied objectively and impartially without personal considerations or bias. A major factor in the effectiveness of discipline is the officer's perception of its applicability to everyone and the appropriateness to deal with the violation. If the areas cited above are known to be entrenched into the manager's application of discipline, his or her subordinates will be much more inclined to accept a disciplinary decision without it adversely affecting morale and/or productivity. However, if there is the slightest concept that there are antagonistic motives to the manager's actions or recommendations, then a counterproductive reaction will develop. In other words, a person will be much more receptive to disciplinary action if he or she feels the same standards and efforts are applicable to all other department members; also, if the manager's motives for the act are not personally motivated or slanted for some reason.

The need for a perceived uniformity in administering discipline is necessary if the desired effect is to be achieved. As has been previously stated, **discipline is a training tool** of management and should be used only for that purpose. Therefore, if the actions taken to correct or prevent a reoccurrence of an error or misconduct is not uniformly applied, then the primary purpose will not be achieved. A functional-level police employee is like any other animal: if he or she is beat often enough for little or no reason, then the beating will soon become meaningless and thus will lose its effectiveness. However, as reasoning and thinking animals, human beings are able to avoid the personal anguish of discipline through the evasion of certain actions that will bring about its implementation. But an unbiased objectivity is essential to the workability of any training effort, including discipline. The perception of fairness and objectivity is critical in the management of police personnel because of the nature of law enforcement and the self-assertiveness that the job requires. It is a clear fact that anything less than obvious uniformity and non-discriminatory discipline will negatively affect the officers' behavioral performances.

The effective and efficient operational-level police manager will be aware of the aforementioned conclusions and assure that his or her disciplinary actions or recommendations are unencumbered by personality or inequitable application. A functionally effective operational positional leader should also document and maintain a record of disciplinary action taken.

2. **Assure that the articulation of established departmental procedures will be utilized for recording and maintaining documented disciplinary actions**. To be truly effective as a deterrent or training tool, disciplinary actions, especially negative types, should be implemented on a **graduating scale**. By graduating scale, it is meant that the minimum disciplinary action considered necessary to effect a change is initially applied, with the severity of the training exploits increasing with each repetition of the misbehavior. In other words, if a person is late without a valid reason, the first occasion would result in a verbal warning, the second such occasion would graduate up to an oral counseling, the third to a written reprimand, and so on. The graduating effect will, theoretically, deter future violations of the same or similar nature. However, it should be stated that for any corrective actions to be effective, it must be clearly articulated to all departmental personnel. These expressed departmental policies and procedures for administering discipline must be adhered to by the positional leader who recommends or implements the actions. It must be remembered that an employee's violation of an unknown or unestablished policy is comparable with a person committing a crime that has not been documented or listed as an offense until after it has been committed. Generally, an action can be recognized as wrong, but if not documented there is no basis for formal punitive or corrective actions. Therefore, it is incumbent upon the operational police manager to assure that departmental directives and procedures for dealing with violations are clearly identified to subordinate personnel. An efficient and effective police manager must be aware that it is not only essential to make the procedure known but also that record keeping of noted violations are just as important. In this societal age of the sue-prone mentality of workers, it is essential that documented facts attest to all actions that may adversely affect an employee's economic and/or job prospects, etc. Most managerial or leadership schools will foster maintaining a personal notebook of interactions with subordinate personnel where corrective comments or directions are issued. This is usually in conjunction with whatever formal documentation process is set into place by the department. However, it must be noted that if the formal documentation is complete, accurate, and permanent, then a personal note file is less important. This author recommends, however, that a current, accurate, and comprehensive personal note file be maintained in addition to the department's formal process. This personal note file maintenance should be articulated to a positional leader's subordinates from the beginning, thereby eliminating any misconception that the positional leader is maintaining some type of secret diary to use against them.

Therefore, from the foregoing information, it is readily understandable why establishing departmental policies and procedures must be conspicuously articulated to subordinates, and that the record keeping for disciplinary actions must also be accurately and comprehensively maintained in an atmosphere of general awareness. This does not mean that each subordinate or the particular violator should be specifically made aware of what the manager's file notes state, but each should be aware that on the occasion that the operational manager takes corrective actions for misbehavior or conduct, the event and actions taken will be documented, both formally and informally, in his or her note file. It must be made clear that the documentation referred to should not affect whatever actions the manager deems necessary to appropriately deal with the problem or situation.

The author has chosen not to attempt to deal with the various levels or types of discipline used by police managers. It is perceived that it is an area best left to the individual department through written directives. However, the basic ingredients for making a disciplinary decision were discussed in the chapters detailing the component characteristics of managements, such as decision making, logical inferences, and obtaining followership.

OPERATION STRATEGY AS A LEADERSHIP CONCEPT

When we begin to consider the leadership concept associated with operational mid-level management, the central core of an operation must be analyzed. The foundational essence of a systematized performance program can be broken down into various subsystems or processes, which make up a productive plan of action. The operational mid-level police manager's performance capability falls within his or her ability to manage workers, material resources, and time requirements into an appropriately producing system. The concept being referred to is an overt ability to structure resource input (human and material) to meet service expectations. If viewed from a clinical perspective, this process is generally considered to be the foundational core of operational leadership for a mid-level police manager.

The integration of a production system into the operational aspects of an organization should occur at all levels of the organization, but the mid-level police leadership is the point where it will be most visible. A planned use of manpower and material resources is certainly more productive than a haphazard reactive approach to functional occurrences and events. It must be recognized that every functional/operational problem or concern cannot be anticipated by a leader. However, a planned process that considers and allows for both expected and unexpected occurrences will enhance a primary police leader's performance ability. To better understand the concept of a production system from a mid-level leader's perspective it may be better to consider the whole picture or the results as a total process. An overall view of the process rather than a consideration of each part and then the sum total should provide a better perspective of a mid-level manager's performance. By this, it is meant that it may be more conducive to view the whole picture intact as opposed to analyzing component parts that combine into a finished output system. Perhaps Russell Ackoff said it best when he identified an operational system as: "A system is a whole that can not be taken apart without loss of its essential characteristic, and hence it must be studied as a whole. Now instead of explaining a whole in terms of its parts, parts begin to be explained in terms of the whole." This concept from the study of system theory, as it relates to mid-level police leadership as a service industry like public law enforcement, may be helpful in understanding a mid-level police manager's operational strategy concerning production as a system. Norman Gaither defined Production System as a "system whose function is to convert a set of inputs into a set of desired outputs." Both operational strategy and production systems are important concepts to the functional mid-level police manager. They are intangible relative to quantitative measurement of services provided. They possess no physical form in relationship to goods and services. These processes must be perceived in terms that they cannot be physically stored or possessed, and their consumption is usually at the same time as their production. The formation of functional strategies has been assessed as the starting point for determining operational plans of action. The determining of functional strategies clarifies the basic structure of the production system. All of the other elements of an operation strategy must sequence from the decision relating to the type of service provided toward the final results or accomplishments. The actions of the middle manager of a police operation must assure a cohesive match between strategy and system at the functional level.

Mid-level leadership as emphasized throughout this text is more than a physical hands-on type of worker management. It is also a mental attitude and a focused desire to identify and follow through with the non-tangible aspects of productive managerial performances.

IDENTIFYING LEADERSHIP PERFORMANCE ACTIONS

The leadership performance skills required for a mid-level police manager to be effective are many and varied. Leadership theorists do not agree on any one set of performance skills required for the operational mid-level manager to be effective as a leader. However, there are several skills that most theorists will agree could be considered essential to an efficient and effective leader. These skills are:

1. Communication skills (sending and receiving information);
2. Good judgment (making logical, well-founded choices);
3. Planning and organization (developing a strategy to accomplish a task and implementing a workable course of action);
4. Delegating skills (assigning tasks that may be more effectively handled by a subordinate and will enhance his/her skills);
5. Decision-making skills (deciding courses of actions based on influences and available information);
6. Problem analysis skills (the ability to dissect a situation or concern and develop a logical solution);
7. Management control (utilizing adequacy of information, due dates, and follow-up dates to assure desired results);
8. Command presence (projecting a perceptual ability to lead);
9. Human behavioral skills (displaying maturity, interpersonal sensitivity, adaptability, enthusiasm, patience, etc.).

As can be seen by the above condensed list, the leadership skills needed to be an effective mid-level leader are vast in scope. A supervisor who is viewed as a **multidimensional performance leader** will traditionally operate effectively.

The leadership performance of a mid-level police manager is said to be the *identification, evaluation,* and the *affecting of performance tasks of subordinates,* whether preferred or undesired. It involves the task performance of subordinates to obtain a clear perspective of their job behaviors by their immediate superior.

A leader's performance skills are generally assessed to acquire knowledge and evaluate why relevant behaviors occur and to determine the interaction of the various skills of a mid-level police leader. To adequately analyze the performance leadership skills of a mid-level police leader, we must consider the motivations that affect human behaviors. A majority of persons let influencing motives affect virtually every aspect of their behavior. Thus, a standardization of perceptual performance limits must be articulated before a leader's behavioral skills can be identified. Kepner-Tregoe said, "Analyzing human performance is done by using Antecedents-Behaviors-Consequences (ABC) analysis. ABC analysis is the consideration of events that precede pinpointed behavior (consequences) to try to determine the cause of the behavior." Simply stated, assessing leadership behavior should be based on an analysis of the situation that requires action, the action taken, and the resulting consequence of the action.

A mid-level manager's performance behaviors may best be explained in terms of the leader's perceptual role expectations relative to job responsibility. Every police mid-level leader is expected to provide leadership for all subordinate personnel, but the personal consideration of what one believes his or her functional duties to be may be inseparable from actual performance. Therefore, if a person is to be considered an effective leader, he or she must possess such behavioral traits as honorableness, courageousness, and the capacity to grow and develop as a leader, in addition to a personal motivation to succeed. Also, it has been concluded that an effective mid-level police manager should display reasonable intelligence that is combined with a degree of common sense. An individual leader should demonstrate that he or she is persuasive, yet flexible, if the particulars of a situation change. Knowledgeable management theorists have indicated that efficient and effective leadership skills are not inborn traits but are generally learned and developed. It is said that anyone who possesses a self-assured personality and a degree of assertiveness can develop the skills to be an effective leader. A developing leader should cultivate the capability to adopt and adapt the desirable leadership traits observed in others to their own individual style. By so doing, the person can develop the skills necessary to be an efficient and effective mid-level police leader.

GENERAL PERFORMANCE BEHAVIORS

As a general rule, mid-level police leaders have what may rightfully be termed an inherent position expectation to inspire subordinates through the use of positive incentives and job challenges that will encourage enhanced job performance. It is generally recognized that most persons want to be perceived as achievers and have desires to maintain a high level of performance efficiency. An effective leader should provide subordinates with an opportunity for personal and professional growth within the organization. Persons of all levels of the organization need to feel that they are progressing toward an attainable personal and/or professional goal objective. An effective mid-level police leader can aid subordinates to achieving desired objectives by providing appropriate information, encouragement, and effective leadership practices. As a positional leader within the organization, a mid-level police leader must attempt to overcome a personal resistance to change that may at times be an impediment to efficient operation of the unit or organization. There should be a total and comprehensive effort put forth by the mid-level police leader. No detail or task influence should be overlooked or bypassed, despite its magnitude or lack thereof, if it affects the leader's subordinates' performance. A leader at any level of the organization must give careful consideration and performance efforts, whether or not he or she agrees with the concept of directed performance action. The moral standard that is expected of a mid-level police leader is no different for a leader than for any other member of the organization. But certainly a person in such a position of leadership must continually uphold elevated morality, both personally and professionally. The quality expectations of a mid-level police manager are compatible with the leader in other fields of employment.

WORK ATMOSPHERE/ENVIRONMENT

Much has been written and emphasized about the atmosphere of leadership and the trait characteristics of effective leaders. The nature and complexity of public law enforcement requires leaders in the field to be especially conscious of work environment. The work environment as referred to in this text has to do with the performance atmosphere created by mid-level leaders. Since the early 1950s, many studies have referred to the importance of the work environment established by leaders. The influence patterns and undeniable effect that mid-level leadership or primary management has on the work environment is readily visible. Most, if not all, employees' performance effectiveness in the work setting can be directly linked to the job environment created by the first line supervisor or primary manager.

Recent research studies regarding employee performance and productivity seems to focus on the leader as the prime influence factor. During the 1950s and 1960s, major job performance studies seemed to focus on the workers. In other words, a *worker-centered focus* has been replaced by a *leader-centered focus* concerning performance expectations and production output. This is also true for policing, even though law enforcement is considered a service rather than a product producer. Police mid-level managers cannot be isolated from the same factors or attributes that's associated with product management leaders. The *leader-centered approach,* when analyzing a primary police leader's effectiveness, must not be limited in scope regarding the productivity of operational employees. A product-producing leader is generally assessed by such traits as initiative, interactive dominance, and tenacity. But the effective police leader will have to be more versatile because the clientele of law enforcement is not a constant. Therefore, a worker's efforts to effectively perform must also be adaptable. The need-varying performance efforts and the uncertainty of end results require the mid-level leader to be much more than an enhancer of work output. As noted earlier, there is no universal list of trait characteristics that can be formulated for a mid-level police leader. The individuals who conclude that a standardized list is possible, if the list is comprehensive, have failed to consider the possibility that different circumstantial events will require a trait focus specific for the situation. Circumstantial events may at times require very little in terms of managerial input, while at other instances performance actions could necessitate an autocratic type of leadership control. Thus, the work environment created by a mid-level police leader must be fluid to deal with shifting concerns, but yet stable enough for subordinates to be confident in the consistency of leadership. Most workers, when asked *what they felt was the most important characteristic in a leader's dealing with subordinates answered that they felt the leader must be fair and consistent in his or her dealings with subordinates.* It was felt that subordinates needed to be able to perceive an expectation of the mid-level leader and to positively anticipate actions or reactions. Thus, the aspect of work environment created by a mid-level police leader is quintessential for effectiveness of subordinates and in turn to line management.

LEADERSHIP CONTROLS EXERCISED
BY A MID-LEVEL LEADER

The possession and use of positional power by a mid-level police manager has and will continue to be discussed throughout this text. The exercise of control by a leader is not an easy concept to articulate or visualize by researchers and other knowledge seekers. The term leadership tends to mean different things to different people, as does the consideration of authority and control by positional leaders throughout an organization. This is especially true in the field of public law enforcement, where much of an officer's action is not under the watchful eye and control of primary or secondary leadership. Thus, leadership and control must be exercised prior to and after action situations regarding much of a subordinate's functional duties. In order to gather a prospect of the various aspects of a leader's exercise of power over subordinates that are considered self-motivated, energetic, and committed workers, we should look at the proposed research of John R.P. French and Bertran Raven. They, as social scientists, theorized that there were several major sources of power exercised by leaders. The author has taken the basic essence of their proposal and applied it to leadership in operational mid-level police management. Initially, the concept of Incentive Dominion as a concept in mid-level police leadership means the leader has the ability to compensate another person for performing a desired task(s) in a specified manner. The reward may be real or simply an assumption. It will, nevertheless, produce results. Incentive type rewards, whether monetary or some other form of positive compensation, will have a limited life span as an inducement for task accomplishment and will need to be continually upgraded, which may not be practical in today's atmosphere of declining budgets, etc. Incentive rewards must be properly timed, as well as being continuous as articulated above. Coercive Dominion affects behavior through the ability of the leader to punish or perceptually harm an employee (negative discipline). It is the perceptual force or use of power to intimidate or manipulate tasks through threatened consequences. It is this aspect of a leader's use of authority that offers an employee no perceptual choice of behavioral performance, results, or task accomplishment. Desired results are achieved or the worker will receive a negative sanction. Legitimate Dominion suggests it is an attribute of legal and rightful achievement. To a leader, the legitimate authority is positionally placed and he or she exercises control by virtue of the delegated right of power granted by the organization's hierarchy. Functional-level police generally have a cognitive recognition that concedes that people placed in leadership positions have the right to give orders and expect compliance by subordinates. Law enforcement personnel are traditionally conservative in their approach to life and their jobs. Therefore, it would be unusual to consider that subordinates would rebel in any form to the direction of a positionally placed leader. Leaders must therefore be aware that inappropriate actions as a leader may be very disruptive and damaging to the morale of subordinates. Reference Dominion or the authority to manipulate others is another source of classifying power exercised by a police mid-level manager. This may be in the form of charisma which may be used to get desired behavioral responses because of a perceptual liking or positive consideration by subordinates. The charismatic leader can affect sweeping actions by subordinates if he or she recognizes this personal characteristic and seeks to augment it with leadership knowledge to positively inspire followers, admirers, and devotees. The reference leader should also realize that his or her actions serve as a model for subordinates and the measure by which an organizational leader will be gauged. This type of leader must assure that all personal actions are within the scope of his or her authority and for the positive achievement of organizational goals and objectives. Skill Dominion is the authority or power that is associated with job knowledge. This form of directive control tends to form around leaders that have shown a superior job knowledge that others do not seem to possess. This perceptual superior's job knowledge are learned skills that the leader has generally labored long and hard to obtain. The having and sharing of perceived superior job know-how is restricted to what is viewed as an expertise in the area of focus and based on trust by subordinates in the leader's performance ability.

The Skill Dominion leader should also be aware that his or her perceived expertise may not only be presumed by subordinates in the area of actual job knowledge but assumed to exist in other areas as well. Thus, the leader must

A LEADER MUST RECOGNIZE THAT THE WORK ENVIRONMENT IS ESSENTIAL TO EFFECTIVE EMPLOYEE PERFORMANCE AND MOTIVATION.

assure that the accuracy of information shared is in all areas so as not to damage subordinates' perceptions of his or her expert knowledge in the arena of actual job know-how. Lastly, the area of Presumption Dominion suggests that a leadership or administration which is based upon coercive force is viewed as illegitimate by those who are controlled. Moral authority appears to have the staying power to keep subordinates manipulatively under control.

The positional leader who has a little power, but can generate an illusion that he or she has a great deal, will frequently be as effective as the leader who possesses the real or actual power. Thus, it is sensible in police mid-level management to attempt to create the impression of absolute power, which at its best is undetectable by subordinates. As an effective leader you must be ready to take action or to project actions that will enhance the perception of your dominance as a leader. Remember that leadership power can be dangerous if it is perceived as being non-existent or very limited regarding a positional leader by subordinates. This perception, whether real or imaginary, may lead to inappropriate actions or reactions by subordinates which may tear a situation to shreds and reduce a mid-level leader's power to ineffectiveness.

EMPLOYEE MOTIVATION AND HANDLING

Relative to all of the areas that should be examined concerning an operational police manager's trait characteristics as an effective and efficient midlevel positional leader, none could be considered more critical than the motivation and handling of subordinates. However, since the basic scope of this text has been written and expressed in terms of a leader's interaction with subordinates, it would be redundant to state here what is interwoven throughout this book. Thus, it appears appropriate by stating the following: **The traditional aspects associated with an operational manager's directing and controlling of the behavior of subordinate personnel via functional leadership are directly attributable to the dimensional trait characteristics discussed. Typically, appropriate employee actions are inspired through motivation or behavior modification and directing efforts through the use of sanctions by the leader. Of all the components and dimensions described and analyzed in this text, the associative aspects of dealing with subordinates is certainly the most important and critical to an operational midlevel manager, relative to a police department's achievement of its goals and objectives.**

Chapter Eighteen

PROJECTING AN EFFECTIVE LEADERSHIP PERSONALITY

To begin our discussion of what Leadership Personality image a mid-level police leader should project in his or her role as an effective manager, we must assess each component separately as to their foundational meaning when applied in a management setting. **Leadership** as a term has been studied and utilized in so many fashions that the use of the word in a managerial or organizational environment almost becomes self-explanatory. We then move to the term **Personality**, which can simply be set-forth as the individualized behavioral traits of a person in response to a situation or influence action. When considering mid-level police management, we must combine Leadership and Personality to get a useful grasp on what is being discussed and what is the significant of establishing an effective Leadership Personality for a managerial leader. Consequently, it should be noted for consideration at this point, that **Approach** as used in this text, often stresses the manner or method of beginning, especially one calculated to evoke a certain response or a desired effect. The reader should also understand that in this text, Approach and Style, as they apply to leadership, do not have the same connotation or meaning. Approach, as used in this text, refers to method or consideration that one uses to formulate the actual way that his or her leadership style or mode of expressing functional traits will be originated.

The clinical definition of leadership personality must then be grasped and conveyed relative to the desired behavioral traits as essential performance characteristics to achieve managerial effectiveness. Typically, when discussing management the term is used in many contexts related to a person's trait skills to affect or lead others; also the term is utilized to refer to attributes that project or convey an image to superiors, peers, and subordinates. Thus, we can infer from the above that leadership personality as a stand-alone phrase is a concept related to behaviors that project a desired image to others. Some theorists have conjectured that it is not totally feasible to clinically define leadership personality in the absence of considering the scope in which the individual's personal characteristic is being viewed and by whom.

We have discussed to some degree in a prior chapter and later in this text leadership styles and why a managerial leader should choose the best one(s) for his or her effectiveness. Consequently, the author has attempted to project a leader's personal behaviors (personality) as a subjective factor in a mid-level police manager's formulation or development of his or her functional approach. It is recognized that a person's biological makeup such as voice, intelligence, physical build, etc. generally cannot be altered. Therefore, these factors, the person's positional situation, and certain other influences will impact the image or approach that the mid-level police manager should use to be effective. It is continually repeated in discussions regarding leadership and management that "Personality Traits" of people involved in the managerial behavioral will always impact the directing person's effectiveness and that "**leaders are made not born.**" In other words, individuals with basic personal characteristic can be taught and learn to be an effective leader. Obviously, a person blessed with what we term as natural charismatic projection or an appearance of forceful dominance will have an edge toward becoming a leader, but those factors alone will not ensure that the person will be an effective leader. Thus, a person who is perceived to have average attributes but is aware and displays the dominant skills of a leader is much more like to achieve leadership effective.

To further grasp the importance and critical nature of developing an effective leadership approach, we must explore the primary concept of the personality that a managerial process should consider. The concern here is not to project any specific action that should be taken by a person in a directing or controlling position. The basic criteria being referred to here is the self-image of the individual and what perceptions conveyed to others will affect his or her leadership characteristics. Virtually, everyone has some kind of self-image of the way he or she should behave in a certain position and the stated perception has been identified as the person's functional concept. The individual may also recognize that he or she does not function in isolation; therefore, the actions taken by him or her will influence the behavior of others. From the in-charge projection of the person's actions, the subordinates, peers, and superiors that he/she interacts with perceive an image of leadership effectiveness, etc.

Personality characteristics being addressed in the context of the personal concepts that an effective mid-level police manager should project and utilize when interacting with others is a continuously evolving process. No mystical or dynamic formula for developing into a productive managerial leader exists. Managerial leadership is a committed task requiring a dedicated effort that has various duties and obligation changes that mandate desired behaviors. When we talk about effective leaders being made and not born, this does not mean that everyone possesses the personality characteristics to be efficient as a leader or manager. For example, some people who are extremely introverted, immoderately shy, psychologically or emotionally not equipped will not deal well in directing and controlling other as an effective leader. Thus, everyone cannot be taught to be an effective leader. In reviewing a number of theories regarding management, some theorists have observed and conjectured that it would be a great boost to the study of leadership if someone could conceive of a method to identify early authoritative characteristics in individuals that would reflect potential for success as a managerial leader.

Mid-level police management is the focus ability to control and direct the task behaviors of others toward specific goals and objectives. It is clear in our concept that management and leadership are so closely related that they can be and are used interchangeably in this text. Consequently, leadership and management reflect the dynamics of the interaction of a leader's functioning and his or her subordinates' reaction. Therefore, as we set-forth discussing Effective Leadership Personality as an essential performance approach, that should be considered and established by mid-level police management, the dynamics of the terms must clearly be understood.

DEVELOPING A PRODUCTIVE PERSONALITY APPROACH

Every mid-level police manager should establish an organized and formatted program that clearly projects his or her personality approach to leadership. The directed behavior set-forth should be structured in an easily understood projection of the personal procedural approach the he or she will employ. The hierarchy of each leadership characteristic to the systematic managerial aim should be understandable to each subordinate. The need for an effective action must be established to insure appropriate leadership in all situations. Also, the collectiveness of a leader's personality approach to effective leadership must be based on the available information and management style that will foster subordinate coordinated actions toward productive and measurable results.

Managerial approaches have been described and defined in many ways during the past several decades. There have been several insightful studies regarding the various aspects relative to the Principals of Management. However, it appears clear that a mid-level police manager's leadership and attributes associated with and individual personality characteristics greatly influence his or her performance abilities. Thus, a mid-level police manager must continually strive to understand what inherent tendencies that he or she should to develop and maintain for a continuously effective functional leadership approach. Therefore, a position ally placed leader who functions with any degree of effectiveness must have some kind of self-concept of the image that he or she projects and recognize how those actions will affect the behavior of subordinates. Such a self-perspective or concept will more readily focus a functional performance approach that will enhance the individual's effectiveness as a managerial leader. A mid-level police manager should also be aware that others (superiors and subordinates) would also perceive an image perspective and expectation from the projected behavioral approach of the leader. The personal behavioral expectations of the manager and others interacted with are critical to the self-analysis that a leader must consider before formulating the leadership personality or functional approach that is most conducive to his or her trait characteristics.

Some other leadership theories have set-forth the concept that: (1) management is a product of its environment; (2) management must inter-relate with superiors and subordinates; and (3) managerial leadership occurs primarily in operational situations that will affect a leader's personality approach. Consequently, managerial behaviors occur whenever these factors encounter one another in an organizational setting. However, the views of the theory stated above are limited and will therefore offer a more expansive and believed better perspective as to the aspects of an effective leadership personality, as they apply the mid-level police management.

Management is a product of its environment. There is virtually no aspect of managerial leadership that excludes a great deal of personal or introspective consideration and environmental interaction by the leader involved. This is even more so concerning a mid-level police manager because of the nature of his or her job and the expectations of what performances that should be obtained from subordinates. It is important to recognize that interpersonal expectations are acquired through a leader's need for self-gratification and previous influences fostered by the anticipations of his or her environment. Perhaps the most important aspect of the interpersonal influence on a manager's leadership personality depends upon prior successes or failures as a leader. As an example, if we consider the performance of a beaver building a dam, if the dam is washed away during the first heavy rain, it is only natural that the next dam built by the beaver will be constructed to withstand the force of a heavy rain. Similarly, if a managerial leader's actions or the personality projected in a prior situation were not effective, then we would anticipate that future procedural behaviors would account for the prior failure as well as the expectations to deal with predictable concerns. Thus, it should be clearly understood that a manager's personal approach to leadership is significantly influenced by his or her self-concept perspective and prior experiences.

Management must interrelate with superiors and subordinates. A simple consideration of the functional aspects of mid-level police management clearly reflects that it is essential that an effective managerial approach must be formulated to be interrelated with the goals and objectives of the organization. This is made plainly evident by defining the functional aspects of police leadership at all levels of the organization. Many of the trait characteristics affecting a leader's personality have been stated and delineated in numerous managerial studies in the past and therefore will be only be limitedly articulated in this text. Several of the more notable factors that influence a leadership personality are *resource management, communicating, coordination,* and *strategy development.* A few other traits that this author views as significant to the ability of a leader are *implementation of plans of action, directing, controlling the behavior of others,* and *team working with other organizational elements.* From the functional responsibilities set-forth above it is evident that any effective personality approach contemplated by a mid-level police manager must positively interact within the organization. Consequently, considering a systematic procedure for the development of an effective personality approach to managerial leadership may be most feasible concerning the interrelated aspects of organizational mid-level police management.

Managerial Leadership occurs primarily in operational situations that will affect a leader's Personality Approach. Principally, middle-level police managers operationally function within an environment that is clearly aligned with a formalized Autocratic Leadership Structure. Most semi-military edifices such as police agencies are interactively connected, even if the link is buffered by several other elements. The focused aim of the organization is the same and is dependent on many of the same resources. Plus, underlying the comparability of the organization's goals and objectives is that each component of the agency is ultimately governed by the same set of rules and guidelines. Further, the availability of subordinate resources for each element of a police agency is obtained from the same pool of selected employees. Therefore, managerial or leadership encounters will always fall under the structural guidelines and focused aim of the organization. And as such, any functional task approach implemented by a police leader is job related and should be considered as procedurally linked and governed by the organization's guidelines for achieving its goals and objectives.

BASIC APPROACHES TO FORMULATING A MANAGER'S PERSONALITY

The principal areas from which mid-level police manager should obtain his or her procedural process for developing an effective leadership personality approach is derived from managerial actions. Several of the most notable efforts that pertain to the establishment of a course of behaviors akin to leadership performances are (1) **projecting employee interactions**, (2) **providing operational support**, (3) **emphasizing goals and objectives**, and (4) **facilitating task accomplishments by subordinates**. The aforementioned processes should interact quite smoothly with the (so titled) "Five Approaches to Leadership" which were set-forth by Fred Romanuk in his Internet published article, dated 19 April, 2010. Romanuk in his writing indicated that the insight for the article was developed over 30 years of reviewed information and his participation in Leadership Development Training. The article's first area noted and addressed "The 'Learning About' Leadership Model" with adjective information. This author believes that "Knowledge about Leadership" would be a key component in the development of an effective managerial process to the establishing of a realistic and workable stylized approach to management. Second, he indicated a program used by many to enhance performance behaviors as a manager; this concept involved emergence of the developing manager into the problem, apparently a sort of sink or swim approach to knowledge acquisition. This process has been the principal method used since the first person took the role of leading and directing others. In a more basic context, it is a trial-and-error method of deciding and utilizing whichever action best gets the job done. The third area addressed referred to "Learning the Gaps" which was viewed by the author as referring to strategic knowledge gains referred to learning about problems that confront management as a method of developing a leadership awareness to formulate a leader's personal approach. This involves the concept of observing; analyzing and then implementing appropriate behaviors as a process of learning management. Unlike the pure trial-and-error process, the method seems to involve watching the on-going interactions and assessing which best solution will resolve or effectively deal with the situation before any managerial actions is taken. It appears basically to suggest that before the job performance behaviors a leader will use this technique of experience comprehension as a method of deciding an effective management approach to leadership. As with the trial-and-error process, the "Learning Gap" method must plan for and implement some form of adjustment or adaptability to ensure optimal results. Romanuk's fourth area associated the most preferred method of developing a personal leadership approach through teaching and learning. It involves information acquisition from knowledge gained through a teaching or guiding process. The term used by Romanuk was "Mentoring," which virtually every leader or student of management is aware that the expression or use of the word in such a context refers to a knowledge advisor. A mentor can be viewed in the manner that a guide leading someone through a maze may be perceived. However, in terms of a leadership approach, the advisor would not only offer information on the actions a managerial leader should take, but why he or she should do so, as well. By suggesting that an advisor (an effective leader) be utilized to assist in developing a workable managerial approach to a mid-level police manager, it is concluded that the results would be positive and also that the use of a mentor will prove successful as a teaching technique that could later be used by the person being advised. The fifth suggested process set-forth by Romanuk for developing management skills was the knowledge gains through being interactive, by participating as a member on a Leadership Team. Utilizing this suggested process, the author concludes that a mid-level police manager by serving on such a team or committee would benefit in several areas and could better formulate an effective leadership approach. The individual could acquire a knowledge expansion and leadership development through his or her interaction with other leaders by absorbing their ideas, techniques, and perspective for action. An interactively involved middle manager would have an opportunity to express personal ideas and perceptions, etc. and then to have those concepts assessed by others, thus, allowing for managerial knowledge growth. An interactive Leadership Group, while typically slow in coming to a final decision, is very worthwhile for knowledge sharing and allowing a leader to develop a degree of comfort in being creative in his or her consideration in developing a personally effective approach to leadership.

THE NEED TO DEVELOP A MANAGERIAL
APPROACH TO LEADERSHIP

The information set-forth in this text regarding essential traits and characteristics of mid-level police management will to some degree discuss Creating Plans of Actions, Leadership Strategies, Decision Making, Setting Goals and Objectives, along with several other facets of managerial actions. Each of these factors is critical to police management, as is the essential establishment of a focused approach that integrates these actions a leader's personal attributes into an effective implementation to achieve optimum results. It has long been recognized that foundational leadership approaches are not a typically immediately conceived concept but rather a learned or observed process. The processes acquired through the basic approaches set-forth previously in this chapter require some time for development and acceptance. There is little doubt or challenge to the awareness that managerial leadership is becoming more complex. The ever-expanding complexity of societal changes and the continuing explosion of technical advances have mandated that established management approaches be able to cope with the increasing dynamics of interactive concerns.

The ongoing dynamics of mid-level police management relationships and exchanges must effectively correlate with subordinates, peers, superiors, external influences, personal concepts and desires, as well as obtainable resources. The productive leader must join these factors with the need to be innovative in his or her demonstrative skills to direct employee behavior to effectively achieve organizational goals and objectives. All of the aforestated factors come together to formulate the core of why it is essential that a mid-level police manager develop and implement a leadership approach that will both be effective and correlate smoothly with his or her personality.

Mid-level police management's formulation and utilization of an effective leadership approach are necessary to ensure implementation of a primary responsibility that is foundationally essential to Management By Objective (MBO). And, even though Management By Objective is only one aspect of a mid-level manager's functional skills that are necessary to his or her operational effectiveness. It is never the less important in as much as productive results and performance outcome are the essence of what leadership is all about. Management By Objective is explored in some detail in this text and is identified at this juncture to articulate the critical nature of developing a serviceable managerial approach.

The author considered identifying each dimensional skill considered essential to a mid-level police manager and setting forth an approach that had previously been effective. But a further consideration concluded that the personality traits and image projection of each Managerial Leader might be different. Thus, an effective approach for a mid-level police manager, "Leader A," when used by, "Leader B," may not produce the same results.

Also, critical to the consideration of developing a viable functional personality approach to leadership should be the consequential results it has on subordinates. Unlike the perception of worker motivation during early 1900s the employees of today is viewed as desiring to achieve more than a method of earning a living from the employment he or she chooses. They appear to require some level of self-satisfaction beyond the earning of a monetary livelihood. This conjecture appears obvious by the number of persons who change jobs each year, unlike the employees of a few decades ago where it was much more common for a worker to remain at one job or place of employment for his or her entire working career. Today's employee willingness to change employment is an indication that the person is seeking economic attainments, self-esteem, a sense of accomplishment, recognition, and self-gratification from the workplace and the leadership of the tasks they perform.

COMPONENTS OF A PRODUCTIVE
LEADERSHIP PERSONALITY

The traditional managerial or leadership approach focuses principally on productivity and achieving goals and objectives. In the past, this was acceptable even though over time, the concept of employee motivation, innovative techniques, and creative worker input has steadily increased. However, currently perceived workers' motives and projections of future trends require new thinking and insightful mid-level police managerial actions. Some of these insightful behaviors, as perceived by the author as essential components for formulating a workable Management Approach, are:

1. The mid-level police manager needs to realistically view his or her personal image and personality traits that he or she exhibits, both from a self-view and the perceptual conclusion of others. The approach established by the leader should first ensure a personal admiration relative to his or her trait characteristics and the ability to be effective as a leader. The aforestated behavioral approach feeds the manager/leader's need to feel good about his or herself and the method, task, and performance effort that he or she is putting forth. This self-perception is readily discernible to others and will thus affect the person's effectiveness in leading and directing others.

2. A leader at any level needs to perceive a measure of prestige for the job he or she is doing. Thus, the development of a managerial approach must factor in the person's need for recognition by others. Most people at one time or another have thought that their self-assessment should not be based on the perception of others and to some degree, that may be accurate, but the reality is that in nearly all cases, a person's success or failure as a leader, cook, painter, or whatever is

dependent on the conclusion of others observing his or her performance. If the subordinates, peers, or superior of a mid-level police manager conclude that he or she is not doing an effective job, then the leader has failed. The aforestated factors clearly articulate that a consideration and/or including a recognition component as part of developing a leader's personality is significant in the establishment of one's managerial approach to effective leadership is mandatory.

3. The ultimate purpose of a mid-level police manager's job is to control and direct the efforts of subordinates to achieve the organization's goals and objectives. Therefore, it may easily be said that the quintessential factor to any leader's personality or effective managerial approach must be the ability to tangibly direct workers toward task achievement. The approach should be developed with the idea to exploit the actions of subordinates' task performance direction to efficiently get the job done. In the past, many leaders have deemed this the only factor worth considering when formulating the guiding criteria when directing and controlling the performance behaviors of subordinates.

4. A clearly delineated approach that projects the authority, power, and control of mid-level police management is a very necessary aspect of a leader's assertiveness. The approach, although projecting a focused control and clear display of authority should not convey an expression of perceptual dominance. As has previously been stated and noted in many managerial studies, a primary Autocratic Leadership style is not effective in all situations; however, we must recognize that it is paramount that a leader needs to project that he or she is in command and control. But Organizational Police Management and its subordinates should view the display of power and control as necessary for effective job performances. Consequentially a mid-level police manager will be aware that an appropriate leadership approach should not convey disrespect for others or any form of self-gratification for the assertive authority that an effective approach must engender.

5. An adequately established personality approach to leadership should have some aspects of the mid-level police manager's desire to demonstrate perfection in his or her job performance. The leader must not be fearful, but yet he or she should be very concerned with his or her personal ability to function as flawlessly as possible. Consequently, the developmental process used to structure and implement an effective personal leadership approach should, if possible, be mistake free while at the same time versatile to appropriately interact with the various factors encountered. A leader must be operationally functional and

always consider the need for his or her job behaviors to be purposeful toward ensuring the accomplishment of organizational goals and objectives. Ideally, the leader should function with a concept that his or her Leadership Approach cannot be criticized for its effort to be effective. To a large degree, the mid-level police manager must seek to make his or her personal managerial actions infallible. A truly effective and continuously productive leader is constantly examining his or her managerial approach for flaws, so that they may be altered to enhance operational behaviors.

6. The projected personality approach decided upon and used by mid-level police management must be developed with the awareness and behavioral recognition that his or her elements or units do not function in a vacuum. Although an effective managerial leader will display some aspects of self-sufficiency and independence, the utilized approach by an organizational manager to the directing of others must have a satisfactory functioning relationship that is unanimously interactive with the police agency. There is an unquestioned need for coordinating operational functions within a police organization that will be influenced by the extent to which the elements interact toward overall achievement of goals and objectives. The mid-level police manager must be aware that when developing of an individualized operational approach that he or she is responsible for his or her personal actions, as well as the conduct and performance of subordinates. The police manager's action and approach to job behaviors should be an example for subordinates.

7. An effective mid-level police manager will project an organizational personality that will promote agency interdependency or an almost symbiotic-type relationship with both peers and subordinates. These relationships are concluded to be a partnership where coordination and cooperation are both joined to ensure that the elements must interact to achieve the department's goals and objectives. A close interaction as well as the necessary cooperative behavior are recognized as a parasitical partnership, although not in the traditional perception, one gets when the term parasite or parasitical is used. The parasitical partnership for which this author refers engendered in a police organization is most typically a model of effective and efficient interdependency. The development of a mid-level police manager's personality should be unalterably tied to his or her cooperative behavior with others. Therefore, when establishing a personality approach or projection of leadership, a mid-level police leader must consider the interdependency of his or her personal job behaviors with those of other

organizational components. However, a self-aware police manager's recognition of the need for an individualized personal task performance will avoid the tendency to get overly dependent on the interactive actions of other elements. A leader's primary personality approach must be based on a stand-alone projection, although he or she realizes the reality that organizational partnerships are necessary to accomplish established goals and objectives.

8. Much of an operational mid-level police manager's leadership personality, like that of virtually every effective leader, is composed of a degree of ambitious desire for personal achievement. When we analyze the behaviors of managers and leaders in most organizations, we find that a majority of those in managerial or leadership positions are there because they want to be there. Therefore, in the development of a personality approach to management, a leader must recognize and seek to project a desired effort to do the best job he or she can. The person's behavior as a manager should be evident to others that a greater organizational achievement is a prime motivator of an effective mid-level police manager. The ambitions and achievements necessary in a positive personality projection by a managerial leader are closely akin to the top step of Abraham Maslow's (1954) "Hierarchy of Needs Theory," which he termed "Self-Actualization." When viewed from a perspective of "Self-Actualization" regarding a functional establishment of a personality approach, a manager's focus appears to be somewhat self-centered. The mid-level police manager's performance behavior focuses on the person's desire to produce creativity that allows for a great deal of self-satisfaction. It is apparent from the recognition that self-actualization is a key component of a middle manager's personality projection and that he or she should also possess a motivation to perform efficiently and effectively.

9. An essential component of a mid-level police management personality includes the need for the leader to limit the scope of his or her individual characteristics. The aforestated often proves to be most difficult because the effective Personality Traits of managerial leaders include all on-the-job behaviors that contribute to leadership success. Many projected characteristics of efficiency or productive behavior are thus more focused and controlled within certain parameters. In other words, an effective and efficient leader should perform tasks that can be accomplished while limiting performance ventures into areas where negative outcomes are likely. By this, the author does not infer that innovation or creative efforts in areas of uncertainty should not be made. However, it is most likely that a leader will prove more effec-

tive and obtain a higher degree of employee motivation where task success is more often achieved than are job failures.

Personality characteristics as being addressed regarding the personal concept of an effective mid-level police manager should be noticeably projected and utilized when interacting with others in an evolving process. There is no mystical or dynamic formula for developing into a productive manager. Managerial leadership is a commitment to performance tasks requiring a dedicated effort involving a variety of duties and alternating obligations that mandate the desired behaviors. As previously stated, "leaders are made, not born," and this does not imply that everyone possesses the personality traits or characteristics to be an effective leader. For example, there are persons so introverted as to be unable to direct or control the behavior of others; likewise, there may be other factors such as extreme shyness, or individuals whose psychological or emotional makeup would limit their managerial skills and thus appear to make them ineffective as a leader. Consequently, everyone cannot be taught to be an effective leader. Many theorists have viewed and conjectured that it would a great boost to the study of management if someone could conceive of a method for early identification of leadership traits in individuals. The conjectured identification method would reflect the potential for success of a person as a managerial leader.

Mid-level police management is the focus ability to control and direct the task behaviors of others toward specified goals and objectives. It is clear in our concept that management and leadership are so closely related, that they can be used inter-changeably in this text. Thus, both leadership and management reflect the dynamics of the interaction of a leader's functioning and the subordinates' reaction to the direction/controls. Therefore the author will conclude this discussion on the importance of a mid-level police manager's development and projection of an effective personality approach when providing leadership.

The makeup of a mid-level police manager's basic performance personality is a composition of all of his or her trait characteristics for leadership. These trait characteristics play a major part in the development of personal leadership ability and effectiveness to function as a mid-level police manager. Most leaders in the management field of study recognize that many people truly have the capability to perform in a leadership role but lack the basic knowledge of how, as well as the opportunity to do so. As previously noted, the individual needs to recognize the areas of weakness in his or her personality and use the appropriate techniques to strengthen those trait areas and to give him or herself the confidence that is very necessary for an effective mid-level police manager. He or she should remember that the successful characteristics observed in other positional leaders should be reviewed and studied in an effort to refine his or her own developed techniques.

SYNOPSIS

In concluding this text's presentation on establishing a functional approach for Middle Management, it is important to remember that simply because an effective mid-level police manager operates within the organizational structure does not necessarily mean that every peer status leader must do everything the same way. When this author talks about the practice of effective leadership characteristics, it is meant that personal projected traits should be performed in a manner that is conducive to the positive functioning of the individual and his or her subordinates. The significant issue that focuses the importance of this chapter is the fact that leadership influences, if not, direct and control the functioning of all groups, whether subordinate workers or peer group interaction. Therefore, it is essential that a mid-level police manager to whom leadership expectation is traditionally vested by virtue of the position he or she be assigned within a law enforcement organization. The question often arises concerning the designated positional leader's leadership ability and authority versus the individual skills and actual performance behaviors in the role. Much of this chapter focused on the leader's ability to develop and project an effective personality and individual performance approach to his or her task as a managerial leader within the organization. There have been a number of theories and concepts distinguishing the characteristics of leaders relative to a clear difference between their exercises of authority, based on their position level within the organization. Information coming forth from some of these theories is that leadership is often fluid within a particular group with the topic area and prior experience or knowledge determining who will be perceived as the leader at that time. Of course, we are referring to the unofficial leader because it is recognized that in law enforcement organization, the positional leader does not and cannot abandon his or her assigned leadership control and direction of subordinates. Thus, the concept of a leader's personality approach and the utilization of a participatory leadership style to gather productive input from subordinates without relinquishing his or her positional authority or responsibility to assure that the assigned tasks of subordinates are effectively and efficiently accomplished. A close analysis and focus on goal-oriented managerial efforts by functioning managers is a meaningful look at the personality characteristics that most consider unique to leaders. Throughout this text's assessment of a managerial leader's approach to establishing an effective leadership personality that will be both effective and productive, the text has attempted to articulate productive management characteristics to direct and control the performance behavior of subordinates. It is also significant to note that the organizational environment is considered important to the effectiveness of a mid-level police manager's dealing with subordinates. Likewise, it is clear that whatever managerial approach adopted and implemented must interact positively with the other organizational elements and contribute to the achievement of the over all goals and objectives of the agency. A number of other areas were touched upon during the text's consideration of an effective personality approach that management leaders should consider, some of the areas briefly mentioned or referred to were having a knowledge of subordinates and their motivational requirements; interactive behaviors that included some participatory input; not limiting personal task knowledge and behaviors to only to personally assigned positional duties; and initiating and directing actions that will reflect that the leader has developed or has the ability to professionally perform as an effective and efficient mid-level police manager.

BIBLIOGRAPHY

1. Lynch, R. G. *The police manager: Professional leadership skills.* Boston: Holbrook Press, 1978, pp. 47–65.

2. Argyris, C. *Personality and organization.* New York: Harper & Row, 1957.

3. Baron, R. A., & Greenberg, J. *Behavior in organizations.* Needham Heights, MA: Allyn & Bacon, 1990, pp. 384–395.

4. Iannone, N. F. *Supervision of police personnel.* Englewood Cliffs, NJ: Prentice-Hall, 1970, pp. 8, 55, & 68.

5. Hersey, P., & Blanchard, K. *Management of organization behavior.* Englewood Cliffs, NJ: Prentice-Hall, 1972.

6. Editorial Staff. *Funk & Wagnall standard desk dictionary.* New York: Funk & Wagnall Co., 1966, p. 23.

7. Roth, W. *Problem solving.* New York: Praeger, Inc., 1985.

8. Lussien, R. *Human relations in organizations.* Homewood, IL: Irwin, 1993, p. 15.

9. Coleman, J. L. *The security supervisor's handbook.* Springfield, IL: Charles C Thomas, 1987, p. 48.

10. Buckingham, C. Ethics and the senior officer: Institutional tension. *Parameters, 3* (Autumn) pp. 23–32, 1985.

11. Pfiffner, J. M., & Fel, M. *The supervision of personnel.* Englewood Cliffs, NJ: Prentice-Hall, 1964.

12. Coleman, J. L. *Operational mid-level management for police* (1st ed.). Springfield, IL: Charles C Thomas, 1988, pp. 126–127 and 129–133.

13. Hayes, A. How the court defines harassment. New York: *Wall Street Journal.* October 11, 1991, p. Bl.

14. Outten, W. N., & Kinigstein, N. A. *The rights of employees.* New York: Bantam Books, 1984, p. 10.

15. Westin, A., & Salisbury. *Individual rights in the corporation: A reading on employee rights.* New York: Pantheon Books, 1980, p. 67.

16. Lawrence, L. *What makes a good job?* New York: Personnel, 25 (January), 1949.

17. Whisenand, P. M., & Ferguson, R. F. *The managing of police organizations.* Englewood Cliffs, NJ: Prentice-Hall, 1978, p. 146.

18. Melnicoe, W. B., & Mennig, J. *Elements of supervision.* New York: Glencoe Press, 1979, pp. 99–103.

19. Spriegel, W. R., Schultz, E., & Spriegel, W. B. *Elements of supervision.* New York: John Wiley, 1957.

20. Drucker, P. *Management.* New York: Harper & Row, 1974, pp. 103–120.
21. Hodgetts, R. *Modern human relations at work* (4th ed.). Chicago: Dryden Press, 1990, p. 576.
22. Coleman, J. L. *Practical knowledge for a private security officer.* Springfield, IL: Charles C Thomas, 1986, p. 37.
23. Ackoff, R. A note on system science. *Interface II,* August 1972, p. 4.
24. Gaither, N. *Production and operation management* (4th ed.). Chicago: Dryden Press, 1990, p. 47.
25. Shostack, G. L. Designing services that deliver. *Harvard Business Review,* January/February 1984, p. 133.
26. Kepner, C., & Tregoe, B. *Project management.* Princeton, NJ: Kepner-Tregoe, Inc., 1987, pp. 82–83.

SELECTED REFERENCES

Adizes, I. *How to solve the mismanagement crisis.* Homewood, IL: Dow Jones, 1979.

Argyris, C. *Executive leadership.* Hamden, CT: The Shoe String Press, Inc., 1967.

Argyris, C. *Personality and organization.* New York: Harper, 1957.

Arnold, J. D. *Make up your mind.* AMACOM, 1978.

Baxter (Orrick, Herrington & Sutcliff). *Sexual harrassment in the workplace.* New York: Executive Enterprises Publication, 1981.

Beckman, R. O. *How to train supervisors.* New York: Harper & Brothers, 1952.

Behn, R., & Vaupel, J. *Quick analysis for busy decision makers.* New York: Basic Books, 1982.

Bellows, Gilson, & Odiorne. *Executive skills.* Englewood Cliffs: Prentice-Hall, 1962.

Berlew, D. E. *Organizational psychology: A book of reading.* Englewood Cliffs: Prentice-Hall, 1974.

Blanchard, K., & Johnson, S. *The one minute manager.* New York: William Morrow, 1981.

Block, P. *The empowerment: Positive political skills at work.* San Francisco, CA: JosseyBass, 1989.

Bonge, J. L., & Coleman, B. P. *Concept for corporate strategy.* New York: Macmillan, 1972.

Bradford, D. L., & Cohn, A. R. *Managing for excellence.* New York: John Wiley, 1984.

Brown, R. E. *Judgment in administration.* New York: Macmillan, 1972.

Brown & Cohn. *The study of leadership.* Danville, IL: Interstate, 1958.

Canton. *Employee counseling.* New York: McGraw-Hill, 1945.

Certo, S. C., & Peter, J. P. *Strategic management: Concepts and application* (7th ed.). New York: McGraw-Hill, 1991.

Cohen, A. R., Frank, S. L., Gadon, H., & Willits, R. D. *Effective behavior in organization.* Homewood, IL: Irwin Publications, 1980.

Coleman, J. L. *Police assessment testing.* Springfield, IL: Charles C Thomas, 1987.

Coleman, J. L. *The security supervisor's handbook.* Springfield, IL: Charles C Thomas, 1987.

Comerford, R. A., & Callaghan, D. W. *Strategic management.* Boston: Kent, 1985.

Daft, R. L. *Management* (2nd ed.). Chicago: Dryden Press, 1991.

Dale, E. *Management: Theory and practices.* New York: McGraw-Hill, 1965.

Deal, T. E., & Kennedy, A. A. *Corporate cultures.* Reading, MA: Addison-Wesley, 1982.

Drucker, P. *Management: Tasks, practices, responsibilities.* New York: Harper & Row, 1974.

Drucker, P. *The effectiveness executive.* New York: Harper & Row, 1967.

Eastman, G. P., & Eastman, E. M. *Municipal police administration.* Washington, DC: Institute for Training in Municipal Administration, 1969.

Ewing, D. W. *Freedom inside the organization.* New York: E.P. Dutton, 1977.

Frederick, W. C., Post, J. E., & Davis, D. *Business and ethics* (7th ed.). New York: McGraw-Hill, 1992.

Gaither, N. *Production and operations management* (4th ed.). Chicago: Dryden Press, 1990.

Gardner, N., & Davis, J. *The art of delegating.* New York: Doubleday, 1965.

Glover, J. D. Fundamentals of professional management. Republic Book Co., 1954.

Gourley, G. D., & Bristow, A. P. *Patrol administration.* Springfield, IL: Charles C Thomas, 1970.

Hagan, J. T. *A management role for quality control.* New York: American Management Association, 1968.

Hall, C. S., & Lindzey, G. *Theories of personality* (3rd ed.). New York: John Wiley, 1970.

Hayel, C. *Management of modern supervisors.* New York: American Management Association, 1962.

Hersey, P., & Blanchard, K. *Management of organizational behavior.* Englewood Cliffs: Prentice-Hall, 1972.

Herzberg, F. Be efficient and be human. *Industry Week.* June 1970. pp. 46–48.

Hodnett, E. *The art of problem solving.* New York: Harper, 1955.

Hunsaker, P. L., & Alessandra, A. J. *The art of managing people.* Englewood Cliffs: Prentice-Hall, 1980.

Iannone, N. F. *Supervision of police personnel.* Englewood Cliffs: Prentice-Hall, 1970.

Jackson, K. F. *The art of solving problems.* New York: St. Martin's Press, 1975.

Janaro, R. P., & Alshulter, T. C. *The art of being human* (3rd ed.). New York: Harper & Row, 1989.

Jenks, J., & Kelly, J. *Don't do, delegate!* New York: Franklin Watts, 1985.

Jones, E. E. *Attribution: Perceiving the causes of behavior.* Morristown, NJ: General Learning Press, 1972.

Jucius, M. J. *Personnel management.* Homewood, IL: Richard Irwin, 1959.

Kanter, R. M. *Men and women of the corporation.* New York: Basic Books, 1977.

Kanter, R. M. *The change masters: How people and companies succeed through innovation in the corporate era.* New York: Simon & Schuster, 1983.

Kidder, T. *Soul of a new machine.* Boston: Little, Brown, 1981.

Kleinmuntz, B. *Problem solving.* New York: John Wiley, 1966.

Koontz, Harold, O'Donnel, & Cyril. *Principles of management.* New York: McGraw-Hill, 1959.

Kreitner, R. *Management* (5th ed.). Boston: Houghton Mifflin, 1990.

Likert, R. Effective supervision: An adaptive and relative process. *Personnel Psychology, I*(43) , 1958.

Likert, R. *New pattern of management.* New York: McGraw-Hill, 1961.

Likert, R. Measuring organization performance. *Harvard Business Review, XXXVI*(2) 1958.

Lincoln, J. F. *Incentive management.* Cleveland, OH: Lincoln Electric Co., 1956.

Lussier, R. *Human relations in organization* (7th ed.). Homewood, IL: Richard Irwin, 1993.

Lynch, R. G. *The police manager: Professional leadership skills.* Boston, MA: Holbrook, 1978.

Lytle, G. W. *Job evaluation methods.* The Ronald Press, 1949.

Maier & Hayes. *Creative management.* New York: John Wiley, 1962.

Maier, N. *Problem solving and creativity in individuals and groups.* Belmont, CA: Brooks/Cole, 1970.

Mann, F. *Leadership and productivity.* Chandler Publishing, 1965.

Margerison, C. J. *Managerial problem solving.* New York: McGraw-Hill, 1974.

Massie, J. L. *Essentials of management.* Englewood Cliffs: Prentice-Hall, 1964.

Melnicoe, W. B., & Mennig, J. *Elements of police supervision.* New York: Glencoe Press, 1969.

Miller, Jim/Kaye, Beverly & Knowles, Malcolm. *Managers as mentors.* San Francisco: Berrett-Koehler, 1996.

Mintzberg, H. *The nature of managerial work.* New York: Harper & Row, 1973.

Morell, R. W. *Managerial decision making.* New York: Bruce Publications, 1960.

Muczyk, Jan P. Dynamics and hazards of MBO application. *The Personnel Administration 24.* May 1979 , p. 52.

Odiorne, G. S. How to manage by objective. *Industrial Week.* June 1070, p. 46.

Odiorne, G. S. *Management by objectives.* Pitman. New York, 1965

Outten, W., & Kinigstein, N. A. *The rights of employees.* New York: Bantam Books, 1984.

Parry, J. *The psychology of communication.* London: University of London Press, 1967.

Payton, G. T. *Patrol procedures.* Legal Book Corp., 1967.

Perrow, C. *Complex organizations* (3rd ed.). New York: McGraw-Hill, 1986.

Peters, T. J., & Waterman, R. H. *In search of excellence.* New York: Harper & Row, 1982.

Pfiffner, J. M., & Fel, M. *The supervision of personnel.* Englewood Cliffs: Prentice-Hall, 1964.

Pigors, P., & Myers, C. A. *Personnel administration* (8th ed.). New York: McGraw-Hill, 1977.

Preston, P., & Zimmerer, T. W. *Management for supervisors.* Englewood Cliffs: Prentice-Hall, 1983.

Reif, W. E., & Newstrom, J. W. Integrating MBO and OBM–A new perspective. *Management By Objective 5,* no. 2 (1975), pp. 34–42.

Roberts, W. *Leadership secrets of Attila the Hun.* New York: Warner Business Books, 1987.

Rogers, C. R. *Client centered therapy.* Boston: Houghton Mifflin, 1942.

Romanuk, F. *Five approaches to leadership.* Roxburgh Mission Network. April 14, 2010.

Rubin, T. I. *Overcome indecisiveness.* New York: Harper & Row, 1985.

Sarason, I. G. *Personality: An objective approach.* New York: Wiley, 1966.

Sargent, A. G. *The androgynous manager.* AMACON, 1981.

Sarnoff, M. *Personality dynamics and development.* New York: Wiley, 1962.

Shanahan, D. T. *Patrol administration: Management by objectives.* Boston: Allyn & Bacon, 1975.

Spriegel, W. R., Schultz, E., & Spriegel, W. B. *Elements of supervision.* New York: John Wiley, 1957.

Towler, J. E. *Practical police knowledge.* Springfield, IL: Charles C Thomas, 1960.

Vaill, P. B. *Leadership: Where else can we go?* Durham, NC: Duke University Press, 1976.

Verderber, R. F. *Communication* (5th ed.). Belmont, CA: Wadsworth, 1987.

Vemon-Wortzel, H. *Business and society: A management approach* (5th ed.). Boston: Irwin, 1994.

Vroom, V. H., & Yetton, P. W. *Leadership and decision making.* Pittsburgh: University of Pittsburgh Press, 1976.

Watson, H. J., Carroll, A. B., & Mann, R. I. *Information systems for management* (4th ed.). Homewood, IL: Richard Irwin, 1991.

Westrum, R., & Samaha, K. *Complex organizations: Growth, struggle, and change.* Englewood Cliffs: Prentice-Hall, 1984.

Wheeler, D., & Janis, I. *A practical guide for making decisions.* New York: Free Press, 1980.

Whisenand, P. M., & Ferguson, R. F. *The managing for police organizations* (2nd ed.). Englewood Cliffs: Prentice-Hall, 1978.

INDEX